Theatrical Legitimation

THEATRICAL LEGITIMATION

Allegories of Genius
in Seventeenth-Century
England and France

TIMOTHY MURRAY

New York ✳ *Oxford*
OXFORD UNIVERSITY PRESS
1987

Oxford University Press

Oxford   New York   Toronto
Delhi   Bombay   Calcutta   Madras   Karachi
Petaling Jaya   Singapore   Hong Kong   Tokyo
Nairobi   Dar es Salaam   Cape Town
Melbourne   Auckland
and associated companies in
Beirut   Berlin   Ibadan   Nicosia

Published by Oxford University Press, Inc.
200 Madison Avenue, New York, New York 10016

Oxford is a registered trademark of Oxford University Press

Library of Congress Cataloging-in-Publication Data

Murray, Timothy.
Theatrical legitimation.
Bibliography: p.
Includes index.
1. Drama—17th century—History and criticism.
2. Theater—England—History—17th century.
3. Theater—France—History—17th century.   4. Literature,
Comparative—English and French.   5. Literature, Comparative—
French and English.   6. Jonson, Ben, 1573?–1637—
Criticism and interpretation.   7. Aubignac, François-
Hédelin, abbé d', 1604–1676.   Pratique du théâtre.
I. Title
PN1831.M87 1987   792'.0941   86-33132
ISBN 0-19-504268-9

10 9 8 7 6 5 4 3 2 1

Printed in the United States of America
on acid-free paper

For Renate and Ashley

✒ Acknowledgments and Textual Note

> The following, and voluntary Labours of my Friends . . .
> have relieved me in much, whereat (without them) I
> should necessarily have touched: Now I will only use
> three or foure short, and needfull Notes, and so rest.
>
> BEN JONSON, "To the Readers," *Sejanus*

True to the English Renaissance model of the dramatic text, this is a manuscript "wherein a second Pen had good share." With very warm thanks, I wish to acknowledge the hands that provided commentary on this text and lent legitimation to the project.

I am especially grateful to Louis Marin and Stephen Orgel whose detailed suggestions and caring encouragement contributed immeasurably to the dissertation from which this book sprung. I owe more than words of thanks to Victoria Kahn, Daniel Brewer, and Mária Minich Brewer who read and reread the entire manuscript. Their individual contributions, along with those of Neil Saccamano, are scattered over the following pages. These four collaborators have indeed "relieved me in much" since this book's sketchy inception. Throughout my research and writing in Ithaca, Paris, and Baltimore, numerous other colleagues and teachers have left their individual touch on my work. I thank: Reeve Parker, David Novarr, Leonard Green, Christopher Pye, Cynthia Koepp, Scott McMillin, Laura Brown, Jean-François Lyotard, Philip Lewis, Jacques Derrida, Jonathan Culler, Katharine Eisaman Mauss, Martha Ward, Geoffrey Waite, Stephen Greenblatt, Herbert Blau, David

Marshall, Michael Fried, Richard Macksey, and Susan Weinberg. At Oxford University Press, I am grateful to Susan Meigs for her editorial contributions and to William Sisler for his confidence and long-term support; he too has crossed paths with this book many times since its beginnings.

Research trips to Paris, London, and Washington, D.C. were made possible by grants from the College of Arts and Sciences at Cornell University, The Fulbright Commission, the Alliance Française de New York, and The Johns Hopkins University Humanities Center.

Finally, my most profound debt is to Renate Ferro. Her labors of practical aid, moral support, humor, and patience gave renewed energy to my writing whenever it was infirm. She knows only too well the complex allegory enframing *Theatrical Legitimation*.

I have retained the original spelling of all quotations, except for three reciprocal standardizations of orthography: u & v, f & s, i & j. Translations are provided in the footnotes; they are mine, unless otherwise noted.

Shorter drafts of several chapters have already appeared in print. "From Foul Sheets to Legitimate Model: Antitheater, Text, Ben Jonson," *New Literary History*, 14 (Spring 1983), 641–64, contains sections of Chapters 2–5; a brief part of Chapter 4 appears as "Ben Jonson's Folio As Textual Performance," in *Acts of the Tenth Congress of the International Comparative Literature Association*, ed. D. W. Fokkema (New York: Garland Press, Spring, 1985), II, 325–330. Very different versions of Chapter 7 have been published as "Theatrical Legitimation: Forms of French Patronage and Portraiture," *PMLA*, 98, No. 2 (March 1983), 170–82, and "Richelieu's Theater: The Mirror of a Prince," *Renaissance Drama*, NS 8 (1977), 275–97. "Non-Representation in *La pratique du théâtre*," *Papers on Seventeenth-Century French Literature*, 9, No. 16 (1982), 57–74, includes parts of Chapter 10. I am grateful to the publishers for their permission to publish revisions of this material.

Contents

PART TWO.   THEATRICAL PORTRAITURE, OR FIGURAL PATRONAGE

PART THREE.   DESIRE AS SPECTATOR

List of Illustrations

Theatrical Legitimation

1

Introduction
Allegories of Legitimation:
History, Desire, Interpretation

> How the objectness of what presences is brought to appearance and how what presences becomes an object for a setting-before, a representing [*Vor-stellen*], can show itself to us only if we ask: What is the real in relation to theory, and thus in a certain respect also in and through theory? ... The word "theory" stems from the Greek verb *theōrein*. The noun belonging to it is *theōria*. Peculiar to these words is a lofty and mysterious meaning. The verb *theōrein* grew out of the coalescing of two root words, *thea* and *horaō*. *Thea* (cf. theatre) is the outward look, the aspect, in which something shows itself, the outward appearance in which it offers itself. Plato names this aspect in which what presences shows what it is, *eidos*. To have seen this aspect, *eidenai*, is to know [*wissen*]. The second root word in *theōrein*, *horaō*, means: to look at something attentively, to look it over, to view it closely. Thus it follows that *theōrein* is *thean horaō*, to look attentively on the outward appearance wherein what presences becomes visible and, through such sight—seeing—to linger with it.

> MARTIN HEIDEGGER, "Science and Reflection"

During the past two decades, the discipline of Comparative Literature has generated a spirited, ongoing debate concerning its motivations and scholarly aims. Many scholars argue for the preserva-

3

tion of Comparative Literature's traditional ties to its roots in literary history and the history of ideas. Comparison in this context leads to an appreciation of the likenesses and differences of national literatures as mirrors of an historical and ideational past. Focusing on genres, topoi, and themes of literature shared by or influencing different national cultures, the traditional pedagogy of Comparative Literature works to maintain a legitimate canon of texts and methods for scholarly exchange. This approach remains heavily invested in the study of the classics, from the Greeks to the Great Books, and privileges the *eidos* of generic and hermeneutic concerns.

English and French seventeenth-century drama has proven to be a particularly fertile field for recent historical projects in comparative studies. Revisionist approaches to historicism as well as a rekindled interest in Renaissance rhetoric have generated many refreshing analyses of the relation of historical drama to culture and politics. Critical energy has been given to reconsiderations of Renaissance individualism, courtly literature, women's writing, and the loosely attendant patterns of authorship, patronage, and reader response. Alongside the more traditional fields of comparative inquiry, these efforts, labelled as the "new historicism," have generated a significant number of studies that attempt to expand the comparative canon to include sociological discussions of the role of literature, art, and drama in nascent capitalism, colonial expansionism, and the related program of the cultural and economic oppression of women and peoples of color.

While such historical critique is highly laudable for its political aims, it relies on particularly traditional assumptions about critical writing that may well undercut the project's sensitivity to the ideology of literary form. Much of this scholarship reasserts, for example, the force of the traditional "master-narrative" by analyzing how texts generate singular, "master" discourses. Two of the most pervasive "new historical" strategies can be cited for organizing and comprehending textual data in terms of centralizing paradigms which a critic would find universally applicable. Revived interest in seventeenth-century Christian tracts, for instance, has resulted in "new" readings of Christianity's influence on literature. This reconsideration of the impact of Christian doctrine has been especially fruitful in Shakespeare studies where many critics now read the Christian ethos as having a negative, instead of positive, influence on drama. In the wake of "new historical" readings, Christianity is understood to inform, if not prescribe, disturbing cultural formations, such as the repressive power of sovereignty, the restrictive concept of the family, the oppression of women, etc. But even when these studies stress their own alienation from Christianity, say in exploring the Christian influence on such fundamental literary relations as gender politics and political service, they continue, with few exceptions, to inscribe textual interpretation in the dominant narrative tradition of Renaissance Christianity. What follows is a critical blocking out (or repression) of other significant, even if marginal, psycho-political conditions, such as conflicting Oriental representations in *Othello* or *Macbeth*. On a different plane, the Marxist narrative elaborates on Marx's passing reference to the Renaissance as an anxious period of economic transition. Marxist criticism has been especially influential in recent studies of Renaissance drama and theatre history. The central, and, too often, single issue here concerns theatre's formation and articulation of the class conditions of early capitalism. Necessarily cast aside by this particular "master-narrative," for instance, is attentiveness to epistemological formations that the competing classes of late Renaissance and early-modern drama shared and were equally enslaved by, like "master narration" itself. In its differing quests for sociological reconstruction, the "new historicism" must defer rigorous critique of the psycho-epistemological filament sustaining the differing expressions of confidence in critical mastery.

This deferral stems to a great degree from the fact that the majority of these single, "master" discourse analyses reassert confidence in the "master-referent," the metaphysical signified. This metaphysical referent of the "new historicism," as I will suggest in the following pages, finds itself sustained by today's concomitant embrace of the seventeenth-century, epistemological legacies of Reason and Logic. But since these "masterly" referential constructs provided a good bit of the philosophical and conceptual material for cultural oppression in and around seventeenth-century theatre, scholars might want to be wary of working toward their methodological reconstruction. By forging ahead in a spirit of renewed hope in the narrative recovery of cultural and literary history, the "new historicism" might easily end up replicating oppressive, seventeenth-century narrative and epistemological paradigms.

In response to such possible iteration of the dominating paradigms of historicism and critical narration, this book stresses the imperative of a reevaluation of the theoretical grounds of the comparative enterprise. Instead of privileging narrative recovery as the end of scholarly study, the aim of such a theoretical program in Comparative Literature is to critique the discipline's foundation in historical and hermeneutical paradigms. Analyzing the epistemological and ideological grounds shaping and determining the study of national, historical literatures, Comparative Literature here focuses not only on *what* historical material it discovers but also on *how to read it* and *how* attendant critical narratives *shape its reading*. Indeed, the comparative enterprise works to highlight and ponder the differences and shifts of the act of reading.

Such study attunes itself to the analysis of method. At stake is less the discovery of "new histories" than the re-presentation of familiar methodologies, less an aesthetic appreciation of the aspects in which historical artifacts offer themselves than a theoretical deconstruction of the epistemological structures shaping historical narrative. Informed by developments in poststructuralist thought, this comparative project turns aside from mere academic appreciation of the truths of the past. Instead it reflects on institutional investments in telling *certain* stories and in shaping a disciplinary corps of *truthful* readers who are satisfied by the genius of their recuperative, comparative methods.

Legitimate Anxiety

The title of this text, *Theatrical Legitimation: Allegories of Genius in Seventeenth-Century England and France*, places the disparate seventeenth-century phenomenon which I will call *theatrical legitimation* in the context of its theoretical narration. Although this book does pay special attention to literary aspects of seventeenth-century French and English dramatic literature (the form and shape of the printed text, the figural elements of dramatic representation, the format of printed epistles, and the critical heritage of authorial intentionality), it does not aim to clarify the constitutive meaning of drama. Rather, in a series of ideological/epistemological analyses, it comments on performative aspects of theatricality underlying the narrative re-presentation of seventeenth-century French and English theatre: the relation between ideology and theatrical representation, the display of authority, the rhetorical structures of ideological performance, and the complex discourse of the antitheatrical prejudice poised against both the theatre and the psychology of the spectator.

I stress the relation of ideology and epistemology, moreover, to set in motion an open concept of aesthetic production. This plays off, yet still resists, the "master-referents" underlying two theoretically perceptive, Marxist analyses of the ideology of art and literature which I have found to be compatible with the motivating concept of my project. First is Louis Althusser's familiar thesis: "l'idéologie représente le rapport imaginaire des individus à leurs conditions réelles d'existence."[1] Second is Fredric Jameson's reinscription of this thesis in the realm of the "political unconconscious": "ideology is not something which informs or invests symbolic production; rather the aesthetic act is itself ideological, and the production of aesthetic or narrative form is to be seen as an ideological act in its own right, with the function of inventing imaginary or formal 'solutions' to unresolvable social contradictions."[2] While steering clear of Jameson's insistence on Marxism as the only narrative structure viable for critical praxis, my book's division into three intersecting ideological/epistemological frames—Authorship, Patronage, and Spectatorship—provides for the representational study of different strategies of narrative production, all as ideological activity.

Because this book discusses ideological strategies shaping the contemporary reception of seventeenth-century literature and culture, I think it important to spend time at the outset broadly introducing and clarifying the conceptual margins of critical concern and narration informing the chapters that follow. I place special emphasis on the significance of this book's attentiveness to a particularly demonstrative, aesthetic enterprise, theatre, one known to favor outward forms of exhibitionism, deceit, seduction, and trickery. While recognized in some circles as an effective tool of moral and political pedagogy, theatre also has been criticized throughout history for generating playful combinations of unfulfilled desire and emotional identification that counterbalance lasting standards of reason and morality. At issue in this book is how the pervasive wariness of theatricality stems as much from epistemological concerns as from generic ones.

This anxiety over theatricality's epistemological impurities surfaces in a wide variety of seventeenth-century texts, from religious tracts to treatises on government and education. It is especially acute in *The New Organon*, where Francis Bacon summarizes

the Idols which have immigrated into men's minds from the various dogmas of philosophies, and also from the wrong laws of demonstration. These I call Idols of the Theatre, because in my judgment all the received systems are but so many stage plays, representing worlds of their own creation after an unreal and scenic fashion. Nor is it only of the systems now in vogue, or only of the ancient sects and philosophies, that I speak; for many more plays of the same kind may yet be composed and in like artificial manner set forth.[3]

The "Idols of the Theatre" critiqued by Bacon are, of course, more a product of theatricality, a particularly performative mental posture and narrative result, than of particular historical forms of the drama. Indeed, questions of epistemology and psychology, instead of literary form or historical fact, dominate the antitheatrical discourse. Bacon's dismissal of the "wrong laws" of theatrical idols, moreover, is germane to my study's dialogue with a broad field of critical exchange extending far beyond the proper bounds of theatre and literary history. Evident in his argument are seeds of a burgeoning debate over critical "systems" per se. Consider, for instance, how today's advocates of traditional methodology often dismiss "theory" as if it were the progeny of Bacon's "Idols of the Theatre," or another example of the theoreticians' "representing worlds of their own creation after an unreal and scenic fashion." Opponents of "theory," similar in approach to seventeenth-century antitheatricalists, frequently challenge poststructural practice for performing stylistic exhibitionism, unproductive linguistic play, and ahistorical fantasies of desire and libidinal gratification. The alleged self-absorption of "theory" is cited frequently by many comparative scholars of seventeenth-century literature as a justification for maintaining strict academic borders between deconstruction and the research of historical narratives.

Responding to such cultural anxieties over both "theory" and theatricality, this book seeks to unravel the unstable codes of critical legitimation valorizing theatre as an important commodity of literary study. One productive point of departure might be to consider in more detail the status of legitimation as an ideological/epistemological paradigm. Defined generally in John Bullokar's *An English Expositor: Teaching the Interpretation of the hardest words used in our Language* as anything "lawfull, lawfully begotten,"[4] legitimation issues forth prescriptions of progeny and legality. As suggested above, the issue of "lawfully begotten" dogmas of philosophy is an important concern of Francis Bacon's, one turning to the question of legitimation as its implicit, critical foundation. Closer consideration of this question in Bacon yields interesting results. Bacon states outright in *The Great Instauration* that his texts depart from traditional conventions of authority and legal issue: "I do not endeavor either by triumphs of confutation, or pleadings of antiquity, or assumption of authority, or even by the veil of obscurity, to invest these inventions of mine with any majesty."[5] In setting aside philosophical assumptions of authority and theatrical veils of obscurity, Bacon establishes his deviant position as a *new* scientist, one slow to embrace the "Idols of the Theatre" and "the wrong laws of demonstration." Still, Bacon turns more quickly than his peers to an elaboration of the rule of legitimation as the modern standard of judgment. In *The Great Instauration*, for example, he writes that "the intellect is not qualified to judge except by means of induction, and induction in its legitimate form."[6] Later he cites the supplemental authority of legitimation in describing how "the sixth part of my work (to which the rest is subservient and ministrant) discloses and sets forth that philosophy which by the legitimate, chaste, and severe course of inquiry which I have explained and provided is at length developed and established."[7] The ordering figure of legitimation surfaces at key moments in Bacon's treatises to qualify his skeptical assertions concerning intellectual authority.

Bacon's readers might note, however, that he develops and establishes almost everything in *The Great Instauration* except the precise boundaries of legitimation itself. An excellent example of Bacon's own evasive prescription of legitimation is apparent in his negative declaration, "I interpose everywhere admonitions and scruples and cautions, with a religious care to eject, repress, and, as it were, exorcise every kind of phantasm."[8] If this intensely anxious passage can be cited as exemplary of Baconian legitimation, it is only because Bacon's strategy of recovering lost scruples through the exorcism of phantasms, of theatrical idols, is very much in keeping with his dismissal of tainted, philosophical authority. Passionate prescriptions of ejection and repression might be said to comprise the Baconian enterprise of critical legitimation. But since the reader can turn only to the forces of repression to pinpoint Bacon's authoritative concept, legitimation stands out as the most noticeable phantasm that evades the critical exorcisms of the new scientist.

This is nowhere more evident than in *The New Organon*'s important discourse on the margins of critical analysis. In summarizing the aims of his method, Bacon clearly steps aside from the conventional citation of legitimation as a figure of sovereign authority or legalized progeny. Taking a leap in the conceptualization of legitimation, Bacon aligns it with his culture's growing interests in method. "My course and method, as I have often clearly stated and would wish to state again, is this—not to extract works from works or experiments from experiments (as an empiric), but from works and experiments to extract causes and axioms, and again from those causes and axioms new works and experiments, as a legitimate interpreter of nature."[9] Bacon here highlights his science as a method of interpretation in addition to being an experiment with assemblage and cause and effect. Legitimation, Bacon might say, begets a certain experiment in reading. Prefiguring the twentieth-century critical analysis of Jürgen Habermas and his colleagues, this pioneer of modern philosophical reading frames legitimation as an obscure aspect of interpretation, the repressed phantasm of the lawfully begotten.

My analyses in later chapters put critical pressure on similar assertions of legitimation built on the very structures of fantasy they wish to repress. My readings suggest that legitimation is but a phantasm of an interpretational authority sustained by little more than layers of fiction, desire, and exhibitionistic theatricality. Although I prefer at this point to veil the particular features of theatrical legitimation for later exposure, a broader theoretical illustration of this structure might now be sketched in terms of the link between Bacon's concept of legitimation and Habermas's contemporary study, *Legitimation Crisis*. Habermas opens his book by remarking on the double structure of linguistic communication underlying legitimation praxis. He maintains that communication about propositional content may occur only with simultaneous metacommunication concerning interpersonal relations. Intentional content transforms "needs and feelings into normative expectations (precepts and values). This transformation produces the distinction, rich in consequences, between the subjectivity of opinion, wanting, pleasure and pain, on the one hand, and the utterances and norms that appear with a *claim to generality* on the other. Generality means objectivity of knowledge and legitimacy of valid norms. Both insure the *community or shared meaning* that is constitutive for the socio-cultural life-world."[10]

In the practice of literary science, moreover, objective truth traditionally has been thought to keep in check any libidinal deviancy from the hermeneutic aims of the critical community. Through the ideology of community or consensus, the transformation of feelings into normative expectations coalesces in the laws of literary history and criticism, laws describing and prescribing the act of reading.[11] In Habermas's language, "we must also conjecture an inner logic through which a hierarchy of non-reversible sequences is fixed from the outset. Limits of a rationally reconstructible pattern of development are reflected in the trivial experience that cognitive advances cannot be simply forgotten as long as the continuity of tradition is unbroken, and that every deviation from the irreversible developmental path is experienced as a regression that exacts its price."[12] Until recently, the obligation of the literary historian was to respect these legitimate limits of reason, to bolster the continuity of tradition, and to yield to the force of criticism's irreversible developmental path. In sum, literary historians have followed the lead of the likes of Francis Bacon who began to map out the boundaries of critical legitimation.

I must now admit, however, that my comparison of the projects of Habermas and Bacon has been more strategic than precise. For readers of Bacon might recall his care not to inscribe, as Habermas does, legitimate interpretation in the hierarchy of non-reversible sequences of tradition and history. Rather Bacon stresses the folly of any critical dependence on such determinacy: "I candidly confess that the natural history which I now have, whether collected from books or from my own investigations, is neither sufficiently copious nor verified with sufficient accuracy to serve the purposes of legitimate interpretation."[13] Very much unlike Habermas, Bacon accents the noticeable gap between the project of history and the codes of legitimation. He acknowledges, even if in the guise of a critical lament, the impotency of history, whose paradigms of performative, dominant authority and constitutive narration fail to serve Bacon's purpose. No matter how copious or verifiable, historiography performs only its insufficiency as a method of analyzing the processes and attendant phantasms of seventeenth-century legitimation.

The seventeenth century is a particularly fertile period for theoretical study precisely because its texts openly express skepticism of the continuities of tradition, of any unbreachable laws of the past. In fact, a great number of texts dwell uncomfortably on the seeming ease with which developmental paths can be reversed. With profoundly different postures, texts by the Bacons and Hobbes in England and the Descartes and Nicoles in France interest themselves in the structures of regression per se and in the precarious repression of desire which so profoundly begets the laws of legitimation. Rather than overlooking the seductions of desire, many seventeenth-century writers, especially practitioners of theatrical enterprises, turn their attention to mental and linguistic forces of reversibility, those forces focusing the critic's attention on the disruptive manifestations of desire and persuasion standing alongside the veil of historical continuity.

Allegorical Deconstructions

In re-positioning the place of seventeenth-century historicism in view of its epistemological relation to the repression of desire and fantasy, I wish to cite the precedent of Walter Benjamin's study, *The Origin of German Tragic Drama*. In this book, which has received far too little attention from contemporary scholars of the baroque (and which prefigures in many ways the recent, differing theoretical projects of Paul de Man, Louis Marin, Jean-Francois Lyotard, and Jacques Derrida), Benjamin examines the strategy of historical recuperation in the context of the performativity of a conflicting style of academic narration, that of allegorization. Benjamin broadly explicates the seventeenth-century view of natural history in terms of the baroque *method of viewing* it. "From the point of view of the baroque, nature serves the purpose of expressing [teleology's] meaning, it is the emblematic representation of its sense, and as an allegorical representation it remains irremediably different from its historical realization. In moral examples and in catastrophes history served only as an aspect of the subject matter of emblematics. The transfixed face of signifying nature is victorious, and history must, once and for all, remain contained in the subordinate role of stage-property."[14] When history is transformed into a declining and ineffective stage prop, much as natural history is in Bacon's *The New Organon*, allegorical representation displaces the act of legitimate interpretation. At issue is not the status of historical facts and structures, but how they are assembled in and through narrative in a philosophical collation of allegory (emblem) and allegoresis (reading).[15] In Benjamin's succinct words, "the object of [such a] philosophical criticism is to show that the function of artistic form is as follows: to make historical content, such as provides the basis of every important work of art, into a philosophical truth. This transformation of material content into truth content makes the decrease in effectiveness, whereby the attraction of earlier charms diminishes decade by decade, into the basis for a rebirth, in which all ephemeral beauty is completely stripped off, and the work stands as a ruin. In the allegorical construction of the baroque *Trauerspiel* such ruins have always stood out clearly as formal elements of the preserved work of art."[16]

The representational object of such an allegorical construction might be identified as the ideological/epistemological *truth-claim*. An analysis of seventeenth-century theatrical legitimation will want to account not only for historical data concerning drama and its representations but also for the figures re-positioning such content into textual narratives bearing claims of authority. We need but to turn to Paul de Man for a concise clarification of this critical difference. In *Allegories of Reading*, he questions whether the pattern of certain narratives are "'historical,' i.e., revelatory of a teleological meaning, or 'allegorical,' i.e., repetitive of a potential confusion between figural and referential statement."[17] De Man would ask us to consider whether we can account in the narration of seventeenth-century theatrical legitimation for something other than historical process or philosophical "becoming." Can we recognize instead legitimation's rhetorical phantasms of repetition and preservation? Might not repressed figures of desire—whether of pleasure or fear, of power or paranoia—underlie legitimation's claims to irreversible development and cognitive advance? Might not figural marginality and deviation from the norm be constitutive of theatrical legitimation in a way that re-positions regression as the essence rather than what Habermas negatively calls the "price" of critical constancy and authority? In sum, might we agree with de Man that the burden of allegory is "to articulate an epistemological order of truth and deceit with a narrative or compositional order of persuasion"?[18]

Such questions perform allegory's rhetorical deconstruction of its own deceptive moves toward narrational and institutional authority. They ask us to take seriously the complex structure of allegory which de Man subtly summarizes in "Pascal's Allegory of Persuasion":

> Allegory is sequential and narrative, yet the topic of its narration is not necessarily temporal at all, thus raising the question of the referential status of a text whose semantic function, though strongly in evidence, is not primarily determined by mimetic moments; more than ordinary modes of fiction, allegory is at the furthest possible remove from historiography. The "realism" that appeals to us in the details of medieval art is a calligraphy rather than a mimesis, a technical device to insure that the emblems will be correctly identified

and decoded, not an appeal to the pagan pleasures of imitation. For it is part of allegory that, despite its obliqueness and innate obscurity, the resistance to understanding emanates from the difficulty or censorship inherent in the statement and not from the devices of enunciation. . . . The difficulty of allegory is rather that this emphatic clarity of representation does not stand in the service of something that can be represented.[19]

Analysis of the allegorical status of seventeenth-century theatrical legitimation requires a critical operation other than the scientific gathering of literary history. It involves the study of the philosophical and ideological status of history as representation, as composed of multilayered rhetorical structures, narrations, and enunciations.

Special attention to the subtle interplay of allegorical statement and enunciational device (rigorously developed by Émile Benveniste and Louis Marin) will extend the scope of such an analysis beyond the limiting site of the allegorical ruin to the twofold performance of representational power. In addition to allegory's forceful attempts to effect lasting presence rather than absence and death, the enunciational apparatus of theatre enacts its own "pouvoir d'institution, d'autorisation et de légitimation."[20] It encodes itself in devices of representation whose formal properties, in their accumulative repetition alone, sanction institutional authority. In observing the structure of theatrical legitimation, my study will pay theoretical attention to both the referential content of the allegorical construction and the enunciational structures of its institutional, ideological authority.

Although few of the theatrical constructs I will consider are openly explicit about the legitimating codes underlying them, they tend as a group to privilege a particular figure empowered with epistemological authority: the critical *genius*. Both an allegorical and enunciational construct, the figure of genius ushers in the field of subjectivity sustaining seventeenth-century expressions of theatrical legitimation. Presented in the different aspects of Authorship, Patronage, and Spectatorship, allegories of genius will be shown to re-present historical content in the guise of the Subject speaking its truth-claim and transcending its status as ruin. Altering the hermeneutical chain through theatrical legitimation, this is the form, as Bacon would have it, of the Phantasm, the Philosopher, the Legitimate Interpreter.

Allegorical Transference

Highlighted differently in France and England, but in ways reflecting and recalling the ideological representations that bridge and distinguish these two cultures, seventeenth-century figures of genius exemplify how particular manifestations of allegory and enunciation, along with more universal structures of law and desire, intersect to present persuasive fictions of theatrical legitimation. In this context, it might be appropriate to mention one other theoretical characteristic of theatrical legitimation before moving on to outline the subject matter of the following chapters. I am thinking of the dependence of legitimation on the combined process of historical and contemporary reception. The breadth and allusiveness of fictional categories as broad as Authorship, Patronage, and Spectatorship may be attributed to the kinship of their refiguration as genius to the representational paradigms of reception per se. Legitimation, as suggested above, is dependent on the allegorical re-positioning or re-generation of objects and Subjects through their narration. This happens through a process of *allegorical transference*, whether from an author's material shift of authority from stage to page, from a patron's self-aggrandizement through the agency of the poet, or from a spectator's re-presentation of the spectacle. To accrue the force of legitimation, these refigurations depend as well on their reading or narrative re-presentation, their being acknowledged as allegories of genius. This complicated structure of legitimation calls to mind Freud's notion of transference, elaborated by Lacan, in which the psychoanalytic exchange between analyst and analysand results in a reshaping of past desires into an altered reality of present narration that has bearing on the future. Different from, but engaged in the initial manifestations of desire, narrative transference actualizes the past of the speaker through representation to the listener. But since the ego of the psychoanalytical subject is no longer identical with the presence which is speaking, "all of the patient's symptoms," writes Freud, "have abandoned their original meaning and have taken on a new sense which lies in relation to the transference."[21] This "new sense," of course, blocks or hinders the patient from acknowledging the original desires (the motivating ideological/epistemological structures) reshaped through the discourse of transference. Lacan goes one crucial step farther than Freud by attributing hermeneutical failure to the entire dialectical situation, to the prejudices, passions, and difficulties of the analyst as well as of the analysand.[22] The dilemma of interpretation that transference poses has provoked more recent narrative theorists to discuss this psychoanalytical process as a possible model of text and reading, one especially well-suited to the dilemmas of historical narration.[23] Indeed, the structure of allegorical transference, discussed above as endemic to theatrical legitimation, can be understood as generating a disjunction of signification (content) and presentation (enunciation), a crisis of reading for all parties.

The first part of this book examines transference in the context of "Authorship as Material Form." Focusing on the different personas of authorship displayed by the public theatre and the printed text in early seventeenth-century England, this discussion looks attentively at the epistemological transfer performed by an author's move from stage to page. Whereas the domain of the public theatre might be understood to nurture significational free play and intertextuality, the printed text offers the playwright the opportunity to transcend authorial anonymity and linguistic ruin through various operations of textual self-representation. The textual materialization of authorship thus enacts the regeneration of the figure of the Self through its objectification in the printed text. This section pays close attention to the editorial activity and critical methodology of Ben Jonson, the first English playwright to publish his own collected plays. Discussing Jonson's marginal position in the dramatic and theoretical institutions in which he participated, I analyze how Jonson's refashioning of his texts into printed plays depended on rational methods of editing and grammar, practices of iconography and textual layout, and subtle strategies of legitimation through the art of dedication and epistle. At stake in this analysis is the relation of differing methodological positions and narratives rather than the discussion of one author's contributions to aesthetic evolution and historical development.

In so distinguishing itself from recent historical overviews of Jonson's interests in poetics and theatre, my analysis not only recounts Jonson's strategies of authorial self-reference but also deconstructs the methodology of authorship. Of particular interest is how critical authority depends heavily on the playwright's trust in semiotic practices and representations. In the final chapter on authorship, "The Critic's Standard," I go on to outline the methodological relation of Jonson's activities to the eighteenth-century formulation of the academic discipline of dramatic literature and its standards of authorial reason.

Part Two illustrates the widening field of dramatic source and method confronting the theoretical comparatist. In developing a literary concept of "Theatrical Portraiture," this section recounts allegorical features of seventeenth-century French patronage and legitimation. It analyzes a combination of rhetorical and practical figures of theatre that confuses the lines between legal and literary legitimation. "Phantoms of the Theatre" places the theatrical interests of Cardinal Richelieu in the philosophical context of the Jansenist attack on theatre and the political context of ideological centralization. "The Printed Portrait" discusses how the rhetoric of French printed portraits and dedicatory epistles formulates a language of passions that allows historical figures to memorialize themselves as textual "figures." Both chapters exemplify the charged concern of seventeenth-century French theorists with the figural in both art and literature. Is the figural a rhetorical trait to be manipulated and controlled in the expression of philosophical speculation and ideological centralization? Or is it a theatrical feature accentuating the fictions of speculative power and the regenerative strength of desire?

This section on "Theatrical Portraiture/Figural Patronage" sketches the dual scene of any theatrical figuration of genius. On one hand, the transference of theatrical portraiture regenerates the agency of drama—author, spectator, player—through the omniscient figure of the Prince. On the other hand, this allegory highlights how the Prince thereby transfers to the agency of spectators and readers the re-presentation of Self and portraiture. Once again the phantasm of legitimate interpretation surfaces as allegory's principal reference.

Part Three turns more directly than the previous discussions to the phantasmatic allegory of "Desire as Spectator." Its opening two chapters pursue a deconstructive reading of the Abbé d'Aubignac's *La Pratique du théâtre*, the treatise traditionally accepted as a theoretical key to neoclassical theatre and ideology. By elaborating on d'Aubignac's critical trope of "color," and by relating it to painting theory, the analysis suggests that this treatise endorses the ideology of rational, artistic centralization (for Richelieu and later for Louis XIV) while simultaneously undercutting it with a competing theory of spectatorship. The theoretical precepts of this notion of spectatorship aim at stimulating libidinal responses, which Lyotard theorizes as the dizzying energies underlying narration per se. In displacing the theatre of sovereign politics with a praxis of "nonrepresentation," they endorse a differing aspect of theatrical legitimation, "plaisirs légitimes."

The book's concluding chapter extends this allegory of a subliminal theatre in a short reflection on the late seventeenth- and early eighteenth-century French aesthetic of the sublime. This discussion positions, perhaps more openly than the preceding chapters, the critical stakes posed by the traditional tendency to rein seventeenth- and early eighteenth-century literary study in the harness of speculative rationality and authorial legitimation. It specifically addresses the implications of literary history's institutionalization of the figure of genius. Written partially in view of the differing aspects of Neil Hertz's writings on the sublime, Julia Kristeva's theory of the "abject," Lyotard's work on subliminal aesthetics, and Derrida's recent analysis of invention, the book ends by presenting energetic spectating as an alternative deconstructive and ideological praxis of comparative criticism.[24]

In some respects compatible with the efforts of the "new historicism" to dismantle the canon, my readings of seventeenth-century theatrical legitimation may work to disfigure many conventions prescribed by the academic tradition of the comparative study of drama. The four chapters on authorship cover a wide range of primary sources, forging the way for the book's continual implosion of the canon of dramatic literature. To maintain even an elementary vision of the complex theatrical representations of seventeenth-century England, contemporary readers might want to consider the sociology of early printed plays, the philosophical importance of antitheatrical tracts, the iconology of printed front matter, the strategy and ideology of dedicatory texts, and the legitimating presence and role of the new science. In a similar fashion, the chapters on French portraiture and spectatorship weave intricate and somewhat unfamiliar patterns of written portraiture, artistic representation and theory, philosophical and theological sources, and formal rhetorical theory and practice. But rather than presenting a "new" version of historical narrative and the cultural similarities of French and English artifacts, these varied and interdisciplinary references illustrate the frenetic mental environment that fashioned seventeenth-century theatricality and now frustrate its (post)modern reconstruction.

In regenerating historical facts through theoretical narration, allegorical transference derails overconfidence in critical authority. My theoretical enterprise assumes that its analysis of theatrical legitimation will catalyze future critical dialogue regarding its gaps in traditional modes of comparison. Illustrating the futility of claims of narrative mastery over any particular allegory, economical necessity limits this book to close analyses of some very idiosyncratic features of the allegories in question: Ben Jonson's editing in England, Richelieu's theatrics and d'Aubignac's deconstructions in France, among others. Clearly the diversity of French seventeenth-century theatre extends beyond the self-legitimation of Richelieu and the sometimes eccentric writings of d'Aubignac, just as the scope of Jonson's peculiar activities in the theatre goes far beyond the anti-theatrical nature of his obsession with print. It could be argued, moreover, that I understate the obvious kinship of notions of Authorship, Patronage, and Spectatorship in England and France for the sake of emphasizing the critical differences between particularly extreme and theatrical allegories of genius. Acknowledging the insufficiencies of narration per se, this study of seventeenth-century theatrical legitimation depends primarily on the relative openness of allegorical discourse. What Lyotard might call "petites histoires," the chapters to follow dis-play and re-present the ideological structures of text and performance.[25]

If this book can be said to have a dominant aim, then, it is to unveil masks of critical domination. In view of the preceding remarks on the seductive, contemporary discussion of consensual legitimation, this introductory chapter ends with recollections of Lyotard's response to Habermas: that critical narration generates more attention to agonistic fluidity than to normative modes of deliberation.[26] It thus displays how the epistemological certainties of interpretation remain shaped by the deceits of desire and the ruptures of ideology. Inscribed in the condition of (post)modern "theory," these readings aim to reveal the instabilities of their own conventions. Not denying the presence or political force of dominating notions of literary consensus, this book wishes only to re-present critical commonplaces in the vulnerable ideological frames of their institutional legitimation. In view of Lyotard's critique of Habermas, they flush out the very theatricality of critical legitimation:

En s'intéressant aux indécidables, aux limites de la précision du contrôle, aux quanta, aux conflits à information non complète, aux "*fracta*," aux catastrophes, aux paradoxes pragmatiques, la science postmoderne fait la théorie de sa propre évolution comme discontinue, catastrophique, non rectifiable, paradoxale. Elle change le sens du mot savoir, et elle dit comment ce changement peut avoir lieu. Elle produit non pas du connu, mais de l'inconnu. Et elle suggère un modèle de légitimation qui n'est nullement celui de la meilleure performance, mais celui de la différence comprise comme paralogie.[27]

 PART ONE

AUTHORSHIP AS MATERIAL FORM

2

Theatre's Obscene Counterfeiting

When Philip Sidney praises dramatic poetry as an art of imitation, he speaks of it as "a representing, counterfetting, or figuring foorth" whose dual purpose is "to teach and delight."[1] Sidney is not unique, of course, in extolling poetic representation, figures, and counterfeits as didactic devices. He is speaking from within a tradition of texts by Aristotle, Horace, and Scaliger. Nor is Sidney's *An Apologie for Poetrie* the sole treatise in Renaissance England to ponder the significance of counterfeiting as a poetic norm and model teaching method. The pens of a group of polemical writers—John Northbrook and Stephen Gosson among others—spilled much ink in evaluating what and how counterfeiting teaches. Yet the intent of these essayists was not, like Sidney's, to link representation "to the highest end of the mistres Knowledge . . . in the knowledge of a mans selfe, in the Ethicke and politick consideration, with the end of well dooing and not of well knowing onely."[2] Rather, writers who defined themselves as critics of the theatre, such as Northbrook, Gosson, and their seventeenth-century counterpart William Prynne, recognized the end of dramatic counterfeiting to be the imitation of "noysome" lust, the visitation of stews, and the solicitation of dolls common rather than the knowing and well doing of mistress knowledge.

These critics of the theatre do not debate Sidney's claim that dramatic poetry is an art of imitation, that its counterfeiting teaches the spectator how to know and perform things. The persuasiveness of such teaching is the source of their antitheatrical fear and their critique of dramatic counterfeiting. In admitting that plays teach even the art of counterfeit that so motivates drama, John North-brook worries about the dangerous and infectious consequences of such instruction: "If you will learne howe to bee false and deceyve your husbandes, or husbandes their wyves ... howe to beguyle, howe to betraye, to flatter, lye, sweare ... to disobey and rebell against princes ... shall not you learne, then, at such enterludes howe to practise them?"[3] So potent is the theatrical infection described by Northbrook that it cannot be attributed to any one aspect of dramatic spectacle and life. Discourse, intention, action, gesture, music, and expression find themselves equally tainted. "This open corruption," as Gosson terms it, "is a pricke in the eyes of them that see it, and a thorne in the sides of the godly, when they heare it. This is a poyson to beholders."[4] Even the dramas of this period, especially those of Shakespeare, Marlowe, and Jonson, express anxieties about the poisons of their own theatricality.[5] The antitheatrical prejudice nurtured fears that morality, social order, and political hierarchies could be undermined by the public's imitation of the innumerable counterfeits performed on the stage. The stage's opponents believed that mimetic models of behavior and thought presented to the theatregoer were counter to the moral virtues and practices fitting to "Governours, Government, Religion, and Devotion."[6]

Textual Counterfeits

One concrete source of Renaissance English theatrical corruption remains especially pertinent to our own contemporary reflections on matters of legitimacy. Textuality—the status of the authoritative dramatic text and the attendant problem of authorship—is a sensitive issue for both modern theoreticians and early critics of English drama. From Roland Barthes to Michel Foucault, contemporary thinkers have been pondering anew the notion of authorship as a reflection of standards of intentionality and textuality.[7] Similar theoretical reflection on the stakes of Renaissance textuality should enable us to highlight the ideological and representational implications of early notions of authorship. A contemporary summary of the form and production of the Renaissance dramatic text might well suggest that the textual matter of Renaissance theatre provides historical documentation not only for the traditional academic focus on aesthetics and attribution, but also, and more important, for our critical reception of the concepts of authorship, intentionality, and production. These are concepts that highlight the dependence of the dramatic artifact on the activities of transference: they inscribe poetic identity in the public's determination of authority as well as in the writer's private purposes; they rely on codes of reading as well as on standards of writing.

Especially problematic to the drama's early critics was how the production of a text often occluded any possibility of confident attribution. The Renaissance stage practice of imitating, feigning, and counterfeiting often concealed the identity of authors and sometimes led to fraudulent performances of an author's text. Stephen Gosson, for instance, was haunted by the latter custom:

> I was enformed by some of you which heard it with your ears, that since my publishing the *Schole of Abuse*, two Playes of my making were brought to the Stage. . . . These they very impudently affirme to be written by me since I had set out my invective against them. I can not denie, they were both mine, but they were both penned two yeeres at the least before I forsoke them, as by their owne friends I am able to prove: but they have got suche a custome of counterfaiting upon the Stage, that it is growen to an habite, & will not be lefte.[8]

Gosson links the illicit representation of an author's script and the feigning of an author's intentions to the sickening habit of theatrical counterfeiting—a habit affecting (infecting) the authors of plays as well as the spectators. If Gosson's problem was commonplace in Renaissance England, the modern critics of early English stage plays face a weighty dilemma. How do we identify *noncounterfeited* plays? Or more to the point of the ideology of Renaissance studies, how do we understand the theoretical context of our discipline's strong motivation to identify *original* or *authentic* dramatic texts? Why do we often stress the originary production of writing over the shifting, even counterfeiting representations of reading?

The problem of textual purity is hardly new to literary criticism. Since before Samuel Johnson, editors of dramatic texts have been obsessed with exorcising the corruption inherent in any text of the early English public theatre. In "PROPOSALS For Printing, by

SUBSCRIPTION, THE DRAMATICK WORKS of William Shakespeare," Johnson asserts an editorial concern that still remains a standard of textual reconstruction: "The business of him that replenishes an ancient book is, to correct what is corrupt, and to explain what is obscure."[9] To perfect a faulty text, according to Johnson, requires the identification of parts foreign to the author's manuscript, lines which have been fitted onto the text apart from or even counter to the original. Johnson adamantly proposes the purgation of Shakespearean humors through an editorial cleansing of Shakespeare. "He that undertakes an edition of Shakespeare, has all these difficulties to encounter, and all these obstructions to remove. The corruptions of the text will be corrected by a careful collation of the oldest copies, by which it is hoped that many restorations may yet be made."[10]

Concurrent with the belief that an original text can be deciphered is the critical imperative to explain faithfully the author's ideas and intentions that the illicit text has obscured. In Johnson's words, "with the causes of corruption that make the revisal of Shakespeare's dramatick pieces necessary, may be enumerated the causes of obscurity, which may be partly imputed to his age, and partly to himself."[11] It is now a commonplace that the recovery of an ancient text—its words and its meaning—should constitute the true business of a textual scholar. But even cursory consideration of the dramatist's profession in Shakespeare's time—or better, a detailed study, as performed by Bentley[12]—will challenge the possibility of ever being able to master a dramatic text of the Renaissance. For the author's copy was always the first source of corruption, ruin, and counterfeit in the English public theatre.

Samuel Johnson bemoans two aspects of theatrical counterfeit that discolor the authorial sources of dramatic literature. One is the art of imitation practiced by the players and their pen-wielding accomplices. Renaissance dramas were written as well as played according to the principle of theatrical plunder. To begin with, the Tudor/Stuart dramatists shared a vast information network of classical models, set pieces, and popular plots. The subtle poet worked these many sources into a verisimilar fable whose unity disguised the disparity of its textual roots. In praise of Ben Jonson, Dryden writes, "he invades Authours like a Monarch, and what would be theft in other Poets, is onely victory in him."[13] Jonson's *Discoveries* explicitly recommends such intertextual weaving as the art of the dramatist:

that, which wee especially require in him is an exactnesse of Studie, and multiplicity of reading, which maketh a full man, not alone enabling him to know the *History*, or Argument of a *Poeme*, and to report it: but so to master the matter, and Stile, as to shew, hee knowes, how to handle, place, or dispose of either, with *elegancie*, when need shall bee. . . . to Nature, Exercise, Imitation, and Studie, *Art* must bee added, to make all these perfect. And, though these challenge to themselves much, in the making up of our Maker, it is Art only can lead him to perfection, and leave him there in possession, as planted by her hand.[14]

The passage suggests that dramatic poetry is deficient if it only imitates and invokes classical and contemporary sources. What the dramatist must master is the multiplicity of reading, whose perfection involves the re-presentation of textual "possession, as planted by her hand."

Although Ben Jonson himself did not always disguise his sources in order to enjoy confident possession of ancient texts, his comments on artistic perfection remind us that the creativity of most Renaissance playwrights was particularly apparent in their craftsmanship at acquiring and dissembling mimetic debts. In Puttenham's *The Arte of English Poesie*, this theatrical ability to reshape, as if new, "any president or paterne layd before them" elevates the dramatists to the level of "truly the most excellent imitators and counterfaitors of all others."[15] Still, this dual act of poetic appropriation and dissemblance, which was second nature to Renaissance playwrights, tends to irritate certain sensibilities first voiced by the enlightened readers of the eighteenth century. Mr. Mason, for instance, admonishes Ben Jonson for the art that Jonson so proudly called his own:

Jonson's writings are one continued series of Imitation and allusion: where he not only translates the ancients, many passages from whom are translated in his performances, and chime in as regular and as if they were the product of his invention: but he gleans as freely, and without reserve, from the moderns when they make for his purpose. . . . In a word, such a one was *Johnson*, that he seems to have made it his study to cull out of others sentiments, and to place them in his works as if from his own mint. This is surely an odd species of improvement from reading, and savours very little of Invention or Genius: It borders very nearly upon, if it is not really plagiarism.[16]

And while Mason charges that the thefts and lies of Ben Jonson darken the luster of poetic genius, another eighteenth-century critic,

Samuel Johnson, understands intertextuality to be the sublime, or better yet, the subliminal factor behind the obscurity of Shakespeare's genius: "Shakespeare is the first considerable authour of sublime or familiar dialogue in our language. Of the books which he read, and from which he formed his stile, some perhaps have perished, and the rest are neglected. His imitations are therefore unnoted, his allusions are undiscovered, and many beauties, both of pleasantry and greatness, are lost with the objects to which they were united, as the figures vanish when the canvas has decayed."[17] The "figuring forth" or "representing" of the dramatic genius is in fact the disfiguring of a wide body of texts manipulated by playwrights to their advantage and sometimes to the disadvantage of their baffled readers.[18] The multiplicities of a writer's reading constitute the clarity and obscurity of the dramatic text.

Concerning obscure reception, Stephen Gosson's antitheatrical texts speak directly to the eighteenth-century consideration of plundering as a shaper of mental and moral confusion. His *Playes Confuted in Five Actions* approaches the subject of poetic plundering almost as if it were a direct reflection of the stage's lying bawds and changelings: "The *Palace of pleasure*, the *Golden Asse*, the *Aethiopian historie*, *Amadis of Fraunce*, the *Rounde table*, *baudie Comedies* in *Latine*, *French*, *Italian*, and *Spanish*, have beene throughly ransackt, to furnish the Play houses in London. How is it possible that our Playemakers headdes, running through *Genus* and *Species* & every *difference* of lyes, cosenages, baudries, whooredomes, should present us any *schoolemistres of life, looking glasse of manners, or Image of trueth*?"[19] Considering Gosson's charge, we might say that a play's immoral content reflects only too well its sensual sources and its plunderous making. The poets' greed not only induces them to pillage an entire body of texts but also attracts them to carnivalesque sources reflecting theatrical plunder and counterfeiting. Whether or not we can verify Gosson's claim with convincing "historical facts," we can readily acknowledge and dwell on the allegorical implications of his troubled remark. Regardless of the fact that ribald literature might have influenced other poetic genres, or that poets as well as playwrights might have readily confused creativity and plagiarism, Gosson projects the threat of all slippage onto the limited space of the theatre. He correlates the loss of the mythical, mimetic looking glass of truth to the misleading seductions of theatrical "*Genus* and *Species* and every *difference* of lyes, cosenages."

In so promoting generic differences as well as the slippage of what Derrida calls conceptual *différance,* the dramatic texts of early seventeenth-century England, like the methods of their invention, bred an hysteria among antitheatricalists which remains familiar to us today on a different stage of debate. We might well appreciate the psychological and epistemological motivations of such antitheatricality in view of today's critical anxieties over "theory."[20] These concerns turn around the anxiety that textual lewdness and looseness—matters of style and its complex levels of performative transference—might lead audiences astray from any direct perception of hermeneutical reality, from any gratifying embrace of the "schoolemistres of life."[21] In striving for a credible, humanistic alternative, the opponents of deconstructive, theoretical *différance* join the earlier Renaissance polemicists against theatrical difference in focusing their attention on the phantasmic relation of textual practice to the "Image of trueth." As I suggest in the previous chapter, such a belief in "any schoolemistres of life, looking glass of manners, or Image of trueth" counts on the fact that all writers and readers desire to find themselves in the same schoolhouse. As the following chapters will note in discussing the ideological differences between the theatre of authors, patrons, and spectators, this trust in a humanistic sameness depends on the certainty of a community of readers, all sharing common codes of practice, performance, and agreement.

In the terms of the early discussions of the Renaissance theatre, we might say that the issue of common agreement turns our attention to the matter of method. Similar to contemporary adversaries of "theory," the earlier critics of theatre, be they the Church leaders of Tudor/Stuart England or the enlightened brethren of eighteenth-century taste, were bothered more by theatrical method, its custom, and its imitation outside the playhouse than by the actual condition of stage plays and corrupted texts. A significant amount of William Prynne's *Histriomastix* preaches against the imitation of theatre's profane discourses ("frothy excrements" and "swelling words") whose "play-house phrases . . . [are] too frequent in our sermons."[22] Indeed, Prynne and his Tudor successors had plenty of reason to be concerned. For the proliferation of the polysemy of dramatic figures and counterfeit phrases beyond the bounds of the playhouse constituted one of theatre's most significant influences on the period's social and monarchical order.[23]

Courtiers and dramatists alike generally acknowledged, if not always without ambivalence, that theatricality was the bedrock of political action and social thought. An important section of Jona-

than Goldberg's *James I and the Politics of Literature* recounts the
frequent seventeenth-century citation of the commonplace "*Qui
nescit dissimulare nescit regnare,* He who does not know how to
dissimulate does not know how to rule." Goldberg reminds us that
this "motto of dissembled rule" appears not only in *Cabinet-Coun-
cil Containing the Chief Art of Empire and Mysteries of State; Dis-
cabineted* but also in a text bearing strong implications for the analysis of allegories of genius, Puttenham's treatment of "the Courtly
figure *Allegoria.*"[24] The proliferation of courtly allegoresis and
authoritative dissemblance was fueled by the many guides written
specifically for the courtier on how to operate both inside and outside of court. Robert Dallington's *Aphorismes,* to cite one particularly eloquent example, spins an allegory of the most effective political comportment of the age: "He that weareth his heart in his fore-
head, and is of an ouvert and transparent nature, through whose
words, as through cristall, ye may see into every corner of his
thoughtes: That man is fitter for a table of good-fellowshippe, then
a Councelltable: For upon the Theater of publick imployment either
in peace or warre, the actors must of necessity weare vizardes,
and change them in everie Scene."[25] Change, sometimes merely
for the sake of change, governed the manners and methods of
Tudor politicians both in combat and in repose. The "vizarde"
replaced the mirror as the dramatic accessory of effective courtly
performance.

A Crisis of Transference

It might be interesting, moreover, to note the displacing effect of the
seventeenth-century discomfort with theatricality's many guises. By
focusing on the theatrical fabrications and the sexual and/or textual
fabrics of the playhouse and its extended political arena, the antitheatrical anxiety failed to recognize, or simply refused to admit,
that the problem of referential obscurity was not limited merely to
the stages of theatre and court but was characteristic of a crisis of
transference in general. The ease of counterfeiting an author's intentions implied a culture-wide breakdown of linguistic signification.
Concurrent with the popularity of public theatre in Renaissance
England, Europe witnessed a resurgence of philosophical skepticism
and scientific reevaluation. In *The New Organon,* to return to a
familiar source, Bacon develops his intricate theoretical allegory

linking theatricality and philosophical carelessness: "this admiration of men for knowledges and arts—an admiration in itself weak enough, and well-nigh childish—has been increased by the craft and artifices of those who have handled and transmitted sciences. For they set them forth with such ambition and parade, and bring them into the view of the world so fashioned and masked as if they were complete in all parts and finished."[26] Along with texts by a large number of philosophers as divergent as Montaigne, Ramus, and Hobbes, Bacon's essay questions the natural accuracy of human understanding. Concealed behind the masks of artifice and the folds of appearance, the chains of knowledge are no longer trusted as sound and unbreakable.

Bacon attributes this breach of mimetic representation to a pedagogical and sociological overemphasis on matters of style and rhetoric. "An affectionate study of eloquence and copie of speech," he writes, "grew speedily to an excess; for men began to hunt more after words than matter; more after the choiceness of the phrase, and the round and clean composition of the sentence, and the sweet falling of the clauses, and the varying and illustration of their works with tropes and figures, than after the weight of matter, worth of subject, soundness of argument, life of invention, or depth of judgement."[27] In attributing the demise of content to an excess of eloquent phrasings and reshapings, Bacon locates the crisis of representation in theatrical strategies of linguistic presentation and the flamboyant or performative use of tropes and figures. He expresses a similar distrust of theatrical and rhetorical counterfeit in *The New Organon*, which maintains that the seductive force of tropes eclipses the bare powers of truth. In discussing "the idols and false notions which are now in possession of the human understanding," Bacon openly attributes the distemper of learning to the confusion of words. As discussed earlier, he places much of the blame for this cancerous situation on the philosophical tradition, which he summarizes as "Idols of the Theatre, because in my judgment all the received systems are but so many stage plays, representing worlds of their own creation after an unreal and scenic fashion."[28] Texts by Bacon and many other seventeenth-century writers, from Hobbes to Ben Jonson, all acknowledge that the methods of learning had become too akin to the mental and textual practices of theatre. They caution their readers not to be duped into blindly accepting ancient or modern philosophers' books. The verity of what books say—their signification—falls under suspicion. At issue, then, is confusion over legitimacy itself. How can one determine and verify any dependable standard of legitimate interpretation?

If we now redirect our attention back to Samuel Johnson and his other reservation concerning textual counterfeiting, we will appreciate the extensiveness of the legitimation crisis peculiar to English Renaissance drama. In and around the Renaissance playhouses, the codes of authorship and reception were undercut not only by theoretical and textual uncertainties stemming from theatrical style and performance but also by legal relationships endemic to theatrical culture. Authority over the period's dramatic texts belonged by English custom to the licensed possessor of the manuscript.[29] The text both literally and figuratively passed out of the author's hands upon its receipt by the acting company. As a rule, a playwright of the public theatre neither published nor released his manuscript to private parties before submitting it to his patrons, the players. What became of the text from the moment of its receipt was at the discretion of the commissioning players. The manuscript was usually vetted, revised, and occasionally even printed by the company presenting it.[30] An author's handwritten copy often became unrecognizable after the company and its freelance writers made innumerable alterations. These disguises of Shakespeare's texts provoked the scorn of Samuel Johnson:

> But of the works of Shakespeare the condition has been far different [from that of writers who publish their own works]: he sold them, not to be printed, but to be played. They were immediately copied for the actors, and multiplied by transcript after transcript, vitiated by the blunders of the penman, or changed by the affectation of the player; perhaps enlarged to introduce a jest, or mutilated to shorten the representation; and printed at last without the concurrence of the authour, without the consent of the proprietor, from compilations made by chance or by stealth out of the separate parts written for the theatre.[31]

In the theatrical workshops there was nothing sacred about an author's manuscript. A text which might have been precious to its maker was but a theatrical commodity to its players.[32] The intentions of the poet were not as important to the company as was the theatrical product that resulted from revision, collaboration, and subsequent ventriloquism through gesture and voice.

Any reference to an "original" text, Alexander Pope notes, pertained to

the *Original Copies*; I believe they meant those which had lain ever
since the Author's days in the play-house, and had from time to time
been cut, or added to, arbitrarily . . . no better copies than the *Promp-
ter's Book*, or *Piece-meal Parts* written out for the use of the
actors. . . . The Plays not having been before so much as distinguish'd
by *Acts* and *Scenes*, they are in this edition [Shakespeare Folio, 1623]
divided according as they play'd them; often when there is no pause
in the action, or where they thought fit to make a breach in it, for the
sake of *Musick, Masques,* or *Monsters*.[33]

In its own context, any critical assertion of "originality" by Renaissance readers and performers lacked the complimentary status it
has in today's more traditional literary circles. Only by *performing*
the author's script—in the sense of "to complete or make up by
addition of what is wanting" (O.E.D.)—could the players achieve a
drama, a spectacle that provoked wonder and delight.

By the same token, a rigid reproduction or imitation of the
author's script can be understood to have been detrimental to the
health of the Renaissance theatre. Numerous factors contributed to
the alteration of the text for its liberal dramatic presentation: its
contents might have required tailoring for approval by the censors;
prologues and epilogues might have been added for the seduction
or edification of the audience; the parts had to fit the members of
the company; and the actors were allowed some interpretive freedom for their histrionic expression; the script, furthermore, was
revised frequently to whet the palates of an audience hungry for
novelty and bored by reproductions of the same drama.[34] Reflecting
the priority of theatrical originality over textual fidelity, the dramatic company thought of the author's draft as its "foul sheets." W.
W. Greg explains that the author's sheets were "foul" because they
were "not to be understood [as] a first sketch but a copy representing
the play more or less as the author intended it to stand, but not itself
clear or tidy enough to serve as a prompt-book. . . . The author
would know that his text was likely to undergo further alteration to
meet the demands of the censor and the exigencies of the stage, and
. . . he might leave occasional tangles and loose ends to be dealt with
by the book-keeper or settled in rehearsal."[35] That Shakespeare's
unblotted, handwritten text is "foul" may seem preposterous to
modern guardians of authorial rights and intentions. After all, some
critics still choose to follow Samuel Johnson's instructions to shed
from the dramatic text its numerous counterfeit authors, collabo-

rations, alterations, and disguises. But recent debates over Gary
Taylor's newly discovered "long lost lines," or the more complicated questions posed by the divided text of *King Lear*, continue to
cast doubt over the cleanliness of even Shakespeare's foul sheets.[36]
And while the discussions of an author's handwritten drafts tend to
focus primarily on the theoretical issue of intentionality, their most
crucial implications extend to matters fundamental to the epistemological relation of English Renaissance theatre with its society.
Like the use of counterfeited warrants in Ben Jonson's *Bartholomew
Fair*, such decentralized authorship sanctioned freedom of interpretation and action for the players. It is precisely this decentralization
and interpretational liberty revolving around textuality that constitutes, in my opinion, the lasting theoretical legacy of Renaissance
theatricality.[37]

Foul Plays

It might be said that antitheatrical forces would disapprove of the
foul sheets of any author. In a play by Jonson, such scornful distaste
is expressed for poetasters, "a sort of poore starv'd rascalls; that are
ever wrapt up in foule linnen, and can boast of nothing but a leane
visage, peering out of a seame-rent sute."[38] Alongside writers, Renaissance plays were commonly attacked for being "dirty," "foul,"
and "obscene." Today these charges might be extended to pertain
not only to the content of a play but also, as I have noted, to its
methodological status as script. The author's copy is foul primarily
because it is ob/scene: to the purpose of, or on account of (*ob*), its
performance on stage (*scaena*). Were a play penned only for reading, William Prynne would have approved of it. The presentation
of such a text would be limited to the supposedly neutral act of reading and would make only the author accountable for the play's performance. Citing the classical tradition of recitation, Prynne sanctioned plays "read or *recited by the Poets themselves,* or some others
of their appointment before the people, not acted on the Stage by
Players, as now they are."[39] Authorial intentions and good will are
here to be trusted and verified, whereas the stage often disguises the
author behind an ungovernable and frequently anonymous collec-
tivity of pens.

   Denoted by the players as "foul" are the notions of intention
and accountable authorship. Even the Master of the Revels recog-

nized the author's diminutive status in the theatre by making the company's bookholder responsible for upholding the laws of censorship. In the case of any violation of the law, an author was but an accomplice of the *bookholder's* "original." This was because the authorities of Renaissance theatre expected the performative utterance of a play to deviate from a mimetic representation of its author's words, if not thoughts. Even an unblotted text would have been supplemented on the stage, so Prynne warned, by "effeminate amorous, lustfull gestures, complements, kisses, dalliances, or embracements."[40] The obscene text is one completed through the staging of uncontrollable counterfeits and floating signifiers. The potential public imitation of this brand of theatrical foulness compelled critics like Prynne to enter vigorously into combat with theatrical impurities "*by applying some speedy corrosives, and emplaisters to them.*"[41]

On a more practical level—that of the circulating text—the theatre's concept of "foul sheets" exemplified an even wider state of a general dissolution in confident intentionality. Just as a playwright's manuscript was performed and disguised by the players, any Renaissance text was subject to being counterfeited through print. The rapid rise of printing in sixteenth- and early seventeenth-century England left publishers with the rights of ownership over any texts licensed in their possession. In the short time between 1590 and 1602, there were 103 plays printed in England, which marked a surge in the publication of English plays. During Elizabeth's reign, 168 printed quartos, octavos, and duodecimos contained plays.[42] Under solvent conditions, the acting companies stored licensed scripts in their archives and withheld them from publication. The theatrical companies believed that the value of a stage play was enhanced by this process, since the surprise and delight of a play's performance would not be diminished by the text's having been widely circulated beforehand. Because printed plays released by the companies were the exception, printers usually acquired manuscripts from dishonest players who reconstructed the text from memory, from patrons the company favored with private transcripts, or even from the authors, who lacked legal authority over the manuscripts they had submitted to the players. That texts were procured by so many means strongly illustrates the lack of concern in early seventeenth-century England for a standardized dramatic manuscript. If obtained from authors and patrons, the printed books might not bear an exact resemblance to the copy approved by the Master of the Revels[43]; if reproduced by the memories of players, the manuscripts might be radically revised versions of the prompt-copies. Even when the companies did allow their prompt-copies to be published, the players were generally interested less in the literary edification of an anonymous readership or in the poetic stature of any particular play than in the acquisition of needed funds for new theatrical attractions.[44] In all of the above cases, the publication process can be said to reflect the fickle standards of the playhouse. If the text was not transmitted to the printer through theatrical acts of dissemblance and deceit, the printer could be assured that the manuscript bore the imprimatur of the acting company, which, in essence, if not in fact, effaced the proprietary signature of the author.

Even when everything remained above board, the printer still could exercise his own rights to re-produce and even counterfeit the text according to his tastes. In a note to the anonymous *Tamburlaine* (1590), for example, the printer boasts of his own poetic prowess: "*I have (purposely) omitted* and left out some fond and frivolous Iestures, digressing (and *in my poore opinion*) far unmeet for the matter, which I thought, might seeme more tedious unto the wise" (my emphasis).[45] Not only were words thought to be uncertain during this period, but the authorship of books, especially printed plays, could not be assumed with confidence to correspond to the signature owning up to a book. This is why George Chapman complains in one of his printed masques that "these following [lines] should in duty have had their proper places, after every fitted speech of the Actors; but being prevented by the unexpected haste of the Printer, which he never let me know, and never sending me a proofe, til he had past those speeches; I had no reason to imagine hee could have been so forward."[46] From the author's point of view, aspects of publishing bore a very strong resemblance to manners of acting; both were tainted by habitual feigning and counterfeiting.[47]

The format of the early English printed play reflects, moreover, the theatre's notion of the "original" text. Regardless of the means by which the printer acquired a play and whether or not the printed version was true to the prompt-copy, it was common for title pages of plays, often used as advertising propaganda, to boast of a text's faithfulness to its successful performance. As Jonas Barish calls to our attention, a title page that did not read, "As it hath sundry times been playde" or, "As it was lately plaid" was not likely to contribute to the sales of its book.[48] Or when releasing a new edition of a play already published, the printers made sure to announce the play as revised for its current representation on the stage. Of the editions of *Mucedorus and Amadine* listed in Greg's *Bibliography*, for example, the last fourteen continue to advertise the printed play's 1610 augmentation in keeping with the most recent stage production: "*Amplified with new additions, as it* was acted" (my emphasis).[49] Publicizing the printed play's fidelity to the current stage version was apparently so important to sales that many unrevised plays were falsely advertised as having been newly corrected. This deceit appears to have been performed to seduce readers to return to already familiar plays.[50] Although we are not sure whether or not the consumers of printed plays also attended the stage representations so boldly advertised on title pages, the publishers' sly marketing techniques indicate a universal interest in the theatrical tradition of counterfeit and revision.

During the period of theatre's rise in England, cautious thinkers were increasingly wary of being deceived by their changing culture and their own distorted senses. As the theatrical achievements of Iagos, Volpones, Helenas, and Faces amply demonstrate, any act of speech could be clothed either intentionally *or* unintentionally in tangled fabrics of deceit. Bacon writes that human understanding, being comparable to the workings of the theatre, is "framed like a labyrinth, presenting as it does on every side so many ambiguities of way, such deceitful resemblances of objects and signs, natures so irregular in their lines and so knotted and entangled."[51] The dramatist's foul sheets with "tangles and loose ends" were indeed images of the mind.

Theatre, the admitted playing of deceits and ambiguities, was threatening to authors and critics alike. It played the inconstancy of meaning sometimes as comedy, sometimes as tragedy. What was humorous and inviting to some people was threatening and downright frightening to others. Among the antitheatrical forces, some panicked and spent all of their energy on ineffectual attacks on the theatre, an institution which was in essence only one of many possible symbols of inconstancy. Still others took the time to become thoroughly familiar with their opponent of foul play. They then set about carefully and scientifically to work toward a new world of textual constancy.

The latter approach to "the loathèd stage" was practiced by Ben Jonson. The man known by his broken compass recognized the counterfeits of the stage to be indicative of his society's customs of thinking, speaking, and acting with flawed methods. Through editorial practices and a strong motivation for authorial legitimation (which was more naïvely sincere than Bacon's), Ben Jonson tried hard to give rise to a method and form of writing that would be inviolate to the cozenings and cheatings of the stage. In the following elaboration of these general remarks on "Authorship as Material Form," I will discuss Jonson's achievement in view of the form of a book, a textual apparatus symbolic of the intellectual constancy and authorial legitimation which he so desperately sought throughout his career.

3

From Ben's Foul Sheets to Jonson's Parented Text

> If Reader thou hast of this Play been an auditour? there is lesse apology to be used by intreating thy patience. This *Tragi-Comedy* (being one reserved amongst two hundred and twenty, in which I have had either an entire hand, or at the least a maine finger) comming accidentally to the *Presse*, and I having Intelligence thereof, thought it not fit that it should passe as *filius populi*, a Bastard without a Father to acknowledge it.
>
> THOMAS HEYWOOD, *The English Traveller*

No one was more familiar with the public theatre in all of its counterfeits than Ben Jonson. His services to the stage ranged from those of copy hack to collaborator to solicited author. We know through Henslowe's *Diary* that Jonson wrote additions for Kyd's *Spanish Tragedy* and Nashe's *Isle of Dogs*. In collaboration with Chapman and Marston, Jonson penned *Eastward Ho!*, joined Dekker and others for *Page of Plymouth* and *Robert II, King of Scots*, and worked with Fletcher and Middleton in the composition of *The Widow*. Jonson came into his own as a solicited author in Henslowe's circle with the 1598 production of *Every Man In His Humour*.[1] Beyond writing for the players, his frequent interaction with them also led to the sort of crime feared by the antitheatrical polemicists. Jonson theatrically killed Gabriel Spencer in a duel. Jonson's apparent attraction to things dramatic even worked in his favor when he was subsequently convicted of murder and scheduled for capital punishment at Tyburn. For he was able to plead benefit of clergy by read-

ing aloud a psalter to prove his literacy.[2] Upon his release with the
Tyburn brand on his thumb, Jonson once again directed his talents
toward the evil pits of the theatre. This man so theatrical in customs
as in texts must have confirmed the deepest doubts of the stage's
many critics.

Yet Jonson's intimacy with the theatre was the direct cause of
his contempt for it. In an elegant and substantial essay, "Jonson and
the Loathèd Stage," Jonas Barish analyzes the complexity of Jonson's ambivalent relationship with the theatre. Barish identifies
Jonson as one of "a galaxy of talented playwrights who at a given
moment in their careers have seen their whole enterprise as hollow."[3] Although there are many reasons for Jonson's renowned
retreat from the public theatre, Barish relates them to the antitheatrical tradition. On the one hand, Jonson felt compromised by
fickle and corrupt audiences, which are often the subject of ridicule
in his plays. On the other hand, counterfeit itself bothered Jonson.
He was troubled by the inconstancy of the players, by the imper-
manence inherent in poetic conventions of the theatre, and by the
stage's valorization of disguise, change for change's sake, and
"heathen language."

Most pertinent to my discussion of allegories of genius is Jonson's discomfort with his own scene of writing. His epistle prefacing
the printed text of *Volpone* deplores a time "when a Name, so ful
of authority, antiquity, and all great marke, is (through their insol-
ence) become the lowest scorne of the age. . . . This it is, that hath
not only rap't me to present indignation, but made me studious,
heretofore; and, by all my actions, to stand off, from them."[4] In
order to exert authority over the production of his plays, Jonson
stood off from the theatrical workshops where so many pens bore
no name, where so many speeches blurred the image of their par-
ents. He was, so far as is known, the first public dramatist to oversee
actively the printing of his plays. The printed book provided him
with a relatively easy solution to his loss of authorial control. Quite
literally, Jonson's supervision of the printing of his sheets diminished the possibility that they would be "soiled" through the production of a counterfeit bearing an author's name but not his
authority. For print, in Barish's words, "offered the chance to expa-
tiate on critical questions, to debate disputed points, affix post-
scripts, and append emendations."[5]

Jonson's complex mistrust of public theatricality surfaces
throughout his printed writings in references to the Renaissance

dramatist's conception of textuality and the seventeenth-century perception of language. In Epigram 56, "On Poet-Ape," to cite a very familiar example, Jonson unmasks in a bitter tone the plunderous customs of playwriting:

> Poore POET-APE, that would be thought our chiefe,
>   Whose workes are eene the fripperie of wit,
> From brocage is become so bold a thiefe,
>   As we, the rob'd, leave rage, and pittie it.
> At first he made low shifts, would picke and gleane,
>   Buy the reversion of old playes; now growne
> To'a little wealth, and credit in the *scene*,
>   He takes up all, makes each mans wit his owne.
> And, told of this, he slights it. Tut, such crimes
>   The sluggish gaping auditor devoures;
> He markes not whose 'twas first: and after-times
>   May judge it to be his, as well as ours.
> Foole, as if halfe eyes will not know a fleece
>   From locks of wooll, or shreds from the whole peece?[6]

This epigram summarizes my previous argument that the construction of a dramatic text involves as much imitation as creative energy. Counterfeit, the appropriation of texts and the concealment of their sources, is the mainstay of theatrical writing, acting, and viewing, all mistrusted by Jonson for their many "low shifts" and thieveries. Jonson's printed plays, poems, and prose texts berate the gleanings and pickings of the Renaissance playwright for their degradations of poetry and authors. The irony, of course, is that Jonson's texts are also guilty of the same counterfeiting traits they chastise.

Bringing home the depth of this paradox, *Discoveries* relates the disorder of the stage's texts and actions to the perilous health of language in general. Sensitive to the crisis of signification in seventeenth-century England, Jonson writes that any inconstancy of meaning and authorial intention reflects poorly on the state of mind of the commonwealth: "The shame of speaking unskilfully were small, if the tongue onely thereby were disgrac'd: But as the Image of a *King*, in his Seale ill-represented, is not so much a blemish to the waxe, or the Signet that seal'd it, as to the Prince it representeth; so disordered speech is not so much injury to the lips that give it forth, as to the disproportion, and incoherence of things in themselves, so negligently expressed. Neither can his mind be thought to be in tune, whose words doe jarre."[7] Much like the essayists writing against theatre, Jonson acknowledges the representational force of style: it provides both the image and message of the words represented. "Negligent speech doth not onely discredit the person of the Speaker, but it discrediteth the opinion of his reason and judgement; it discrediteth the force and uniformity of the matter, and substance."[8] Words fashioned in loose speech and the fast-changing talk of the stage add much to the threat of linguistic chaos. Yet Jonson does not limit his suspicion of the language of theatre, in whose baseness and looseness his texts are surely implicated, to the manner of speech. In the case of theatre, Jonson perceives linguistic disarray to be as much the responsibility of the writer as a problem of the speaker. "If it be so then in words, which fly and escape censure, and where one good *Phrase* begs pardon for many incongruities, and faults; how shall he then be thought wise, whose penning is thin and shallow? How shall you looke for wit from him, whose leasure and head, assisted with the examination of his eyes, yeeld you no life, or sharpenesse in his writing?"[9] An ordered text, thought true to its author's thoughts and unchanging in its transmission, contributes more to a tuneful community of meaning than do the shrieks and groans of the best players. The sharpness of Jonson's pen etches a figure of authorship begotten legitimately by natural wit and wisdom. "*Language* most shewes a man: speake that I may see thee," *Discoveries* contends. "It springs out of the most retired, and inmost parts of us, and is the Image of the Parent of it, the mind. No glasse renders a mans forme, or likenesse, so true as his speech."[10]

Tanquam Explorator

Earlier studies of Ben Jonson, by critics such as L. J. Potts, D. J. Gordon, Richard C. Newton, Don Edward Wayne, and Lawrence Manley, have documented Jonson's commitment to the rigorous control of inventive methods and his affinity with the new philosophers.[11] The promotion of unconventional methods of scientific selection and discovery was commonplace in late sixteenth- and early seventeenth-century intellectual circles, in groups extending far beyond the bounds of those concerned mainly with poetic fables and narratives. From Ramus to Bacon, thinkers experimented with methodological notions to work beyond their skeptical suspension of traditional models of thought, philosophical investigation, and textual (re)construction. Through their controlled contemplation and observation of isolated entities, the new scientists hoped that new groups and pairings of things and ideas could be discovered that would better represent nature's actual order and man's ability to govern this order. Another look at Jonson's relation to the new science, from a perspective more distinctly allegorical than is apparent in previous secondary discussions, might help to clarify how method, printing, and antitheatricality were intricately linked together in Jonson's representational package.

The early development of mechanical printing was, in Bacon's mind, symbolic both of technological progress and of a technique of restoring lost mastery over words and their implementation.[12] Printing enabled man to think conceptually about his *use* of language. Through the reduction of language to physical properties organized visually on the page, words could be conceived as objects to be touched, tabulated, seen, and thereby secured, improved, perfected, and rationally taught.[13] Bacon sought similar techniques for organizing and objectifying human understanding, for controlling the natural world. He and his contemporaries proposed methods that would restore to man his lost confidence both in his ability to control the natural world and in his own understanding, unbalanced as it was by the emotional and representational vagaries of the imagination. Providing printing with a script as ordered in its thought and presentation as it would be fixed spatially on the page, the various philosophical experiments were invested with hopes of producing mental texts as fully "impressing and lasting" as those sought by Jonson in the print shop.

Ben Jonson's personal motto was *Tanquam Explorator*. His obsession with the practice of strict principles of examination is now a well-documented fact, thanks partially to the work of the above critics. His editing and printing of plays posited a new way of controlling the theatrical text and of reordering the priorities of its use. Yet, we would delimit the significance of Jonson's antitheatrical activities in relegating them entirely to the scene of the new science. Paramount to Bacon's method is the skeptical suspension of traditional models of thought and philosophical investigation. While Bacon stresses the potential fruits of novelty, Ben Jonson is not a writer to break away easily from the habits of tradition.[14] Instead of spurning custom, Jonson's critical projects often arrest custom's flow in order to manipulate it, not so much in the interest of science as to create systems of mechanical reproduction over whose corruption and foulness he can assert control.

Jonson's ambivalent adherence to custom in the wake of the new science is especially evident in *The English Grammar*. In undertaking the construction of a general grammar, Jonson exercised a method of induction common in the seventeenth century. His grammar, moreover, maintains an important place in the grammatical tradition on historical and methodological grounds. Historically, *The English Grammar* is only the second extant grammar written primarily in the interest of the English tongue.[15] The first English grammar penned in the vulgar was fashioned by William Bullokar in 1580 for a double reason: "to no small commoditie of the English Nation, not only to come to easie, speedie, and perfect use of our owne language, but also to their easie, speedie, and readie entrance into the secretes of other Languages."[16] Early English grammars generally emphasized the compilation of etymologies and syntaxes that might facilitate the students' ability to move beyond their native tongue through the acquisition of a foreign language. In fact, most early grammars were written only for the scholarly purpose of "the more certaine Translation of the English tongue into Latine."[17] But Jonson's grammar is unique in its loyalty to the vernacular; it is "for the benefit of all Strangers, out of his observation of the English Language now spoken and in use."[18] Jonson's text is not so much a universal grammar through which an Englishman might escape the feebleness of his own tongue and customs as it is a vehicle for the communication of the rules of the vernacular to its speakers and its hearers from abroad.[19]

Methodologically, *The English Grammar* comes close to serving as an English paradigm of Ramistic grammar.[20] With many direct citations from Ramus, the *Grammar* follows the Ramistic pattern of etymologies and syntax. But the text's preface calls attention to a mixture of influences which is indicative of Jonson's methods of textual construction:

> The profit of *Grammar* is great to Strangers, who are to live in communion, and commerce with us; and, it is honourable to our selves. For, by it we communicate all our labours, studies, profits, without an Interpreter.
>
> Wee free our Language from the opinion of Rudenesse, and Barbarisme, wherewith it is mistaken to be diseas'd; We shew the Copie of it, and Matchablenesse, with other tongues; we ripen the wits of our owne Children, and Youth sooner by it, and advance their knowledge.

Confusion of Language, a *Curse.*

> Experience *breedeth* Art: *Lacke* of Experience, Chance. Experience, Observation, Sense, Induction, are the fower Tryers of Arts. It is ridiculous to teach any thing for undoubted Truth, that Sense, and Experience, can confute. So *Zeno* disputing of *Quies*, was confuted by *Diogenes*, rising up and walking.
>
> In Grammar, not so much the Invention, as the Disposition is to be commended: Yet we must remember, that the most excellent creatures are not ever borne perfect; to leave Beares, and Whelps, and other failings of Nature.[21]

Unlike Ramus, Jonson bases his grammar on the history of a language's use as well as the experience, observation, and sense that breed art. Furthermore, Jonson's favoring of disposition over invention as the primary category of grammar is the opposite of the Ramistic valorization of invention. Jonson's grammar is difficult to place because it is just as aligned with the English logical tradition of John Seton, Thomas Wilson, and Ralph Lever, which favors disposition over invention, as it is a reminder of Ramus's universal grammar divided into the uncomplicated groupings of etymology and syntax.[22]

Still, the most interesting aspect of Jonson's grammar is its unabashed and unique commitment to custom. Jonson's grammatical endeavors aim for a minimum of linguistic confusion and for a freedom from the diseases of signification common to the stage. But does this mean, as it does for Bacon and almost all universal grammarians, the exclusion of language from its historicity, from the customs of its use? The unusual feature of *The English Grammar* is its frequent reflection on the mixed merits of custom as the arbitrary fashioner of the English tongue. Although Jonson's text is not a speculative grammar concerned most with the significational attributes of language, it does seriously and openly ponder the impact of custom upon signification:

> The *Accent* (which unto them [the Latins, Greeks, and Hebrews] was a *tuning* of the voyce, in lifting it up, or letting it downe) hath not yet obtained with us any signe; which notwithstanding were most needfull to be added; not wheresoever the force of an *Accent* lieth, but where for want of one, the word is in danger to be *mis-tuned.* . . . But the use of it will be seene much better by collation of words, that according unto the divers place of their *Accent*, are diversly pronounc'd, and have divers significations.[23]

Jonson's aim, similar to his relation to the public stage, is to know intimately the diverse uses of language before combatting their curses and confusions. Not interested in formulating a pure grammar based upon nominal and objective principles of linguistics, his first consideration is "not now to quarrell *Orthographie*, or *Custome*; but to note the powers."[24]

Ben Jonson sees in his vulgar tongue a rich body of untapped resources which, with the care of grammarians and editors, can be tuned as finely as the great tongues from which it derives. "For what was the ancient Language, which some men so doate upon, but the ancient Custome? Yet when I name Custome, I understand not the vulgar Custome: For that were a precept no lesse dangerous to Language, then life, if wee should speake or live after the manners of the vulgar: But that I call Custome of speech, which is the consent of the Learned; as Custome of life, which is the consent of the good."[25] The thrust of Jonson's grammar is very comparable to that of his dramatic editing: to profit from the blemishes of experience and custom, he transforms confusion into the authoritative regions of typographical art. He understands stable semiotic meaning to derive from syntactic and orthographic order and stability—achieved by consent of the learned. Rather than expurgating, for example, the unusual and awkward second conjugation of the English verb, Jonson the grammarian transfers it from the loose habits of vulgar custom to the rigid order of the grammatical method: "That which followeth, for any thing, I can find (though I have with some diligence searched after it,) intertaineth none, but naturall, and home-borne words, which though in number they be not many, a hundred and twenty, or thereabouts; yet in variation are so divers, and uncertaine, that they need much the stampe of some good *Logick*, to beat them into proportion."[26] In Jonson's view, home-born words bear their fruits only when supported by the frame of grammatical method. Freedom from disease and confusion is to Jonson not so much a matter of invention and purity as a cleansing of a word's natural blemishes of ordering and proportioning.[27]

Although *The English Grammar* claims mainly to serve the interests of the English people by classifying the vulgar tongue, its unusual tone also calls attention to its author's investment in the text's formation. Most early seventeenth-century grammar books present grammar as a universal system based only on univocal patterns and structures of language.[28] But there is more to Jonson's grammar than the factual identification of universal rules of grammar. It places rhetorical emphasis on the source of this English grammar—not custom but the shaper of custom whose authorial voice surfaces strategically in the text, "hoping that I shall be thought sufficiently to have done my part, if in towling this Bell, I may draw others to a deeper consideration of the matter."[29] Although a debate concerning the motivations behind Ben Jonson's *Grammar* might appear to lead us far astray from the matter of theatrical legitimation, I believe they were analogous to the antitheatrical thrust of Jonson's printing: the use, shape, and receptivity of language reflects the method of its organizer through textual manipulation and control of custom. The self-referential tone of *The English Grammar* is best summarized by Jonson himself: "We have set downe that, that in our judgement agreeth best with reason, and good order."[30] Jonson's personal interest in ordering language and text stems, of course, from his belief that "no glasse renders a mans forme, or likenesse, so true as his speech."[31]

Jonson collected texts in the same way that he ordered language. Another method regularly practiced by the new scientists of his time was the compilation of commonplace books. I have already relied on many passages from *Timber: or, Discoveries* to illuminate Jonson's thought. But since a commonplace book illustrates its owner's thoughts mainly through the collection of others' writings, the fact of the book is often more interesting than its contents. If a person wishes to train himself in inductive reasoning (or discovery), he must have, according to Bacon, "a muster or presentation before the understanding of all known instances which agree in the same nature, though in substances the most unlike. And such collection must be made in the manner of a history, without premature speculation, or any great amount of subtlety."[32] Jonson's withdrawal from the public theatre was to some degree in response to a challenge similar to Bacon's. Renaissance public theatre valued the transient, spectacular moment over the history of dramatic texts, authors, and their ideas. The goal of the theatre was delight, not contemplation. As his keeping of commonplace books exemplifies, Jonson's thought process might be said to be antitheatrical. For it is predicated on the conservation of literary history: the recovery and ordering of lost masterpieces and their authors' intentions.

The regular use of a commonplace book in the seventeenth century has been understood to have strengthened the author-as-editor's powers of cognition.[33] Practice in the science of induction comes not only from collecting innumerable authors and passages but also from methodologically ordering them. "Sorting," "cutting out," "woods," and in this case *Timber: or, Discoveries* are the metaphors used in the Renaissance to suggest the dual process of selecting and grouping together passages for contemplation.[34] Similar to the printing of plays, the common-placing of variant texts unites them in one spatially apprehensible image through which its compiler becomes trained in visually maintaining identities and differences—what is done manually in transcribing the commonplace book. The object of such contemplation is textual (or intellectual) history, and the seventeeth-century popularity of commonplace books sustained the tradition of the recovery of ancient texts and authors. In turn, so D. C. Allen claims, the compilation of these texts enhanced the gatherer's learning and literary stature: "one cannot bring together a collection of pertinent quotations without wide reading and a certain exercise of the powers of criticism."[35] To collect such a text, then, is to fashion one's own place in the annals of intellectual history.

Discoveries differs significantly in style and form from other extant English commonplace books of its period. It is not arranged according to readily identifiable commonplaces whose order is determined by alphabetization or theme. Nor does the text bear an index that enables users "to be well ware how thei reade Common places."[36] And most significant, the authors and sources of the extracts in *Discoveries* are not clearly identified by Jonson. It is important that Jonson's commonplace book stands so far apart from other readily retrievable seventeenth-century examples of this genre that Richard C. Newton associates it with *The English Grammar* as an "expository prose work."[37] Indeed the recognizable sources of *Discoveries* are often paraphrased and intermixed in the book with Jonson's own prose musings in a fashion that resembles theatrical counterfeiting. Even the subtitle of *Discoveries* suggests the peculiarity of Jonson's project: "*Made upon Men and Matter: as they* have flow'd out of his daily Readings: or had their refluxe to his peculiar Notion of the Times."[38] Unlike the printed commonplace books whose encyclopedic order and clarity of sources make them accessible to modern readers as documents of intellectual history, Jonson's *Discoveries* openly flaunts the originality of his editorial project and the uniqueness of his own relation to the literary tradition. *Discoveries* not only represents the fashioner's knowledge of history, "his learning and literary stature,"[39] but also projects the editor's personal and peculiar *allegorical* version of history.

Although *Discoveries* is not of the same class as *The English Grammar*, they both illustrate how Ben Jonson twists the customs of method to suit his own representational needs. While Jonson no doubt benefited intellectually from contemplating the development of grammar and the history of ideas, his carefully modelled texts, be they grammars, commonplaces, or plays, to which I will now turn my attention, suggest that the end of such learning was Jonson's personal usurpation and displacement of literary methods and theatrical traditions. His texts project an image of his originality as an author, not to be easily eclipsed and forgotten by the habits of counterfeit.

Shifting Forms

> We see then how far the monuments of wit and learning are more durable than the monuments of power or of the hands ... the images of men's wits and knowledges remain in books, exempted from the wrong of time and capable of perpetual renovation. Neither are they fitly to be called images, because they generate still, and cast their seeds in the minds of others, provoking and causing infinite actions and opinions in succeeding ages.
>
> FRANCIS BACON, *The Advancement of Learning*

The potency of Jonson's authorial seeds is especially impressive when apparent in the smallest of textual kernels. Consider the marginal example of the title pages of Jonson's printed plays. On their own, they provide poignant testimony of the singular, monumental image of authorship made durable by the publication of his dramas. Departing from the customs of early English play printing, Jonson's title pages minimize the conventional appeal to the public's desire for a printed reproduction of the performed version. The title page of the 1600 quarto edition of *Every Man out of his Humour* italicizes Jonson's disregard for the public stage instead of emphasizing his play's run on the bankside: "The Comicall Satyre of EVERY MAN OUT OF HIS HUMOR. AS IT WAS FIRST COMPOSED by the AUTHOR B.I. *Containing more than hath been Publickely Spoken or Acted.* With the severall Character of every Person."[40] By rudely flaunting his "foul sheets," this book clearly publicizes Jonson's own text, not its public performance. For an example much more to the point of alienating both the theatrical community and the common purchaser of quartos, I turn to the title page of *The Alchemist* (1612), whose only reference to the theatre is a Latin epigraph:

> ———Neque, me ut miretur turba, laboro
> Contentus paucis lectoribus.[41]

Content to be deciphered by few readers, this epigraph blatantly snubs both the public spectator, "the sluggish gaping auditor," and the greedy booksellers pandering to low tastes. Contrast the title page of *The Alchemist* with that of, say, *The Merchant of Venice* (1600): "The most excellent Historie of the *Merchant of Venice*. With the extreame crueltie of *Shylocke* the Jewe towards the sayd Merchant, in cutting a just pound of his flesh: and the obtayning of *Portia*, by the choyse of three chests. *As it hath beene divers times acted by the Lord Chamberlaine his Servants.*"[42] This title page is an advertisement designed to compete in the bookstalls with other cheap quartos, joke books, almanacs, and coney-catching pamphlets. Jonson's texts and title pages provide clear indications of his efforts to stand apart from the theatrical scene, printed or performed.

Moreover, the "Induction" of *Bartholomew Fair* openly challenges the public theatre's emphasis on exaggeration and spectacle: "If there bee never a *Servant-monster* i' the *Fayre*; who can helpe it? he sayes; nor a nest of *Antiques*? Hee is loth to make Nature afraid in his *Playes*, like those that beget *Tales*, *Tempests*, and such like *Drolleries*, to mixe his head with other men's heeles."[43] Theatrical appeals to the fantastic and irrational were not, for Jonson, the ends of dramatic poetry.[44] Rather, his efforts in the print shop illustrate his textual concerns with linguistic and rhetorical clarity as well as with visual order and uniformity. These interests favor authorial standards over theatrical wonder.

Printing, as a symbolic act, provided Jonson with a material frame adequate in itself for the performance of his image. Through his attentiveness to the strategy of editing for print, Jonson constructed a stable *forme* of punctuation, spelling, and style that offers its viewers the visual system of dramatic representation particular to his cautiously assembled books. *Sejanus* provides a perfect example of how Jonson produced a printed quarto that surpasses in literary detail its performance on the stage. Fixed in print, this text's detailed marginal notes identify the literary sources of Jonson's play. In the preface "To the Readers," moreover, Jonson stresses his personal concern for the marginalia: "least in some nice nostrill, the *Quotations* might savour affected, I doe let you know, that I abhor nothing more; and have onely done it to shew my integrity in the *Story.* . . . Whereas, they are in *Latine* and the worke in *English*, it was presupposed, none but the Learned would take the paynes to conferre them, the Authors themselves being all in the learned *Tongues*, save one, with whose English side I have had little to doe: To which it may be required, since I have quoted the Page, to name what Edition I follow'd."[45] Such careful literary citation, which boasts of its author's erudition, indicates Jonson's unusual concerns as an editor. Print enhanced Jonson's trust that his dramatic literature, not to mention his personal image, would profit from stylistic and intellectual constancy.

Jonson's transference of texts and methods from stage to book set a precedent that redirected the focus of English theatrical representation. *The WORKES of Benjamin Jonson, 1616* was not only the first collection of one English playwright's plays and poems edited by the author but also the first to appear in folio. This collection prepared the way for the later publication of the folios of Shakespeare (1623), Beaumont and Fletcher (1647), and the posthumous second Jonson (1640). Along with this change of scene and form of dramatic production went a shift of representational purport. Whereas Renaissance dramatic treatises portray the stage as a vehicle of delight and didacticism, the dramatic folio favors the representation of an author. In his dedicatory poem to Shakespeare's 1623 folio, Jonson is quite explicit about his appreciation for such a book:

> Soule of the Age!
> The applause! delight! the wonder of our Stage!
> My *Shakespeare*, rise; I will not lodge thee by
> *Chaucer*, or *Spenser*, or bid *Beaumont* lye
> A little further, to make thee a roome:
> Thou art a Moniment, without a tombe,
> And art alive still, while thy Booke doth live,
> And we have wits to read, and praise to give.[46]

The collected writings of playwrights, especially when encased in folios, assume the stature of literary corpora. Shakespeare finds himself in the elite company of Chaucer and Spenser—in addition to classical authors, theologians, historians, and scientists whose texts were often entombed in folios. The magnificent shape of these books embodies particularly well the increasing system of "self-crowned laureates" which Richard Helgerson depicts as the dominant literary tradition of Jonson's age, a tradition directing the poet "toward the monarch, who is central to the higher and truer poetic identity that he seeks."[47] Yet, as suggested by Jonson's *Poëtaster*, the folio collections might also signify the distinction between a bookish dramatic tradition and the laureate status that poets acquired through identification with the monarch:

> Let us now behold
> A humane soule made visible in life;
> And more refulgent in a senselesse paper,
> Then in the sensuall complement of Kings.[48]

Suggesting a relation different from Helgerson's equation of laureate and princely subject, the folios assume, in many respects, their own sovereign right of authorial succession. Or as Bacon would phrase it, they spawn a legitimate line of textual authority by casting their own seeds in the minds of writers and critics to come.

The monumental stature of the dramatic folio is represented explicitly and implicity in the *WORKES* of 1616. The form and layout of Jonson's collection emphasizes the image of the author and immortality of his texts. In the epistle "To the Most Noble and Most Equall Sisters, The Two Famous UNIVERSITIES," preceding both quarto and folio editions of *Volpone*, Jonson addresses the issue of a special form intended for his printed plays: "if my *MUSES* be true to me, I shall raise the despis'd head of *poetrie* againe, and stripping her out of those rotten and base rags, wherwith the Times have adulterated her form, restore her to her primitive habit, feature, and majesty, and render her worthy to be imbraced, and kist, of all the great and master-*spirits* of our world."[49] The cover of the folio clothes Jonson's plays in a majesty altogether different from the players' costumes of rotten and base rags. For the book's format distinguishes the work of Ben Jonson from that of other playwrights performed on the stage and reproduced in the printed book.

To begin with, there is the matter of the folio's size. Why do Jonson's *WORKES* appear in folio when plays were normally printed in octavo or quarto editions affordable by the general reading public? A folio's large format was, according to Bentley, "generally reserved for sermons, geographies, the classics, royal books like *The Works of King James,* and other such literature thought to be of permanent significance."[50] Representing permanence and status, the physical form of Jonson's *WORKES* is symbolic in itself. From its initial stages as an edited manuscript to its production as a book, the seventeenth-century folio demanded the full attention of anyone involved with it. No other book required all the resources of the printing house for its publication. Financially, it was a risk compared to the publication of quartos that "made for a quick sale, and required but a slender outlay of capital."[51] In the production of Jonson's folio, the printer, Stansby, utilized all of the inventions of printing, from design technique to the most detailed typography. In assembling this volume, Stansby combined layouts as diverse as the ornate opening page of *Poëtaster* (Figure 1) and the reduced-type commentary bordering *The Masque of Queenes* (Figure 2). Even the paper was of such quality that it caused William Prynne to lament, "*some Play-books since I first undertooke this subject, are growne from* Quarto *into* Folio; *which yet beare so good a price and sale, that i cannot but with grief relate it, they are now new-printed in farre better paper than most Octavo or Quarto* Bibles, *which hardly finde such vent as they.*"[52] Considered as a material commodity, the folio of 1616 presents its dramatic literature in a package deemed more worthy than its content by the antitheatrical spokesperson, Prynne. In this context, Jonson's folio requires close critical attention not only because it is a playwright's collection of his own texts, but also because of the social status of the physical object. This folio has been handed down literally through generations of readers as a valuable sovereign monument of Renaissance drama.[53]

The monumental character of Jonson's folio lies not only in its shape and weight but also in the layout of its pages. The folio's texts follow in detail the format of the early printed editions of classical plays. As Herford and Simpson document, the plays in the folio, unlike Jonson's quartos and other English plays printed in early quartos, conform to "the setting of the old Greek and Latin comedians originally adopted in the first editions of Plautus (Venice, Merula, 1472), Terence (Strassburg, Rusch, 1470), Aristophanes (Aldus, 1498). The speeches in dialogue are printed continuously, running on in even lines."[54] Also following the system of classical editions, Jonson's folio groups the names of all speakers at the beginning of each scene. Finally, in keeping with the European stan-

POËTASTER.

After the second founding.

ENVIE.

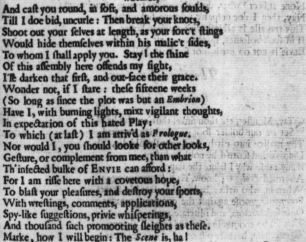

ight, I falute thee, but with wounded nerves:
Wifhing thy golden fplendor, pitchy dark-
neffe.
What's here? TH'ARRAIGNMENT? I: This,
this is it,
That our funke eyes have wak't for, all this
while:
Here will be fubject for my fnakes, and me.
Cling to my necke, and wrifts, my loving
wormes,
And caft you round, in foft, and amorous foulds,
Till I doe bid, uncurle: Then break your knots,
Shoot out your felves at length, as your fore't ftings
Would hide themfelves within his malic't fides,
To whom I fhall apply you. Stay! the fhine
Of this affembly here offends my fight,
I'le darken that firft, and out-face their grace.
Wonder not, if I ftare: thefe fifteene weeks
(So long as fince the plot was but an *Embrion*)
Have I, with burning lights, mixt vigilant thoughts,
In expectation of this hated Play:
To which (at laft) I am arriv'd as *Prologue*.
Nor would I, you fhould looke for other looks,
Gefture, or complement from mee, than what
Th'infected bulke of ENVIE can afford:
For I am riffe here with a covetous hope,
To blaft your pleafures, and deftroy your fports,
With wreftings, comments, applications,
Spy-like fuggeftions, privie whifperings,
And thoufand fuch promooting fleights as thefe.
Marke, how I will begin: The *Scene* is, ha!

ROME?

Y

arifing in the midft of the ftage.

Figure 1. Opening page of *Poëtaster, The WORKES of Benjamin Jonson, 1616.*

some on their shoulders; others with ointment pots at their girdles; all with spindles, timbrels, rattles, or other *veneficall* instruments, making a confused noyse, with strange gestures. The deuice of their attire was Master Jones his, with the Inuention, and *Architecture* of the whole Scene, and Machine. Only, I prescrib'd them their *Properties* of Vipers, Snakes, Bones, Herbs, Roots, and other ensignes of their *Magick*, out of the authority of ancient and late *Writers*, wherein the faults are mine, if there be any found; and for that cause I confesse them.

These eleven Witches beginning to dance (which is an usuall ᵃ *Ceremony* at their *Conuents*, or meetings, where sometimes also they are vizarded, and masqu'd) on the sodaine, one of them missed their *chiefe*, and interrupted the rest, with this speech.

ᵃ See the *Kings Maiesties book,* (our *Soueraign*) of *Dæmonology, Bodin Remig. Delrio. Mal. Malef.* And a world of others, in the generall: But let us follow particulars.

SIsters, stay, we want our ᵇ *Dame*;
Call upon her by her name,
And the *Charme* we use to say;
That she quickly ᶜ anoynt, and come away.

ᵇ Amongst our vulgar Witches, the honor of *Dame* (for so I translate it is giuen with a kind of preeminence to some speciall one at their meeting: which *Delrio* insinuates, *Disquif. Mag. lib. 2. quest. 9.* quoting that of *Apuleius lib. de Asin. aureo. de quadam caupona, Regina Sagarum.* And addes, *ut scias etiam tum quasdam ab iis hoc titulo honoratas.* Which is the M. *Phlippe Ludouigus Elich, Dæmonmagie, quest. 10.* doth also remember. ᶜ When they are to be transported from place to place, they use to anoynt themselues, and sometimes, the things they ride on. Beside *Apul.* testimony, See these later, *Remig. Dæmonolatria lib. 1. cap. 14. Delrio, Disquif. Mag. L. 2. quæst. 16. Bodin. Dæmonomam. l. 2. c. 4. Barthol. de Spina. quæst. de Strigib. Philippe. Ludouigus Elich. quæst. 10. Paracelsus in magic. & occul. Philosophia,* teacheth the confection. *Vnguentum ex carne recens natorum infantium, in pulmenti formam tostum, & cum herbis somniferis, quales sunt Papauer, Solanum, Cicuta, &c.* Abul Lea. Bapt. &c. *lib. 2. Mag. Natur. cap. 16.*

1 CHARME.

DAME, DAME, the watch is set;
Quickly come, we all are met.
ᵈ From the lakes, and from the fens,
From the rocks, and from the dens,
From the woods, and from the caues,
From the church-yards, from the graues,
From the dungeon, from the tree
That they die on, here are wee.

Comes she not yet?
Strike another heate.

ᵈ These places in their owne nature dire, and dismall, are reckon'd up, as the fittest from whence such persons should come: and were usually obserued by that excellent *Lucan,* in the description of his *Eristho. lib. 6.* To which we may adde this corollary out of *Agrip. de occult. Philosop. l. 1. c. 48. Saturno correspondent loca quævis fœtida, tenebrosa, subterranea, religiosa & funesta, ut cœmiteria, busta, & hominibus deserta habitacula, & vetustate caduca, loca obscura, & horrenda, & solitaria antra, cauerna, putei: Praterea piscina, stagna, paludes, & ejusmodi.* And he *lib. 3. c. 42.* speaking of the like, and *lib. 4.* about the end, *Aptissima sunt loca plurimum experientia visorum, nocturnarumque incursionum & consimilium phantasmatum, ut cœmiteria, & in quibus fieri solent executiones criminalium, & in quibus recentibus annis publice strages factæ sunt, vel ubi occisorum cadauera, nondum expiata, nec ritè sepulta, recentioribus annis subhumata sunt.*

2 CHARME.

THe weather is faire, the wind is good,
Vp Dame, o'your ᵉ horse of wood:
Or else, tuck up your gray frock,

ᵉ Delrio *Disq. Mag. lib. 2. quæst. 16.* has a story our of *Triezius* of this horse of wood: but that which our Witches call so, is sometimes a broome-staffe, sometimes a reede, sometimes a distaffe. See *Remig. Dæmonol. lib. 1. cap. 14. Bodin. l. 2. cap. 4. &c.*

And

Figure 2. The Masque of Queenes, The WORKES of Benjamin Jonson, 1616.

dards of printing classical dramas, entrances and exits are not noted.[55] The textual layout of Jonson's collection handily contributes to the classical formalism with which Jonson identifies himself.[56] Indeed, the format of the folio, unique among English printed plays of the same period, symbolizes the representational shift the volume as a whole embodies. It can be considered as a literary phenomenon portraying not only a playwright but also an architect of the printed text—an author in the monumental sense of the term.

Jonson's method of writing for the print shop—of producing dependable text—is exemplified by his thorough revision of the quarto texts of *Cynthia's Revels*, *Poëtaster*, and possibly even *Every Man in His Humour* for their folio edition. His bibliographers have determined that "there is mechanical proof that Jonson was still revising copy for the folio months after printing had started."[57] Jonson's folio regularizes punctuation, capitalization, scenic division, and diction in ways that often depart from seventeenth-century standards of printing plays. Even more significant is how Jonson adopted the mechanics of printing as a method of final stylistic tightening. The printer's proofs afforded the author a final opportunity to polish any rough spots that he could not see as clearly in manuscript form. In a study of the folio variants of *Epicoene*, L. A. Beaurline maintains that the resetting of the first twelve pages of text "shows obvious authorial revisions."[58] Also, the folio "Argument" of *Sejanus*, as Johan Gerritsen notes, "was fairly extensively revised by Jonson at the proof stage," and the earlier *Sejanus* quarto, in the opinion of Herford and Simpson, is such a text composed partially on the printer's forme.[59] To a certain extent, then, Jonson was not as far from the textual standards of the playhouse as he would have desired. His method was to revise his texts right up to the final moment of their production. The crucial distinction, however, is that Jonson, not the players, asserted his authority over the text's reconstruction in the print shop. And unlike the method of the playhouse, what directed all of Jonson's editorial activities was not "counterfeiting" but the princely and performative "most high, and heartie *inventions*" thought by him to furnish the aura or presence of a work.

In view of the extent to which Jonson's poetics reflects a deep sensitivity to the mechanics and style of material production, it is somewhat surprising that it has taken critics so long to pay careful heed to his early interest in printing.[60] Further discussions of the theoretical implications of Jonson's project would portray him as an early formulator of what Walter Benjamin describes as the art of representation through mechanical reproduction. In his influential essay, "The Work of Art in the Age of Mechanical Reproduction," Benjamin discusses the technical reproduction of art in terms which are closely akin to the tradition of Renaissance theatre that gave rise to Jonson's printed texts. This is particularly apparent in Benjamin's reflections on an artifact's originality: "The presence of the original is the prerequisite to the concept of authenticity. Chemical analyses of the patina of a bronze can help to establish this, as does the proof that a given manuscript of the Middle Ages stems from an archive of the fifteenth century. The whole sphere of authenticity is outside technical—and, of course, not only technical—reproducibility. Confronted with its manual reproduction, which was usually branded as a forgery, the original preserved all its authority."[61] An interesting correlation can be established between the authority of a medieval manuscript attributable to a certain archive and the originality of a prompt-book held in the vaults of an acting company. Their place or location of holding—their physical presence—determines authenticity. When the players could still produce their "original," they labeled as forgery any attempt to transfer the prompt-book from the theatre by memorization or manual transcription. Benjamin points out, moreover, that the issue of authenticity and originality is immaterial vis-à-vis technical reproduction. "First, process reproduction is more independent of the original than manual reproduction. For example, in photography, process reproduction can bring out those aspects of the original that are unattainable to the naked eye yet accessible to the lens."[62] Technical reproduction allows the artifact to be seen by the viewer in a perspective unattainable in the environment demarcating authenticity and authority. The transfer of a text from playhouse to printed book displaces almost completely the textual invisibility prescribed by the stage. "Secondly, technical reproduction can put the copy of the original into situations which would be out of reach for the original itself. Above all, it enables the original to meet the beholder halfway, be it in the form of a photograph or a phonograph record."[63] When a Renaissance performance of a play was made into a book, it underwent similar alienation from its original. The Renaissance actors sometimes were concerned, in fact, that too many viewers would meet their plays halfway, thus leaving the audience on the wrong side of the bank. The complete displacement of performance from stage to book would lead to the absence of theatregoers.

Yet Jonson's relation to printing is much more complicated than the binomial relations of original:presence, reproduction:absence. Jonson used the reproductive process of printing *to form* his manuscript. Plays written by Jonson for the acting companies were not embodied in secure and authentic manuscripts; their foulness precluded their "presence" as stable dramatic "originals." Custom meant for dramatic scripts to be changelings whose many transformations attracted viewers to players, not to authors. It was especially in the print shop that Jonson could assert his presence as an author and arrest the flow of textual bastardization by placing a hand on manuscripts that belonged legally to either the players or the printer. Jonson's efforts outside of the playhouse aimed at diminishing the inconstancy of textual repetition by establishing a standard text, a literary concept which has developed since Jonson's time to captivate the attention of historians of dramatic literature. Although the following assertion may sound strange to critics accustomed to considering a printed text as an alien, if not corrupted, form of dramatic writing, Ben Jonson influenced the domain of originality and legitimation more by his editing for the press than by his writing for the theatre.

References to printing's contribution to orderly habits of Renaissance thought and expression bring immediately to mind the innovative work of Walter Ong and Elizabeth Eisenstein. Ong's texts ask us to ponder the spatial relation of print to the more orderly philosophical systems—especially Ramism—prevalent during the early expansion of printing.[64] In contrast to studies by Ong, Eisenstein's *The Printing Press as an Agent of Change* emphasizes the sociological impact of printing, not to mention printing's contribution to comparative methods of collecting and thinking about literature.[65] Such studies of the influence of printing on literary issues raise important questions about Jonson's ideological/epistemological relation to print.

Especially pertinent to the discussion of Jonson, who stood tall among the immediate descendants of Ramus in England, is Ong's analysis of printing as a Ramistic device. "At the heart of the Ramist enterprise," Ong writes,

> is the drive to tie down words themselves, rather than other representations, in simple geometrical patterns. Words are believed to be recalcitrant insofar as they derive from a world of sound, voices, cries; the Ramist ambition is to neutralize this connection by processing what is of itself nonspatial in order to reduce it to space in the starkest

way possible. The spatial processing of sound by means of the alphabet is not enough. Print or written words themselves must be deployed in spatial relationships, and the resulting schemata thought of as a key to their meanings. Displayed in diagrams, words transmute sounds into manipulable units like "things."[66]

In brief, the English Ramists would have understood the sounds, voices, and cries of mutable dramatic verse to be transformed by publication into fixed columns of print. Locked into position on the printing forme, imprinted uniformly in any number of books, dramatic language thus would have been thought safe from the players' prerogative to alter its pronunciation, tone, or use. The printed text also provided the Ramistic reader with a method of memorization and hermeneutical understanding unfamiliar to the public theatre. Ong argues in detail how print contributed to an "assiduous cultivation of topical logics" in the Renaissance. Consisting of a spatial diagram on the page, a printed play might be said similarly to offer the reader a framed tableau for memorization and contemplation. Dramatic space, often discussed in terms of pictorial space, would thus be reduced into a literal textual picture.

Through such topical control, Jonson's printed plays can be understood to lend themselves particularly well to the "sovereign worth" of poetry lauded by Tibullus in *Poëtaster:*

> That, which he hath writ,
> Is with such judgement, labour'd, and distill'd
> Through all the needfull uses of our lives,
> That could a man remember but his lines,
> He should not touch any serious point,
> But he might breathe his spirit out of him.[67]

The topical shapes of printing allowed Jonson and his texts to breathe more freely. Through representation in reading, Jonson's printed and therefore lasting texts subscribe to Tibullus's mnemonic and mimetic notion of poetical legitimacy. They also might be said to achieve what Horace defines in *Poëtaster* as the ultimate "*analyticke* summe / Of all the worth and first effects of artes. / And for his *poesie*, 'tis so ramm'd with life, / That it shall gather strength of life, with being, / And live hereafter, more admir'd, then now."[68] Jonson's life through printing allows his twentieth-century readers to appreciate how such a "ramm'd" and "analyticke summe" may well constitute his Ramistic aims. For it is generally agreed that this

author-as-editor worked conscientiously toward both his texts' spatial reproduction on the page and lasting mimetic representation by
their rightful actors—the readers.

Yet, our contemporary understanding both of "writing" and of
Ramism's impact on Renaissance English literature compromises
any predictable equations of conscientious textual editing and faithful reader reception. We might first consider the literary debate over
the extent of the "analyticke summe" of Ramistic theory. Frances
Yates argues that the Ramistic bookish theatre lacks "the emotion-
ally striking and stimulating images the use of which had come
down through the centuries from the art of the classical rhetor. The
'natural' stimulus for memory," adds Yates, "is now not the emo-
tionally exciting memory image; it is the abstract order of dialectical
analysis."[69] In appealing to his readers' use of such reason, Jonson
would ask them to delimit and center his texts in a way that is
unnatural to the public playhouse. Yet, Rosamond Tuve's interpretation of Ramistic poetics reinscribes the paradox of theatrical effect
into the scene of the printed book. In *Elizabethan and Metaphysical
Imagery*, she subtly describes the importance of rhetorical eloquence to the Ramistic system that strove to appropriate rather
than to purge emotive responses. In recalling the Ramistic emphasis
on logical structure and order, Tuve comes close to prescribing an
"analyticke summe" when she remarks how the Ramist "is against
deceitful and frivolous and vainglorious eloquence which does not
delineate the true nature of things." Yet she clarifies this point by
arguing for English Ramism's paradoxical transference of poetic
example to the scene of philosophical didacticism. "That eloquence
should make wisdom manifest did not seem so much a desideratum
as a legitimate and universally discoverable connection; the possibility of a gap between the two results from the falsifications which
imperfect man is always likely to fall into. . . . Ramists were redress-
ing a balance, but they were correcting the abuses of the hundreds
of forgotten writers we have never read, not those of a Spenser or a
Sidney."[70] In a similar way, we might consider Jonson's Ramistic
interests in view of his own somewhat eccentric attempt to redress
the balance of theatrical legitimacy. His printed texts insist less on
the repression of emotion, than on its transference or reinscription
in the space of authorial representation. The fact that orderly forms
of presentation might enhance the rhetorical performativity of
authorship—with its many emotive layers—made printing doubly
attractive to Ben Jonson.

Emphasis on the rhetorical importance of printing, as a performative operation in itself, might change the focus of analysis from recent discussions of the topical semiotics of print to consideration of printing as exemplary of the mechanism of transference. The particular example of Jonson's complex relation to the printed word provokes us to reflect on recent histories of print not merely as source books but also and more crucially as indicators of the methodological and philosophical stakes of the delineation of such a history. Especially important are the problematic and ideologically charged assumptions nurtured by writers like Ong and Eisenstein concerning the uniqueness, permanence, and non-iterability of the printed word. Their texts argue for the importance of printing's vast reproduction of virtually identical copies. In granting special status to textual sameness, dependability, and verifiability, their arguments lend themselves to theoretical assertions regarding the hermeneutical promise of stable signification granted to textuality by the ontological condition of printing. Thanks to printing, this reasoning claims, Ben Jonson's intentional message is now permanently available to all readers in canonical form. The only remaining flaw lies in the interpretational inconsistencies of the community of readers.

In view of these confusions of "writing" with printing, of signification with mechanical reproduction, confusions which have acquired the status of commonplaces in both Comparative Literature and Cultural History, students of Ben Jonson may want to exercise caution in making assumptions along with, say, Richard Dutton about a "consistent set of attitudes, a 'vision', humanist and conservative" signified by Jonson's printed folio.[71] Trust in such consistency is undercut by the philosophical and historical contradictions weakening the overall enterprise of the history of printing. I have in mind the critique of this historical project by a fascinating range of writers, who are interested in how the study of the history of printing remains motivated by a trust in the indisputable impact of the *invention* of print, a romantic trust in the *ideology of the new*. Disputing claims that printing conceived a new form of topics, Frances Yates succinctly reminds us that spatial visualizations "are a transfer to the printed book of the visually ordered and schematised lay-outs of manuscripts."[72] Yates's remarks in *The Art of Memory* emphasize the *transference* of text from one scene of authority to another, rather than the *invention* of a new "topics" of textuality; that is to say, she stresses the structure of textual displacement rather than the multilayered hope in the "*new.*" Her remarks may here serve as a warning that any interest in the printed text will bear more fruit in light of the epistemological conditions of the printed word: textuality per se.

From a philosophical perspective, Derrida insists convincingly on the inherent iterability of any textual system, whether in script or print. *Limited Inc a b c . . .* addresses the conflation, which I think is apparent in both Ong's and Eisenstein's discussions of printing, of the material presence of text with its hermeneutical "permanence."

> Sans doute la "permanence" ou la "survie" du document (scripta manent), quand et dans la mesure (toujours relative) où elles ont lieu, impliquent-elles l'itérabilité ou la restance en général. Mais l'inverse n'est pas vrai. La permanence n'est pas l'effet nécessaire de la restance. J'irai plus loin: la structure de la restance, impliquant l'altération, rend impossible toute permanence absolue.[73]

In analyzing the textual structure of iterability, Derrida clarifies the issue of authorial intentionality which conceptual histories of printing tend to privilege. Commenting directly on the resistance of the textual to any rigid notion of intentionality, he writes:

> L'intention ou l'attention dirigée sur un itérable et déterminée par lui en itérable a beau se tendre vers la plénitude actuelle, elle ne peut, par structure, y atteindre; elle ne peut en aucun cas être pleine, actuelle, totalement présente à son objet et à elle-même. Elle est d'avance divisée et déportée, par son itérabilité, vers l'autre, d'avance d'elle-même *écartée.* Cet écart est sa possibilité même. Autre manière de dire que si cet écart est sa possibilité, il n'attend pas, il ne lui survient pas comme un accident ici ou là. L'intention est *a priori* (aussi sec) différante.[74]

Derrida's emphasis on the structure of language as deferral, "d'avance d'elle-même *écartée*" ("*re-moved*" [trans-ferred?]), stands in vivid contrast to the hermeneutical and metaphysical constancy which Father Ong asks us to embrace in the printed word.

The epistemological analysis of the printed word, which lays bare the textual structure of deferral, both highlights and problematizes Ben Jonson's antitheatrical investment in editing and publishing. For Jonson labored in the print shop to reconcile, somehow, the irreconcilable view of textuality as iterable yet "permanent." The margins of a printed play, like those of a grammar and commonplace book, provided Jonson with unchangeable borders to preserve the fiction of the originality of his text, or "the Image of the Parent of it." This author's apparently deep sensitivity to the complexities of linguistic representation may be credited as the catalyst for the arrival of a different, perhaps we can say *allegorical,* custom of drama: textual editing and subtle reproductive transference with the end of effecting or re-presenting authorial presence. This futile manipulation of textual form, one that inevitably deconstructs itself, will be the focus of the following chapter. For now, I wish to conclude these exploratory remarks on foul sheets and parented texts by suggesting a motto more fitting for Jonson's project. I would recommend *Tanquam Texplorator.*

4

The Textual Apparatus
of Jonson's Authorial Genius

This Figure, that thou here seest put,
   It was for gentle Shakespeare cut;
Wherein the Grauer had a strife
   With Nature, to out-doo the life:
O, could he but haue drawne his wit
   As well in brasse, as he hath hit
His face; the Print would then surpasse
   All, that was euer writ in brasse.
But, since he cannot, Reader, looke
   Not on his Picture, but his Booke.

BEN JONSON, "To the Reader"
(Shakespeare, 1623)

It is somewhat ironic to speak of Ben Jonson as a textual technician, as one who constructed his image as a playwright through attentiveness to the architectonics of the printed text. In so viewing Jonson we may bring his method close to the artistic practice of his adversarial collaborator, Inigo Jones. Jones encapsulated his image as an artist in the spectacular form of his architectural shapes and mechanical devices. His designer's pencil, much like the editor's pen, fused itself in the rhetorical colors and accented forms of technical reproduction. Jonson's many critical differences with Jones and the poet's ambivalence about the unequal praise received by the designer need not be recounted in detail here.[1] Still, an empathetic look at Jonson's apparent fascination with new means of mechanical reproduction attests that he matched his designer Jones in concern for artistic shape and material delight. As Stephen Orgel insists, "as a poet, he was bound to assert that 'the Pen is more noble, then the Pencil.' But he continues almost at once, [in *Discoveries*] 'Picture is the invention of Heaven: the most ancient, and most a kinne to Nature.' Paradoxically, Jonson claims for the visual arts precisely that divinity that had constituted, for Sidney, the chief defence of poetry."[2] The fusion of poetry and picture in the printed plays accords to Ben Jonson's drama the status of the ideal, preserving both the purity of his poetic invention and the stable order of its mechanical form.

We might remain suspicious, however, of descriptions of Jonson's textual form as one promoting artistic purity. In many respects the folio of 1616 calls to mind the image of an independent poet dangerous to the platonic republic of letters rather than the figure of a neoplatonic priest of purity and beauty. I do not mean to say that Jonson's poetry is in itself necessarily subversive in undermining the classical, neoplatonic code—in many respects Jonsonian drama and verse do appeal, as Jonson claims in the *Masque of Queenes*, to the timelessness of Fame and the "all-daring Power of Poetry."[3] Rather, in terms of the semiotics of his textual architecture, the codes of printed title pages, front matter, epistles, frames, borders and marginalia, I wish to suggest that the author-as-editor supplements the form of Sidney's poetic divinity with the spatial figures of authorship, editorship, interpretative authority, and judgmental excellence. In asking readers to acknowledge the "figurative" as a process of tranference from image to code, or signifier to signified,[4] the many textual images of Ben Jonson function semiotically to divide the readers' reception of one commodity—dramatic poetry—from their re-presentation of a newer theatrical commodity: textual genius. Through this division of re-presentation enters the allegorical process of reading Jonson. For in reshaping dramatic poetry to allow for the figuration and even fetishization of authorial genius, Ben Jonson openly displays the all-daring Power of the Folio. Allegorical form is presented to the viewer through the performative frames of editorial prowess and authorial sharpness.

The Image of Work

A striking picture of Jonson's textual architecture is provided by the title page of *The WORKES of Benjamin Jonson, 1616* (Figure 3). Addressed to the wise and studious viewer, this emblematic title

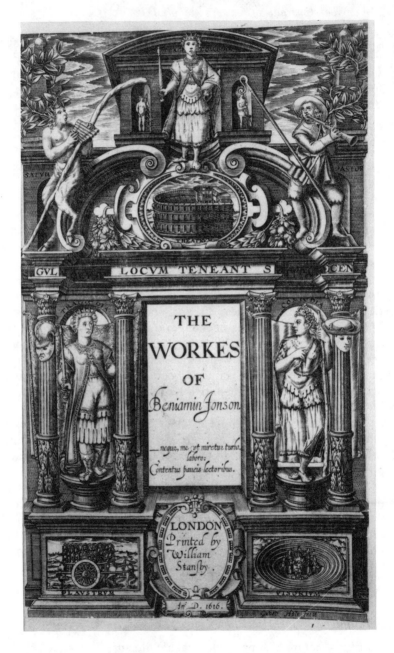

Figure 3. Title page, *The WORKES of Benjamin Jonson, 1616.*

page is an image of the book, its status, and its editor's method. The architectural design of the frontispiece depicts a triumphal arch whose antique form celebrates both the folio's link to the classics and Jonson's status as a contemporary author whose name is worthy of inscription within a commemorative monument. The classical lineage of Jonson's *WORKES* is suggested by the two scenes on the plinth signifying the beginnings of Greek theatre. The image on the right depicts the origins of classical drama: the chorus performing in honor of Bacchus. On the left is an emblem of the first winner of the prize for tragedy at the Dionysia—Thespis and his cart with a jar of wine and tethered sacrificial goat. Directly above these images, the figures of comedy and tragedy stand in niches flanking the central arch. They represent pictorially the classical tradition which Jonson's texts imitate in structure.

The three main figures above the central pediment represent the newer forms of drama that interested Ben Jonson. TRAGI COMOEDIA clearly identifies the genre with which Jonson experimented. Corbett and Lightbown, moreover, identify SATYR as part of "the world of the Entertainments which fill the last part of the first volume of the *Workes*," and PASTOR as the shepherd of pastoral poetry.[5] Semiotically attuned readers might find this generic emblem of pastoral to be somewhat confusing since no work of this genre appears in the folio. The prefatory image of the PASTOR provokes the readers to contemplate how it functions in view of the absence of what it obviously signifies. This is one of the many floating signifiers in the folio that opens up an allegorical disjunction between classical reference and contemporary transference. What might this lacuna suggest about the Jonsonian design accompanying this frontispiece? Some readers argue that Jonson intended to have completed his pastoral, *The Sad Shepherd*, for inclusion in the 1616 volume. Or, in the less hypothetical context of Louis Adrian Montrose's suggestion that the Elizabethan pastoral created an elite authorial image contributing to the domain of courtly authority,[6] Jonson's ambiguous gesture to the genre may be taken as yet another sign of his literary withdrawal from the common domain of the public theatre. The direction of my argument to follow, moreover, prompts me here to read PASTOR less as a sign of the Jonson's poetic alignment with the court than as a figure of his own editorial project, a figure that betokens the literary strategy of a shepherd of straying texts, one intent on protecting dramatic poetry from the fleecings of poet-apes, regardless of their social rank. And if PASTOR is taken as an allegorical figure of the antitheatrical tone of Jonson's book, the figure SATYR which accompanies PASTOR might also ask to be imagined allegorically. As such, it could be read to figure the third form of drama described by Puttenham and the dramatic form developed so intensely by Jonson to critique counterfeits, changelings, and actors: Satire. Joined by the sovereign of contemporary theatre, TRAGI COM-OEDIA, PASTOR and SATYR might be taken as figures overseeing the evil pits of the public theatre, as depicted in the upper cartouche. Read allegorically in the exaggerated spirit of the antitheatrical treatises, this emblematic title page could be imagined as a prefatory figure of Ben Jonson's peculiar practice of dramaturgical transference.

Yet I need not blindly follow the lead of Gosson, Rankins, and Prynne by jumping to exaggeration for evidence of authorial presence on the title page. Although such iconographic presence is much more latent than blatant, Jonson's representation as author clearly manifests itself in a traditional textual format on the frontispiece's central aperture, which appropriately resembles a proscenium arch. This space presents us with the book's title and an adjoining epigraph: "*THE WORKES of Benjamin Jonson* —neque, me ut miretur turba laboro: contentus paucis lectoribus." The name of the author is identified in terms *of his* (textual) *WORKES* and the book's limited ambitions as a public commodity. The epigraph, recognizable from *The Alchemist* quarto, emphasizes selective reception: only the ambitious few need subscribe. Every detail of the *WORKE*'s frontispiece makes quite explicit its book's monumental character. As Corbett and Lightbown conclude in their analysis of this pictorial text, even its ornamental detail, such as "the presence of the obelisks, which are monuments, and the laurels, the traditional crown of the poet, is surely to signify the author's desire that the folio may bring him a poet's immortality."[7] While Ben Jonson's *WORKES* are listed as a collection in the Stationer's Register, his book enters its author among the roles of the celebrated laureate. The title of the folio is encapsulated within an emblem celebrating the entry of a cultural hero come home.

Under normal circumstances, a printed book might have been the key to a seventeenth-century poet's entrance into elite circles, and the prefatory matter would include a dedication of the book to a patron.[8] By conforming to the etiquette of patronage, Jonson would have confirmed, as L. C. Knights claims, that he "accepted an hierarchical system and found nothing dishonourable in seeking the favour of the great."[9] His book would be—or at least would claim to be—dependent on a patron. In Helgerson's literary hierarchy, moreover, Jonson's "entry into the system of patronage was a sign of his poetic elevation, testimony to his attainment of that laureate status for which he strove. Patronage associated him with the gentleman amateurs, whose nonliterary advancement depended equally on the assistance of the wealthy and well-placed, and it dissociated him from the mere professionals, particularly the play-writing professionals."[10] Although Jonson's book dissociates him from his fellow playwrights and includes dedications of individual texts to various patrons, the sign system of its title page actually diminishes his dependence on the honorable system of patronage. Containing no poems dedicated to a princely patron of the project, the front matter of the folio functions as a further pronouncement of titular illustration. In the front matter, the reader sees poems praising *only the author*, especially notable since such encomiums normally follow the poet's dedication to a particular patron. As if a sign of the folio's method, this collection departs from the customs of prefatory dedication, thus suggesting that the folio is an iconic symbol of Jonson's peculiar drive for authority.

More important than authority itself is the matter legitimized by this book. The title *WORKES* could signify almost anything. It gives no indication of the specific contents of the folio. Included under its rubric are Jonson's poems and masques, as well as individual plays. And the second volume of the 1640 *WORKES* contains *The English Grammar*, *Discoveries*, and Jonson's translation of the *Ars Poetica*. A term much more suggestive than its obvious corollary "writings," *WORKES* signifies design as well as literary system. Implying as much, Thomas Heywood is said to have asked, "where doth the mistery lurke, / What others call a play you call a worke."[11] One obvious response to this challenge lies in Francis Bacon's *The New Organon*, which distinguishes *words* from *works*. The players fall into the category of those who rely on *words* for mere "affectation and parade . . . but leaned too much to the ambition and vanity of founding a sect and catching popular applause." Their performances lack serious direction or purpose. "Assuredly they have that which is characteristic of boys: they are prompt to prattle, but cannot generate; for their wisdom abounds in words but is barren of works."[12] Players are here said to be lacking because they do not generate—in the sense of giving rise to—products that bear the clear mark of their progenitor or source. In fact, Bacon's

criticism of actors is faithful to the customs of the Renaissance playhouse. The identification and glorification of sources was not a convention cherished by the players, who preferred disguised sources,
collaboration, and alterable texts. In contrast, the folio's title aligns
the book with Jonson's other literary projects, which pretend to be
motivated by the inductive imperative to delineate clearly human
nature and its textual sources. What could be considered a neutral
and even customary title, *WORKES*, actually stands forth as a
charged sign of Jonson's editorial method and authorial productiv-
ity. And if we accept Bacon's distinction between the barren playhouse and the potent author, the *WORKES* helps to place Jonson
among the heroes of his age. In Bacon's words, "fruits and works
are as it were sponsors and sureties for the truth of philosophies."[13]
Work(s) precludes play in Jonson's editorial endeavors, through
which he promotes himself as the authority figure par excellence of
poetry and language. Or, in the words of "a friend," "*Bens* plays are
works, when others works are plaies."[14]

Cataloguing Dramatic History and Method

To Jonson authority meant acumen in the methods of selection.
Inscribed on the frieze of the frontispiece is a slogan advertising this
scientific trait: *singula quaeque locum teneant sortita decenter*, or as
Jonson translates it, in *Horace, His Art of Poetrie*, "Each subject
should retaine / The place allotted it, with decent thewes."[15] The
selection of this particular verse from Horace as the motto of the
WORKES is extremely significant. Neither comedy, tragedy, poetry,
nor poetic theory is extolled explicitly by this motto. Issues intrinsic
to classical dramatic form are here supplanted by contemporary
philosophical notions of selection, placement, and arrangement.
The folio advertises itself as an exemplum of the *ars inveniendi*.
This art form of collecting and arranging finds itself linked in Benjamin's *The Origin of German Tragic Drama* to the exercise of sovereignty, one often practised by Ben Jonson: "The [baroque] notion
of the man of genius, the master of the *ars inveniendi*, is that of a
man who could manipulate models with sovereign skill. . . . The
writer must not conceal the fact that his activity is one of arranging,
since it was not so much the mere whole as its obviously constructed quality that was the principal impression which was aimed

at."[16] The folio's motto, in brief, opens the book with veiled, allegorical references to the genius within.

The second page of the folio exemplifies this reference to sovereignty through the methodological performance of arrangement. "The Catalogue" (Figure 4) lists the contents of the volume in a diagrammatic fashion indicative of Jonson's method. If we begin an analysis of this page by considering its method of entitling, we will note that "The Catalogue" lists neither a specific masque nor a particular poem. The titles "The Forrest," "Entertaynments," "Panegyre," "Masques," and "Barriers" evoke a titular neutrality comparable to that of *WORKES*. Although "The Forrest" is an obvious reference to a collection of poems, this title suggests more about the method of inductive gathering than the subject matter of poetic content. Similarly, "Entertaynments" and "Masques" are generic titles promising a certain convention of organizing texts.

The plays, on the contrary, are listed individually by title. A quick perusal of "The Catalogue" will assure the readers that their favorite plays are included in the *WORKES*. A closer look, moreover, reveals that the overall presentation of plays in "The Catalogue" is markedly different from their representation in the theatre. Although Jonson catalogued the plays in the order of their original performances on stage, his dramatic poems were not written as a single textual unit, harmonious in its synchronic order. They were commissioned by different companies, representing the wants of the Fortune's common theatregoers on one side and the Blackfriar's aristocratic tastes on the other. Denoting as much about the social history of the theatre as about the chronology of their authorship, the plays are highly significant of the unique context of their individual transformations on the stage. "The Catalogue," in contrast, displays a particularly textual progression that effaces the heterogeneity of the individual plays and their many staged and printed siblings. By so ordering the plays chronologically, Jonson fabricates a lasting textual temporality transcending the sporadic moments of theatrical performance and quarto publication.[17] The chronology shown by "The Catalogue" represents Jonson's unique history of the theatre.

Semiotically, "The Catalogue" provides the readers with the sort of diagrammatic apparatus which Crites (reputed to represent Jonson) requests in *Cynthia's Revels*: "Sir, I feare I may doe wrong to your sufficiencies in the reporting them, by forgetting or misplac-

The Catalogue.

Euery Man in his Humor,	To Mʳ. CAMBDEN.
Euery Man out of his Humor,	To the INNES of COVRT.
Cynthias Reuells,	To the COVRT.
Poëtaſter,	To Mʳ. RICH. MARTIN.
Seianus,	To ESME Lo. Aubigny.
The Foxe,	To the VNIVERSITIES.
The ſilent Woman,	To Sir FRAN. STVART.
The Alchemiſt,	To the Lady WROTH.
Catiline,	To the Earle of PEMBROK.
Epigrammes,	To the ſame.

The Forreſt,
Entertaynments,
Panegyre,
Maſques,
Barriers.

¶ 3

Figure 4. "The Catalogue," *The WORKES of Benjamin Jonson, 1616.*

72

ing some one; your selfe can best enforme him of your selfe, sir: except you had some catalogue, or list of your faculties readie drawne, which you would request mee to shew him."[18] Were we to adopt Crites's attitude toward catalogues, we would interpret Jonson's table as a list not only of contents but also of faculties. "The Catalogue" can be said to operate in many respects as a representation of Jonson's Self.

However, Jonson curiously forgot or at least misplaced some of his labors in assembling his list of dramatic sufficiencies. *The WORKES of Benjamin Jonson, 1616* contains only one early play in which Jonson collaborated. Symbolically abandoned by the folio are Jonson's plays of mixed parentage, such as *The Case is Altered* (1597), *The Isle of Dogs* (1597) with Thomas Nashe, *The Widow* (1607) with Fletcher and Middleton, *The Spanish Tragedy* which Jonson probably revised for Henslowe in 1601–02, and, significantly, *Eastward Ho!* with Chapman and Marston, for which Jonson was imprisoned.[19] Although the revised *Sejanus*—a collaboration in its original versions—is printed in the folio, Jonson deleted the quarto note "To the Reader" in which he says, "lastly I would informe you, that this Booke, in all numbers, is not the same with that which was acted on the publike Stage, wherein a second Pen had good share: in place of which I have rather chosen, to put weaker (and no doubt lesse pleasing) of mine own, then to defraud so happy a *Genius* of his right, by my lothed usurpation."[20] In displacing his collaborations and in so dishonoring the rights of *Sejanus*'s other genius, Jonson more firmly establishes the picture of his own textual sovereignty. As shown by "The Catalogue," the folio flaunts but one image: its own *intra*textuality, or Jonson's own version of his textual history.[21]

Diagrammatic Nomination

In addition to the fictional history of Jonson's play writing, "The Catalogue" provides further clues to the method of its making. This page highlights Jonson's concerns as an editor as well as his prowess as an author. His *Epigrammes*, listed in the same column as the plays, are visual reminders of his personal investment in textual order and classification. The *Epigrammes* are carefully selected short poems grouped in the text as one spatial body.[22] The place allotted to each epigram is delineated clearly by numerical ordering.

To a certain extent, the order of the epigrams, their place in the epigrammatic cataloguing system, signifies more than their subject matter. For example, the titles of the epigrams are inefficacious as dependable denominating devices, even though they all denote their subjects. There are nine epigrams entitled "To the Same," and numerous epigrams bear exactly the same heading: "On Sir John Roe" (27 and 32), "To William Roe" (70 and 128), and "On Playwright" (68 and 100), etc. Due to such duplication, it is best to identify an epigram by referring to its number. The numerical "place allotted it" functions in essence as an epigram's nomination. Any discussion of a particular poem automatically points to the place of its arrangement in the whole and to the editorial act of its ordering.

What might be termed the epigrammatic relation *nomination:arrangement* also serves as the linguistic code signifying and embodying the form of "The Catalogue." The referential complexity of dedications in the right-hand column provides a colorful illustration of this semiotic system. On one level, the dedications of individual texts obviously express Jonson's gratitude to particular patrons (missing on the folio's title page and in its dedicatory poems). A detailed historical account of each play's relation to its patron would bring forth much provocative material. Richard Martin, to mention but one interesting reference, intervened on Jonson's behalf in the Star Chamber where a prosecution was threatened for character defamation in *Poëtaster*. First, the dedicatory mention of Martin evokes Jonson's theatrical vulnerability—slander and character defamation were prime targets of antitheatrical potshots.[23] Second, this dedication is a sign of Jonson's subsequent transfer of his plays from stage to book. The dedication is above all a *textual* event. And it is this textual event—the act and art of dedication—that sheds light on the new conventions of theatrical representation instituted by the folio of 1616.

On a semiotic level, the fundamental significance of such a catalogue of dedications derives from its naming of a particular readership for the folio. Missing from the *WORKES* are the general appeals "To the Reader" which follow the dedicatory epistles in the *Sejanus* and *The Alchemist* quartos. In the folio, Jonson's focus is directed away from a mass of readers to a select collection of proper names. Still, it should be stressed that "The Catalogue" goes beyond the mere identification of a few socially prominent figures like Lady Wroth and the Earl of Pembroke. Jonson names social *groups* which are best suited as the recipients of his texts. The Inns of Court, the

Universities, the Court are significant neither for what they are, nor for the particular individuals belonging to them, but for what they represent as social units: an ideal. This ideal designates what Richard C. Newton has called "a community of readers,"[24] an early-modern phantasm of consensus whose image stands in sharp contrast to the polyvalent *common* theatregoers named by Stephen Gosson: "the common people which resorte to Theaters being but an assemblie of Tailers, Tinkers, Cordwayners, Saylers, olde Men, yong Men, Women, Boyes, Girles."[25] And just as Gosson uses the nomination of tailors, cordwainers, sailors, and even women to sully the image of theatregoers, Jonson uses nomination as a means of legitimizing the image of his plays.

Nomination in "The Catalogue" works two ways. Besides naming the ideal audience for his plays, Jonson renames the texts themselves. As they are arranged in "The Catalogue," the titles of the plays read ambiguously. The play alternatively entitled *The Fountain of Selfe-Love*, for instance, is listed both as *Cynthia's Revels* and *Cynthia's Revels, To the COURT..* The symbolic addition (arrangement) of a comma, followed by a period after COURT, suggests that the separate parts—title and dedication—can be considered as a whole.[26] The title *Every Man out of his Humour, To the INNES of COURT.* enhances this association. Unlike the other sets of title and dedication, this pair's textual spacing is contiguous, thus stressing the title's minimizing the difference between play and dedication. Spatial contiguity here catalyzes the nominal association of Jonson's plays with the ideal reading public of courtly society.

Because nominality stands forth as such a fundamental element of "The Catalogue," its significance begs to be clarified. Meaning "existing in name only, in distinction to *real* or *actual*; merely named, stated, or expressed, without reference to reality or fact" (O.E.D.), the *nominal* association of plays with certain groups of readers emphasizes the fictitious nature of Jonson's enterprise. As he writes in "To the extraordinary Reader" of the *Catiline* quarto (a text missing from the folio), Jonson does not expect to attract a superior reader simply by reserving the folio *Cynthia's Revels* for the Court: "you I would understand to be the better Man, though Places in Court go otherwise."[27] This better man is probably not as well known to Jonson's printed texts as is the "Reader in Ordinairie," who "for the most commend[s] out of affection, selfe tickling, an easinesse, or imitation."[28]

Still, Jonson's cautious use of names evokes their most ideal connotations. These might be explained by taking a detour through Claude Lévi-Strauss's discussion of name-giving in *The Savage Mind*. Lévi-Strauss writes that "dans un cas, le nom est une marque d'identification, qui confirme, par application d'une règle, l'appartenance de l'individu *qu'on nomme* à une classe prédonnée (un groupe social dans un système de groupes, un statut natal dans un système de statuts)."[29] In this context we can appreciate the significance of Jonson's nomination of, say, "the INNES of COURT." The name has a highly valorized and preordained ideal status. Still, Lévi-Strauss adds that "dans l'autre cas, le nom est une libre création de l'individu *qui nomme* et qui exprime, au moyen de celui qu'il nomme, un état transitoire de sa propre subjectivité. Mais peut-on dire que, dans l'un ou l'autre cas, on nomme véritablement? Le choix, semble-t-il, n'est qu'entre identifier l'autre en l'assignant à une classe, ou, sous couvert de lui donner un nom, de s'identifier soi-même à travers de lui."[30] I believe that we can go one step beyond Lévi-Strauss by saying that the self-referentiality of name-giving applies to both author and text—Jonson, the name-giver, and "The Catalogue," the textual presentation (giving) of names and titles. It may be true that Jonson's naming of Aubigny and Cambden implies his self-identification through them.[31] Even more certain is what Lévi-Strauss suggests about the sign structure of "The Catalogue." Nomination through arrangement in "The Catalogue" legitimizes plays by identifying them with the Court and its institutions. In the folio, scenic representation of a play is superseded by typographical and nominal presentation. The art of dramatic representation no longer depends on the combined talents of collaborators, actors, bookholders, and scriveners, but on Ben Jonson's careful naming and arrangement through editorial practice. This sets a precedent, in turn, for the continued identification of the editor-author throughout the folio's subsequent design, typesetting, distribution, and reading.

The Countenance of Reason

> Neither is the modern dedication of books and writings, as to patrons, to be commended: for that books (such as are worthy the name of books) ought to have no patrons but truth and reason.
>
> FRANCIS BACON, *The Advancement of Learning*

We might want to endorse Bacon's challenge of dedications by questioning the relation of Jonson's method to the tradition of prefatory epistles. Henry Peacham goes so far as to suggest that the epistle is often the literary highlight of a seventeenth-century volume. "Ere you begin a booke, forget not to reade the Epistle; for commonly they are best laboured and penned. For as in a garment, whatsover the stuffe be, the owner (for the most part) affecteth a costly and extraordinary facing. . . . So it is with our common Authors, if they have any wit at all, they set it like velvet before, though the backe, like (a bankerupts doublet) be but of poldavie or buckram."[32] Written after the composition of a book—or a play—but preceding it in textual order, the epistle is a particularly effective device of authorial commentary on the artifact to follow. In Angel Day's words, "an Epistle therefore, is that which usually we in our vulgar doe tearme a Letter, and for the respectes thereof is called the messenger, or familiar speach of the absent, for that therein is discovered whatsoever the minde wisheth in such cases to have delivered."[33] Though absent in the playhouse full of apes, the familiar speech of the Renaissance playwright displays itself as present in the epistle. As Jonson writes in "TO THE COURT," "it is not pould'ring, perfuming, and every day smelling of the taylor [the theatregoer], that converteth to a beautiful obiect: but a mind, shining through any sute."[34] Especially as utilized by Jonson, the dedicatory epistle provides an opportunity for the mind of the author to forewarn the readers about the intentions, the power, and the strategy behind the artifact to follow.

Jonson's rhetorical posture in his epistles works to enhance in style and statement the endeavors of an author-as-editor anxious about his invisibility in the playhouse. In "The Catalogue" every play is listed adjacent to the title of an epistle fundamentally antitheatrical in message. While "To the UNIVERSITIES" and "To Sir Fran. STUART" rail against the theatre's textual inconstancy and apery, "To Esme. Lo. Aubigny" and "To the Earle of PEMBROK" make insinuations about the judgmental incompetence of the theatregoer:

> why should they remit any thing of their riot, their pride, their selfe-love, and other inherent graces, to consider truth or vertue; but, with the trade of the world, lend their long eares against men they love not: and hold their deare *Mountebanke*, or *Iester*, in farre better condition, then all the studie, or studiers of *humanitie*? For such, I would rather know them by their visards, still, then they should publish their faces, at their perill, in my *Theater*.[35]

Published for the first time in the *WORKES*, this epistle to "To the
Earle of PEMBROK" can be read as a foreword to both the
WORKES and the *Epigrammes* which it prefaces. It announces the
transfer of Jonson's texts from the fickle, feigning space of the stage
to a bookish theatre in which "all the studie, or studiers of human-
itie" are held in higher repute than the histrionic devices of a Scoto
Mantuano.

In the case of the 1616 folio, the dedicatory epistle establishes
dramatic performance as an act of reading. For the epistle seeks to
establish a quality of reception better than is possible on the stage.
As Barish understands it:

> In preface and dedication and apologetical epistle, moreover, Jonson
> appeals to readers over the heads of playhouse audiences. The latter
> cannot truly measure the worth of what is offered them; they are bent
> on instant gratifcations of a kind he has little wish to supply, and are,
> in the nature of things, prone to be swayed by opinion rather than
> reason. Readers, simply by virtue of literacy, possess a certain irre-
> ducible minimum of knowledge and discipline. In addition, they are
> removed from the passions of the playhouse. They can ponder,
> instead of reacting blindly, and so bring cool heads and sound judg-
> ments to the act of evaluation. The end result of such considerations
> is to make the printed script rather than the live performance the final
> authority.[36]

Although Jonson's epistles clearly perform his authority, we might
want to be cautious about glossing their particular notion of "readership." Jonson's apparent attentiveness to the packaging of his
printed plays indicates his recognition that not all Renaissance readers of plays were necessarily free from the passions of the stage. Jonson knew his medium better than did the antitheatrical critics who
shared Barish's contention that reading is necessarily much less
passionate than viewing. Most seventeenth-century purchasers of
printed plays, I am sure Jonson would remind us, sought in reading
to repeat the instantaneous emotional gratification experienced in
the theatre. Being attracted to printed plays by the same desires that
lured them to coney-catching pamphlets and other base forms of
popular literature, they hoped to be cruel to Shylock and to obtain
the pleasures of Portia. It is important, as Barish suggests, to recognize Jonson's desire to sway his readers away from pleasure to the
practice of discipline and reason. But even though Jonson's texts try
to manipulate a select readership into leaving—or never entering—
the theatre "giddie with change," his many epistles and prefaces

voice his suspicion that readers "simply by virtue of literacy" can bring sound judgments to his books. While the epistles train readers to acknowledge Jonson's historiographic and philological presence, as Newton argues, they suggest that Jonson neither desired nor encouraged "evaluation" of his texts by their readers.[37] Rather, his goal was to restrict the act of evaluation by offering to the readers an authoritative and stable terrain of text, one whose constancy and consistency would contrast strongly with the fluid ways of players and the polysemous interpretations of readers. In this respect, his subtle references to "a community of readers" tend to be more parodic and agonistic than accommodating. In reinscribing his texts in the formal codes of the epistolary tradition, Jonson struggles against any ideology of communal consensus, which he often critiques for cultivating more promiscuous judgment than theatrical legitimation.

We might better understand how Jonson could have expected his books to withstand evaluation by giving further consideration to the codes of reading woven into his epistles. In "To the Earle of PEMBROK," facing the *Epigrammes*, Jonson intertwined a reference to the transparency of his text with his praise of Pembroke's valor, equally constant and transparent:

> MY LORD. While you cannot change your merit, I dare not change your title: It was that made it, and not I. Under which name, I here offer to your Lo: the ripest of my studies, my *Epigrammes*; which, though they carry danger in the sound, doe not therefore seeke your shelter: For, when I made them, I had nothing in my conscience, to expressing of which I did need a cypher. . . . I must expect at your Lo: hand, the protection of truth, and libertie, while you are constant to your owne goodness.[38]

While Jonson obviously opens communication with his Lord by paying homage to a title, he points the reader away from the conventional gesture made in epistles to a patron's interpretational authority over the dedicated text. Jonson undercuts his apparent declaration of subservience to his lord with this passage's references to the sound, the reception of the text. The author does not ask Pembroke to shelter the text by passing judgment on its meaning. Jonson's interesting distinction between shelter and protection indicates his belief in his text's fidelity to its author. In what is almost an empty gesture, he requests the patron to protect only the liberty and inherent truth of the text, whose transparent intentions efface the need for polysemous interpretations: "I had nothing in my conscience, to expressing of which I did need a cypher." In protecting the text, Pembroke fulfills Jonson's subtle offer to match it in goodness. This missive both flatters the title of the recipient and represents the truth-claim of the adjoining text. The writer of the epistle here directs the reader's gaze toward his own authorship under the cover of addressing another's authority.

Jonson clarifies the bounds of his personal authority in the same epistle to Pembroke: "But I foresee a neerer fate to my booke, . . . that the vices therein will be own'd before the vertues (though, there, I have avoyded all particulars, as I have done names) and that some will be so readie to discredit me, as they will have the impudence to belye themselves. For, *if I meant them not, it is so*" (my emphasis).[39] The poet now suggests that the text means nothing when considered apart from its author. Any effort to "read" the text—to interpret and to judge the text in an insightful way—will only reflect the infelicity of interpretation through which impudent readers will belie themselves.[40]

Such a firm pronouncement is curious in view of Jonson's laudatory reference to Pembroke's judgment in his other epistle to the patron, which precedes *Catiline*:

> Posteritie may pay your benefit the honor, & thanks: when it shall know, that you dare, in these Jig-given times, to countenance *a legitimate Poeme. I must call it so*, against all noise of opinion: from whose crude, and ayrie reports, I appeale, to that great and singular faculty of judgement in your Lordship, able to vindicate truth from error. It is the first (of this race) that I ever dedicated to any person, and had I not thought it the best, it should have beene taught a lesse ambition. Now, it approcheth your censure cheerefully, and with the same *assurance*, that innocency would appeare before a magistrate. (my emphasis)[41]

In this epistle, Jonson appears to defer to the faculties of his patron. But while making a gesture toward judgment and consensus, Jonson establishes the terms for a discourse that very severely delimits the flexibility, if not the essence, of judgment: "it approcheth your censure cheerefully, and with the same *assurance* that innocency would appeare before a magistrate." His presentation of *Catiline* to Pembroke actually constitutes yet another challenge to the patron to recognize textual purity. In appearing to offer itself up for judgment, the innocent text turns the tables on its patronly judge, on its reader whose reputation for irrefutable judgment is here on the line.

As in the epistle to the *Epigrammes*, Jonson predetermines for Pembroke the difference between poetic truth and error, "a legitimate Poeme. I must call it so." The (nominational) powers of textual legitimation here lie less with Pembroke the patron than with Jonson the author. In moving from foul sheets to printed word, Jonson himself sets (arranges) the rules of reading. Correct reading affirms Jonson's sole authority to declare his text "legitimate." As Newton also suggests, Jonson's printed texts thus "reflect on and intensify the impression of authority and textuality that, in their printed form, he seeks to give them."[42] At stake is Jonson's silencing of the crude polysemy of interpretation and the subsequent manipulation of his countenance—"feigned or assumed appearance" (O.E.D.)—of legitimate, authorial presence.

I need not stress the novelty of Jonson's use of the concept of "legitimation" as a quality of dramatic authorship. Although legitimacy is a notion which we have readily come to associate with theatre, it was rarely evoked in Renaissance England, even in terms of its common reference to the rights of succession and the genius of sovereignty. Nor was it commonly understood to refer dialectically to the bastardy of the foul sheets penned for the theatre's pits.[43] Still, Jonson's choice of "legitimation" contributes to the spirit of his overall disdain for readers and their attempts "to adopt" his texts through judgment and interpretation. His writings are almost obsessed by fears of "the sinister application / Of the malicious, ignorant, and base / Interpreter: who will distort, and straine / The generall scope and purpose of an authour, / To his particular, and private spleene."[44] Jonson's epistolary presence continually asserts a strong distrust of even his best readers' abilities to achieve a faithful philological or historiographical reception of his work, which Newton argues to be the aim of Jonson's printed texts. I suggest, moreover, that the Jonsonian strategy of countering inconstant reception nurtures, ironically no doubt, the allegorical sensibilities of his readers which one might expect him to have diminished. For Jonson's readers must learn to recognize how the Jonsonian strategy undercuts the conventions of epistolary form normally designed to empower the addressees.

To counterbalance his "invading interpreters,"[45] Jonson worked fanatically to formulate a persuasive allegory of authorial legitimation. In his epistle "To the *UNIVERSITIES*," he boldly asserts the poet's own sovereignty over interpretation of any sort, whether philological or historiographical:

if men will impartially, and not à-squint, looke toward the offices, and function of a Poet, they will easily conclude themselves, the impossibility of any mans being the good Poet, without first being a good man. He that is said to be able to informe yong-men to all good disciplines, inflame growne-men to all great vertues, keepe old-men in their best and supreme state, or as they decline to child-hood, recover them to their first strength; *that comes forth the interpreter, and arbiter of nature*, a teacher of things divine, no lesse than humane. (my emphasis)[46]

As legitimate *arbiters* of their own texts, poets are here said to assume an almost prophetic stance. To clarify this function of the arbiter within the context of Occidental law and judgment, I would like to turn to Émile Benveniste's discussion of the concept in *Le Vocabulaire des institutions indo-européennes*. An arbiter, Benveniste writes,

> décide non d'après des formules et des lois, mais par sentiment propre et au nom de l'équité. L'*arbiter* est en réalité un *iudex* qui agit en tant qu'*arbiter*; il juge en survenant entre les parties, en venant du dehors comme quelqu'un qui a assisté à l'affaire sans être vu, qui peut donc juger librement et souverainement du fait, hors de tout précédent et en fonction des circonstances. Cette liaison avec le sens premier de "témoin qui n'était pas en tiers" permet de comprendre la spécialisation du sens d'*arbiter* dans la langue juridique.[47]

Not only do arbiters have "the power to decide or ordain according to [their] own absolute pleasure" (O.E.D.), but arbiters also present themselves in the guise of disinterested parties, as allegorical representatives of justice. It is toward the presentation and acknowledgment by the readers of such an allegory of invisible and impartial authorial justice that Jonson craftily fashioned his printed texts. His brash representation of absolute control over the reception of his texts even leads to his declaration, in the printed text of the *Masque of Queenes*, that "now, so secure an Interpreter I am of my chance, that neither praise, nor dispraise shal affect me."[48]

Likewise, Jonson counsels other authors to be similarly sure of the worth of their work: "For, though but early in these pathes thou tread, / I find thee write most worthy to be read. / It must be thine owne iudgement, yet, that sends / This thy worke forth: that iudgment mine commends."[49] In this poem dedicating Browne's *Britannia's Pastorals* (also published in 1616), Jonson frames his reading of the text in terms of its author's own arbitration. Similarly, Jonson opens his 1619 poem to Beaumont with laudatory verse which would be equally appropriate as an epigraph to the folio of 1616. "This Booke will live; It hath a *Genius*: This / Above his Reader, or his Prayser, is."[50]

The Masques of Genius

As a diagram of Jonson's textual genius, "The Catalogue" displays an image of lasting authorial presence—a material presence transcending brief and inconstant exchanges with both readers and patrons. "The Catalogue" presents the binomial, almost Ramistic, pairs of play-epistle, stage-book, actor-editor in one pictorial unity serving the ends of an allegory of authorial mind.[51] And while the plays and epistles are contrasted and unified by "The Catalogue's" spatial tableau, the poems and masques remain centered below. One common method of reading this centralized column is to understand it as the presentation of a privileged group of poetic texts, as the apex of a hierarchy of genres. Thus "The Catalogue" can easily be read as depicting Jonson the laureate over Jonson the playwright. For even greater specificity we might turn to Jonathan Goldberg's argument suggesting that the mere presence of the masques in the folio is an allegory of Jonson's aims as a *political* poet: "Jonson's decision to include the masques in his *Workes*, to transform scripts for performance into permanence of print, provides one place of meeting between the monarch and the poet."[52] In addition to such readings of the masques as a presentation of the balanced image of poet laureate and poet prince, we might also reconsider how their privileged positioning in "The Catalogue" places further emphasis on the allegory of printed genius. The highlighted position of the column of poems and masques might work as well to evoke a conceptual synthesis of play and epistle, thus accenting the literary activity central to Jonson's concerns in publishing the folio.

While this activity is clearly ideological, I prefer to think of it as exemplifying a system of representation more extensive than the poet's localized loyalty to the politics of James I. "The Catalogue" and the subsequent semiotic system of the printed masques illustrate very well the condition of "writing" presented by Derrida in his analysis of eighteenth-century theoretical formulations of such systematization of text. "The Catalogue" provides perhaps the most poignant example of Jonson's fascination with textual formalization and geometric ordering. Introducing the *WORKES* as an important volume in the allegorical history of knowledge, its table of contents-in-tableau pictures a system of self-representation performing, in Derrida's words, "le mouvement de l'idéalisation: formalisation algébrisante, dé-poétisante, dont l'opération consiste à refouler, pour mieux le maîtriser, le signifiant chargé, l'hiéroglyphe lié."[53] What becomes all too apparent in the formulae of the printed masques is how these texts are framed in a phantasmatic, semiotic system, one allowing the spectators of the folio to read only allegorically, one requiring acknowledgment of their dependence on the unfathomable genius of the book.

In many respects, the printed masque functions similarly to the dedicatory epistle. It demarcates the difference between theatrical performance and printed re-presentation as well as the hermeneutic deferral, *différance*, of Jonsonian textuality. As Jonson admits in his description of *Hymenaei*, the richness of a masque's spectacle "cannot by imagination, much lesse description, be recovered to a part of that *spirit* it had in the gliding by."[54] The aim of the Jonsonian printed masque is not, then, to recapture and codify the revels, their dances, music, and machines. Rather, Jonson developed a descriptive poetry to be reproduced imaginatively and differantly through reading.

In printing the masques, as Stephen Orgel explains, Jonson had specific literary ambitions: "for Jonson the masque was a poem as well as a spectacle, so that on the printed page the move into the world of the court became an assertion of those moral virtues of order and nobility that the court embodied. . . . By 1616, when Jonson presented nineteen masques and entertainments to a reading audience in the first volume of the *Workes*, the success of the masque as literature was clearly of considerable importance. . . . The masque as a poem has its own independent virtues. Jonson's text directs the reader's attention to the prince by means of a richly imagined dramatic scene."[55] Orgel does not mean to suggest, however, that the most important elements of the masque—songs and dances—are of no consequence to the printed masque. Rather, he writes that "to a reader, such theatrical elements of the work exist only through their literary counterparts; harmony, order, courtliness, grace—the values expressed by music and dance—must be established by Jonson's poetry. So while the characterizations, descriptions, everything that gave substance to the ideal world and its prince served to justify the revels in performance, they essentially replace the revels when the masque becomes a poem."[56] Orgel's sophisticated textual analyses of the masques demonstrate the affinity of the performative forms of spectacle to the Jonsonian masques as literature, as poetic personifications of the many values associated with dance and music in Tudor/Stuart England. Goldberg goes even one step farther to develop the ideological relation between a masque's writing and how it reads as the king. "For Jonson, then, the performed masque aimed at the condition of writing. This was an implicitly royal and royalist aim. Text and monarch stood in the same relationship to the performance onstage; at the masque, there was another silent text, the king himself.... The masque as text, the masque that reproduces and represents the performance in an unchanging form, assumes the ideal form of the king."[57] Goldberg's discussion of the interrelation of a masque's text and performance highlights the ideological stakes of writing in the realm of James I. Yet, his and Orgel's discussions hint at one narrative form which is a common element of the performed and printed sovereignty of the masque as well as the factor accenting the sharp disjunction between the two. *Description*, as a strategy of both the performance and writing of masques, works in the folio of 1616 to differentiate sharply between two allegories of (1) royalist loyalty, and (2) authorial genius legitimizing Jonsonian textuality.

As a narrative device, description was an inherent element of the performance of the Renaissance masque. In *The Haddington Masque*, for instance, "VULCAN went forward, to describe" the masquers who represented the twelve signs of the zodiac.[58] Such a descriptive performance enhances the role of the masquers as allegorical personifications of themselves. The mixture of descriptive commentary with poetic allegory serves the apparent political ends of the masque to represent the virtue and centrality of the prince. Jonson points out, moreover, that description in such a case is only a small part of a larger representational whole:

> The nature and propertie of these Deuices being, to present alwaies some one entire bodie, or figure, consisting of distinct members, and each of those expressing it selfe, in the owne active sphaere, yet all, with that generall harmonie so connexed, and disposed, as no one little part can be missing to the illustration of the whole: where also is to be noted, that the *Symboles* used, are not, neither ought to be, simply *Hieroglyphickes*, *Emblemes*, or *Impreses*, but a mixed character, partaking somewhat of all, and peculiarly apted to these more magnificent Inventions: wherein, the garments and ensignes deliver

the nature of the person, and the word the present office. Neither was
it becomming, or could it stand with the dignitie of these shewes (after
the most miserable and desperate shift of the Puppits) to require a
Truch-man, or (with the ignorant Painter) one to write, *This is a Dog*
or, *This is a Hare*: but so to be presented, as upon the view, they
might, without cloud, or obscuritie, declare themselves to the sharpe
and learned.[59]

The role of description in such a masque is not to reveal the
obvious—to say, for instance, *This is a Prince*. Rather it purposes
to enliven the figural quality of the virtues of such a prince.

In the printed masque, the function of description is sometimes
similar but even more fundamental to the structure of the whole.
As suggested by such printed masque titles as Jonson's *The Description of the [Haddington] Masque* and Campion's *The Description of
a Maske: Presented in the Banqueting room at Whitehall*, description might well constitute the aesthetic foundation of the printed
masque. Long and detailed descriptions of masquers and machines
often dominate the space and figure of the poetry, performing visually and linguistically as the dominant element of spectacle.

The Masque of Queenes illustrates this point. Jonson disrupts
the poetic flow of this masque with a four-page, erudite description
of the masquers enclosed in Inigo Jones's House of Fame. The strategic nature of this description fails to make good Jonson's promise
to his readers that "here, wee cannot but take the opportunity, to
make some more particular description of the *Scene*, as also of the
Persons they presented."[60] This is because his descriptions of the
masquers avoid the particulars of dramatic performance in
the interests of a poetic production of a different kind. Concerning
the fifth masquer, to cite one example in full, Jonson writes:

The fifth was the fayre-hayrd Daughter of *Ptolomaeus Philadelphus*,
by the elder *Arsinoë*; Who (maried to her brother *Ptolomaeus*, sur-
nam'd *Euergetes* was afterward *Queene* of *AEgipt*. I find her written
both *Beronice*, and *Berenice*. This Lady, upon an expedition of her
new-wedded Lord, into *Assyria*, vowed to *Venus*, if he returnd safe,
and conquerour, the offring of her hayre; W^ch vow of hers (exacted by
the success) she afterward pform'd: But her Father missing it, and
taking it to heart, *Conon*, a *Mathematician*, who was then in house-
hold w^ih *Ptolomaee*, and knew well to flatter him, perswaded the
King, that it was tane up to Heaven, and made a *Constellation*; shew-
ing him those *seven starres, ad caudam Leonis*, wch are since call'd
Coma Beronices. W^ch Story, then presently celebrated by *Callima-*

chus, in a most elegant *Poëme, Catullus* more elegantly converted; wherein they call her the *Magnanimous, from a Virgin*: alluding (as *Hyginus* sayth) to a rescue she made of her Father, in his flight, and restoring the honor, and courage of his Army, even to a victory.[61]

Curiously, Jonson's description tells us nothing about the masquer's attire or actions in the performance. Reading more like a performative of its author's erudition than an account of theatrical performance, this particular group of descriptions in the *Masque of Queenes* is so digressive that recent editors have relegated much of it to the footnotes of their editions. One problem faced by the editors of Jonson's masques has been when to differentiate descriptive verse from digressive description. This is partly because Jonson's frequent digressions distinguish his masques printed in the folio of 1616 from other printed accounts of spectacles and masques. Printed descriptions of masques normally focus on loyal reports of the events, costumes, and scenery without lapsing into interpretation or discussion of historical precedents. While most descriptive reports call attention to the figure of the prince, Jonson's annotative accounts display the presence of the author.

This might be a timely moment to mention the paradoxical fact that Jonson prepared the learned annotations of the *Masque of Queenes* at Prince Henry's request. Orgel hypothesizes that similar annotations in other masques of the same period reflect "the relation between Jonson's artifice and the requests of his employers."[62] I would like to suggest, however, that in addition to illustrating the power of the relation of patron and author, the printed masques function much like the folio's printed epistles in calling particular attention to the craft of the author-as-editor: in this case, to the annotator and architect of textual form.

The *WORKES* provides its readers not only with performative prosaic descriptions, but also, and most significantly, with visually striking layouts of text in which mechanical form functions to embody authorial mind. The elaborate marginalia and footnotes accompanying many of Jonson's printed masques tend to distract the reader from concentrating on an imaginative reconstruction of the revel itself. While *The Masque of Darkenesse* and *The Masque of Beauty* direct their readers' eyes to lettered marginalia documenting Jonson's many sources, *Hymenaei* shows its readers a literal textual collage whose framed layouts of marginalia invade the space of the text. In Figure 5, for instance, the colon of the line "At which, HYMEN, troubled, spake:" leads to Jonson's framed com-

These reprefented the foure [*] *Humors, and foure Affections, all glori-*
oufly attired, diftinguifht only by their feuerall Enfignes and Colours; and
dancing out on the Stage, in their returne, at the end of their dance, drew
all their fwords, affured to encompaffe the Altar, and difturbe the Cere-
monies. At which HYMEN *troubled, fpake:*

is more than *Grammar* to releafe it. For, befides that *Humors* and *Affections* are both *Mafculine in Genere*, not one of the *Specials*, but in fome language is knowne by a *Mafculine* word: Againe, when their *infuences* are common to both *Sexes*, and once generally impetuous in the *Male*, I fee not, why they fhould not, fo, be more propetly prefented. And, for the *Allegorie*, though here it be very cleare, and fuch as might well efcape a candle, yet becaufe there are fome, muft complaine of darkneffe, that haue but flicke eyes, I am contented to hold them this Light. Firft, as in *naturall bodies*, fo likewife in *minds*, there is no difeafe, or diftemperature, but is caufed either by fome abounding *humour*, or perverfe *Affection*; after the fame manner, in *politick bodies* (where *Order, Ceremony, State, Reverence, Devotion,* are parts of the *Mind*) by the difference, or prædominant will of what we (*metaphorically*) call *Humors,* and *Affections,* all things are troubled and confufed. Thefe, therefore, were *tropically* brought in, before *Marriage*, as difturbers of that *myfticall body*, and the *rites,* which were *foure* unto it; that afterwards, in *Marriage,* being dutifully tempered by her *Power*, they might more fully celebrate the happineffe of fuch as live in that fweet *Vnion*, to the harmonious lawes of Nature and Reafon.

HYMEN.

SAve, fave the *virgins* ; keepe your hallow'd lights
Untouch'd; and with their flame defend our *Rites*.
The foure untemp'red *Humors* are broke out,
And, with their wilde *Affections*, goe about
To ravifh all Religion. If there be
A Power, like REASON, left in that huge Body,
Or little *world of Man*, from whence thefe came,
Look forth, and with thy bright and [b] numerous flame
Inftruct their darkneffe, make them know, and fee,
In wronging thefe, they have rebell'd 'gainft thee,

Hereat, REASON, *feated in the top of the Globe (as in the braine, or higheft part of Man) figur'd in a venerable Perfonage, her haire white, and trayling to her wafte, crowned with lights, her garments blue, and femined with Starres, girded unto her with a white bend, fill'd with* Arithmeticall *figures, in one hand bearing a Lampe, in the other a bright Sword, defcended, and fpake:*

REASON.

FOrbeare your rude attempt; what ignorance
Could yeeld you fo prophane, as to advance
One thought in act, againft thefe *Myfteries* ?
Are UNION'S [c] *Orgies* of fo flender price ?
Shee that makes *foules,* with *bodies,* mix in love,
Contracts the *world* in one, and therein JOVE ;
Is [d] *fpring* and *end of all things:* yet, moft ftrange !
Her felfe nor fuffers *fpring,* nor *end,* nor *change*.
No wonder, they were you, that were fo bold;
For none but *Humors* and *Affections* would
Have dar'd fo rafh a venture. You will fay
It was your zeale, that gave your powers the fway;
And urge the *mafqued,* and difguis'd pretence,
Of faving blood, and fuccring innocence ?

M

So

Figure 5. Hymenaei, The WORKES of Benjamin Jonson, 1616.

88

mentary on grammar and "Allegorie" ("though here it be very cleare, and such as might well escape a candle").[63] Supplementing and deferring the text of the masque, this frame disrupts the readers' imaginative recreation of the scene and its royal figures, and forces them *to see Jonson's own performance* of "the harmonious lawes of Nature and Reason." This also happens when the text introduces the appearance of Juno's throne. In Figure 6, the readers' desire to know what "upon the discovery, REASON made narration of" is delayed and satisfied metonymically by an editorial frame. This time, the frame demarcates Jonson's notes on *his* reasonable interpretation of the scene's antiquity. This marginalia, moreover, is shaped in the form of a right angle border dissecting the text at the moment of REASON's discovery. Such examples of typographical disruption enact a poetics of description somewhat alien to the royalist purpose of the printed (and performed) masque: "to direct," in Orgel's words, "the reader's attention to the prince, by means of a richly imagined dramatic scene."[64]

The typographical disruption of the poetry of Jonson's masques might be said to be similar to the alienation effected by the montage of the modern avant-garde. In "The Author as Producer," Walter Benjamin stresses the ideological formations revealed by montage's "principle of interruption." "The interruption of action, on account of which Brecht described his theater as *epic*, constantly counteracts an illusion in the audience.... Epic theater, therefore, does not reproduce situations; rather, it discovers them. This discovery is accomplished by means of the interruption of sequences. Only interruption here has not the character of a stimulant but an organizing function. It arrests the action in its course, and thereby compels the listener to adopt an attitude vis-à-vis the process, the actor vis-à-vis his role."[65] In addition to provoking the readers to reflect on their reproduction of the ideology of the masque, Jonson's typographical disruptions of text display the author's own attitude vis-à-vis his role.

His technique of marginal interruption often serves as a method of authorial commentary. *Part of the Kings Entertainment in Passing to his Coronation* ends with a marginal frame that introduces a self-conscious reference to his own sovereignty over texts: "For our more authoritie to induce her thus, see . . .".[66] Referring to the polysemous nature of *Hymenaei*, Jonson frames one of Reason's speeches with the parenthetical aside: "*Macrob* (to whose interpretation, I am specially affected in my Allusion) considers it

For ¹ *five* the speciall *number* is,
Whence hallow'd UNION claimes her blisse;
As being all the summe, that growes
From the united strengths, of those
Which ᵐ *male* and *female* numbers wee
Doe style, and are *first two*, and *three*;
Which, joyned thus, you cannot sever
In equall parts, but one will ever
Remaine as common; so we see
The binding force of *Vnitie*:
For which alone, the peacefull *gods*
In number, alwayes, love the oddes;
And even parts as much despise,
Since out of them all discords rise.

¹ Plutarch. in Quæst. Rom.

m See Mart. Capel. lib. 6. de Nupt. Phil. & Mer. in numero Pentade.

Here, the upper part of the Scene, which was all of Clouds, and made artificially to swell, and ride like the Rack, began to open; and, the ayre clearing, in the top thereof was discovered ⁿ JUNO, *sitting in a Throne, supported by two beautifull* ᵒ Peacocks; *her attyre rich, and like a* ᵖ *Queene, a* q *white Diadem on her head, from whence descended a* Veile, *and that bound with a* ʳ Fascia, *of severall coloured silkes, set with all sorts of jewels, and raised in the top with* ˢ Lillies *and* Roses; *in her right-hand shee held a Scepter, in the other a* Timbrell, *at her golden feet the* ᵗ *hide of a Lyon was placed: round about her sate the spirits of the ayre, in severall colours, making musique: Above her the region of fire, with a continuall motion was seene to whirle circularly, and* JUPITER *standing in the top (figuring the Heaven) brandishing his thunder: Beneath her the* Rain-bov, IRIS, *and, on the two sides, eight Ladies, attired richly, and alike in the most celestiall colours, who represented her* Powers, *as shee is the* ᵘ Governesse *of marriage, and made the second Masque. All which, upon the discovery,* REASON *made narration of.*

n With the Greekes, Iuno was interpreted to bee the aire it selfe. And so Macr. de som. Scipia. lib. 1. cap. 17. calls her. Mar. Cap. surnames her Aeria, of reigning there.
o They were sacred to Iuno, in respect of their colours, and temper, so like the Aire. Ovid. de Arte Amand. Laudatæ ostendit

avis Iunonia pennas. And M.t. lib. 2. Habili Saturnia curru Ingreditur liquidum pavonibus æthera pictâ. p Shee was called Regina Iuno with the Latines, because she was Soror & Conjux Iovis, Deorum & hominum Regin. q Reade Apul. describing her, in his tenth booke of the Asse. r After the manner of the antique Bend, the varied colours implying the severall mutations of the Aire, as showers, dews, serenitie, force of winds, clouds, tempest, snow, haile, lightning, thunder, all which had their noises signified in her Timbrell: the faculty of causing these, being ascribed to her by Virg. Æneid. lib.4. where he makes her say, His ego nigrantem commista grandine nimbum Desuper infundam, & tonitru cælum omne ciebo. f Lillies were sacred to Iuno, as being made white with her milke, that fell upon the earth, when tout tou'te Hercules away, whom by stealth he had laid to her brest: the Rose was also called Iununia. t So was she figured at Argos, as a Step-mother insulting on the spoiles of her two Privigni, Bacchus and Hercules. u See Virg. Æneid. lib. 4. Iunoni cui omnes cui vincla jugalia curæ: and in another place, uant, signum primi & Tellus, & Pronuba Iuno: And Ovid, in Phil. Epist. Iunonem terris quæ præsidet alma Maritis.

REASON.

ANd see, where, JUNO, whose great name
Is UNIO, in the *Anagram*,
Displayes her glistering State, and chaire,
As shee enlightned all the *ayre!*
Harke how the charming tunes doe beat
In sacred concords 'bout her seat!
And loe! to grace what these intend,
Eight of her noblest *Powers* descend,

M 2   **Which**

Figure 6.   Hymenaei, The WORKES of Benjamin Jonson, 1616.

90

thus ...".[67] Furthermore, the readers of *The Masque of Queenes* view the introductory description of the DAME through a framed commentary beginning, "This *Dame* I make to beare the person of *Ate*, or mischeife (for so I interpret it) out of *Homer's* description of her."[68] I want to suggest that these assertions of authorial legitimation, especially when their frames violate the figural space of the princely masque, contribute to an imaginative reconstruction—or more likely to an *attempted recuperation*—of the many allusions behind the making of the masques.[69]

Consider for a moment how a particular note to *Oberon* contributes to the readers' appreciation of the economics of the Jonsonian masque:

> Insomuch as the most learned of Poets, *Virgil*, when he would write a Poeme of the beginnings, and hidden nature of things, with other great Antiquities, attributed the parts of disputing them, to *Silenus*, rather then any other. Which whosoever thinkes to bee easily, or by chance, done by the most prudent writer, will easily betray his own ignorance, or folly.[70]

When we reflect on this passage as a statement of the ideology of the masque, we appreciate Jonson's oblique reference to sovereignty as "the beginnings, and hidden nature of things." But this passage also reveals the poet's strong notions of the sovereignty of his craft. While the prince may embody the idea of the source, only the most learned laureates of an age, so the argument goes, allow this idea to be conceptualized and nurtured. Like Virgil, and Silenus before him, only Jonson (so he implies) can write of, can recreate, the sources which the prince merely represents.

In revealing his debts to the lines of accession, Jonson encloses his masques in a frame of multiple conventions: conventions of poetry as well as conventions of judgment, of interpretation, of the limits of poetic authority and legitimacy. The Renaissance poet read Virgil, Virgil cited Silenus, ad infinitum. While it is unlikely that Jonson looks all the way back to Silenus primarily because the ancient writer's histories are exemplary for their "digressions in the Hellenistic fashion,"[71] digression is once again asserted to be the cornerstone of successful verse and its reception. Jonson presents to his readers a text which is not unlike a commonplace book in being woven and rewoven, read and reread "out of fullness and memory of my former readings."[72]

Still, the framing of these former readings inscribes Jonson's

printed masques in what Derrida terms "l'économie de l'abîme."
Such an economy banks on the poet's claim to reestablish the exact
intellectual boundaries of his text through the framed presentation
of analogies and poetic debts. However the continual expansion and
intertextual multiplication of these references work mainly to "fait
violence à l'intérieur du système et distord ses articulations
propres."[73] Unlike a proscenium arch, which encloses a relatively
controlled vision of a masque, Jonson's many frames intersect and
multiply each other and their various codes. These techniques of
violating the clarity of a masque's message defer the readers' confident framing and reappropriation of the Jonsonian masque. Rather
than providing a clear point of semiotic perspective, multiple
frames function similarly to anamorphic pictures, whose differing
perspectives distort and prevent the viewer's recovery of only one
harmonious image in a single picture.[74] We might even say that Jonson's printed masques present themselves to the readers much like
the antimasques of *The Masque of Queenes*: "not as a Masque, but
a spectacle of strangenesse, producing multiplicity of Gesture, and
not unaptly sorting w'h the current, and whole fall of the Devise."[75]

To conclude the discussion of Jonson's textual apparatus in
view of this analogy (as the text asks us to read analogously), we
could say that the readers of Jonson's masques are presented with
striking representational alternatives. They might choose to partake
in the semiotic free-fall set up by the Jonsonian *mise-en-abîme*.
Such a choice would, in effect, defer or displace any centralized representation from the pages of the folio, not to mention any reproduction of a consenting community of readers. Or else, and as Jonson would prefer, they might imitate the viewers of the courtly
antimasque by growing structurally and, indeed, allegorically
dependent on the presence of the personage who alone possesses the
power to make strangeness and multiplicity seem illusory.[76] Akin to
the performances in court, Jonson's texts are structured to evoke
and personify the figure of authority sustaining their inconstant
margins. As one character pleads in *Mercurie Vindicated*:

> The *Genius* of the place defend me! You that
> are both the *Sol* and *Iupiter* of this spheare,
> *Mercury* invokes your majesty against the sooty Tribe
> here; for in your favour onely, I growe recover'd
> and warme.[77]

As the allegorical genius behind *The WORKES of Benjamin Jonson,
1616*, Jonson subtly presents himself as the legitimate majesty of

interpretation. While his masques as poems may direct the reader's attention to the figure of the prince, the printed dramatic poems work *as productions of texts*. At their semiotic best and worst, they perform the countenance of their particular editorial sovereign. The *WORKES* presents its genius as an author in deed and, most important, in authority. Or, as Jonson writes in *Discoveries*, "as it is fit for grown and able Writers to stand of themselves, and worke with their owne strength, to trust and endeavour by their owne faculties: so it is fit for the beginner, and learner, to study others, and the best . . . which hath an Authority above their owne."[78]

5

The Critic's Standard: From Jonson & Johnson

Actor. Author. Authority. Of persons artificial, some have their words and actions *owned* by those whom they represent. And then the person is the *actor*; and he that owneth his words and actions, is the AUTHOR: in which case the actor acteth by authority. For that which in speaking of goods and possessions, is called an *owner*, and in Latin *dominus* ... is called author. And as the right of possession, is called dominion; so the right of doing any action, is called AUTHORITY. So that by authority, is always understood a right of doing any act; and *done by authority*, done by commission, or licence from him whose right it is.

THOMAS HOBBES, *Leviathan*

As for *Johnson* ... I think him the most learned and judicious Writer which any Theater ever had. He was a most severe Judge of himself as well as others.

JOHN DRYDEN, *Of Dramatick Poesie*

Ben Jonson's folio of 1616 left a lasting impression as a standard for the editing and ordering of dramatic texts. Preceding the publication of Jonson's *WORKES*, printed plays were more likely to be found in the company of cheap joke books than among the tomes cherished by the literati. Plays were even excluded from the prestigious Bodleian Library by Sir Thomas Bodley.[1] But, as Bentley states, "probably no other publication [than Jonson's *WORKES*] before the Restoration did so much to raise the contemporary estimate of the generally belittled form of plays."[2] In the aftermath of Jonson's *WORKES*, the plays of Shakespeare, Beaumont and Fletcher, and others were edited in folios similar to the standard-bearer of 1616. Although the intent and method behind these other folios vary somewhat from Jonson's, the form is virtually the same: it organizes dramatic texts in a fixed fashion and assigns them, correctly or not, to readily identifiable authors.

In our day, the dramatic folios of the seventeenth century have assumed an authority second to no other theatre texts issued in the Tudor and Stuart period. The theoretical and methodological standards of this tradition provide a foundation, however hollow, for a broad range of contemporary discussions of theatre and of textuality in general. The folio's format and contents have been promoted since the late seventeenth century as models to be copied and imitated. In searching "for the pattern of a perfect Play," John Dryden turns to "*Ben. Johnson*, who was a careful and learned observer of the Dramatique Lawes."[3] Dryden valorizes Ben Jonson's *WORKES* not for its histrionic or courtly action but as a scriptural (or, better yet, classical) model. As a commodity and as a collection of "complete" works, the folio has attained the status of a Book. We might say, following the cynical suggestion of William Prynne, that Jonson's folio is analogous to the Bible. A reading of the *WORKES* enlightens the beholder and carries on the sacred tradition of Jonsonian genius. Possession of the folio grants the holder personal rights to its illustrations and expositions of Jonson's legitimate authority.

Possession and exclusion are the two primary critical categories implicit in the folio. They valorize the individual author above the social institutions of either theatre or court. Excluded from the folio are the sustaining features of public theatre: joint authorship, decentralized authority, theatrical dialogue, social intercourse, and textual alterability. Also suggested in the format of the *WORKES* is the exclusion of the conventional seventeenth-century notion of patronage as a literary prerequisite and referent. Patronage does not legitimize Jonson's dramatic literature. Instead, the valor of an aristocrat is merely compared in the folio to the assumed truth and beauty of a text. *The WORKES of Benjamin Jonson, 1616* symbolizes the wit of its author-editor, not the magnanimity of a patron. The folio, then, signifies yet another level of allegorical transference:

the transference of textual property rights and intellectual authority from the communal structures of the court and theatre to the private domain of the author and subsequent possessor of his folio.[4]

Jonson's editorial method, moroever, set a specific precedent for critical evaluation and individual assertions of intellectual authority. His folio represents the successful gathering together of his own texts by his own hand. He established a model of speaking for himself, of believing himself to be able to limit the meaning of his texts through the publication of his book, through the mechanical reproduction and literary institutionalization of *writing*. Thus, the performance of Jonson's text presents an image of the author's genius in its own right, in its own literary succession through the life of the book.

These intellectual rights are analogous to the property rights to the folio. As an historical phenomenon, the folio stands alongside John Locke's essay "Of Property" in its promotion of literature, philosophy, and art as intellectual commodities bearing the marks of their progenitors.[5] These associations allowed the economic success of a dramatist's book to be equated philosophically with the quality of the author's mind. Alongside the late seventeenth- and eighteenth-century proliferation of new editions of individual authors' collected plays, the notion of authorship as an indicator of the worth of a commodity became more and more important (Shakespeare being the exemplary case). The representation of the powers of individual genius began to surpass in market value that of the communal knowledge of the public theatre and its many textual workshops.[6]

Splitting Genius

Ironically, but true to the legacy left by Ben Jonson, the allegory of a Renaissance playwright's authorial genius acquired more representational worth in the eighteenth century than did the actual theatrical pursuits of these playwrights in the Tudor and Stuart playhouses. Samuel Johnson's "Preface to Shakespeare" (1765) is a monument to "the comprehensive genius" of the poet. It is interesting that the focus of Johnson's praise is not so much the poetics of the Shakespearean text as the method of its making, the powers of Shakespeare's invention. "Perhaps it would not be easy to find any authour, except Homer, who invented so much as Shakespeare, who so much advanced the studies which he cultivated, or effused so much novelty upon his age or country."[7] According to Johnson's prefatorial advertisement, Shakespeare's ability to appropriate and improve on books and nature stemmed from his epistemological prowess, from "observation impregnated by genius."[8] In Johnson's appreciative words, "there is a vigilance of observation and accuracy of distinction which books and precepts cannot confer; from this almost all original and native excellence proceeds. Shakespeare must have looked upon mankind with perspicacity, in the highest degree curious and attentive."[9]

The fruits of this curious perspective return us to a consideration of the allegory, or perhaps we should here say phantasm, of authorial method as constituting the underlying worth of a dramatic text. Johnson lauds Shakespeare for the opposite of creative fiction. As Johnson represents him, Shakespeare is above all writers "the poet of nature; the poet that holds up to his readers a faithful mirror of manners and of life . . . the dialogue of this authour . . . seems scarcely to claim the merit of fiction, but to have been gleaned by diligent selection out of common conversation, and common occurrences."[10] Representing something other than "originality," Shakespeare's genius, like the figure of genius discussed in previous chapters as the auto-portraiture of Ben Jonson, lies in his execution of empirical method.[11] This genius manifests itself in the persuasive imitation (or even plagiarism) of the dramatic subject.[12]

Samuel Johnson's correlation of genius with method is significant not merely because it attests to the legacy of Ben Jonson but also because it reflects the eighteenth-century development of genius as a legitimizing concept. Johnson admits that his preface's image of Shakespeare is more an allegory of the editor's own "critical sagacity"[13] than any true representation of the genius of Shakespeare's own age:

> it must be at last confessed, that as we owe every thing to him, he owes something to us; that, if much of his praise is paid by perception and judgement, much is likewise given by custom and veneration. . . . He has scenes of undoubted and perpetual excellence, but perhaps not one play, which, if it were now exhibited as the work of a contemporary writer, would be heard to the conclusion. I am indeed far from thinking, that his works were wrought to his own ideas of perfection; when they were such as would satisfy the audience, they satisfied the writer.[14]

Johnson's preface here mimics Pope's of 1725, which attributes the faults of the Shakespearean text to "our Author's being a *Player*, and forming himself first upon the judgments of that body of men whereof he was a member . . . most of our Author's faults are less to be ascribed to his wrong judgment as a Poet, than to his right judgment as a Player."[15] In publicizing the genius of Shakespeare, Johnson and Pope turn away from Shakespeare's deformed genius as an Elizabethan player, thereby transforming notions of originality fundamental to Renaissance theatre. The critics of the eighteenth century, many of whom were editors and marketers of text, compulsively refined their notion of genius in terms of authorial originality. The gradual repression of Shakespeare's status as a player facilitated the critical praise of his performance as a poet. John Dennis's claim of 1712 that "*Shakspear* was one of the greatest Genius's that the World e'er saw for the Tragick stage"[16] was followed by Pope's appraisal, "if ever any Author deserved the name of an *Original*, it was *Shakspear*."[17] By the time of Johnson's edition, Shakespeare's creative reputation had been confined to his image as a writer. This critical splitting of the genius of Renaissance theatre— the spirit, wit, genius of the player from the image, product, genius of the author—resulted in the institutionalization of what we know today as "dramatic literature."

In seeking to eliminate the playful aberrations of Renaissance stage history from a presentation of the authoritative text, Samuel Johnson promoted a fictional concept of genius which was far more antitheatrical than was Ben Jonson's editorial withdrawal from the theatre. This suggestion of antitheatricality behind Samuel Johnson's project may sound incongruous with his own lively interests in the theatre, exemplified by his complex relationship with Garrick, as well as the production of his own play, *Irene*, which suffered the ridicule of its Drury Lane audience. Yet even the briefest excerpt of Boswell's account of the production history of *Irene* highlights the discomfort Johnson, the author, experienced in the professional arena of Garrick, the player. Boswell writes that

> Garrick being now vested with theatrical power by being manager of Drury-lane theatre, he kindly and generously made use of it to bring out Johnson's tragedy, which had been long kept back for want of encouragement. But in this benevolent purpose he met with no small difficulty from the temper of Johnson, which could not brook that a drama which he had formed with much study, and had been obliged to keep more than the nine years of Horace, should be revised and altered at the pleasure of an actor.[18]

Boswell includes in his biography other telling examples of Johnson's anxieties over playhouse authority. The case of Johnson's *Life of Savage* seems to impress Boswell as the most blatant illustration of a very general bias: "It is remarkable, that in this biographical disquisition there appears a very strong symptom of Johnson's prejudice against players. . . . At all periods of his life Johnson used to talk contemptuously of players; but in this work he speaks of them with peculiar acrimony."[19]

Yet, Boswell's accounts of Johnson's delight in frequenting the Drury Lane's Green Room and Johnson's deep friendship with Garrick suggest that he exercised his prejudices more in theoretical terms than in practical ones. It is, thus, in the theatre of dramatic theory and criticism that Johnson focused his venom against the practices of the players. In his notes and prefaces to Shakespeare's plays, Johnson's antitheatrical bias reveals not only his preference for poets, but also, and more significantly, the conservatism of his dramatic standards.[20] Philosophically, many of Johnson's passages praising Shakespeare echo the regressive positions of Prynne, Gosson, and their confrères. Consider, for instance, Johnson's praise of Shakespeare for developing a drama which

> is the mirrour of life; that he who has mazed his imagination, in following the phantoms which other writers raise up before him, may here be cured of his delirious exstasies, by reading human sentiments in human language; by scenes from which a hermit may estimate the transactions of the world, and a confessor predict the progress of the passions.[21]

This eighteenth-century position held that the passions are tempered, not aroused, by the drama of a genius. Imaginary phantoms and delirious ecstasy have no place in the theatre of the book, unless, of course, they work to represent a phantom of authorship and an ecstasy of editorial profit and control. Johnson's editorial bias against unruly sentiments and the seductions of the public stage echo loudly and clearly the positions of the earlier tracts against theatre. As Leopold Damrosch, Jr. summarizes Johnson's position, "even though Johnson was fond of applying Shakespearean passages to his own emotional needs, his considered view of the plays can almost be said to repudiate that emotional experience. In assessing his conception of Shakespeare's tragedies, one should probably take the word *rational* as the keynote, as in the program set out in 1756 in the 'Proposals' for an edition: as the editor 'hopes to leave his authour better understood, he wishes likewise to procure him more rational approbation.' "[22]

Combatting Feminine Arts

This editorial stress on reason in the age of the affective tragedy reveals a critical bias not only favoring poets over players but also recommending against theatrical emotions of a particular kind. Johnson's notion of an authoritative and univocal Shakespearean text necessarily brackets the many amorous spectacles inherent in Shakespearean drama. To cite one serious example, Johnson praises Shakespeare above other poets for erasing the confusions of love from his texts:

> Upon every other stage the universal agent is love . . . to bring a lover, a lady and a rival into the fable; to entangle them in contradictory obligations, perplex them with oppositions of interest, and harrass them with violence of desires inconsistent with each other . . . is the business of a modern dramatist. For this, probability is violated, life is misrepresented, and language is depraved. But love is only one of many passions, and as it has no great influence upon the sum of life, it has little operation in the dramas of a poet, who caught his ideas from the living world, and exhibited only what he saw before him.[23]

Perhaps it is endemic to the editorial notion of collected plays that the reader posit authorial genius over and against any critical admission of a text's oppositions of interest, violence of desires, depravity of language, and misrepresentations of any kind that might detract from the notion of the ideal. But even more telling, if the above statement is considered as even a partial indicator of the editorial program of Samuel Johnson, is the hint of a misogynist alignment with the earlier, Tudor/Stuart opponents of the stage.

Consider the critical context of Johnson's dismissal of love. Among the antitheatricalists, one of the most passionate charges against theatre was that it aroused womanly passions. In condemning cross-dressing, for instance, William Prynne qualifies the threat of costuming by stressing women's amorous roles in the theatre. "This putting on of woman's array (especially to act a lascivious, amorous, whorish, love-sick Play upon the Stage) mus needs be sinfull, yea abominable; 'because' it not onely excites many adulterous filthy lusts, both in the Actors & Spectators; and drawes them on both to contemplative and actuall lewednesse ... 'but likewise' instigates them to self-pollution."[24] The violence of desires, as Johnson might say, provides the antitheatricalists with ample reason to keep their distance from woman's array and love-sick plays. Even in the entirely different context of a positive assessment of drama, John Dryden praises Shakespeare for avoiding lascivious, amorous scenarios. "The excellency of [Shakespeare] was ... in the more manly passions; Fletcher's in the softer. Shakespeare writ better betwixt man and man; Fletcher, betwixt man and woman: consequently, the one described friendship better; the other love."[25] In wanting to silence Shakespearean love, Johnson appears to follow Dryden as well as Prynne in promoting the purer scenarios of fraternity.

We hear further resonances of this discourse in Johnson's curious, qualifying remark in the preface, that "Shakespeare has no heroes; his scenes are occupied only by men, who act and speak as the reader thinks that he should himself have spoken."[26] While this passage might well be written too casually to suggest that Samuel Johnson's school of dramatic literature is open only to men (or at least only to manly passions), we might also reflect on his summary of *Antony and Cleopatra*, in which he states that "for except the feminine arts, some of which are too low, which distinguish Cleopatra, no character is very strongly discriminated."[27] Johnson's enigmatic notion of "the feminine arts" distinguishing Cleopatra's violent desires calls to mind his critical discomfort with the passions of love.[28]

As if gauging the severity of Johnson's own affective response to "the feminine arts," Kenrick and Barclay dwell on his attitudes toward female characters as a substantive issue in their debate over the merits of Johnson's edition of Shakespeare. Barclay defends the integrity of Johnson's commentary on *Measure for Measure* by restating the editor's position:

> Does man mar his creation in profiting by female weakness? God forbid! The meaning then is, Women, they are such frail fantastical mortals, that man, by endeavouring to recommend himself to the notice of his fellow-creatures, by an imitation of their manners, by profiting by their ways, mars his creation; that is, derogates from the dignity of his species, and frustrates one of the ends of his Maker, who originally intended him to hold a due superiority over them. Perhaps the reader may think it somewhat strange, that *Isabel* should rail so bitterly against her own sex; but he would do well to consider that it was the weakness of a woman which gave her all this trouble.[29]

It might be said that even Barclay misses the importance of his own misogynistic point by limiting it to the context of *Measure for Measure*. For in his preface, Johnson identifies these same fantastical, "feminine arts" as the general source of critical impurities in Shakespeare:

> A quibble is to Shakespeare, what luminous vapours are to the traveller; he follows it at all adventures; it is sure to lead him out of his way, and sure to engulf him in the mire. It has some malignant power over his mind, and its fascinations are irresistible. Whatever be the dignity or profundity of his disquisition, whether he be enlarging knowledge or exalting affection, whether he be amusing attention with incidents or enchaining it with suspense, let but a quibble spring up before him, and he leaves his work unfinished. A quibble is the golden apple for which he will always turn aside from his career, or stoop from his elevation. A quibble, poor and barren as it is, gave him such delight, that he was content to purchase it, by the sacrifice of reason, propriety and truth. A quibble was to him the fatal Cleopatra for which he lost the world, and was content to lose it.[30]

Samuel Johnson's original and rational version of Shakespeare discredits the threatening devices of Cleopatra and the quibbling, "feminine arts" of the Renaissance and even Restoration theatre. In so displacing theatre from the passionate world of the historical stage to the dignity of the utopian page, Johnson's edition of Shakespeare belies the misogynistic interests of its dramatic methods and critical priorities.[31]

It is difficult to plot a direct ideological line from Jonson to Johnson. But their various displacements of theatre into book share common antitheatrical prejudices concerning authorship, linguistics, and the promotion of an ideal concept of genius, one sustained by reason, propriety, and truth. Whether or not these concerns necessarily breed a defensive patriarchal academy is difficult to discern. It might possibly be the case, for example, that the eighteenth-century debate over the merits of Elizabeth Montagu's *Essay on Shakespear* stem from discomfort with her gender. Johnson is reputed by Boswell to have remarked that "when Shakespeare has got [Robert Jephson] for his rival, and Mrs. Montagu for his defender, he is in a poor state indeed."[32] I am tempted to suggest a subliminal misogyny in this passage in view of the later remarks of George Kirkbeck Hill, Boswell's nineteenth-century editor: "that [Mrs. Montagu's] dull essay, which would not do credit to a clever schoolgirl of seventeen, should have had a fame, of which the echoes have not yet quite died out, can only be fully explained by Mrs. Montagu's great wealth and position in society."[33] These passages might be understood as weak traces of a tradition of male defensiveness in the face of female critical writing. But it is much easier to focus on the more clearly identifiable, antitheatrical legacy of "The Jonson and Johnson School," one that legitimizes the critical production and possession of textual authority. This tradition evaluates the Renaissance play far too often as a rationalized, poetic text offering a limited and ordered model for moral behavior. The ambiguity of theatrical spectacle and counterfeit is forgotten in and for the clarity of reasoned, critical presentation. Thus, the theatrical precedent of what Johnson labelled as "feminine arts"—constant dialogue, free exchange, troubling desires, and textual inconstancy—is often delimited by the critic's intransigent tendency to make textual monuments out of plays, as well as princely poets out of playwrights, many of whom preferred to be called players.

But does this monumentality of authorial presence reflect the disparate and often chaotic nature of Renaissance theatre? Or does it indicate the critic's historical tendency to "marginalize" theatre by glorifying authors and texts to be possessed and reproduced in a restrictive hermeneutical context of genius? Unfortunately, the latter case is more representative of today's (marginal) relationship to seventeenth-century drama. I emphasize (marginal) because the critical dependency on the textual glorification of Renaissance drama has worked to rigidify the boundaries or margins of the institution of historical dramatic study. Jacques Derrida addresses these margins in an essay concerning Antonin Artaud, whose theatrical project resisted the legacy, the chains and bonds of such a tradition. In discussing Artaud's forceful struggle against theatre's modern bonding with authorial legitimation and forms of textual hegemony, Derrida writes that

l'Europe vit sur l'idéal de cette séparation entre la force et le sens comme texte, au moment même où . . . croyant élever l'esprit au-dessus de la lettre, elle lui préfère encore l'écriture métaphorique. Cette dérivation de la force dans le signe divise l'acte théâtral, déporte l'acteur loin de la responsabilité du sens, en fait un interprète se laissant insuffler sa vie et souffler ses mots, recevant son jeu comme ordre, se soumettant comme une bête au plaisir de la docilité. Il n'est plus alors, comme le public assis, qu'un consommateur, un esthète, un "jouisseur" (cf. [Artaud] IV, p. 15). La scène alors n'est plus cruelle, n'est plus la scène, mais comme un agrément, l'illustration luxueuse de livre. Dans le meilleur des cas un autre genre littéraire.[34]

In the worst case, on the other hand, I wish to suggest that such a transformation of play into book constitutes the essence of anti-theatricality. The valorization of rational literary codification dismisses the dissonant, libidinal experience of theatrical spectacle and the dialogical discourse of its study. Any reader who chooses to be only a *Son* of Ben, who opts for the intellectual *possession* of a manuscript and its inherited "line," stands forth as an unquestionable *critic* of the theatre. For a study of drama to ponder the disguises of theatricality, univocal monologue need give way to playful dialogue, illuminating in its passionate duplicity.

PART TWO

THEATRICAL PORTRAITURE, OR FIGURAL PATRONAGE

6

Pre-Face

> Un portrait est un tableau assez indifférent pour ceux qui
> ne connaissent pas la personne qu'il représente; mais ce
> portrait est un tableau précieux pour ceux qui aiment la
> personne dont il est le portrait.
>
> ABBÉ DU BOS, *Réflexions critiques sur la
> poësie et sur la peinture*[1]

Ben Jonson's editorial project aimed at the legitimation of dramatic
authorship. The folio shows the allegorical portrait of an ideal
author readily perceivable through the image of his method, stable
in its presence on the page. This image shows itself as different from
the slippery world of collaborative authorship, textual alteration,
double dealings, and playhouse changelings. In England, Ben Jonson stood out as an author eager to relegate theatre to the world of
a book and as an editor desiring to restrain the multiple images projected on the stage to a single condensed portrait of an author.
Theatre to Jonson was best achieved by its impression, or re-pres-
sion, in the sheets of a folio.

Had Jonson practiced his trade in neighboring France, especially during the period of the revival of neoclassical drama, he
might not have been so unique. In France, plays were often printed
simultaneously with their presentation on the stage, and the rights
of the playwright were much more secure in the French public playhouse than they were in England. Jonson's concern for order and
the new science, unusual within the walls of the English theatre, was
commonplace among French playwrights. The French dramatist
did not feel Jonson's need to withdraw from the public theatre in
order to exercise linguistic constancy and methodological consis-

tency. Unlike the French playwrights Corneille and Molière, Jonson
appears not to have been confident of being able to communicate
his theoretical beliefs through the performance of his comedies and
tragedies. Although Jonson's drama illustrates his interest in unified
representations of time, place, and action, he shared neither the
French commitment to the unities nor the French trust in the unities' ability to reform the viewer's role in the public theatre.[2] Judging
from his later comedies, especially *Bartholomew Fair* and *A Tale of
a Tub*, Jonson's interests lay more in the satirization of confusion
on the stage than in the presentation, so admired by the French, of
images clarified by the three unities. For effective unity and stable
imagery, Jonson resorted to the allegorical margins of the book and
to his self-referential ways of editing.

Yet, both Jonson's bookish theatre and the entire realm of early
French theatre profited from a similar formula: the development of
forms of portraiture whose legitimization of theatre enhanced the
power of the dramatic subject. Jonson's *WORKES* altered theatre's
stature in part by portraying the image of authorial genius, which
gave shape to the paradigm of source-study and its attendant critical
ideology. Although the seventeenth-century French author fell short
of achieving Jonson's bookish prominence, the French process of
legitimation was similar to that enacted by Jonson's *WORKES*. In
the face of sharp attacks by religious leaders, French theatre was
legalized primarily as a means of portraying figures of political stability and order. But the heroes of early French drama were often
more realistic than stock dramatic characters. The choice roles in
French theatre were played by patrons who nurtured theatricality
for the purpose of their own self-representations in the playhouse
and in printed plays.

As an introduction to this section on French patronage, I would
like to reflect for a moment on the political context of portraiture
and artistic representation in seventeenth-century France. In *Les
vrais PORTRAITS des ROIS DE FRANCE* (1636), Jacques de Bie
explicates the portrait of his patron, Louis XIII:

> je m'asseure que ceux, qui verront vostre Nom au frontispiece de cet
> admirable bastiment, ne pourront s'empecher d'y entrer, pour en con-
> siderer les merveilles avec ravissement. Que s'ils les sçavent gouster
> comme il faut, ils avouëront, que vostre Image, que j'ay placée au
> fonds de ce Sanctuaire, comme au lieu le plus honnorable, est, à vray
> dire, l'ornement parfait & le Tutelaire Genie de tout cet ouvrage. Je
> sçay, SIRE, que le Temps, quelque puissant qu'il soit, n'a point d'em-

pire sur vos Royales Vertus, qui d'elles-mesmes sont plus durables, que les Medailles des ALEXANDRES & des CESARS. Aussi n'ay-je mis la vostre en ce Livre, qu'afin de la proposer comme un modelle de ce qu'il y eut iamais de plus Auguste dans le Monde, & comme un exemple sur lequel se doivent former les plus grands Rois de la Terre.[3]

Reflecting the sentiments of his age, de Bie theorizes that a portrait bears the traces of its subject's genius. Much like the figure of Jonson's authorial genius, that of a portrait is represented as transcending the limits of time and the decomposition of natural matter. Whether painted or written, a portrait's depiction of ideal models of comportment, virtue, and behavior are said to provoke contemplation and ultimately (what could only be an attempt at) emulation by the viewer.[4]

Profiting from the political emblematics of earlier Italian and English masques, pageantry, and painting, seventeenth-century French theatre was especially proficient in mythologizing portraiture as a perfect way to represent political figures and their accomplishments. The production of various genres of portraiture was so important to the mythology of the Sun King that Louis XIV and his ministers centralized the artistic academies to assure unified and consistent representation of the king. From 1663 on, the Académie Royale de la Peinture et de Sculpture, the Petite Académie des Médailles, and even the academies of dance and music were administered essentially to propagate an ideology of portraiture, imagery, and culture. The academies' discussions of the most effective means of visual and oral representation resulted in official doctrines concerning these matters which led to the liberal commission and dissemination of artifacts depicting the king and his ministers in war, contemplation, and play. The Petite Académie des Médailles, for instance, was founded solely to create and produce a series of medals commemorating the history of Louis XIV's reign.[5] Of primary importance to the ministers of the academies were the artist's conformity as well as the artifact's harmony with the representational aims of the government: the complimentary display of the king through the simultaneous depiction of his royal servants. In every artistic field, from painting to tapestry, the referential message of cultural artifacts conformed to a carefully conceived ideology of representation. Motivated by the theory of narrative transference, the regeneration of fact through figural representation, the production of artistic figures was in many instances the sovereign's most efficient means of portraying force and power.

As early as thirty years before Louis XIV's reorganization of the academies, the Cardinal de Richelieu officially founded the Académie Française as a means of centralizing literary etiquette and standardizing the rules and styles of literature. As Charles-H. Boudhours describes the project, "il ne faut pas oublier que dès sa fondation l'Académie Française a promis une *Grammaire* et une *Poétique*. Régler la langue, classer les 'ouvrages d'esprit', définir les 'genres', c'est l'effort constamment poursuivi. Ce qui n'est plus à nos yeux que décevante et illusoire ambition passe alors pour légitime et nécessaire mesure de progrès et d'ordre."[6] In striving to formulate a legitimate measure of aesthetics, the early academies gave special attention to the status of the dramatic text.[7] Richelieu recognized theatre, more than medals or tapestries, as an ideal form of political representation. His campaign to centralize theatre was very similar to Colbert's and Le Brun's shaping of the arts in the 1660s. But unlike the aims of his descendants, Richelieu's was to institutionalize theatre as an ideological medium of "his" court, as an allegory of self-representation. Analysis of the complex nature of theatrical legitimation in the age of Richelieu leads me away from the figures of English authorship to specific French "phantoms of the theatre."

7

Phantoms of the Theatre

The pathos of poses does *not* belong to greatness; whosoever needs poses at all is *false.*—Beware of picturesque men!

NIETZSCHE, *Ecce Homo*

The French notion of legitimation refers to two distinct but not always different processes. In a legal sense, legitimation is the "reconnaissance des pouvoirs (d'un souverain, d'un envoyé)."[1] Legal powers represent themselves in seemingly univocal conventions of speech, action, and heraldry—"seemingly," because univocality is less important to legitimation than is the act of acknowledging power. In the process of legal legitimation, the interlocutor must recognize the force of conventions and acknowledge institutional authority; there is little room for discussion of the extent or implications of power's many conventional manifestations. In the law, legitimation diminishes the possibilities for interpretation. But in a seventeenth-century French literary context, legitimation engenders dispute, "action de légitimer, de justifier."[2] Debates over literary legitimacy consider issues of univocality, propriety, signification, convention, and efficacy. The arguments work to determine rather than to acknowledge the powers and effects of a text.[3]

In seventeenth-century France, both these processes of legitimation contributed to the image of patrons of the theatre. Patrons made grandiloquent efforts to be recognized as powerful for their contributions to theatre, and friends as well as foes of the stage often mediated their analyses of the theatre by reflecting on the points of view or the activities of theatre's underwriters. Especially during the early formation of French neoclassical theatre, a distinction between theatre's literary legitimation and a patron's legalistic legitimation was often indiscernible. The endorsement of a dramatic project by a person recognized as powerful sufficed as the rationale for literary and artistic merit. Conversely, as I will demonstrate in touching upon the legitimizing activities of two important patrons of the early French theatre, Louis XIII and the Cardinal de Richelieu, the patronage of theatre often gave rise to various forms of portraiture that contributed to the public acknowledgment of a patron's influence over culture and society.[4]

The legal and literary aspects of legitimation are not clearly differentiated in the Académie Française's original definition of *légitimer:* "déclarer légitime par authorité souveraine, faire reconnaistre publiquement pour légitime."[5] Since, as this definition suggests, the recognition of the sovereign's legal power of declaration determines textual propriety, the most fundamental act of legitimation in the seventeenth-century was its pronouncement. Louis XIII, for example, contributed immeasurably to the repute of French players by approving the Act of April 1641, wherein he states, "nous voulons que leur exercice, qui peut innocemment divertir nos Peuples de diverses occupations mauvaises, ne puisse leur être imputé à blâme, ni préjudicier à leur réputation dans le commerce public."[6] The legal implications of this decree are significant because they extend beyond the simple literary matter of approving the theatre's moral content and the actors' stature in public. For such a declaration of theatre as a legitimate means of entertainment is synonymous with the speaker's assertion of sovereign authority to make decrees. Legitimation of theatre is in this sense performative. It is a royal speech act that legalizes theatre for the participants through decrees or public expressions of patronage. Concurrently, legitimation entails not only a statement but also its reception by the interlocutors who thus recognize the status or power of the speaker. In the seventeenth century, the enactment of the king's office depended partially on the public's acknowledgment (legitimation) of his declarative authority.[7]

Louis XIII also performed his authority by endorsing the players at the Hôtel de Bourgogne, known as the Comédiens du roi. Every time the troupe performed they presented themselves as the company declared official by the king. Their performances, then, represented both the king's patronage of theatre and the public acknowledgment of his power to legitimize. By patronizing the theatre, by performing the royal act of legitimation, the king presented a symbolic image of his authority to the public. I might go so far as to call this image an allegorical portrait of his self. For the person of the king was recognized only through the act of inter-subjective transference, that is, only through the re-presentation of his sovereignty by his subjects.[8]

Unlike many of his ministers and advisers, Louis XIII openly frequented the Hôtel de Bourgogne, thereby establishing himself as the physical image of his legitimizing powers. I should note, however, that the type of performance given by the company at the Bourgogne tarnished the allegorical portrait of Louis XIII as royal patron. Although the title reflecting the troupe's legitimation, Comédiens du roi, represented the king's declarative authority, the drama played on the early Bourgogne's stage did not always complement the image of a prince. The Comédiens du roi had a penchant for slapstick and farce rather than for the higher and more princely genres of tragedy and tragicomedy. By favoring dramatic genres that portrayed common life, the Bourgogne attracted audiences attuned more to mean manners than to royal portraiture, theatregoers who "ne cessent aussi de parler, de sifler, & de crier, & ... ne viennent-là qu'à faute d'autre occupation."[9] Louis XIII, much like Shakespeare's young Hal, solicited company unbefitting the station of a king.

Even the scenery and staging used by the Comédiens du roi were below the neoclassical standards set by the Académie Française. For scenery, the Hôtel de Bourgogne used *décor simultané*, which consisted of up to five compartments placed side by side depicting different locations. To establish the locale of a scene, actors placed themselves in or in front of a certain compartment. The compartment then served as the spatial referent for the entire scene—even if the actors moved downstage.[10] The locale could be changed in the same act by a player's moving to another compartment. Such scenic displacement did little to preserve the unities of time, place, and action so cherished by the early French theoreticians of drama. In this context, it could be said to exemplify Louis XIII's enjoyment of unsophisticated forms of drama. His preference for comedy, farce, and the scenic disorder accompanying them did not contribute to the legitimizing image of a king as someone dependable for his stability and mental perspective.

In contrast to Louis XIII, the Cardinal de Richelieu was careful to promote himself as the patron of a theatrical environment compatible with his courtly image. Richelieu favored the actors of tragedy at the Théâtre du Marais. The seriousness of the Marais's drama provided a representational alternative to the farce of the early Hôtel de Bourgogne.[11] The Marais showed mainly tragic portraits of princes steeped in respect and glory—the sort of image with which Richelieu preferred to be associated. And if the historical accounts are at all accurate, the environment of the Marais was also tamer than the riot of the Bourgogne. The audience's attentiveness to the representation on the stage was probably influenced by the seriousness of the drama and by the theatre's ordered and unified machinery. All of these factors heightened the image of the theatre's patron.

Even Richelieu's performance as a patron differed significantly from Louis's viewing and open endorsement of the comedies at the Bourgogne. Although Richelieu was forthright in his patronage of the company installed at the Marais, he did not explicitly lend his title to the acting company nor did he frequent the public theatre. Had he done either, he still would have lacked the king's power to "legitimize" in the strict sense defined by the Académie Française. Richelieu's strength as a patron derived from his recognition of the cultural importance of *literary* legitimation and of the public's potential confusion of legal and literary authority. The cardinal took an active role in determining the mechanics of the Marais's theatrical representation and in formulating the images to be shown on the stage. He personally oversaw the work of many of the Marais's playwrights, dictated the structural and thematic quality of the plays, and solicited revisions of scripts destined for the Marais. To cite but one case, the Abbé d'Aubignac received Richelieu's "ordre exprès" to rewrite the fourth act and the catastrophe of Tristan's *Panthée*.[12] Richelieu was also known to apply his own pen to unfinished and imperfect scripts—if he did not secretly write many scripts himself. In addition, the princely characters portrayed on the Marais's stage reflected the image of their patron. By determining the conventions of the company, Richelieu established himself as a sometimes secret but very influential authority over what transpired at the Marais. He was the figure most responsible for the literary legitimation of early French theatre.

Apparently Louis XIII was neither blind to the superiority of the Marais's drama nor incognizant of the powers of legitimation being subtly amassed by Richelieu. By 1634, Louis XIII used his prerogative of decree in a way that might have diminished Richelieu's gain from the Marais troupe. The king transferred four principal members of Montdory's troupe—Le Noir, his wife, Jodelet, and Jodelet's brother l'Espy—from the Marais to the Bourgogne.[13] But the king's legal method of dispersing Montdory's company indicated Louis XIII's lack of appreciation for Richelieu's particular skill at legitimation. While Louis relied on his sole legitimizing tool, his sovereign powers of decree, Richelieu worked behind the scenes to cover Montdory's losses by improving the quality of drama performed at the Marais. The subsequent resilience of the Marais attested to the resourcefulness and literary strength of its patron, Richelieu.

The extent of Richelieu's influence over the poetic conventions of the public stage is well documented by the dispute concerning *Le Cid*. Although Richelieu did not openly express his exact position in the debate regarding *Le Cid*'s verisimilitude and unity of time, the texts documenting the controversy consistently display widespread deference to the cardinal's judgment. Lancaster reports that Corneille cooperated with the Académie Française's review of *Le Cid* only after learning that Richelieu wished the matter to be handled by the Académie.[14] *Le Cid*'s proponents, moreover, stressed the significance of the play's presentation at the Louvre and Richelieu's Palais Cardinal. The supplementary performance of a play at court theatres (representations that were usually promoted and sponsored by Richelieu as a favor to the queen) were sometimes cited in the early seventeenth century as a substantial criterion of the play's artistic legitimacy. In this vein, "l'ami du *Cid*" chastises Claveret for his brashness: "vrayment cela est bien ridicule que . . . vous vouliez escrire, & faire comparaison avec un des plus grands hommes de nostre siecle pour le Theatre, & douter encores de l'approbation que le Cid a receu au Louvre & à l'Hostel de Richelieu."[15] Corneille himself counters Scudéry with the same sort of barb:

> Ne vous estes-vous pas souvenu que *le Cid* a esté representé trois fois au Louvre, & deux fois à l'Hostel de Richelieu. Quand vous avez traitté la pauvre Chimène d'impudique, de prostituée, de parricide, de monstre; Ne vous estes pas souvenu, que la Reyne, les Princesses, & les plus vertueuses Dames de la Cour de Paris, l'ont receüe & caressée en fille d'honneur?[16]

Corneille argues that the play was legitimized by its performance on the royal stage and by the approval of the women at court. A play's selection by Richelieu and the grateful acknowledgment of his choice by the courtly audience weighed heavily in its defense.

When Corneille defended *Le Cid* on textual grounds, he again acknowledged the judgment of Richelieu. One of the issues in the dispute was the text's actual legitimacy—Corneille was accused of merely translating the Spanish play *Las mocedades del Cid*, by Guillen de Castro (1618). Although Corneille's texts do not deny his debt to de Castro, they staunchly defend *Le Cid* as the product of Corneille's own creative powers. To verify the legitimacy of his text, Corneille turns directly to the person responsible for the approval of texts played before either the public or the court: "que mesme j'en ay porté l'original en sa langue à Monseigneur le Cardinal, Vostre Maistre & le mien."[17] To Corneille, Richelieu's approval suffices as proof of the text's legitimacy. The challenges to *Le Cid*'s originality, as well as the critiques of the play's adherence to the strict conventions of the neoclassical stage, are here rebuffed by the acknowledgment of one patron's sovereign authority over the laws of the theatre.

Playing Spectator

Although Richelieu did not believe in making his sovereign self a spectacle for the Marais's common theatregoer, he was nevertheless concerned with showing himself as a spectator at the theatre. For this purpose he formed a theatre company of his own and presented plays in the privacy of the Palais Cardinal. To ensure the quality of the plays performed, Richelieu solicited the combined talents of five esteemed dramatists—Rotrou, L'Estoille, Corneille, Boisrobert, and Colletet—who collaborated on the development of sketches made by Chapelain, the supervisor of Richelieu's theatrical interests. It goes without saying that Richelieu gave final approval to these scripts after he helped Chapelain's company plan and write them. Although such a workshop atmosphere bears some resemblance to the English acting companies, the individual authority over Richelieu's troupe was never in doubt. This particular drama collective operated "sous la contrainte d'un génie impérieux."[18]

In addition to ruling over his own workshop, Richelieu constructed a theatre that was designed especially for extravagant spectacles to enhance the image of their patron's genius. The first French private structure of major proportions to have a permanent stage,[19] the Salle de la Comédie provided the French aristocrat in the early seventeenth century with an ordered and hierarchical setting for the serious contemplation of drama. Blondel's "Plan du Palais Royal"

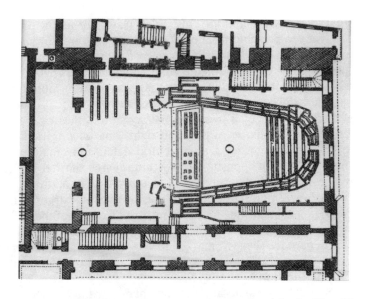

Figure 7. Plan of Richelieu's Salle de la Comédie, in Blondel, *Architecture Française,* 1754.

Figure 8. Michel Van Lochon, *Le Soir.*

(Figure 7) depicts the auditorium, which was sixty feet wide and seventy feet long, excluding the proscenium stage area of similar dimensions. Although Blondel's design is a plan for the modification of the Salle de la Comédie undertaken in the 1670s,[20] the dimensions of both the *salle* and the stage area were most likely comparable before renovation. In the design phase, equal concern seems to have been given to the spatial layout and theatrical effectiveness of the two spaces of play and sight. The *salle* itself offered to the viewer a spectacle of architectural detail and "majestueux ornamens." The wall opposite the proscenium arch showed a splendid arcade of three arches painted in *trompe-l'oeil*. In addition, the roof beams were "poutres de chêne d'une longueur si extraordinaire & si prodigieuse" that they too were intrinsic features of the Salle's spectacle.[21] The Salle de la Comédie, whose decorations shared the elegance of baroque scenery, marked the beginning of an aristocratic trend away from the French public theatre toward the grandeur of the court auditorium.

As an architectural addition to the Palais Cardinal, the Salle de la Comédie reflected Richelieu in his domestic surroundings. On the opening night of the Salle de la Comédie, Richelieu, the genius responsible for its conception, whom we might as well call its author, showed off an interior of such splendor and architectural harmony that it would have equaled the *grande salle* of any court. In fact, we can take this analogy one step further. Like any courtly domain, the Salle de la Comédie exhibited important people as well as "majestueux ornamens." For Richelieu, an essential element of serious drama was the careful construction of an audience. Not only did he plan the theatre but he also hand-picked the spectators: "On n'y entroit que par billets, & ces billets n'étoient donnés qu'à ceux qui se trouverent marqués sur le Mémoire de son Eminence, chacun selon sa condition; car il y en avoit pour les Dames, pour les Seigneurs, pour les Ambassadeurs, pour les Etrangers, pour les Prélats, pour les Officiers de la Justice & pour les Gens de guerre."[22] Richelieu gave such careful attention to the constitution of this premier audience that "les généraux Jean de Werth, Enkenfort et Dom Pedro de Léon, prisonniers de guerre, en eurent leur part, y ayant été conduits du bois de Vincennes."[23] The theatrical presentation of both war captives and esteemed courtly personages was a sure referent of Richelieu, the genius behind the military and domestic strategies of France.

The author of this spectacle placed his well-mannered, highly

significative audience in the center of the hall on a striking amphitheatre of twenty-seven tiers of stone steps.[24] When movable
benches for the spectators were placed on this structure occupying
most of the hall (51¾ feet), the Salle de la Comédie boasted a rec-
tangular auditorium that provided a strong contrast to the unruly
parterre of the public theatre. Because the amphitheatre was not
amphitheatrical in the general sense of the term—everything points
to straight rows of steps rising backwards—it accented the hierarchy
of both seating and perspective even more.[25] The higher one's rank,
the closer one sat to the cardinal, who enjoyed the place of honor.
The audience attending Richelieu's theatre was thus a "living and
visible emblem of the aristocratic hierarchy."[26] Only in the Salle de
la Comédie it was Richelieu—and not Louis XIII—who sat symbolically, if not always literally, at the center of this allegorical
arrangement.[27]

   Although "center" may appear a misnomer in describing the
architectural heights of a hierarchy, it reflects the strategic layout of
the Salle de la Comédie. Richelieu and any royal guests sat on an
échafaud located in the visual and verbal center of the hall. This
dais would have been constructed on the amphitheatre to be equal
in height with the raised stage, thus achieving a balance between the
theatre of the stage and that of the prince. In this position, the cardinal and his party would have been the focus of attention from all
sides. The overall sign system of the architecture of the Salle de la
Comédie represented a synchronic movement from *architectonic
spectacle* (the figural significance of building materials and design)
to *inter-subjective spectacle* (the guests and their overpowering signification as subjects of a surrogate monarch) to the cardinal himself
as *spectacle of sovereign genius*. Richelieu's theatre handily contributed to the visual legitimation of his place at the pinnacle of a hierarchical society.

   But what about the cardinal's place in relation to the role of
dramatic spectacle? Would the Salle de la Comédie's elaborate
mechanical and visual dramaturgy have distracted the audience
from acknowledging the cardinal's authority, centrality, and legitimacy in this playhouse? Perhaps one should wonder whether the
material splendor of the stage eclipsed the figural presence of the
patron?

   Judging from the records, the ornateness of the Salle's performances could be seen to have competed with Richelieu for the
attention of his audience. Accounts of this theatre's magnificent

spectacles indicate that Richelieu spared no expense in staging his plays. The audience for Desmarests de Saint Sorlin's *Mirame* (the play that opened the Salle de la Comédie) marveled at "des machines qui faisoient lever le Soleil & la Lune, & paroître la Mer dans l'éloignement, chargée de Vaisseaux."[28] Pellison-Fontanier suggests that Richelieu built this great hall of his palace mainly to facilitate the performance of such extravagant spectacles, "dont la représentation luy cousta deux ou trois cents mille escus."[29] Still, Richelieu did not go to such expense for the mere purpose of entertaining his guests. Such liberal use of machinery in the Renaissance theatre turned the spectators' thoughts back to their appreciation of the lavishness of the play's benefactor. As Sebastiano Serlio proclaimed, "the more such things cost, the more they are esteemed, for they are things which stately and great persons doe, which are enemies to niggardlinesse."[30] Like the construction of the Salle, the elaborate scenic devices in Richelieu's theatre exemplified the princely virtue of magnificence.[31] An audience viewing such spectacle acknowledged the cardinal's powers and means to perform theatre lavishly.

The Salle de la Comédie's exaggeration of scenic perspective also contributed to the audience's recognition of Richelieu's resources. The Salle's scenery was carefully designed and constructed to show sharp, fleeting lines of perspective heightened by the frame of a proscenium arch.[32] The delight of partaking in the optical illusion of perspective was as much a part—if not the greater part—of the Salle de la Comédie's spectacle as was the acting.[33] The cardinal's dais, located in the middle of the Salle and centered by the proscenium arch, placed Richelieu in the only position of perfect perspective in the house. For the other spectators, the theatrical experience was directed away from the stage toward the one point in the playhouse from which the perspective achieved its greatest effect. They could enjoy the vanishing point only by imagining how it must look from Richelieu's place.[34] The theatrical function of Richelieu's vision was an essential element of the spectacles at the Palais Cardinal. In fact, if any one prop in the Salle de la Comédie can be said to symbolize Richelieu's performance as patron of his theatre, it would not be the scenery and its perspectival system but the *eyes* witnessing such a sight. With his eyes serving as an intermediary focus between the spectators and the stage, Richelieu portrayed himself as a model of perfect perspective, which Alberti termed *perspectiva legitima*.

The Salle de la Comédie's stress on optical perspective is extremely significant in the light of seventeenth-century artistic doctrines. Art theory understands the perspectival system as a metaphor for the spectator's quality of vision and judgment. Roland Fréart's *Idée de la perfection de la peinture demonstrée par les principes de l'art* discusses perspective in terms of the notion of "optique": "cet Art si necessaire, que les scavans ont nommé l'Optique, et que les Peintres, et tous les Desseignateurs appellent communement la Perspective, donne des moyens infaillibles de representer précisément sur une surface (telle qu'est la toile d'un tableau, une parois, une feuille de papier, ou telle autre chose) tout ce que l'oeil void et peut comprendre d'une seule oeillade, pendant qu'il demeure ferme en un mesme lieu."[35] Perspective is here synonymous with "optique" because the perspective represented on the canvas (or on the stage) refers as much to its viewer as to its own structural space. Fréart's first "Axiome de la Perspective," for example, insists "que le poinct de Veüe represente l'oeil qui void le Tableau."[36] This juxtaposition of the perspective viewed and the viewing eye leads to a second level of "optique," one concerned specifically with the epistemological prowess of the viewer:

> les Geometres, qui sont les vrais maistres de cette question, pour en exprimer l'Intelligence, se servent du nom d'Optique, voulant dire par ce terme-là, que c'est l'Art de voir les choses par la raison, et avec les yeux de l'Entendement: car on seroit bien impertinent de s'imaginer que les yeux du corps fussent d'eux-mesmes capables d'une si sublime operation, que de pouvoir estre juges de la beauté, et de l'excellence d'un Tableau.[37]

To Fréart, the eyes are signs of intelligence, of the sublime powers of reason and judgment. The maintenance of perspective, moreover, requires a person's ability both to see the perspectival plan and to understand the geometrical significance of perspective.[38] Returning to the Salle de la Comédie, we can say that Richelieu, poised in the visual center of the hall, maintained symbolic control over the epistemological power of the eyes. The beholders were asked to acknowledge the face of Richelieu as a simulacrum of optical potency.

I wish to stress the word "simulacrum" because it suggests how Richelieu presented himself allegorically and how his beholders could potentially represent him as a patron of theatre.[39] Just as Richelieu the prince showed himself as Richelieu the patron in the

Salle de la Comédie, his countenance doubled as something representationally different from the form of its physiognomy. To its
beholders, Richelieu's face reflected the vision of his perspective.
And the actual depth of the cardinal's perception was not as significant as was the allegorical image of perspective—reason, judgment,
and power—which the viewer was asked to perceive, indeed, was
asked to acknowledge, as Richelieu. In a manner of speaking, the
spectator had at hand sufficient representational elements to construct from Richelieu's pose an imaginary composite portrait—the
simulacrum of an ideal order of vision.[40]

From Play to Model

> Le Poëte Comique nous entretient donc des aventures de
> nos égaux, & il nous présente des portraits dont nous voy-
> ons tous les jours les originaux. Qu'on me pardonne
> l'expression: il fait monter le parterre même sur la scène.
>
> ABBÉ DU BOS, *Réflexions critiques sur la
> poësie et sur la peinture*[41]

This hypothesis concerning the spectator's abstract portrait-making
derives from seventeenth- and eighteenth-century French texts
stressing the relation of theatre and portraiture. Corneille, for
instance, writes in "Au lecteur," preceding *La veuve*, that "la comédie n'est qu'un portrait de nos actions et de nos discours."[42] The
Abbé d'Aubignac reminds his readers that tragedy has been considered since its inception "comme un portrait magnifique et sensible
de la fortune des Grands."[43] Both these statements are derived from
Aristotle's *Poetics*, which cites the portrait painter as the source of
the dramatic image. Those involved in rejuvenating early French
drama profited from this correlation of theatre and portraiture.
Richelieu, for example, ordered Desmarests to execute a play
emphasizing the exaggerated features of five characters. The result
was *Les visionnaires*, described by Antoine Adam as a play representing "un certain nombre de personnages bizarres, probablement
bien connus des gens renseignés. Il ne s'agissait donc, ni d'une
comédie d'intrigue, ni d'une comédie de moeurs, ni d'une étude de
caractère. Ce que Richelieu attendait, c'était à peine une pièce. Mais
une série de portraits."[44]

Such blatantly exaggerated portraiture was accompanied on the French stage by a more subtle theoretical convention that stressed the interpretation of portraits as signs of particular character traits. D'Aubignac's *Le martyre de Ste Catherine* emphasizes the varying abilities of the antagonists to read the hero's features like a book:

> Ha! Madame, voicy de quoy vous esprouver,
> Valere, sans dessein ne vient pas vous trouver.
> L'Arrest de vostre perte est peint sur son visage.
>   FLAVIANE IV. iii[45]

> Je n'ose soupçonner ton esprit d'autres charmes,
> Il n'a point en recours à de si lâches armes;
> Tout le sort qu'il pratique est écrit dans tes yeux.
>   MAXIMILIAN V. ii[46]

This play ends with Catherine's summons of both Maximilian and the spectators to read her portrait as the image of her soul:

> Toy qui vois le plaisir que j'en reçois dans l'ame,
> Incomparable objet d'une eternelle flâme!
>   CATHERINE V. iii[47]

Catherine's trust that the recognition of her facial expression could lead the viewer to decipher her soul is indicative of the seventeenth-century emphasis on the significance of portraits. As Ariste explains to the Grand Admiral de France in d'Aubignac's novel *Le Roman des lettres*, "tous les yeux qui s'arrestent sur vôtre personne, y cherchent moins les traits de vostre visage, que les secrets de vostre ame."[48]

The early French theatre trained spectators to read portraits as signs of particular character traits. In a lecture to the Académie Royale de la Peinture et de Sculpture, for instance, Antoine Coypel emphasized the representational effectiveness of Molière's portraiture:

Molière a tellement su peindre le caractère des hommes, que beaucoup des gens à qui il n'avoit jamais pensé ont pris pour leurs portraits particuliers ceux qu'il avoit peints d'après la nature en général; et tels ont fui ses spectacles, pour s'épargner le déplaisir secret qu'excitoient en eux les vives peintures des défauts qu'ils connoissoient avoir & qu'ils avoient eu le malheur de trop chérir.[49]

Molière's theatre was effective partially because his plays offered clear portraits of the human character. These portraits, moreover, helped to legitimize theatre through an indirect process of transference. Their representation provoked the viewers to self-reflection.

The dominant role played by Richelieu in his own theatre altered somewhat the public theatregoer's traditional identification with characters on stage. The priorities of theatrical portraiture in the Salle de la Comédie are suggested by Campion: "le Cardinal . . . avait tant d'attention au récit de sa comédie qu'il ne pensait qu'à s'admirer soi-meme en son propre ouvrage."[50] Campion describes the spectacle of the Salle de la Comédie as a sort of self-portrait of Richelieu. The heroic portraits shown on the stage at the Palais Cardinal were doubled by the live portrait of their princely model. If Campion's habits as a spectator were at all typical, it can be surmised that the cardinal's guests watched the plays mainly in terms of Richelieu's reactions. This sort of diverted spectating is illustrated by Michel van Lochon's engraving, *Le Soir* (Figure 8), that depicts the relative inattentiveness of the courtly beholders to the spectacle being played out before royal patrons. The faces of a good many of the viewers seated in loges along the sides of the parterre are turned away from the stage toward the position of the "prince."[51] In the Salle de la Comédie, the spectators' introspective interpretations of the portraits shown on the stage were mediated by their reflections on Richelieu. The cardinal's portrait, a focus of intense attention, also might have been the primary object of interpretation in his playhouse.

Richelieu's portraiture seriously influenced early French theatre by projecting a continuous, albeit fictional, image of the cardinal as the only legitimate model of dramatic imitation. Corneille discusses this process in his dedicatory epistle to Richelieu preceding the printed text of *Horace*:

> Et certes, MONSEIGNEUR, ce changement visible qu'on remarque en mes ouvrages depuis que j'ai l'honneur d'être à Votre Éminence, qu'est-ce autre chose qu'un effet des grandes idées qu'elle m'inspire quand elle daigne souffrir que je lui rende mes devoirs? et à quoi peut-on attribuer ce qui s'y mêle de mauvais, qu'aux teintures grossières que je reprends quand je demeure abandonné à ma propre faiblesse? Il faut, MONSEIGNEUR, que tous ceux qui donnent leurs veilles au théâtre publient hautement avec moi que nous vous avons deux obligations très signalées: l'une, d'avoir ennobli le but de l'art;

l'autre, de nous en avoir facilité les connaissanc
n'avons plus besoin d'autre étude pour les acquéri
yeux sur Votre Éminence quand elle honore de s;
attention le récit de nos poèmes. C'est là que, lisa
qui lui plaît et ce qui ne lui plaît pas, nous nous i
titude de ce qui est bon et de ce qui est mauvais,
infaillibles de ce qu'il faut suivre et de ce qu'il fau
j'ai souvent appris en deux heures ce que mes
m'apprendre en dix ans.[52]

Corneille's measured letter of praise presents Richelieu as a perfect viewer and mimetic model of princely insight. The passage suggests that authoritative receptions and interpretations of Corneille's plays are possible only by following the dramatic standards set by the cardinal. Unlike those prescribed legally by Louis XIII, these rules of legitimation are purely theatrical, expressed more by the movement of the face ("sur son visage") than by pronouncements on the principles of drama. A mere two hours in front of this image equips the spectator with more rules for theatre than do ten years of book learning. Corneille's introductory epistle, a genre known in seventeenth-century France for its flattering depictions of a patron's many (though often allegorical) qualities and achievements, valorizes Richelieu politically as a simulacrum of theatre's patronage and legitimation. He is a condensed image portraying all of theatre's "règles infaillibles."

All the more interesting is the persuasiveness of Richelieu's performance. Corneille responds to the cardinal's theatricality by imitating it in writing: thus we find Richelieu's authoritative prominence in the theatre, which we are often forced to imagine, embodied in the form of a dramatic text. Corneille further describes the beholder's reception of the codes of theatre as mimetically direct: one only needs to think, write, or, in our case, read about the legitimizing actions and powers of Richelieu to be inspired by "des grandes idées." Richelieu's momentary self-representation in the theatre as an image of optical potency transformed him into an immortal—that is, textual—model of dramatic imitation.

Herein lies the significance of Richelieu's patronage of early French theatre, a significance that we cannot adequately understand merely by retracing historical facts, whether those concerning his involvement with the Théâtre du Marais, his promotion of the Académie Française, or his insistence on the development of dramatic theory. Richelieu's special contribution to the theatre lies in his

ation of what I call theatrical portraiture. The cardinal
d from the theatre how a prince should show himself, and
presented his portrait in a theatrical setting to profit from his
viewers' (and subsequent readers') allegorical acknowledgment of
legitimation. Richelieu seems to have benefited particularly well
from his deep sensitivity to the spectators' wishes to be fooled by
legitimation, to view ideal simulacra of authority instead of fallible
people. He nurtured to his own advantage the theatrical *esprit*
described by Scudéry in his *Observations sur le Cid.* "Ne m'eston-
nay-je pas beaucoup, que le peuple qui porte le jugement dans les
yeux, se laisse tromper par celuy de tous les sens, les plus facile à
decevoir: Mais que cette vapeur grossiere, qui se forme dans le Parterre, ait pu s'eslever jusqu'aux Galleries, & qu'un fantosme ait
abusé le savoir comme l'ignorance, & la Cour aussi bien que le
Bourgeois, j'avoüe que ce prodige m'estonne."[53] Richelieu seems to
have acknowledged that the spectator's phantasmatic transference
of past theatrical portraits into present mimetic models was the fruit
of theatre's patronage and legitimation.[54]

Illegitimate Portraiture

Richelieu was not alone in recognizing the viewer's tendency to
valorize theatrical simulacra as behavioral models. Indeed, the very
process of theatrical portraiture, encouraged and legitimized by
Richelieu, was the focus of the antitheatrical criticism of theatre's
legitimacy. The French tracts against the stage directly challenged
the patronage of theatre for personal legitimation. These treatises by
the Jansenists and their allies focused, moreover, on the spectators'
attraction to this dramatic institution bolstered by the legitimizing
conventions of literature and law. The threat of theatre, they feared,
was not so much the credulity of its models as the blind desire of
its beholders, not so much the institution's legitimacy as the spectator's vulnerability. Conti's *Traité de la comédie et des spectacles*
summarizes the central issue of the French antitheatrical position:

> ce n'est donc plus que dans les livres de Pöetique que l'instruction est
> la fin du Pöeme Dramatique. Cela n'est plus veritable, ny dans l'in-
> tention du Pöete, ny dans celle du spectateur. Le desir de plaire est ce
> qui conduit le premier, & le second est conduit par le plaisir d'y voir
> peintes des passions semblables aux siennes: car nôtre amour propre
> est si delicat, que *nous aimons à voir les portraits de nos passions aussi*

bien que ceux de nos personnes. Il est mesme si incomprehensible, qu'il fait par un étrange renversement, que *ces portraits deviennent souvent nos modeles,* & que la Comedie en peignant les passions d'au-truy, émeut nostre ame d'une telle maniere qu'elle fait naître les nostres, qu'elle les nourrit quand elles sont nées (my emphasis).[55]

Of primary concern to those so opposed to the theatre is the psychology of the viewer: the relation of the passions and pleasure, the abstract notion of self-love, the viewer's confirmation of self-love in the light of the theatrical image, and finally, the danger of the projection of this image as the imitative model for reflection and action.[56] In sum, the danger can be reduced to the dynamics of theatrical portraiture.

Those objecting to both portraiture and theatre claim that portraits tend to distract the beholder from the rationally acquired "connaissance de soi-même." In a complex elaboration of this complaint, the Jansenist Pierre Nicole describes the distracting simulacrum as a veil hiding the defective image of the soul:

L'homme veut se voir parce qu'il est vain. Il évite de se voir, parce qu'étant vain il ne peut souffrir la veüe de ses defauts & de ses miseres. Pour accorder donc ces desirs contraires, il a recours à un artifice digne de sa vanité, qui luy donne moyen de les contenter tous deux en même temps. Cét artifice est de couvrir d'un voile tous ses defauts, de les effacer en quelque sorte de l'image qu'il se forme de luy-même, & de n'y enfermer que les qualitez qui le peuvent relever à ses propres yeux. S'il ne les a pas effectivement, il se les donne par son imagination; & s'il ne les trouve pas dans son propre être, il les va chercher dans les opinions des hommes, ou dans les choses exterieures qu'il attache à son idée comme si elles en faisoient partie; & par le moyen de cette illusion, il est toûjours absent de luy-même & present à luy-même: il se regarde continuellement, & il ne se voit jamais veritablement, parce qu'il ne voit au lieu de luy-même que le vain phantôme qu'il s'en est formé.[57]

Nicole here opposes two notions of reflection. One is clearly identifiable as self-reflection that uses the faculty of reason to produce an honest and balanced image of one's self. Self-reflection depicts the subject's commendable traits as well as its faults and weaknesses. Competing with this self as *res cogitans* is a self engendered by another sort of reflection, but which still does not work in active opposition to the *res cogitans*.[58] It does not negate reason, nor does it deny the subject's faults and weaknesses. Rather, this other self, commonly known as passion, hides, camouflages, and disguises the *res cogitans.* The passions, aided and abetted by a productive imagination, make images (the literal sense of *imagination*) that deflect through transference the rays of reflective vision. As Conti suggests above, the passions flatter and deceive the self with images of desire appealing to the long-sought-after object of self-love. The result is Conti's "étrange renversement," where the images of passion provide models of imitation more desirable than those produced by the discourse of reason. This transformation of the thinking self into the figural image of an object of desire is the same activity described by Corneille as the viewing of Richelieu's simulacrum. Instead of rationally seeing one's self or another object as it is, one beholds its idealized form as one both imagines and desires it.

Although Nicole does not specifically mention the Salle de la Comédie, the Théâtre du Marais, or the Hôtel de Bourgogne, he blames the theatre (as well as the novel) for a great part of the damage caused by such portrait making. In his inflammatory essay, "De la comédie," Nicole criticizes theatre as the significant part of a fictional world of false idols: "cela suffit pour obliger tous ceux qui ont quelque soin de leur salut de fuir les Comedies, le Bal, & les Romans, n'y ayant rien au monde qui fasse sortir davantage l'ame hors de soy, qui la rende plus incapable de l'application à Dieu, & qui la remplisse davantage de vains fantômes. Ce sont d'étranges prieres que celles que l'on fait en sortant de ces spectacles, ayant la teste pleine de toutes les folies qu'on y a vües."[59] Still, no matter how distraught Nicole might have been over the proliferating accessibility of plays, he was ambivalent about condemning the theatre outright. By distinguishing between the artifact and its viewer, he carefully avoided investing theatrical portraiture with a self of its own, with a kind of sinful personification:

> quand il seroit vrai que la Comedie ne feroit aucun mauvais effet sur de certains esprits, ils ne la pourroient pas neanmoins prendre pour un divertissement innocent, ny croire qu'ils ne sont point coupables en y assistant. On ne joüe point la Comedie pour une seule personne: c'est un spectacle qu'on expose à toutes sortes d'esprits dont la plupart sont foibles & corrompus, & à qui par consequent il est extremement dangereux. C'est leur faute dira-t-on d'y assister en cet estat. Il est vray; mais vous les autorisez par vostre exemple . . . plus vous estes reglé dans vos autres actions, plus ils sont hardis à vous imiter dans celle-là . . . & si la Comedie ne vous fait point de plaies par elle-même vous vous en faites à vous-même par celle que les autres reçoivent de vostre exemple.[60]

In Nicole's opinion, it is not so much spectacle that is at fault for weak minds as it is the fault of weak minds to base their conduct on imaginary images.[61] Nicole condemns any acceptance of images as models of imitation, whether they are theatrical images or the images of patrons of the theatre. In both cases, the viewer creates a portrait of a model and then thinks and acts according to the standards determined by that model.

If Nicole's biased text is at all credible, royal models were favored as the subject of seventeenth-century, imaginary portraits: "Que de gens font le portrait d'un Prince! Tout son Royaume, tous les païs étrangers sont pour luy une Academie de Peintres, dont il est le modele."[62] Nicole shows such models, moreover, to be more complex than I have presented them. He argues against theatre in part because actors could become engulfed by the passions of their roles, by how the temporary conditions of theatrical dialogue entice them to think. The danger of such transference is thrust upon anyone taken as a subject for portraiture:

> Pour mieux comprendre de quelle sorte l'homme pourroit estre forcé de se voir luy même par les objects qui sont hors de luy, & ce qu'il fait pour s'en garantir, il faut considerer qu'il ne se regarde pas moins selon un certain estre qu'il a dans l'imagination des autres, que selon ce qu'il est effectivement; & qu'il ne forme pas seulement son portrait sur ce qu'il connoist de soy par luy-même, mais aussi sur la veüe des portraits qu'il en découvre dans l'esprit des autres. Car nous sommes tous à l'egard les uns des autres comme cét homme qui sert de modele aux Eleves dans les Academies de Peintres. Chacun de ceux qui nous environnent se forme un portrait de nous; & les differentes manieres dont on regarde nos actions, donnent lieu d'en former une diversité presque infinie.[63]

Since theatrical portraiture seems to affect the model as much as it does the beholder, it is fairly easy to imagine how Richelieu's image of himself as a legitimizing prince was heightened by those who regarded him as such in the Salle de la Comédie. As Mlle. de Scudéry describes the inter-subjective conditions of self-portraiture, "je me suis vû en autrui, comme on se voit dans un miroir, & beaucoup mieux que je ne me voyais en moi-même."[64] In the site of allegorical transference, the royal player remains just as dependent on his beholders as the spectators are on the prince. Both spectator and prince display themselves as the exaggerated theatrical image created by the conditions of enunciation with the Other. This Other, moreover, is as much a psychological representation as it is a mere character of the dramatic poem or an allegorical convention of royal spectacle. It is simultaneously the phenomenological Other of the subject's *res cogitans* and the subliminal image projected by the theatrical beholder.

Whether or not Nicole can dismiss theatrical portraiture as a legitimate activity, he hit the mark by discussing it as a phenomenon that extends far beyond the boundaries of the dramatic poem and playhouse. As the example of Richelieu illustrates, the psychology of portraiture was integrally related in the seventeenth century to the structure of legal and cultural legitimation. Richelieu's image as the surrogate monarch of France was enhanced by his portraiture as the sole authority over the many facets of writing, staging, and beholding plays. Public acknowledgment of his theatrical achievements contributed to his legitimation as the (legal) caretaker of France. From the less sophisticated Louis XIII to the more able governors, Richelieu and Louis XIV, the validity of a prince was measured to a large degree by the extent of his overall portraiture. And as Louis XIV demonstrated through his centralization of all the arts, theatre and its patronage were but one aspect of a system of allegorical representation whose end was political legitimation. Although the portraits chosen by Louis XIV, Richelieu, and Louis XIII were exaggerated, in keeping with Aristotle's theatrical model, there remained no formal boundaries, whether of poem, playhouse, or decree, limiting the illusion of portraiture. Its phantasmatic force fueled the seventeenth-century French political system, which was sustained by the public's acknowledgment of its leaders' fictional powers.

8

The Printed Portrait:
A Figure of Figures

Pierre Nicole's closing chapter of "De la comédie" contains his most poignant description of the "fantômes" sustaining theatre and portraiture. His charge, simple and to the point, pertains to actors and spectators alike. "Si les choses temporelles ne sont que des figures & des ombres sans solidité: on peut dire que les Comedies sont les ombres des ombres, & les figures des figures; puisque ce ne sont que de vaines images des choses temporelles, & souvent des choses fausses."[1]

The label, "les figures des figures," is significant as more than an ultimate charge directed by Nicole at the institution of theatre. "Figures" is a very resonant concept that might explain Nicole's discomfort with both theatre and a particular form of language:

> Les Comedies & les Romans n'excitent pas seulement les passions, mais elles enseignent aussi le langage des passions, c'est-a-dire l'art de les exprimer & de les faire paroistre d'une maniere agreable & ingenieuse, ce qui n'est pas un petit mal.[2]

It is not enough, insists Nicole, to talk about theatre's passionate production of portraits. That happens outside of theatre as well as within ("un homme du commun ... qui vit dans sa famille n'est peint que par le petit nombre de ceux qui le connoissent, & les portraits qu'on fait de luy, ne sortent gueres hors l'enceinte de sa Ville"[3]). What Nicole claims is unique to both the theatre and the novel is their dangerous ability to teach as well as excite the language of the passions. The threat lies in the representation's combination of different kinds of figures: those of the passions and those of language.

Nicole distinguishes between two distinct applications of theatrical language. Either theatrical language can be multiplied and confounded by the writing of contemporary plays or it can be limited and tempered by the translation of classical texts. As with Nicole's qualifications concerning the relative innocence of spectacle itself, the object of his attack is not so much theatrical texts as their use.[4] Reminiscent of the widespread Jesuit adaptation of theatre for pedagogical purposes, Nicole himself argues for the usefulness of theatrical texts in the context of formal instruction:

> Vous voulez abuser du mot des Comedies, & confondre celuy qui les fait pour le Theatre, avec celuy qui les traduit seulement pour les Ecoles: mais il y a tant de difference entr'eux qu'on ne peut pas tirer de consequence d'un à l'autre. Le Traducteur n'a dans l'esprit que des regles de Grammaire qui ne sont pas mauvaises par elles-mêmes, & qu'un bon dessein peut rendre tres-bonnes: mais le Poëte a bien d'autres idées dans l'imagination, il sent toutes les passions qu'il conçoit, & il s'efforce même de les sentir afin de les mieux concevoir.[5]

In this response to Desmarest's criticism of Nicole's translation of Terence into French, the Jansenist insists that a translation undertaken to enrich the instruction of French grammar is justifiable. Reminiscent of the example of Ben Jonson, the grammarian is here presented as the only "writer" of plays worthy of imitation. What counts is the writer's "bon dessein" and constant application of the grammatical rules of language. Nicole defends translation because he sees it to be fundamentally antitheatrical. His imposition of grammatical rules on the plays of Terence disinfects them as carriers of theatrical humors.[6]

In contrast, Nicole criticizes the dramatic poet for being a veritable "empoissoneur public."[7] The dramatists' inattentiveness to grammatical precision is a sign of weak moral comportment. More concerned with the display of passion than with a demonstration of good grammatical intentions (self-reflection), poets efface their reasoning selves (*res cogitans*) for the sake of the passion of their work. They emphasize the text's image and design (*dessin*) over its grammar and intentionality (*dessein*). Cultivating their imaginative talents—the making of images—and their abilities "de les faire paroistre d'une maniere agreable & ingenieuse," poets are exemplary rhetoricians, not grammarians. Their primary task is to transform imaginary figures into extraordinary language. Or, in the simple terms of the eighteenth-century rhetorician du Marsais, dramatic poets make figures of figures.

> On dit communément que les *figures sont des manières de parler éloignées de celles qui sont naturelles et ordinaires*: que *ce sont de certains tours et de certaines façons de s'exprimer, qui s'éloignent en quelque chose de la manière commune et simple de parler*: ce qui ne veut dire autre chose, sinon que les figures sont des manières de parler éloignées de celles qui ne sont pas figurées, et qu'en un mot les figures sont des figures, et ne sont pas ce qui n'est pas figure.[8]

One of the threats of theatre is its tendency to cultivate a linguistic life of its own through the medium of figural language, whose mimetic distance from its object is feared by Nicole. Dramatists thus make present the linguistic forms of figures while encouraging their repetition through performative transference.

Surprisingly, Nicole does not go much farther than this account in developing his attack against theatre's linguistic subversiveness. Although *La Logique du Port Royal* provides an elaborate definition of legitimate language and its use, Nicole limits his critique of theatre's rhetorical discourse to the examples of imaginary images and artistic portraits. Yet, a discussion of theatrical portraiture would not be complete without due consideration of its own figural language. For it is the rhetoric of theatrical portraiture that keeps the seventeenth-century dramatic image alive in the absence of its physical model.

Take the example of Corneille's epistle to Richelieu discussed in the preceding chapter. We are able to grasp the import of Richelieu's portrait because of the linguistic remnants attesting to it. The figure of Richelieu remains impressive because Corneille and numerous others felt compelled to speak it and, more significantly, to write it. This transference of a three-dimensional visual image into the shape of a written text provides one example of an extensive seventeenth-century French tradition of cross-movement between written, theatrical, and artistic forms of portraiture, a cross-fertilization well-illustrated by the account of the painter Daniel Dumoûtier of an order from Louis XIII: "pour dire, faites mon por-

trait, le prince dit: Ecrivez-moi."[9] Alongside the costly and complex
productions of painted and theatrical portraiture, seventeenth-century French writers developed a written portraiture memorializing
the simulacra once projected in the theatre hall. As Mlle. de Montpensier writes in the preface to her *Recueil des portraits et eloges*,
the written portrait "marque et designe si bien ceux dont il a entre-
pris la vie, qu'il semble que nous les voyons, que nous leur parlions,
& que nous soyons avec eux dans une familiarité tres estroite."[10]
Enhanced by the figural language cultivated by the portraitists, the
written portraits produce a lively and always present picture of their
majestic subjects. In the form of a written text, theatrical portraiture
transfers the site of princely legitimation from stage to page and
thereby permits the reader to sustain prolonged communication
with the figure.

In the world of seventeenth-century French theatre, this transfer occurred most frequently in dedicatory epistles accompanying
printed plays. An examination of plays printed at that time in
France reveals a significant number of epistles concerned more with
the written portraiture of their patrons than with the type of self-
referential, authorial legitimation performed by Ben Jonson. Still,
that a seventeenth-century epistle, whether French or English, is
most often an encomium of a patron would not surprise most critics
of the period. What is important about this literature in France,
however, is that it became formalized as a twofold allegorizing
genre—epistle and written portrait. The rhetorical figures of the
written portrait, moreover, give rise to a specific image of theatrical
presence that dominated the ideological concerns of dramatic practice and theory in seventeenth-century France. Only after considering these particular figures in view of patronage, will I be able to
account, in Section Three below, for the Abbé d'Aubignac's subtle
and curious plea to future practitioners of theatre to depart from
both the figures of theatrical portraiture and the ideology which they
embody.

The Eternal Presence of Praise

> J'aime mieux dire que [Voiture] se joûë agréablement de
> son sujet, & que des Lettres galantes ne demandent pas

une vérité si austére que des Epîtres dédicatoires, qui sont d'elles-mêmes graves & sérieuses.

DOMINIQUE BOUHOURS, *La Maniere de bien penser dans les ouvrages d'esprit*[11]

The portraiture in epistles of printed plays lends itself to theatrical legitimation not just because it is written, but primarily because it embodies the prince in a literary form whose generic principles fuel the ideology of absolute patronage. Reshaping the countenance of the patron into the allegory of a literary persona, the codes of this genre work toward the transformation of the subject into a paragon of fictional perfection. It is precisely the representation of the fictional that constitutes the political value of the carefully posed portrait. For the written portrait avoids any detailed narration of the personal history of the subject portrayed, any careful recounting of past deeds, or even any prediction of future exploits. The portrait is a phantasmatic tableau, a sweeping and all-inclusive statement of praise.

Take as an example La Calprenède's dedication of a play to Richelieu, written partially in the style of a portrait:

> Et certes, MONSIEUR, quand je considere les prodiges de vostre vie, je ne crois plus qu'il soit au pouvoir des hommes descrire des choses si infiniment au dessus d'eux, il n'en peuvent parler que comme les Perses du Soleil, & les plus prudens à l'imitation du Peintre couvriront sans doute d'un voile ce qu'ils ne pourront assez bien exprimer, aussi quelle satisfaction peut on retirer de ses veilles en mettant au jour ce que la posterité ne prendra que pour des fables puisque les merveilles qui leur serviront de matiere semblent assez esloignées de la verité qu'elles font de l'apparence . . . & tout l'Europe est une table ou l'histoire de vostre vie est gravée en des caracteres eternels. C'est sur cet ample Theatre que vous avez paru avec tant de pompe, & que vous avez obligé toute la terre à suspendre ses propres interets pour regarder avec quelle prudence & quelle conduitte vous desmeslez les nostres.[12]

The image of Richelieu sketched here is so praiseworthy that La Calprenède calls it indescribable.[13] Any attempt to imitate it requires the portraitist, in the tradition of Protegenes and Apelles, to think of it as if covered with a veil circumscribing and mediating the writer's perception of an image too perfect to be represented.[14]

This veil metaphor also reminds us of Alberti's commentary on the activity of reading portraits. The veil fixes the image in an unchanging plane which "is always the same thing in the process of seeing."[15] One effect of this constancy is its accessibility, its observability to all readers, much unlike the vanishing point in Richelieu's theatre which delimits ideal vision to the princely position. But, similar to the vanishing point, the written portrait of Richelieu presents itself to all readers as an illusion of grandeur "que la posterité ne prendra que pour des fables puisque les merveilles qui leur serviront de matiere semblent assez esloignées de la verité qu'elles font de l'apparence." The well-wrought portrait enacts the fiction of self-legitimizing drama, the kind described by Nietzsche as showing itself as veiled, as masked, as the "mere appearance of mere appearance."[16]

This accentuation of the image's accessibility through fictionality also manifests itself in the time structure of the portrait. The temporal actions of Richelieu, "les prodiges de vostre vie," are mentioned as former actions, wondrous for their theatrical pomp and splendor—"c'est sur cet ample Theatre que vous avez paru avec tant de pompe." Yet, these unspecific past events merely qualify another image in which the cardinal's entire personal history—past, present, and even future—is reduced into one figural portrait, forever present "gravée en des caracteres eternels." This transference of the temporal into an eternal or durative present is also represented in La Calprenède's text by the entire world's suspension of its activities, its temporal motion, in order to remain fixed and spellbound in beholding the portrait of Richelieu.[17] Temporality is thus reshaped into an image of what might be called the eternal presence of praise.

This exaggerated, fictional presence is also a formal trait of epideictic rhetoric and distinguishes the French written portrait from popular seventeenth-century forms of narrative and dramatic fiction. The narratives of both the novel and the drama posit a "dual temporality" marking the difference between narrative time and "reading" time. This is the difference that has provoked theoretical discussions concerning the unities of time, place, and action (prevalent in the seventeenth century and recently resurfacing in the narrative theories of Gérard Genette and Christian Metz[18]). In subscribing to the time structures of epideictic rhetoric, the seventeenth-century French portraitists sidestepped the impossible struggle to make the reader's experience of time as synonymous as possible with that of the fictional character. Extending Aristotle's prescription that the "present" is the most appropriate time for the epideictic, portraitists made this moment eternal by transforming a hero's actions into a textual fable always present to the reader as a laudable fiction, made marvelous by its unspecificity.[19]

The reader's acknowledgment of the lofty character of written portraits derives in part from the rhetorical features of epideictic rhetoric.[20] The anonymously penned *Portrait de Mademoiselle de Beauvais* stresses the portraitist's tendency to weight exaggeration over verisimilitude. "La pluspart des Autheurs se sont moins attachez à la ressemblence qu'à l'amplification."[21] Functioning similarly to Aristotle's concept of tragic heightening, the rhetorical emphasis on amplification and exaggeration shows the portrait to be more than a true representation of the subject. In so doing, epideictic rhetoric prompts the reader to respond to the illusory quality, or better yet, the fictionality of its image. Being something more than a piece of laudatory prose, the text presents the image as a figure of a literary character whose illusory scope defies representation.[22]

Also contributing to the fictionality of written portraiture are its tone and style which, ironically, depend more heavily on structures of negation and denial than on those of affirmation and acceptance. In *Portrait de Madame la Comtesse D. . . . .*, Monsieur Perrin introduces the epideictic figure of his rhetoric only by denying it: "je ferois vostre Eloge, & non pas vostre Portrait, si j'en disois plus; & ce n'est ny vostre intention, ny la mienne."[23] It is a common strategy of written portraiture to deny motivation by praise or blame. Such negation, what an empathetic reader might want to call verbal neutrality, is more than a means of disguising praise. It constitutes the narrative style of written portraiture: "& si jen disois ce qu'elles me donnent matiere de penser, je ne pourrais parler du reste de sa personne sans composer un Livre au lieu d'un Portrait."[24] As an alternative to biographical depictions of the subject (the length of which constitutes a "book"), the written portrait tends to exercise linguistic condensation as a means of "neutral" representation.[25] This is not to say that portraits avoid excessive praise of the subject but that they render this praise by the quality of the condensed representational image rather than by the quantity of laudatory description.[26]

Consider the density of La Calprenède's only description of Richelieu: "& tout l'Europe est une table ou l'histoire de vostre vie est gravée en des caracteres eternels." The biography of this hero turns around its representation in the figural space of a *table*, itself a highly polysemic image. Consideration of the many connotations of *table* listed in the *Robert* may tell us, among other things, that a *table* is "chez Aristote, Leibniz, État de l'esprit 'vierge,' avant toute représentation"—the non-representable source of perfection, the *tabula rasa*, or what we now acknowledge as the representational scene of *Archi-écriture*. Yet also as a figure of representation itself, *table* is an "ensemble de données dont chaque article peut être identifié sans ambiguïté au moyen d'un ou plusieurs arguments (abcise, ordonnée; figures, symboles)." Here, *table* presents us with the complete *list* of all of the qualities, actions, thoughts, figures, etc. of the subject, in the scientific sense of an *inventaire, répertoire, sommaire*. And finally, this image of reason and truth doubles as a figure of the management of reason and truth, "recueil d'information, de données . . . groupées de façon systématique, en vue d'une consultation aisée"—the methodological means of condensing unmanageable material into a *tableau*, what Michel Foucault discusses as the seventeenth-century habit of reordering reality into *tableaux* of signs.[27] In sum, La Calprenède's condensation of the portrait of Richelieu into the figure of a *table* collapses multiple notions into one extremely polysemous signifier: (1) the unrepresentable source of Richelieu's perfection, (2) the citation of all of his qualities which we are asked to recognize as incomplete aspects of the unrepresentable source, (3) the condensational method of their grouping and perception. In the spirit of the genre and its ideological purport, La Calprenède pens a portrait of Richelieu which is nothing, or rather, which is nothing more than a figure of the figure of its representation.

Such abstraction exemplifies the fictional thrust of the written portrait. The abstract quality of the figures *table, Europe, Histoire de vostre vie*, for instance, leaves the dimensions and boundaries of all these images to the infinite representation of the reader's imagination (which is similarly structured to displace everyday narratives into condensed and negated textures of dream images). Through Europe's reduction to the scene of Richelieu's actions, for example, the image of Europe loses its cartographic specificity as the literal portrait of *Europe* and of Europe's *own* history. Effaced by its transformation into the space of the eternal character of Richelieu's biography, Europe becomes conflated with the phantasm of Richelieu.[28]

The impressiveness of this descriptive condensation is espe-

Figure 9. Marcus Gheeraerts the Younger, *Queen Elizabeth I.*

cially evident in relation to the structural differences of painted and written portraits which seventeenth-century French portraitists were keen to discuss. Perhaps no painting stands better in comparison with La Calprenède's portrait than an English example, the Ditchley portrait of Elizabeth I, painted by Marcus Gheeraerts the Younger (Figure 9). This is due to the convenient fact that the Ditchley portrait represents pictorially the same linguistic images penned by La Calprenède in his portrait of Richelieu. Not only does Elizabeth stand on the map of England, but the images of ships coming and going, carefully inserted in each major port of entry, also suggest her desire to expand her kingdom through colonial exploration, trade, and conquest. The Ditchley portrait depicts the entire world as a stage on which is played the history of Elizabeth's reign. The picture's detailed images are accompanied by a cartouche that contains a fragmentary sonnet explaining the hierarchical relation of secular rule to divine order, which is only alluded to by the allegorical figure of the heavens surrounding Elizabeth's likeness.[29] In a way that restricts the beholder's imaginary explication of the image, this graphic text clarifies what is not made evident by Gheeraerts's pictorial representation. To effect such a representation, moreover, Gheeraerts relies on a representational mixture of image and text, one that generates a structure of figural multiplication and accumulation in contrast to written portraiture's economy of condensation and negation. The Ditchley portrait, filled with explicit symbolic indicators such as a portrait, a map, and a poetic table among many other things, lacks the provocative economy of La Calprenède's written portrait of Richelieu. The French writer's brief text suggests in only one line as much as Gheeraerts's cartouche and imagery display together.[30] Most significant is how La Calprenède's abstraction of the images clearly outlined by Gheeraerts leaves them open to a freer imaginative representation (and interpretation) by the reader. Much more than the Ditchley picture, which is representative of a popular mode of royal portraiture, La Calprenède's condensed and abstract portrait of Richelieu compels the beholder to speak, to re-present an infinity of praises.[31]

From Actions to Idioms

It should be noted that the significance of the preceding discussion of written and painted portraits goes far beyond the coincidental nature of the striking similarity of the Ditchley and La Calprenède examples. Comparison of these two genres generated a French conceptual discourse important to matters of theatrical legitimation. In her fascinating theoretical preface to the *Recueil des portraits et eloges*, Mlle. de Montpensier draws on this comparison to delineate particular features of written portraiture believed to enhance its rhetorical force:

> Si les plus difficiles & les plus bizarres [Dames du Royaume] gardent du respect & de la veneration aux Tableaux des Heros & des Heroïnes, qui font d'ordinaire les riches ornamens de leurs Palais? Quelle estime ne doit-on pas faire de nos Portraits, puisqu'ils ne dépeignent pas seulement, comme les autres, les beautez & les traits du visage, mais encore les lumieres de l'esprit, & les belles qualitez de l'ame. Les premiers sont des chefs-d'oeuvres de Peintres excellens en leur Art, qui ne servent qu'à donner de la reputation à l'Ouvrier. Les Seconds élevent les Heros representez, & produisent au grand jour le merite, les inclinations, & les vertus des objets. Ce sont des grands modelles de beauté, de douceur, de piété, de prudence, d'amour, de generosité & de modestie, que l'on donne au public. Comme il y a bien plus de Triomphans que de Sages, & qu'il est bien plus aisé de vaincre que de bien vivre: Nous pouvons dire qu'il est bien plus difficile de bien representer les genereuses inclinations & les grandes qualitez d'une ame divine, comme celle de vostre A.R. que de descrire des combats & des triomphes qui rendent les Heros plus glorieux à la verité, mais non pas toujours plus prudens & plus vertueux: Ainsi l'on peut dire, que dans cét abregé de toutes les merveilles de nostre Cour, nos Princesses & nos Dames, on enchery sur tous nos Poëtes & nos Orateurs.[32]

In addition to Montpensier's suggestive remarks concerning the possible gender differences of the two genres, which Erica Harth discusses in her analysis of the sociological implications of feminine portraiture, two criteria surface in her comparison of painted and written portraits that speak directly to the complex issues of theatrical legitimation: authorship and representationality.

In terms of authorship, Montpensier stresses a crucial difference between the two media. On one hand, the painted portrait is comparable to a literary text, say of the stature of Ben Jonson's grand folio. They both show themselves as "chefs-d'oeuvres . . . qui ne servent qu'à donner de la reputation à l'Ouvrier." The self-consciousness of their design (*dessin* and *dessein*) detracts from the glory of the princely images they depict. Montpensier claims, on the other hand, that the authors of written portraits efface themselves for the sake of their own work. Indeed, a large number of the portraits printed in Montpensier's large collection are even penned anonymously, as if doubly denying their authorship (even the striking exception of the auto-portraiture often listed as "fait par elle-même" seems to suggest that the status of authorship, designated by the third person, is less consequential than the subject of the portrait, always identified by the proper name; Montpensier's collection never lists auto-portraits in the converse fashion, say, "Portrait d'elle-même fait par Mademoiselle de Rohan"). Much like the playwrights criticized by Nicole, the portraitists are said by Montpensier to emphasize the text's imagery and rhetoric over their own intentions and reputations as authors. As a result, the texts call attention to their representationality and rhetoric instead of valorizing the merits of their writers as authors.

For Montpensier, however, the issue of authorship is much less crucial to written portraiture than is the quality of allegorical representation offered by the genre. Discussing the representational structures of painted portraits, Montpensier questions the painters' claims concerning the value of their medium. The implications of her position become especially evident when it is contrasted with that of a seventeenth-century theoretician of the plastic arts, say Roger de Piles. Although Montpensier would agree with de Piles that a painted portrait "consiste à exprimer le veritable temperamment des personnnes que l'on represente, & à faire voir leur Phisionomie,"[33] she would differ on the representational depth of physiognomy. In *Cours de peinture par principes*, de Piles takes elaborate measures to valorize the genre of painted portraiture. One of the most striking passages in his chapter, "Sur la maniere de faire les portraits," makes a strong claim for the profundity of painting:

> Il est sur-tout nécessaire que les figures qui ne sont point occupées, semblent vouloir satisfaire le desir de ceux qui ont la curiosité de les voir; & qu'ainsi elles se montrent dans l'action la plus convenable à leur tempérament & à leur état, comme si elles vouloient instruire le spectateur de ce qu'elles sont en effet; & comme la plûpart du monde se pique de franchise, d'honnêteté & de grandeur d'ame, il faut fuir dans les attitudes toutes sortes d'affectations, que tout y soit aisé & naturel, & que l'on y fasse entrer plus ou moins de fierté, de noblesse & de majesté: ... Je suis ce valeureux capitaine qui porte la terreur par-tout, ou bien qui ai fait voir par ma bonne conduite tant de glorieux succès. ... Enfin les attitudes sont le langage des portraits.[34]

De Piles makes the same assertion for painted portraits that Montpensier reserves for written ones, "qu'il nous semble que nous les voyons, que nous leur parlions."[35] Inscribed in a painted portrait, de Piles writes, is a language that allows the spectator to read the painting, to hold discourse with it concerning the subject's *honnê-teté* and the qualities of the soul. This description of attitudes as a language of painting is a seventeenth-century commonplace, evidenced, for example, by Poussin's earlier claim to Chantelou that "les sept premières figures à main gauche vous diront tout ce qui est ici écrit et tout le reste est de la même étoffe: lisez l'histoire et le tableau, afin de connoître si chaque chose est appropriée au sujet."[36]

But Montpensier depreciates the value of painting's reading experience by contending that the language of painted portraiture does little more than describe bodily features and actions. Her point is that painting lacks the rhetorical force of written portraiture to speak what cannot be drawn: "les lumieres de l'esprit, & les belles qualitez de l'ame." The argument of Montpensier's text, moreover, goes far beyond the frequently cited issues of the debate between mute poetry and speaking pictures.[37] Instead of denying the narrative structures of painting, Montpensier joins Poussin in likening painted portraits to historical narratives. Both are shown by Montpensier to share a common representational style. The language of painted portraits consists of the picture's "attitudes," the poses of the subject. To de Piles, the effect of this language is that the figures "se montrent dans l'action le plus convenable à leur tempérament & à leur état." Painted portraits, then, describe the glorious *actions* of the subject, "je suis ce valeureux capitaine qui porte la terreur par-tout." Historical narratives rely on similar language effects, "de descrire des combats & des triomphes qui rendent les Heros plus glorieux à la verité." They make the hero glorious *by describing his actions* in war.

According to Montpensier, the heroes of written portraits are not so much men of action as exemplary women, "des grands modelles de beauté, de douceur, de piété, de prudence, d'amour, de generosité & de modestie." They are represented not as the fruit of phallic actions but as the paradigm of certain abstract qualities. Written portraiture displaces description of the subject's personal actions and history with the nomination of innate properties. Framed by epideictic rhetoric, not history, the written portrait lies outside of the context of any temporal or pictorial localization. In written portraits, "attitudes" are ornaments of "la merite, les inclinations, et les vertus des objets," not sculptural positions of the body itself. Being suspended from temporality and freed from the referential limits of historical pronouncement and physical depiction, the written portrait is said by Montpensier to be more universal and absolute in assertion.[38]

Exemplary of the abstract ornamentation of written portraiture is de La Serre's miniature portrait of the Duchesse d'Esguillon, which is subtly inserted into his dedicatory epistle prefacing *Thomas Morus*: "je suis fort aise qu'elle [cette Ouvrage] me serve d'occasion à faire voir au Public, que je sçay subir avec toute sorte de respect la Loy de ses Oracles, lors qu'ils publient par toute la Terre, que vous en estes un des plus riches ornements."[39] Limiting his portrayal of the Duchesse to the enunciation of "un des plus riches ornaments," as a limit*less* trait in itself, de La Serre demonstrates the relation of written portraiture to the complex representational codes of seventeenth-century classical discourse. These enunciative structures restrict themselves to nominal maxims of an absolute nature, like the absolutely abstract virtues of *bienséance* and *bon sens*.[40] An abstract phrase, such as "un des plus riches ornaments," functions in a significational system of "mirroring" in which a nominal icon is only a shifting signifier of still another nominal icon.

A striking illustration of nominal mirroring can be found in Dominique Bouhours's *Les Entretiens d'Ariste et d'Eugène*, which describes *bon sens* as a signifier of a person's perfect perspective:

> Il y a encore une autre sorte de beaux esprits, qu'on peut appeller des esprits de negociation & de cabinet. Ce sont des genies éclairez, judicieux, actifs, & propres pour les affaires: d'une veuë ils en penetrent le fond, ils en découvrent toutes les circonstances & toutes les suites; ils trouvent en un instant tous les expediens & toutes les voyes par où l'on peut ménager & faire reüssir les choses les plus difficiles. Mais ils ne voyent que ce qu'il faut voir, & qu'autant qu'il faut, pour prendre un bon parti & faire un choix raisonnable.[41]

Bouhours's explanation of *bon sens* is clouded by a series of synonymous nominations of genius. First, *bon sens* figures as a synonym of *esprit de negotiation*. Clarifying *esprit de negotiation*, Bouhours describes it as the execution of *un bon parti* and *un choix raisonnable*. But in consulting Bouhours further, we learn little more than that *un choix raisonnable* stands as the synonym of *bon sens*. Such extremely circular referentiality restricts the signification of any one nominal assertion to the mirror image of its double, thereby constituting a system of nominal auto-signification. Nothing is signified by this use of language other than the *mise-en-abîme* of the nominal system itself, or in terms more familiar to the dis-

cussion of written portraiture, its own endless fictionality or allegoresis. When represented by these nominal codes, the portrait of a
prince is the fictional embodiment of *bon sens, bienséance, bel
esprit*, etc.—the historical self is reduced to the auto-portrait of a
linguistic system. In this case, the written portrait stands essentially
as an allegory of its own semantic field: the transference of one figure into another (rhetorical) figure.[42]

Personification

Sustained by this seventeenth-century system of nominal auto-signification, the French written portrait embodies a particularly neoclassical praxis of epideictic rhetoric. The portrait's purposive relation to its readers is implicitly mimetic, thus adapting the purpose
of epideictic rhetoric as prescribed by Aristotle to the demands of
the French *doctrine classique*: "the hearer of the epideictic is but a
mere spectator for he has nothing to judge, he merely listens to the
condition of things as they are reported."[43] Although the nominal
rhetoric of French written portraiture is not subject to judgment,
being structured as an unquestionable (ahistorical) truth, it does ask
its audience to function as more than merely passive spectators. In
de La Serre's words, "les plus ambitieuses d'honneur n'aspirent qu'à
de vous pouvoir imiter."[44] The seventeenth-century French written
portrait asks its readers to accept and repeat the nominal codes of
epideictic rhetoric as models of imitation.[45] The quality of portraiture, then, depends on the performative force of the figural image
to generate a rhetorical life of its own. A striking portrait, whether
seen as a simulacrum of a face or read in the form of a text, encour-
ages the spectator to speak the model, to enunciate the figural *personification* of the portrait.

The seventeenth-century French written portrait's performance
through personification is especially significant because it precedes
in practice what had to wait until the nineteenth-century for theoretical explication. It is Pierre Fontanier's *Manuel des tropes* (1830)
that comes closest to elucidating the sort of figural personification
found in these portraits. Going farther than its predecessors, say *La
Logique ou l'art de penser* of Port-Royal (1662–83) or du Marsais's
Traité des tropes (1730), Fontanier's treatise discusses personification as a rhetorical trope, performing the abstract sentiments that
stand, much like the theatrical passions, in vivid contrast to the

rational and grammatical explications of rhetoric.[46] The earlier writer, du Marsais, makes this distinction especially apparent when he writes that "il est bien plus utile d'observer [les fautes] qui pèchent contre la conduite, contre la justesse du raisonnement, contre la probité, la droiture et les bonnes moeurs. Il serait à souhaiter que les exemples de ces dernières sortes de fautes fussent moins rares, ou plutôt qu'ils fussent inconnus."[47] In marked contrast to this antitheatrical position, Pierre Fontanier's description of personification goes into conceptual detail to revive the theoretical understanding of the fictional importance and benefits of rhetorical personification: "la *Personnification* consiste à faire d'un *être inanimé, insensible, ou d'un être abstrait et purement idéal, une espèce d'être réel et physique, doué de sentiment et de vie, enfin ce qu'on appelle une* personne; *et cela, par simple façon de parler, ou par une fiction toute verbale.*"[48] The object of personification, as we have seen practiced by various strategists of seventeenth-century theatrical portraiture, might be either an ideal simulacrum of a prince, brought to life by the theatregoer's "vains fantômes," or a linguistic fiction, sustained by nominal praise and given shape in a written portrait.[49]

Returning to my earlier example of Corneille's epistle to Richelieu, it can now be seen how the simulacrum of a patron is personified in both of these ways. The image of the ideal viewer is brought to life in the text as a portrait that "speaks" the laws of viewing and interpretation. Simultaneously, the linguistic codes sustaining portraiture—*bon sens* and *bienséance*—are personified in the image of Richelieu whose visage depicts clearly and economically "ce qui est bon" and "ce qui est mauvais." The act of writing the portrait posits the simulacrum of both as a figural portrait and as a model of figural language. One implies the other. Furthermore, the reader might recall that Conti and Nicole, in their antitheatrical critiques of portraiture, condemn such ideal portraits because "ses portraits deviennent souvent nos modeles." A written portrait calls on its beholder to personify it as a model, to bring it to life through the process of repetitive imitation, and thus to enact its transference from fiction to reality. The model personified is indeed the ultimate "figure des figures," which can be said to be the real, concrete image of all of its fictional expressions ("de beauté, de douceur, de piété, de prudence, d'amour, de generosité & de modestie").[50] Such a transformation of numerous fictional images into one tangible mimetic model constitutes the strategic aim of written portraiture.

As a genre specializing in the promotion of fictional models of virtue, the written portrait was especially useful in seventeenth-century France as an ideological device for representing the courtly image. Earmarked by the economies of condensation and negation, the representation of the written portrait's image is not contingent on the presence (or even existence) of the princely figure portrayed. Fictional in reality, nominal models are made present and real by their personification as conventions of written portraiture and by their repetition through reading. Yet the portrait's style of condensation works, much like the unconscious, to generate an active allegorical process of the multiplication and dissemination of political fables. The strength of the seventeenth-century French ideological representation depended on such an economical portrayal and the subsequent performative multiplication of fictional, courtly models.[51]

Portraiture's Legitimacy and Deficiency

In seventeenth-century France, the printed play provided one of many excellent representational mediums for the indirect dissemination of written portraits. More than two hundred and eighty new plays were written and published in what might be termed Richelieu's period, from 1635 to 1651. Profiting from the economical rhetoric of written portraiture, playwrights often incorporated portraits of patrons into their dedicatory epistles. These two genres—epistle and portrait—were not exclusive in seventeenth-century France (if they ever have been exclusive).[52] Perhaps the authors felt that a portrait would be received with more grace when presented as a spontaneous gesture in the context of another medium, the dedicatory epistle, than if it were presented as a bare written portrait in which "tous les Hommes sont des Catons ou des Cesars pour le moins; & les Femmes des Lucreces, ou des Octavies."[53] These authors even make claims that they printed plays only as excuses for the presentation of a written portrait (disguised as a dedicatory epistle). In the dedicatory epistle "À Monsieur le Marquis de Richelieu," Boisrobert writes "que je ne l'ay publié que par la seule jalousie que j'ay de l'honneur de vostre amitié."[54] Regardless of the exact reason behind this mixture of genres, if reason alone can ever account for literary mixture, early French plays often appear to have been printed as much for their epistles as for their dramatic poems. Since the large majority of plays printed in individual quartos are prefaced, however economically, by epistles that include written portraits, we might want to dwell momentarily on the representational impact that such portraiture has on the printed presentation of plays.

Montpensier's emphasis on representationality and authorship, as the two crucial criteria of the genre, is echoed by seventeenth-century French tenets concerning the essential elements of dramatic representation. The texts of the two leading early dramatic theorists, Jules de La Mesnardière and the Abbé d'Aubignac, pay close attention to the representational qualities of dramatic prose. La Mesnardière, justifying his rejection of "les Rythmes & la Musique" as modes of the performance of tragedy, calls for the preservation of the essential element of dramatic representation:

> nous bannissons à dessein de nôtre Définition les Rythmes & la Musique, qu'Aristote met dans la sienne; d'autant que nôtre Tragédie ne sert pas de ces beautez comme des choses necessaires, & qu'elle employe seulement pour imiter les Actions, la Réprésentation réelle, accompagnée du Discours.[55]

Because a tragedy sets out to imitate the actions of the hero, La Mesnardière accepts action alone as the necessary element of serious dramatic representation. Dramatic action, moreover, is doubly significant to La Mesnardière's treatise because it often carries the authority of historical narration. As examples we can recall Shakespeare's *Henriad* or the French allegorical history plays in which the lines of fiction and reality are scarcely visible.

Although d'Aubignac also focuses on the quality of staged dramatic action, he spends much time discussing the effects on the dramatic poem of the representation of principal dramatic figures, in addition to that of the hero. Turning his eye to authorship, d'Aubignac suggests that "on les [poëmes] regarde seulement comme les chefs-d'oeuvre d'un bel esprit, & une parfaite imitation de la vertu des Heros."[56] From this perspective a dramatic poem portrays both the image of a hero in action and the image of a *bel esprit*, the nominal figure recognizable as the author of a *chef-d'oeuvre*. There is an interesting similarity here between d'Aubignac's description of a play's representational effects and Montpensier's references to historical narrative and painted portraiture. Merely recall, for example, how she describes the representational image of painted portraits in the same terms d'Aubignac uses to speak of dramatic poems, "des chef-d'oeuvres de Peintres excellens en leur Art, qui ne servent qu'à donner de la reputation à l'Ouvrier."[57] Regarding representation, moreover, Montpensier claims that painted portraits and historical narratives render a hero glorious by means of narrative styles depicting action. It is striking how closely Montpensier's conception of historical narratives and painted portraits resembles the notions of both d'Aubignac and La Mesnardière about the subjects portrayed by dramatic poetry. All three genres show portraits through action, whether the action derives from the sword or the pen.

These same drama theoreticians understand that the zeal of this action is diminished when plays become books. Needless to say, the publication of a play removes the script from the scene of what La Mesnardière calls its *représentation réelle*. And as evidenced by Corneille's explanation to the reader of *Mélite*, seventeenth-century French dramatists who habitually published their own plays expressed negative opinions regarding the status of the printed play: "Je sais bien que l'impression d'une pièce en affaiblit la réputation: la publier, c'est l'avilir."[58] Corneille acknowledges that printing lessens the quality of dramatic representation because narrative action replaces a more emotive, histrionic action. A different writer, André Mareschal, elaborates on the ultimate consequence of printing when he explains to the reader of *Le Railleur ou le satyr du temps* "la raison qui a fait cesser sa representation. Je suis bien plus en peine de sçavoir comme tu la dois recevoir, puis qu'il est vray qu'aux pieces purement Comiques comme est celle-cy, le papier ôte beaucoup de leur grace, et que l'action en est l'ame. Ces vers couppez, & tous ces petits mots interrompus qui sont du jeu Comique, & qui pour estre familiers entrent si facilement dans l'imagination, lors qu'ils sont poussez chaudement, languissent lors qu'ils sont écrits."[59] Lacking a stage for its corporeal representation, a printed play is understood by this writer to be deprived of its soul, synonymous here with action.

One seventeenth-century English dramatist would have claimed just the opposite. Ben Jonson used printing as an opportunity to sharpen the image of drama's soul: authorship. Through his careful manipulation of the nominal codes of dedicatory portraiture, Jonson presented himself both as the image of an author "d'un bel esprit," and as the model of virtuous heroic action—the play should be read as an allegory of his standards. But Jonson's case, we must recall, is atypical. In England, publication of plays reflected more often than not the playwright's minimal status as an independent author. A typical English title page, such as "A / WOMAN / KILDE / with Kindnesse. / *As it hath been oftentimes Acted by / the Queenes Maiest. Servants. Written by* THO. HEY-WOOD," advertises the play's representation and its acting company in addition to the author. Although similar power struggles between playwrights and actors were not the norm in France, the format of a French printed play was also a sign of the standards of authorship. But a representative French title page, such as "LA SOEUR GENEREUSE, / Tragicomedie," provides no information concerning the play's representation on the stage and identifies neither the acting company nor the author. Yet, the particular way of listing this title hints at how written portraiture reflected the status of the dramatic author in seventeenth-century France. The absence of the author's name is not at all uncommon on French title pages, and most French printed plays include a separate introductory text identifying the dramatist. In some instances, the printer published this text as his own apology for revealing the identity of an author desiring anonymity.[60] In other cases, the printer included a text informing the reader that he acted on behalf of an author unable to present himself in the proper fashion.[61] Yet, as a rule, the author's name is revealed by the signature of the dedicatory epistle that normally follows the title page. This transfer of the signature from title page to dedicatory epistle speaks directly to the issue of this chapter. Because the author's signature of the epistle doubles as his signature of the play, the French epistle can be said to usurp the title page as the semiotic space of theatrical legitimation.

This shift might again prompt recollection of the strategy of Ben Jonson. In turning to dedicatory epistles for self-legitimation, his strategy was to use epistles for definition of the limits of his readers' interpretative authority. Yet, readers would be hard pressed to find a seventeenth-century French playwright who consistently bolstered his own authority through the medium of dedicatory epistles. Rather, the nature of legitimation in the French dedicatory epistle is better understood in view of Montpensier's conceptual description of written portraiture. The written portrait, she writes, effaces the image of the author for the sake of the patron personified as a *bel esprit*. Mareschal's dedicatory portrait in *La Cour bergere, ou l'arcadie de Messire Philippes Sidney* quite explicitly compares the writer's authority to that of his dedicatee, Sir Robert Sidney:

Monseigneur, cette piece est si legitiment à VOTRE EXCELLENCE, puis qu'elle porte cét illustre & glorieux Nom de SIDNEY, & qu'elle est mesme de vôtre Maison . . . pour faire voir que la protection de ce Livre est en vôtre bien-séance. . . . Vous en serez le Iuge & le Patron; vous, MONSEIGNEUR, qui avez la doctrine & les lumieres pour en faire le discernement, & assez de bonté aussi pour excuser quelques deffaux, quand vous en treuveriez.[62]

Mareschal describes Sidney, not himself the author, as the model of *bon sens*. Following the conventions of the French dedicatory epistle, the author depicts himself as accident prone, as held captive in the world of human error. His flawed work requires the judgment of a higher, even if fictional, authority. Mareschal thus presents the patron to the reader as the legitimate trustee of dramatic doctrine and perspective.

Often the most obvious demystification of the fiction of portraiture works best to sustain the patron and efface the author. In the dedicatory epistle "À la Reine Régente," Corneille's portrait of the queen is outlined in view of a comparison of her superiority to the fictions of *Polyeucte*:

Ce n'est qu'une pièce de théâtre que je lui présente, mais qui l'entretiendra de Dieu: la dignité de la matière est si haute, que l'impuissance de l'artisan ne la peut ravaler; et votre âme royale se plaît trop à cette sorte d'entretien pour s'offenser des défauts d'un ouvrage où elle rencontrera les délices de son coeur. C'est par là, MADAME, que j'espère obtenir de Votre Majesté le pardon du long temps que j'ai attendu à lui rendre cette sorte d'hommage. Toutes les fois que j'ai mis sur notre scène des vertus morales ou politiques, j'en ai toujours cru les tableaux trop peu dignes de paraître devant elle, quand j'ai considéré qu'avec quelque soin que je les pusse choisir dans l'histoire, et quelques ornements dont l'artifice les pût enrichir, elle en voyait de plus grands exemples dans elle-même.[63]

Corneille here enunciates a portrait of the queen by contrasting her perfect, fictional image with the real but flawed—because historical—pictures of his theatre. By his simple reference to the "plus grands exemples dans elle-même," he presents a condensed written image of his patron that surpasses any possible portrait of her on the stage. The epistle of *Polyeucte* suggests how the written portrait, acting as the preface to the play, presents a mimetic model of a patron who can be represented only partially by the composite images of the play's various fictional characters. All of the expressions of virtue, all of the eloquent manners, all of the descriptions of action read in the play are said by Corneille to be nothing more than signs of what remains hidden "dans elle-même."[64] When it follows the reception of a written portrait, the reading of a French printed play might be described as the reader's figural personification of the epistle's nominal model.

This suggestion, moreover, is less a hypothesis than a theoretical elaboration of seventeenth-century French discussions of dedicatory epistles. Consider that of Dominique Bouhours:

> Que dites vous de ces personnages qu'on introduit dans les Epîtres dédicatoires? Entendez-moy, s'il vous plaist. L'Auteur d'un ouvrage qui traite des conquestes de César, ou des aventures d'Hippolite, ne fait point de difficulté de dire à un Prince, en luy dédiant son livre: *Voicy le vainqueur des Gaules qui vient vous rendre ses hommages. Hippolite sort du fond des bois dans le dessein de vous faire sa cour.*[65]

To Bouhours, the characters of fiction enter into direct dialogue with the hero of written portraiture. Such personification of the prince thus works to transform the nature of theatrical mimesis. It should be evaluated no longer in terms of the players' verisimilar actions but on the basis of the readers' literal repetition and performance of the rhetorical portrait.

It is this rhetorical status of the portrait, more than the portrait itself, that constitutes the allegorical power of written portraiture. In Boisrobert's epistle to the Marquis de Richelieu, to cite one last and fitting example, the importance of the portrait of a particular Richelieu is overshadowed by Boisrobert's emphasis on the performative ideology of portraiture as such:

> Monsieur, comme je dois toute ma fortune au Nom illustre que vous portez, je croy luy devoire encore tous mes projets, toutes mes inclinations & mes pensées, & que je ne dois desormais plus regarder que ce grand Nom dans le monde, par qui j'ay veû fonder avec le salut & la gloire de la France, mon honneur, mon loisir, & mon repos. Ne trouvez donc pas estrange que si j'ose vous dedier ce petit Ouvrage Comique, qu'il semble estre aussi peu digne de ce Nom illustre.[66]

The ultimate effect of theatrical portraiture is to reduce the image of a patron to the phantasm of a figural name, eternally present on the lips of the reader. The many facets of the Marquis de Richelieu's theatrical portrait are transformed by Boisrobert into the form of a linguistic figure of figures sustaining all Richelieus, all theatrical production, not to mention "le salut & la gloire de la France." Clarifying the ideological benefits of theatrical patronage, Boisrobert sharply delineates the scope of the ideal theatrical portrait: "je dois desormais plus regarder que ce grand Nom dans le monde." To Boisrobert, the act of theatrical beholding becomes synonymous with the evocation and personification of a *nom illustre*. The particular historical personage standing behind such a "title" is not as important to the representational structure of written portraiture as is the beholder's visual and mental focus on the allegory of a title, the *real*ization of a fiction of genius.

In concluding this section on theatrical portraiture, I want to reflect for a moment on the advantages and disadvantages of this seventeenth-century figural portraiture as the performance of ideology. It is not difficult to appreciate how in various sophisticated ways theatrical portraiture serves the needs of ideology, especially ideology in the Althusserian sense: "le rapport imaginaire des individus à leurs conditions réelles d'existence."[67] Ultimately, the stage representation of the princely personage is almost superfluous as an ideological tool. For the printed portrait brings alive the fictional perfection of the princely image, so necessarily flawed by the real stage conditions of dramatic and historical representation.

On a seemingly different level, moreover, we might note how the universal features of textuality discussed earlier as those clearly recognized by Ben Jonson—textual inconstancy and the shifts and gaps of iteration—surface poignantly in later revisionist presentations of early seventeenth-century French portraiture. When ideological identifications shifted in late seventeenth-century France, writers continued to evoke early seventeenth-century portraits, but often as a means of adjusting these texts' allegorical nominations and personifications to the altered conditions of their historical reality. Bouhours's *La Maniere de bien penser* (1688) cites a paradoxical example of the shifts of iteration. This text attests to the lasting performativity of theatrical portraiture when it recalls

une Epître addressée au Cardinal de Richelieu, dans laquelle un Ecrivain du regne passé le flatte en ces termes qui me sont demeurez dans la mémoire. "Nos forces defaillent à mesure que nos merveilles croissent; & comme l'on a dit autrefois d'un vaillant homme, qu'il ne pouvoit plus recevoir de blessûres que sur les cicatrices de celles qu'il avoit recûës, vous ne sçauriez estre loué que par des redites; puisque la vérité qui a des bornes, a dit pour vous tout ce que le mensonge qui n'en connoist point a inventé pour les autres."[68]

Later in his text, Bouhours recounts how the ideological conditions of historical truth then resulted in the inconsequential substitution of the figure of one wounded genius with another: "A la vérité, quand le Cardinal fut mort, L'Auteur supprima toutes ces loûanges dans une seconde édition, & dédia mesme son livre à Jesus-Christ, comme pour desavoûër publiquement des pensées flatteuses qui avoient quelque chose d'excessif, & mesme de peu religieux."[69]

PART THREE

DESIRE AS
SPECTATOR

9

Portraits or Pleasures

> Je sçay bien que vous [Richelieu] vous étes mélé de Vers
> & de Prose, que quelquefois vous avez eu part aux
> applaudissemens du Théâtre, & je vous avoüeray, si vous
> le voulez, que le Parnasse est couvert de vos Crea-
> tures. . . . On n'est point responsable icy des sermons que
> l'on fait dans les Epistres Dedicatoires; il est permis d'y
> mentir impunément, & ce n'est qu'une drogue qui se livre
> sans garentie, & qui n'est pas de meilleur aloy que les
> contes de la Fontaine.
>
> GABRIEL GUERET, *La Guerre des auteurs
> anciens et moderns* (1671)[1]

Following my citation of Bouhours's anecdote about the changing
faces of portraiture in late seventeenth-century France, Gabriel
Gueret's warning of the druglike effect of dedications might suggest
a new direction in the latter half of the century in the enunciation
of ideology. This would be the articulation of a subversive, marginal
discourse prevalent during the age of Louis XIV, one suggesting that
the acknowledgment of allegorical portraiture need not entail the
viewers' belief or even loyalty to the historical personage or ideological concept portrayed as the receptacle of genius. Part Three,
"Desire As Spectator," in isolating some fascinating examples of
such disruptive shifts between presentations of portraiture and representations in the activity of reading and viewing them, addresses
the complex role of the spectator in performing ideological diversity
and *différance* in neoclassical France.

   Given the multidimensional nature of the conditions of spectating, I would like to assume a cautious posture from the outset.
For I would not want to pursue this investigation of further abstract

examples of the allegory of genius by underemphasizing the change that took place between the 1630s and the 1670s in actual material and literary conditions. But instead of focusing on the specifics of any transformation of material conditions, this concluding section of *Theatrical Legitimation* investigates the ideological interrelation of certain "real" conditions of spectating and their "allegorical" representations. I make this connection to emphasize the point, latent throughout this book, that allegorical relations of text and reading fuel the heightened ideological representations of literature as much as, indeed more than, do actual poetic and historical conditions. As Gueret's passage suggests, the druglike veils of ideology, capable of being draped over any cultural artifact, determine the conditions of portraiture's allegories of genius. In the context of seventeenth-century French aesthetics, the most fascinating aspect of theatrical legitimation is the very complex packaging of the materials of theatre in carefully designed, ideological representations.

This discussion of spectatorship begins by recalling the textual phenomena best representative of the ideological fabric of allegory: treatises on theatrical representation. In addition to stimulating a surge in the composition of plays and portraits in seventeenth-century France, the literati under Richelieu and Mazarin were responsible for an explosive proliferation of prescriptive writing about theatre. The texts which I have already discussed as exemplary of this phenomenon, such as the antitheatrical attacks, the debates over *Le Cid*, and the theoretical writings of Jules de la Mesnardière and the Abbé d'Aubignac, as well as those by Chapelain, Ménage, and others, gave rise in the later half of the seventeenth century to theoretical classics by Corneille, Rapin, du Pures, and Boileau. Literary historians point to this vast theoretical enterprise as yet another example of the neoclassical effort to codify, classify, and thus ideologize theatre. Ideology should receive particular stress in this context because the theoretical uniformity of the rapidly expanding body of plays was understood by Richelieu and his academic ministers as a mirror image of their power over culture in general.

The texts of François Hédelin, the Abbé d'Aubignac, are especially representative of this seventeenth-century attempt to gain critical control over the French theatre. D'Aubignac played a visible, although somewhat ambiguous, role in Richelieu's vast theatre project. To begin with, d'Aubignac was made responsible around 1632 for the education of Richelieu's nephew, Jean-Armand de Maillé-Brézé. According to d'Aubignac's nineteenth-century biographer, Charles Arnaud, the cardinal himself may have been instrumental in making the appointment.[2] The formal recognition of d'Aubignac's pedagogical talents and his entry into the house of Richelieu might have paved the way for d'Aubignac's later theatrical exploits under the cardinal's patronage. Although the abbé was not included among Richelieu's prestigious group of four playwrights, Richelieu did call upon him to revise Tristan's *Panthée*. D'Aubignac claimed, moreover, that his only play in verse had been commissioned by the cardinal.[3] On at least one other occasion, Richelieu summoned d'Aubignac to the Palais Cardinal to evaluate a play in rehearsal.[4] And if we are to believe the abbé, Richelieu's respect for d'Aubignac's opinion led the Cardinal to commission *La Pratique du théâtre* and the *Project pour le rétablissement du Théâtre François*, which texts, d'Aubignac claims, were meant to serve as the theoretical blueprints for the restoration of French theatre.[5]

In his prefatory comments to the *Pratique*, d'Aubignac is careful to stress the ideological "Necessité des Spectacles." Emphasizing sociopolitical considerations of "magnificence," "puissance," and "authorité," d'Aubignac asserts theatre's fundamental purpose: "Il faut bien certes que les Spectacles soient tres-importans au gouvernement des Estats."[6] The breadth of theatre's legitimate social function—to sustain the image of the state—is illustrated by d'Aubignac's wide-ranging discussion of "necessité." On one level, theatre provides an institutional antidote for unemployment, laziness, and various types of social malaise.[7] While theatre assembles all of society's misfits together in one place where they can be entertained (and watched), it subjects the spectators to the subtle indoctrination of "les belles representations de Theatre que l'on peut nommer veritablement l'Ecole du Peuple."[8] On another level, waging a spectacle, especially during time of war, can demonstrate a country's ability to perform persuasively: "c'est donner des témoignages bien signalez, qu'il a des tresors inépuisables et des Hommes de reste."[9] The abbé emphasizes how his country's capability to stage spectacles is a demonstration of the resources it has available for either the theatre of war or the war of theatre. Such a mounting of spectacle bolsters France's image as a nation of unlimited reserves and unbendable spirit.[10]

Ranging in discussion from pedagogy to propaganda used for war, d'Aubignac's prefatory chapter on the political necessity of spectacle leads finally to the outline of the image of theatre signified by all of its many ideological shades: "les Souverains ne peuvent rien faire de plus avantageux pour leur gloire, et pour le bien de leurs Sujets, que d'établir et d'entretenir les Spectacles et les Jeux publics avec un bel ordre, et avec des magnificences dignes de leur Couronne."[11] To d'Aubignac, the ultimate purpose of seventeenth-century French theatre is to project an image of strong, confident leadership.

Aligned with the glory of the sovereign, the various types of spectacle stand in the *Pratique* as signifiers of their magnanimous sponsors. In prefacing his treatise on theatrical practice with a discussion of the ideology of patronage, d'Aubignac even sketches a flattering portrait of a particular sponsor whose many written faces are now familiar to the reader of this study:

> La Scene a repris un nouveau visage, et les rides que sa vieillesse luy avoit imprimées sur le front, ont perdu beaucoup de leur difformité. Heureuse de n'avoir pas esté desagreable au plus merveilleux Esprit du monde; je veux dire au Grand Cardinal de Richelieu et d'avoir encore eu assez d'agrément pour mériter ses graces. Car ce fut par ses liberalitez qu'elle receut de nouvelles forces, et qu'elle commença de rentrer dans ses anciens droits, sa premiere beauté, sa noblesse et sa splendeur. Et ce fut par ses soins que tout ce que l'Antiquité vid jamais de sçavant, d'ingenieux et de magnifique, revint peu à peu sur nostre Theatre. . . . Mais puisque la mesme main qui lui avoit fait un si bon accueil, n'a pas achevé son rétablissement, il n'y a guere d'apparence qu'il arrive jamais à sa perfection, et qu'il se soûtienne mesme longtemps. Et sa recheute sera d'autant plus dangereuse, qu'il ne se trouve pas en tous les Siecles des Genies pourveus de la suffisance, de la liberalité, de la pureté des moeurs, et des autres qualités necessaires à ce dessein. La vie de ce Grand Homme a fait le Siecle des grandes et des nouvelles choses. Toutes celles qui n'ont point acquis sous luy leur perfection ni l'affermissement de leur estat, auront peine à rencontrer l'occasion de le pouvoir faire. Aussi n'appartenoit-il à personne de donner à la France ces plaisirs legitimes, qu'à celuy-là mesme qui multiplioit de jour en jour ses Palmes et ses Lauriers. Il étoit bien juste que celuy qui s'estoit rendu semblable aux Cesars et aux Pompées dans ses victoires, les imitât encore en la restauration du Theatre et de ces illustres divertissemens. Enfin la gloire et la grandeur des Spectacles ne pouvoit mieux venir que de celuy qui s'estoit rendu luy-mesme le plus glorieux et le plus grand Spectacle du Monde.[12]

In view of the preceding discussion of theatrical portraiture, it is not surprising that d'Aubignac describes French theatre's "nouveau visage" and "plaisirs legitimes" as reflections of the portrait of its protecting genius, the Cardinal de Richelieu. France's achievements on both the stage and the field of war contributed to the cardinal's grandeur as the greatest Spectacle of the World. As for the legitimacy of theatre itself, the abbé here establishes an interesting correlation between ideological portraiture and dramatic spectacle. He goes so far as to suggest that these two institutions are interdependent: the glory of one is contingent on the spectacle of the other.[13]

Yet, we may want to be somewhat cautious in reading d'Aubignac's entire treatise as but an echo of its prefatory portraiture. Gueret, one of d'Aubignac's closer colleagues, reminds us after all that dedicatory fictions can be used for strategy as well as for flattery: "il est permis d'y mentir impunément, & ce n'est qu'une drogue qui se livre sans garentie."[14] In d'Aubignac's *Aristandre ou histoire interrompuë*, moreover, the abbé adopts a similar open sarcasm regarding prefaces: "vous sçavez bien mon cher Lecteur que je ne dois à personne ce que je donne au public, & que vous n'avez pas droit d'examiner un present comme une moyenne que j'emploirois pour acquiter quelque debts."[15] Similar brash outbreaks in d'Aubignac's texts present the profile of a French critic who did not always stand within the privileged space of seventeenth-century *perspectiva legitima*. An early defeat in d'Aubignac's career, his last minute exclusion from the Académie Française, provides a telling example of how the sharpness of his tongue often left him on the margins of political favoritism. Chapelain attributed the controversy surrounding d'Aubignac's candidacy to a weakness in political sensitivity: "Il eût été le premier reçu, s'il n'eut point fait un libelle contre la *Roxane* de M. Desmarets, où il blamait le goût de Son Eminence et de Mme d'Aiguillon qui l'avait estimée."[16] D'Aubignac's passion for critical honesty did not always leave him within the realm of sovereign benefit. Indeed his rejection by the Académie Française later culminated in his permanent social marginality under Louis XIV. In 1663, d'Aubignac complained to Corneille that "m'est commun avec dix mille personnes de naissance, de condition & de vertu, qui meritent mieux que vous, mais qui ne sont pas connus de sa Majesté, non plus que moy, qui depuis dix sept ans n'ay pas seulement veû la porte du Louvre."[17] Exemplifying the stakes of literary legitimation, d'Aubignac's social marginality was directly related to his style of dramatic criticism. The abbé's exclusion from the official bodies of literary politics seemed either to provoke or to be the result of his ambivalence toward the dictates of an ideology of centralized representation.

In the 1660s, d'Aubignac expressed open contempt for the Académie Française as the legitimate institution dictating the policies
of contemporary criticism. Aiming right at the source of theatrical
legitimation, his jabs included sarcastic remarks about the Académie's judgment. In his anonymous but clearly autobiographical *Le
Roman de lettres* (1667), the abbé sneers at the Académie while suggesting his own principles of literary legitimation. Responding to an
author friend, the character Ariste writes, "si j'osois parler [comme]
Balzac en cette occasion, je dirois que vous nous donnez quelque
chose de plus excellent qu'un Roy. [J'AY receu les deux derniers
volumes que vous avez mis au jour.] Mais je laisse toutes ces elevations de pensées à Messieurs vos confreres de l'Académie: Je ne
me sens pas assez de forces pour les faire iustes, & me soustenir."[18]
By comparing the benefits of a fictional novelist to the legacy of a
certain Balzac, most likely the suspect and unfavored absolutist,
Guez de Balzac, Ariste ironically challenges the Académie to question the relationship of absolutism and fiction.[19] Is the Académie the
symbolic body of perfect reason and perspective, or, comparable to
the novelist, the acknowledged promoter of empty fictions?

Further signifying d'Aubignac's own critical marginality (something he shared with Balzac), this passage from his novel is consequential because it stands as the fictional counterpart of an actual
letter which d'Aubignac sent to Louis XIV three years earlier. In
1664, the Abbé d'Aubignac wrote an impassioned plaint to the king
requesting official recognition and subvention of a second literary
academy in Paris. D'Aubignac desired legitimation of his own "Académie des Belles Lettres," which he had formed along with Gueret
and other friends around 1654 (perhaps in response to his exclusion
from the Académie Française). The mere notion of such a request
is both courageous and ludicrous, given Louis XIV's organization
of all of the academies as agencies of the hierarchically centralized
representation of his own portraiture. D'Aubignac's *Discours au
Roy pour l'establissement d'une seconde Académie* directly critiques
the effectiveness of such centralization around only one adjudicat-
ing group with literary authority. In so doing, it also questions the
judgment of the kingly patron and figurehead of the Académie
Française:

> ceux qui se trouvent engagez à cette necessité d'instruire le public, ces
> doctes Maîtres en tant de differentes Facultez, se sont relâchez en
> deux choses qui nuisent au progrez des Sciences, & qui les ont presque

toute defigurées. La premiere est, qu'ils s'attachent opiniastrement aux maximes que les anciens ont laissées dans leur escrits, & se persuadant qu'ils ont la certitude de toutes les veritez, ils ne veulent rien chercher au-delà. Ils condamnent tout ce qui ne s'accorde pas à leurs principes; ils prononcent anatheme contre tous ceux qui les contredisent, & de quelques demonstrations dont les nouveautez puissent estre appuyées, de quelques experiences dont les vieilles erreurs soient confonduës, il suffit qu'une proposition leur soit nouvelle pour estre rejettée.[20]

Even though d'Aubignac warns in the same text against "la revolte contre leur Prince legitime," his plaint for critical difference and novelty challenges not only the Académie but the entire ideology of centralized representation.[21] In particular it tarnishes the portrait of the king which d'Aubignac sketches so faithfully in this *Discours au Roy*:

Ce sont les Sçavans qui connoissent & qui disent que les Souverains sont les images sensibles du Dieu vivant, ou pour parler aux termes de l'Escriture Sainte, qu'ils sont les Dieux visibles de la terre; que jamais on ne peut violer le respect qui leur est deub, sans blesser les ordres de la Providence Divine; & que nous n'avons pas plus de droit d'examiner leurs volontez, que de contredire leur établissement qui n'a point d'autre principe que la main toute-puissante de l'Eternel.[22]

Agreeing with the abbé that the Académie des Belles Lettres did not have the right to examine his will, Louis XIV refused the petition and left d'Aubignac's academy, loyal more to fickle novelty than to the repetition of standardized norms, outside the legitimate and centralized space of the Louvre. In view of the deconstructive implications of this academy's existence, its opponents named it the "Académie des Allegoriques."[23]

There is considerable evidence in d'Aubignac's writings of his personal ambivalence concerning the uniformity of neoclassical standards of theatre, an ambivalence which insists on novelty as an alternative to the aesthetics of centralized theatrical portraiture. In the 1660s, for example, d'Aubignac was embroiled in a literary dispute with Corneille over the interpretation of classical theory. One of the many issues of their debate was the value of d'Aubignac's treatise, *La Pratique du théâtre*. As d'Aubignac recounts their disagreement, Corneille dismissed the *Pratique* as an inept paraphrase of Aristotle's *Poetics*. D'Aubignac also complains that the playwright publicized the abbé's ignorance and misuse of the Italian commentators on the *Poetics,* whom we might note placed special stress on the ideological utility of theatre. The abbé's written response to these charges is flippant and brief:

> Quand j'entrepris cét ouvrage, je resolu de ne rien copier des autres qui nous ont donné l'art poëtique depuis Aristote, & de n'enseigner que des choses nouvelles, ou de rectifier par une docte nouveauté, celles qui estoient connuës, & vous sçavent bien que vous n'avez jamais veu autre part ce que vous avez trouvé dans ce livre, que les habiles des-interessez nomment vrayment un livre, & un livre nouveau.[24]

D'Aubignac insists that his discussion of theatre is meant not to reiterate the Aristotelian position on poetry but to introduce "des choses nouvelles" to seventeenth-century French discussions of theatre. He had already taken a similar position in the *Pratique*: "Quand à moy, sans rebattre en ce discours ce qu'on peut apprendre dans Aristote, dans ses Interpretes et dans les anciens et les modernes, je m'efforceray de ne traitter que des Matieres nouvelles, ou du moins de donner quelques nouvelles instructions sur celles que les autres ont traittées."[25] In promising his readers something different from that found in other treatises on theatre, d'Aubignac tends to turn aside not only from the Italian commentaries but also, and most importantly, from his loyalty to the portrayal of genius as the particular figure of his patron. Although the abbé may open his text with a conventional sketch of portraiture, he asks that his readers notice the more striking character of his treatise's own textuality: "un livre, & un livre nouveau."

How the *Pratique* might bear signficance *as a book* is suggested by a review of its 1715 edition in *Le Journal littéraire.*

> Quoi que ce ne soit ici qu'une réimpression d'un Ouvrage plus ancien peut-être & plus connu qu'aucun de nous, nous ne laisserons pas d'en donner un Extrait étendu. Nous avons dit dans notre Préface, que "nous pourrions bien donner quelquefois des Extraits de certains Livres, qui par leur mérite, ou leur rareté, vaudroient la peine qu'on en donnât une idée éxacte." *La Pratique du Théâtre,* par *François Hedelin,* Abbé d'*Aubignac,* a l'une & l'autre de ces qualitez. Ce Livre a toûjours été fort estimé, & il étoit devenu fort rare. D'ailleurs, nous croyons qu'on ne sera pas fâché de trouver rassemblées dans un seul Extrait les principales régles du Poëme Dramatique. Tout le monde parle des ces régles, mais peu de personnes savent en quoi elles consistent, nous en donnerons ici une idée générale. Ceux, qui voudront s'instruire plus à fonds, auront recours au Livre même.[26]

The writer of this review suggests two ways of approaching "Livres, qui par leur mérite, ou leur rareté, vaudroient la peine qu'on en donnât une idée éxacte." Interested parties can become immersed in the book itself, *or,* as Corneille wished for d'Aubignac, the reader can depend on commentaries dedicated to the task of sniffing out a book's rarity, merit, and novelty. Even the closest readers of d'Aubignac's text have not strayed too far from the subjects extracted in the *Journal*'s legitimation of the *Pratique* as a "rare book." The *Journal* limits its digest to a conventional summary of d'Aubignac's discussion of the three dramatic unities in view of the ideology of neoclassical centralization. Even today, we tend to mimic the method of the early French journal by relying on the *Pratique* as an encyclopedic lending-bank of tidbits that support our conventional assumptions about neoclassical theatre and its hierarchical ideology. Although the *Pratique* continues to be recognized as an important *source book* of seventeenth-century theatre, it has not received many close readings that tend to go "plus à fonds."

D'Aubignac himself prescribes close reading as the most fruitful method of literary analysis. "Il ne faut pas prendre la connoissance exacte des Piéces anciennes par les notes et les distinctions apparentes qui sont dans nos imprimez, mais par une lecture exacte de ces excellens Ouvrages."[27] A "lecture exacte" of the *Pratique* might lead beyond the limits inscribed by its introductory tableau of neoclassical portraiture. In the chapter to follow, it will mean taking a harder look at the text's indirect discussion of theatrical legitimation, at the relation of the "Prince legitime" to theatre's "plaisirs legitimes." Especially when read in view of d'Aubignac's own critical marginality, the *Pratique* is significant for introducing a seventeenth-century French theory of dramatic representation that stresses the pleasure of the spectator in contrast to the ideology of portraiture and the legitimation of authorship. This discussion will then lead to my concluding chapter, which dwells on the late seventeenth- and early eighteenth-century sublime and on deconstructive extensions of d'Aubignac's peculiar allegory of reading.

🐦 10

Showing the Colors: Desire and Ideology in La Pratique du théâtre

In contemplating the complex and somewhat marginal, ideological enunciations of *La Pratique du théâtre*, I find myself returning to the marginal corollary of a seventeenth-century Spanish play exemplifying the paradoxical balance of social ideology and individual desire. In Lope de Vega's *Fuente Ovejuna*, the Red Cross, which Fernando Gómez flaunts in answer to accusations of rape and pillage, is a sign of a flourishing chivalric order. The moral perfection of the institution signified by the Red Cross overshadows the aberrance of its figurehead. As long as Fernando Gómez continues to hold his colors high, the community tolerates his wantonness. As a convincing sign of societal order, color points away from the individual towards the abstract tradition of the Calatrava, which the Grand Commander represents.

But even though colors sometimes signify deeply rooted customs, it would be too reductive to say that colors alone re-present traditions. We might think of colors as *intermediaries* showing, in the case of *Fuente Ovejuna*, neither a particular institution (the Order of the Calatrava) nor the actual knights bearing heraldic colors.[1] Instead, colors indicate the beholder's *belief* in the signified tradition. During the first two acts of *Fuente Ovejuna*, Fernando Gómez is shielded from the citizens' wrath because of their conviction of the potency of the Red Cross. When colors in the material shape of either crosses, flags, or banners portray public opinion, the evils veiled by the colors remain invisible to the believers. Here it can be said that colors perform ideology. As Althusser would say, they depict belief—our imaginary relation to the real condition of things. An institution thrives when the persuasiveness of its representational mode dissembles the frailty of its actual parts. So by showing their colors, figureheads like Fernando Gōmez divert their spectators from potentially damaging character study that would diminish belief in the institution, or, in ideology-as-such.

But showing the colors is not synonymous with believing them. The behavior of a Fernando Gōmez exemplifies the ruse of representation which is always ideological, as Althusser, Marin, Lyotard, and others remind us. Fernando Gōmez deliberately flaunts the Red Cross as an ideological sign in order to dissemble his brazen disrespect for the moral codes of chivalry. By using ideology to serve ends contrary to the public opinion constituting and legitimizing an institution, he turns the ideology against itself. In this respect, his bearing the colors performs a simultaneous display and mockery of public opinion.

Similar paradoxical manipulations of color and ideology span the history of dramatic literature. In both plays and theatre treatises, writers rely on carefully crafted rhetoric to represent the veils of ideology. One extremely sophisticated strategist of rhetorical color is the Abbé d'Aubignac. His *La Pratique du théâtre* provides fecund testimony of his loyalty to the *doctrine classique* and the ideology that it represents. If the *doctrine classique* were known by a particular color, d'Aubignac's text could be said to be painted in it. Yet d'Aubignac's treatise outlines a practice of dramatic coloration that discreetly ironizes the many conventions of centralization and *perspectiva legitima* which I have discussed as governing the theatre's relation to the *doctrine classique*. In a complicated display of critical writing and allegorical strategy, the abbé builds a dramatic system whose representational principles provide the conceptual foundations for the displacement of the centralized, neoclassical ideology by an aesthetic concern for the representation of multiple perspectives in sometimes incongruous shades and colors.

Moving Portraiture

In keeping with its prefatory call for a French theatre dedicated to the enhancement of princely portraiture, *La Pratique du théâtre* provides carefully delineated prescriptions for a dramatic practice true to the codes of the *doctrine classique*. In the tradition of *Le Journal littéraire*, readers of the *Pratique* have been quick to emphasize its alignment of theatrical practice with two important standards of seventeenth-century French representation: *bienséance* and *vraisemblance*. In one frequently cited passage of the *Pratique*, the abbé correlates all dramatic writing with the mores of its audience:

> Il ne faut pas oublier (et ce n'est peut-estre pas une des moindres observations que j'aye faite sur les Piéces de Theatre) que si le Sujet n'est conforme aux moeurs et aux sentimens des Spectateurs, il ne rëussira jamais, quelque soin que le Poëte y employe et de quelques ornemens qu'il le soustienne; car les Poëmes Dramatiques doivent estre differens selon les Peuples devant lesquels on les doit representer; et de là vient que le succez n'en est pas tousjours pareil, bien qu'ils soient toujours semblables à eux-mesmes. . . . Parmy nous le respect et l'amour que nous avons pour nos Princes, ne peut permettre que l'on donne au Public ces Spectacles pleins d'horreur; nous ne voulons point croire que les Roys puissent estre mechans, ni souffrir que leurs Sujets, quoy qu'en apparence maltraittez, touchent leurs Personnes sacrées, ny se rebellent contre leur Puissance, non pas mesme en peinture.[2]

In asking the poet to cater to "le respect et l'amour que nous avons pour nos Princes," the *Pratique* has been said to delimit dramatic subject matter to what flatters the seventeenth-century French notion of monarchy.[3] *Bienséance* serves, in this instance, as an aesthetic barometer measuring theatre's conformity to the requirements of its ideological representation, to the projection and protection of images of powerful persons.

In view of this concern with monarchical propriety, d'Aubignac also focuses considerable attention on the importance of dramatic verisimilitude. "En un mot la Vray-semblance est, s'il le faut ainsi dire, l'essence du Poëme Dramatique, et sans laquelle il ne se peut rien faire ni rien dire de raisonnable sur la Scéne."[4] D'Aubignac goes on to outline two conditions of dramatic subject matter which directly align *vraisemblance*, the essence of dramatic poetry, with the ideological requirements of *bienséance*:

> (1) C'est une Maxime generale que le *Vray* n'est pas le sujet du Theatre, parce qu'il y a bien des choses veritables qui n'y doivent pas estre veuës, et beaucoup qui n'y peuvent pas estre representées: c'est pourquoy Synesius a fort bien dit que la Poësie et les autres

Arts qui ne sont fondés qu'en imitation, ne suivent pas la verité, mais l'opinion et le sentiment ordinaire des hommes.

(2) Le *Possible* n'en sera pas aussi le sujet, car il y a bien des choses qui se peuvent faire, ou par la rencontre des causes naturelles, ou par les avantures de la Morale, qui pourtant seroient ridicules et peu croyables si elles estoient representées.[5]

In excluding both the real and the possible as necessary factors of dramatic production, the abbé frees theatre and its princely image from the contingencies of *truth* and *natural cause*. Not a means of showing what has happened or what could happen, the verisimilar figures of theatre portray what *should* be happening. In d'Aubignac's words, "c'est une pensée bien ridicule d'aller au Theatre pour apprendre l'Histoire. La Scéne ne donne point les choses comme elles ont esté, mais comme elles devoient estre, et le Poëte y doit rétablir dans le sujet tout ce qui ne s'accomodera pas aux regles de son Art."[6] In so framing an ideal condition, situation, or action that is both credible and acceptable to its spectators, *vraisemblance* joins with the codes of *bienséance* to treat the viewers of theatre to pleasing ahistorical fictions of ideological purity.[7]

This displacement of history by the representation of social and political ideals is often cited by the readers of the *Pratique* as constituting the fundaments of d'Aubignac's poetics. Hans Neuschäfer, to cite a particularly astute reader of d'Aubignac, even suggests that d'Aubignac's theatrical codes served especially well as a sort of smoke screen to hide the bitter battles of contemporary history. In the eyes of the seventeenth-century politicians who supported the monarchy, Neuschäfer remarks, the Fronde was best forgotten by such a poetics of ideals that effaced the scars of civil differences.[8] Neuschäfer also emphasizes how the ideological fictions of political harmony influence d'Aubignac's attentiveness to the codes of *bienséance*. This point might well account for d'Aubignac's tendency to illustrate his text with particularly ideological maxims, such as, "Le Sujet qui se rebelle contre son souverain est criminel"[9] or, "vivant dans un Estat monarchique, nous tenons comme sacrée la personne des Roys, quand méme ils seroient injustes."[10] A poetics dedicated to the profession of this sort of rhetoric remains in harmony with the ideology of portraiture outlined in the *Pratique*'s opening chapter. The text often insists that a play's language, mores, and social structures be custom-designed to promote the public's belief in the purest colors of monarchical order and unity.

D'Aubignac's sensitivity to the needs of the spectator also cap-
tured the attention of his cranky nineteenth-century critic and biographer, Charles Arnaud. But Arnaud's care to cite the *Pratique*'s
novelty in addition to its neoclassical conformity leads the reader
away from theatrical portraiture to a consideration of the paradox
of d'Aubignac's own colors. Ironically, the dramatic principles of
the *Pratique* which Arnaud so astutely interprets to be novel are
often at odds with the Romantic critic's own rather conventional
notions of neoclassical theatre. One of the *Pratique*'s sections that
particularly irritates Arnaud concerns d'Aubignac's rule that theatre
must comply with "l'opinion et le sentiment des hommes."
Arnaud's discomfort stems from his disagreement that poetic standards should be set according to the norms of popular taste. He
avoids the tendency of most students of neoclassical literature to
identify "des hommes," whose opinion dictates the codes of theatre,
as necessarily an elitist, highly intelligent class responsible for shaping the ideology of the *doctrine classique*. Arnaud's view differs from
that of Ernst Cassirer, for example, who writes that poetic loyalty to
sens commun guarantees "the highest powers of scientific reason."[11]
Instead, Arnaud maintains, "les oeuvres inspirées de la mode sont
condamnées à être vite démodées et caduques," ruled as they are by
"le complaisant et le complice des préjugés, des passions ou des
ignorances de la foule."[12]

In lodging this complaint, Arnaud is actually more in touch
with the "lecture exacte" of many seventeenth-century French treatises than are those critics who assume that neoclassical dramatic
standards were necessarily elevated. In the *Idée des spectacles
anciens et nouveaux*, the Abbé du Pures sets a precedent for
Arnaud's discomfort: "Nous ne faisons point icy de distinction de
ces divers genres de Jeux, parce que l'Idée vulgaire & universelle le
les confond ordinairement, & que ces connoissances trop fines pour
le Peuple & pour les gens de la Cour, l'embarassent beaucoup plus
qu'elles ne les instruisent."[13] Such an understanding of common
taste as constituting a mixture of class and competence informs
Arnaud's anxiety about the democratic constitution of "la foule."
All theatregoers, according to du Pures, share the tastes and judgments of vulgarity. As the Abbé du Bos noted in 1719, this influence
of common taste on the practice of theatre was not foreign to the
spirit of the *Pratique*. It was d'Aubignac to whom du Bos turned for
an answer to the following riddle of competent spectatorship: "les
Professeurs qui toute leur vie ont enseigné la Logique, sont-ils ceux

qui connoissent le mieux quand un homme parle de bon sens, &
quand il raisonne avec justesse?"[14] In response, du Bos notes that
"le parterre, sans sçavoir les regles, juge d'une piéce de théâtre aussi
bien que les gens du métier. *Il en est du théâtre comme de l'éloquence*, dit l'Abbé d'Aubignac, *les perfections n'en sont pas moins
sensibles aux ignorans qu'aux sçavans, bien que la raison ne leur en
soit pas également connue.*"[15]

In the first chapter of the *Pratique*, d'Aubignac delimits the content of spectacles to what is comprehensible to the common
theatregoer:

> Les esprits de ceux qui sont du dernier Ordre [le Peuple], et des plus
> basses conditions d'un Estat, ont si peu de commerce avec les belles
> connoissances, que les maximes les plus generales de la Morale leur
> sont absolument inutiles. C'est en vain qu'on veut les porter à la vertu
> par un discours soûtenu de raisons et d'autorités, ils ne peuvent com-
> prendre les unes, et ne veulent pas déferer aux autres.
>
> Il y a certes bien loin de la capacité de ces Ames vulgaires aux
> sublimes speculations des Sçavants et aux distinctions ingenieuses
> des Philosophes. . . . Toutes ces veritez de la Sagesse sont des lumieres
> trop vives pour la foiblesse de leurs yeux. Ce sont des paradoxes pour
> eux, qui leur rendent la Philosophie suspecte, et mesme ridicule. Il
> leur faut une instruction bien plus grossiere. La raison ne les peut
> vaincre, que par des moyens qui tombent sous les sens. Tels que sont
> les belles representations de Theatre que l'on peut nommer veritable-
> ment l'Ecole du Peuple.[16]

The abbé speaks of the theatregoer as an animal of the senses.
Unable to respond to the truth of rational discourse, the spectator
reacts only to the pleasures and desires of the baser faculties. In
many sophisticated ways, d'Aubignac shifts the dramatist's focus
away from blatant didacticism, away from bondage to concepts of
rational truth and judgment, to a more emotive and less predictable
level of aesthetic and interpretative experience.

This qualification deserves some elaboration. Although d'Aubignac does not ban logical instruction and moral maxims from the
stage, he insists on paying close attention to the manner of their
expression. They should be presented in a way that both pleases and
seduces the spectator:

> Je n'approuverois pas qu'en parlant à un Souverain, il employast
> beaucoup de vers pour dire,
>   *Qu'un Roy possede un pouvoir auquel nul ne doit resister.*
> Mais je trouverois plus agréable qu'il fist dire,

> *Vous ne connoissez pas les droits de vostre Couronne, vostre pou-*
> *voir n'a point de bornes, et quiconque voudra vous resister, deviendra*
> *criminel.*
> car ces discours s'éloignent en apparence des instructions generales,
> et joignent de si prés l'Action du Theatre, qu'ils ne peuvent pas
> ennuyer.[17]

Reflecting d'Aubignac's care to posit the needs of spectators over
the clarity of ideological maxims, this passage insists that theatre
must maintain, above all else, the attention of the audience. In "Des
Discours didactiques ou instructions," moreover, the abbé emphasizes his stress on spectatorship by aligning it with his claims concerning the novelty of the *Pratique.* "Voicy une matiere nouvelle en
l'Art Poëtique, et dont je n'ay rien trouvé dans les Autheurs qui
nous en ont fait de gros Volumes: Je l'ay observée le premier, et fait
des reflexions qui ne sont point ailleurs, et qui contiennent des avis
que le Poëte ne doit pas mépriser."[18] As the basis of "newness" in
this chapter, d'Aubignac stresses his effort to establish a balance
between the message of the poem and the psychological requirements of the spectator.[19] When push comes to shove, D'Aubignac
sacrifices maxims and moral instructions as a means of placating
the pleasure-seeking theatregoer:

> Il faut poser pour assûré, Que tous ces Discours instructifs, sont ordi-
> nairement defectueux sur le Theatre, parce qu'ils sont de leur nature
> froids et languissans; et que ce sont des Maximes generales qui, pour
> instruire, vont seulement à l'esprit et ne frappent point le coeur; ils
> éclairent et n'échauffent pas; et quoy qu'ils soient souvent assez beaux
> et bien exprimez, ils ne font que toucher l'oreille, sans émouvoir
> l'ame: de sorte que l'Action du Theatre, où nous cherchons quelque
> chose qui remuë nos affections, et qui fasse quelque impression sur
> nostre coeur, nous devient peu sensible, et consequemment peu cap-
> able de nous divertir.[20]

Aimed at the emotions, not at the intellect, d'Aubignac's theatrical
practice elicits an affective response from the viewers. At stake in
the action of theatre is the stimulation of the spectators' libidinal
energy. Merely the possibility of such an energetic re-action was sufficient in itself to provoke the paranoia of Conti and theatre's other
opponents. For a libidinal re-presentation of theatrical action will
most likely fail to duplicate a psychological experience resembling
rational discourse or, on a visual level, perspectival spatialization.

It is important to note that this requirement calls for a particular approach to formulating not only the theatrical *message* but also the material *apparatus* of dramatic poetry. The *Pratique* instructs the dramatic poet to compose the separate parts of a poem for the same referent: "tout de mesme le Poëte en considerant dans sa Tragedie le Spectacle ou la Representation, il fait tout ce que son Art et son Esprit luy peuvent fournir pour la rendre admirable aux Spectateurs: car il ne travaille que pour leur plaire."[21] What counts most in a dramatic poem is neither the ingenuity of plot, the embellishment of character, nor the depth of language. Rather, d'Aubignac asserts time and again that *spectacle* is the most consequential part of dramatic representation. And by spectacle d'Aubignac means the play's libidinal engagement of the spectator.[22]

Emphasizing the epistemological conditions of theatre, the abbé instructs the poet to set his sights on a simulacrum of the spectator that "il les doit avoir en la pensée, quand il travaille pour le Theatre."[23] Whatever can be imagined by the dramatist to displease, bore, confuse, overburden, or disrupt the patience of the spectator should be avoided in writing a play. Stressing the appearance or simulacrum of a concept of spectatorship, not simulacra of real princes or authors, d'Aubignac makes clear his assertion that the end of dramatic technique is the pleasure-filled attention of the spectator. This priority was sufficient to provoke passion of a different sort from d'Aubignac's astute nineteenth-century reader, Arnaud: "tout pour les spectateurs! avait dit d'Aubignac. C'est au nom des spectateurs, de la puissance de leur imagination, de l'impossibilité de se passer de leur concours, qu'il faut repousser la démonstration."[24] If an ideological message or portrait can be sketched without depreciating the viewer's experience, d'Aubignac would recommend its inclusion in the poem. But, above all else, the playwright must attend to the needs of the spectators and their "plaisirs legitimes."

In formulating a method of writing dramatic poetry that corresponds to these legitimate needs of the beholder, d'Aubignac describes two specific epistemological conditions of the spectator's experience. The spectator responds *rationally* and *judgmentally* (*sentiments*) to the part of the spectacle that is independent of performance—the *narrative action* of the poem. But the material and sensual aspects of spectacle evoke an *emotional* (*sensations*) response to the *performance*. When it comes to setting priorities, moreover, attentiveness to theatre's materiality takes priority:

> Pour entendre comment le Poëte se doit gouverner à l'égard des Spec-
> tateurs, et comment ils luy sont considerables ou non, il ne faut que
> faire reflexion sur ce que nous avons dit d'un Tableau. Car en le con-
> siderant comme une peinture, ou un ouvrage de l'Art, le Peintre fait
> tout ce qu'il peut pour le rendre excellent; parce qu'il sera veu, et qu'il
> y fait tout à dessein d'en estre estimé."[25]

The parts of the poem and the material conditions of its representation need contribute to and solicit the *visual* attention and pleasure of the beholders. The viewers' judgmental experience of the
poem corresponds, or perhaps d'Aubignac would say *conforms*, to
their sensual or visual enjoyment of the representation. The playwright writes first to suit the needs of a beholder (*spectateur*) and
only second to attract a reader (*lecteur*, or as Corneille often says,
auditeur).[26]

To Show the Colors

This distinction between reader and viewer and its relation to the
rules governing poetic construction provoke Charles Arnaud to
challenge the *Pratique* for limiting its theatrical prescriptions to the
visual criteria of painting:

> en ce qui concerne la représentation, les *sentiments* des spectateurs
> sont au contraires déterminés, au théâtre même, par les impressions
> organiques, les *sensations* qu'ils y reçoivent. Tandis que le poème
> epique s'adresse directement à l'imagination, le poème dramatique
> est un tableau 'qui tombe sous le sens,' et dont 'l'oeil est le juge,'
> comme disait Chapelain.—La vraisemblance oblige donc à ne jamais
> mettre en contradiction les *sensations* et les *sentiments* des specta-
> teurs, et par conséquent à rendre identique, dans l'action et la repré-
> sentation, tout ce qui tombe sous les sens.[27]

Although we shall soon discuss how d'Aubignac was careful to go
beyond matters which are merely pictorial, the text does concen-
trate on the spectators' visual experience and the requirements of
plastic imagery. A fascinating aspect of d'Aubignac's discussion of
theatrical imagery is his particular manner of comparing it to painting, often in lieu of concerns exclusively literary. There is something
very special about this text's *practical* reliance on pictorial examples
that distinguishes its understanding of the "ut pictora poesis" motif
commonplace in the humanistic theatre treatises indebted to the *Ars
Poetica*.

D'Aubignac expresses a deep belief that certain aspects of the *craft* of painting should be imitated by the dramatic poet. In describing an imaginary picture of a "Magdeleine Penitente," the abbé suggests that the poet needs to be sensitive to the following techniques of the painter:

> Il y employera les plus vives couleurs; afin que l'oeil y trouve plus de satisfaction. . . . Il ne la representera pas dans le fond d'un rocher, parce qu'elle ne pourroit estre veuë; mais à l'entrée d'une Grote, et il s'y gouvernera ainsi, parce qu'il considere son ouvrage comme une peinture qui doit tomber sous les sens et qui doit plaire.[28]

D'Aubignac speaks here not of painting in general, but of particular facets of picture-making, especially those relating to color, those enhancing the quality of pleasure through vision—"afin que l'oeil y trouve plus de satisfaction." It is especially crucial to the craft of playwriting, the Abbé suggests, that the poet maintain control over pictorial color and its projection through both the plastic and linguistic aspects of performance.

The *Pratique*'s first concentrated discussion of painting and color occurs, significantly, in the chapter "Des Spectateurs et comment le Poëte les doit considerer." Here d'Aubignac outlines his stance regarding the artifact's need to provoke a harmonious experience of *sensations* and *sentiments* in the beholders. He begins by linking aspects of painting with the binary experience of theatre:

> Je prens icy la comparaison d'un Tableau, dont j'ay resolu de me servir souvent en ce Traitté, et je dis qu'on le peut considerer en deux façons. La premiere comme une peinture, c'est à dire, entant que c'est l'ouvrage de la main du Peintre, où il n'y a que des couleurs et non pas des choses; des ombres, et non pas des corps, des jours artificiels, de fausses élevations, des éloignements en Perspective, des raccourcissements illusoires, et de simples apparences de tout ce qui n'est point. La seconde entant qu'il contient une chose qui est peinte, soit veritable ou supposée telle, dont les lieux sont certains, les qualitez naturelles, les actions indubitables, et toutes les circonstances selon l'ordre et la raison.[29]

D'Aubignac goes on to relate the illusions of color with dramatic "Représentation," and "la chose qui est peinte," with "la verité de l'Action Theatrale." These associations suggest clearly what Rensselaer W. Lee describes as the "purely formal correspondances between the sister arts: design equals plot, color equals words."[30] In such formal terms, color and its corollary, "la Représentation," give rise to "the ornamental or even frankly decorative appeal of art."[31]

In a dramatic context, this would refer to the embellishment of dramatic poetry with perspectival scenery, carefully designed costumes, props, lighting, and other devices of staging. Color here signifies the various decorative sources of artistic delight.

It is important to note, however, that the *Pratique* rarely posits merely formal correlations between theatre and painting. Further consideration of the chapter on "Des Spectateurs" reveals how d'Aubignac's subtler reliance on color signifies much more than the decorative aspects of theatrical accessories:

> Je scay bien que le Poëte ne travaille point sur l'Action comme veritable, sinon en tant qu'elle peut estre representée; D'où l'on pourroit conclure qu'il y a quelque mélange de ces deux considerations, mais voicy comment il les doit démêler. Il examine tout ce qu'il veut et doit faire connoistre aux Spectateurs par l'oreille et par les yeux, et se resout de le leur faire reciter, ou de leur faire voir; parce qu'il doit avoir soin d'eux, en considerant l'Action comme representée. . . . Il faut qu'il cherche dans l'Action considerée comme veritable, un motif et une raison apparente, que l'on nomme couleur, pour faire que ces Recits et ces Spectacles soient vraysemblablement arrivez de la sorte.[32]

D'Aubignac goes so far as to say that color provides the core foundation of verisimilar spectacle. "Et j'ose dire que le plus grand Art du Theatre consiste à trouver toutes ces couleurs."[33] Rather than being a mere ornamental addition to theatrical action, color is an intrinsic element of the theatrical phantasm, "une raison apparente" of the actions imitated by dramatic representation. Although its exact applications are sometimes obscure in the *Pratique*, color functions as the agent that enhances the libidinal activity of the spectator.

D'Aubignac's conception of the libidinal function of color might be understood in view of color's more clearly delineated role in seventeenth-century French painting. In the French debate over color and design, color was acknowledged to have an effect far greater than the pleasure derived from painting's aesthetic ornaments.[34] The complicated theory of color developed by one critic to whom we have already turned, Roger de Piles, has been astutely summarized by Svetlana Alpers in her essay, "Describe or Narrate?" Alpers's formulation of the role of color in the *Cours de peinture par principes* helps make accessible the implications of d'Aubignac's somewhat vague use of the term:

De Piles in speaking powerfully for color in art is less concerned with the actual use and effect of color than with those general phenomena with which color had come to be identified. On the one hand, color was seen as the ornament of art—mere appeal—and on the other, as the basis of imitation, specifically as in Vasari's account of Giorgione, imitation which appears to be operating in a vacuum—imitation, in other words, as *mere* imitation with no narrative end in view. . . . It is on the basis of the assumed link to imitation that those seventeenth-century artists whom we have already discussed—Rembrandt and Caravaggio, for example—were repeatedly described in the seventeenth century as colorists. Color is used here as a term referring to their absorption in the act of representation or imitation.[35]

As a vital aspect of what Alpers calls seventeenth-century descriptive painting, color undermines the *structural primacy* of narrative action by portraying a credible image steeped in mimetic realism. Descriptive clarity, the visibility of an image, is more important to the artist than any narrative message that might be contained in the picture. This practice of color, as interpreted by Alpers, gauges an artist's commitment to the purity of representation-as-such. In the theory of de Piles, Alpers adds, the corollary of this commitment is color's tendency to attract the eyes of the beholder:

De Piles, and this is the strength and subtlety of his analysis, called both Rembrandt and Rubens colorists for an essentially single reason: because he sees the imitative power of one and the coloristic appeal (what Reynolds was to call the "eloquence") of the other as engaged in an essentially common concern for representational force. De Piles is the first critic to link up in a positive and powerful way the two traditional aspects of color: (1) its link with imitation and (2) its powerful appeal to the eyes. In arguing that imitation leads to a desired end of fooling the eyes and calling on the viewer, de Piles validated imitation in a new way by tying it to a desirable and newly defined end of art. He is thus able to give full recognition and full weight to the representational power of the work of art as such.[36]

In contributing to the visual forcefulness of an image's realism, color is said here to complement imitation. A painting's color attracts and deceives the viewer's eyes so as to transform the cursory glance of a disinterested viewer into the attentive, captivated trance of a beholder. Such a coloristic appeal to the beholder, one that is not so much decorative as structural, was promoted by de Piles as an essential element of effective (affective) artistic imitation.

This primarily representational function of color, as elaborated by de Piles in the late seventeenth century, points toward the paradoxical role of theatrical color outlined by d'Aubignac in the 1640s. According to the abbé, coloration is the process of making a dramatic image fit "pour estre representée":

> C'est travailler sur l'Action en tant que representée, et cela est du devoir du Poëte; mesme est-ce sa principale intention. Mais il la doit cacher sous quelque couleur qui dépende de l'Action comme veritable. . . . Car il n'y a point d'action sur leur Theatre [des Anciens], point de parole, point de recit, point de passion, point d'intrigue qui n'ait sa couleur, à prendre l'Histoire comme veritable, encore qu'elle ne soit inventée par le Poëte que pour estre representée.[37]

Color to d'Aubignac is something that transforms dramatic action and its poetic narration into an image appealing to the libidinal drives (*sensations*) of the spectators. The above passage suggests, moreover, that d'Aubignac has in a mind a very subtle use of color. He does not suggest merely that the dramatist literally add color, in the sense of scenic decoration or linguistic adornment, which would call attention to the representation of a play, to the actual performance by players in front of spectators. Rather, color is a means of dissembling, disguising, and hiding (*semblance*) the reality of stagecraft (*le vrai*) in order to enhance the verisimilitude of the theatrical image. While luring and seducing the spectators' eyes, color reduces the distance between poetic narration and the playing and viewing of spectacle. The poet versed in the technique of coloration weaves a structural veil that permits the spectators to re-act, to make irrationally true, the fictional presence and reality of the action being played out before their eyes. It is in this context that we can appreciate anew d'Aubignac's attentiveness to *vraisemblance*. This dramatic structure might now be understood as something different from the fictional imitation of social truth. Although *vraisemblance* continues to signify truth (*le vrai*), it points to the general condition of spectatorship and theatrical re-presentation: the irrational truth of theatrical desire (*le semblant*).[38]

D'Aubignac's most informative technical discussions of coloration are found in his analyses of the constitution of theatrical images. Concern over the verisimilar quality of the image dominates the *Pratique*'s frequently cited chapters on the unities of time and place. Economy and structural unity function, in the abbé's view, as determinants of imitative potency. Speaking of action, the abbé says that the playwright should limit himself to a principal, but "tellement limitée," historical action. One of the purposes of such poetic economy is to enhance the realistic intensity of the dramatic image. The simplicity of dramatic actions, "les petits sujets," provides the poet with a manageable and malleable substance with which to craft an image steeped in verisimilar allure. Reminding us of de Piles's claims for historical painting, D'Aubignac argues that pictorial concentration on a central act, rather than on a narrational series of actions, enhances the descriptive value of the image. The unified dramatic image is said to be so mimetically efficacious that one action represents a series of contingent causes and effects, "et par la representation d'une seule partie faire tout repasser adroitement devant les yeux des Spectateurs, sans multiplier l'action principale."[39] The quality of such a dramatic image can be evaluated best in terms of its descriptive clarity and its appeal to the beholder for a more elaborate, mental repetition: "toutes les actions, bien que dépendantes en quelque façon d'une principale, estoient si grandes et si fortes, que de chacune on eust pû faire un Poëme."[40] Such an image, so colorful in its own descriptiveness, might be said to give rise to the spectators' own re-presentation or speaking of it. In this instance, the *Pratique* provides us with a very balanced and reciprocal notion of *ut pictura poesis*.

We should now be able to appreciate how d'Aubignac wrote his treatise around a particular maxim: "le Theatre n'est rien qu'une Image."[41] Yet we would miss the complexity of the *Pratique*'s paradoxical colors by failing to emphasize the abbé's clarification of this truism concerning theatre's essence as image: "le Theatre n'est autre chose qu'une representation, il ne se faut point imaginer qu'il y ait rien de tout ce que nous y voyons, mais bien les choses mesmes dont nous y trouvons les images."[42] It is the activity of representation, not merely the dramatic visibility of colorful images, that constitutes theatricality at its best for d'Aubignac. In *La Pratique du théâtre*, moreover, representation includes a wide range of color producing media:

> j'appelle Representation, l'assemblage de toutes les choses qui peuvent servir à representer un Poëme Dramatique, et qui s'y doivent rencontrer, en les considerant en elles-mesmes et selon leur nature, comme les Comediens, les Decorateurs, les Toiles peintes, les Violons, les Spectateurs et autres semblables.[43]

To add color may mean developing the role of decorators or painted

scenery, both "qui peuvent *servir à representer* un Poëme Dramatique." Still, the most striking aspect of d'Aubignac's concept of representation is its inclusion of the spectator as a structural necessity
of color—not merely its aim. Theatrical representation, then, is
equally a matter of the construction and reception of images and
their material support.

To enhance the beholders' imaginative reconstruction of dramatic images, d'Aubignac demands of the dramatic poem carefully
contrived colors of a different sort that transport the images of theatre beyond the pictorial realm of the visible. These colors are especially apparent toward the end of the *Pratique* when d'Aubignac
most explicitly addresses the paradox of his reformulation of the
classical notions of seventeenth-century dramatic representation. In
"Du discours en general," he speaks of the demands of visibility in
view of dramatic dialogue:

> A considerer la Tragédie dans sa nature et à la rigueur, selon le genre
> de Poësie sous lequel elle est constituée, on peut dire qu'elle est telle-
> ment attachée aux actions qu'il ne semble pas que les discours soient
> de ses appartenances. Ce poëme est nommé *Drama*, c'est à dire,
> *Action* et non pas *Récit*; Ceux qui le representent se nomment
> *Acteurs*, et non pas *Orateurs*; Ceux-là même qui s'y trouvent presens
> s'appellent *Spectateurs* ou *Regardans*, et non pas *Auditeurs*; Enfin le
> Lieu qui sert à ses Representations, est dit *Theatre*, et non pas *Audi-
> toire*, c'est à dire, *un Lieu où on regard ce qui s'y fait*, et non pas où
> *l'on Ecoute ce qui s'y dit*. Aussi est-il vray que les Discours qui s'y
> font, doivent estres commes des Actions de ceux qu'on y fait
> paroistre; car là *Parler*, c'est *Agir*.[44]

But even though theatre is described as being based on actions, not
on words, and as visual and sensory, not rhetorical and affective,
silence—except during the intervals—is decreed to be the gravest
error of drama.[45] The paradox is put succinctly by d'Aubignac:

> En un mot, les Discours ne sont au Theatre que les accessoires de
> l'Action, quoy que toute la Tragédie, dans la Representation ne con-
> siste qu'en Discours; c'est là tout l'ouvrage du Poëte, et à quoy prin-
> cipalement il employe les forces de son esprit; et s'il fait paroistre
> quelques actions sur son Theatre, c'est pour en tirer occasion de faire
> quelque agréable discours; tout ce qu'il invente, c'est afin de le faire
> dire.[46]

By substituting words for actions, d'Aubignac displaces visibility
and its corollary of *perpectiva legitima* as the guiding principles of
dramatic color. Although pictoriality continues to be an essential

element of the abbé's theatrical practice, the visual is less a material
and visible apparatus of the stage than an apparatus of representation: the image as re-presented in the mind of the theatregoer. The
Pratique thus extends the notion of the theatrical *scène*, "un lieu où
on regarde ce qui s'y fait," to include the *figural* space of representation-as-such.

The figural apparatus of d'Aubignac's theatricality manifests
itself prominently in the *Pratique*'s emphasis on the importance
of the incompletion of the dramatic image. A finished dramatic
product best represents the picture of its incongruities and
imperfections:

> Le Poëme Dramatique est comme une quinte essence de tous les pré-
> ceptes qui se lisent dans les Autheurs, qui nous ont enseigné l'art de
> bien dire en prose et en vers; parce qu'il les y faut employer avec tant
> de jugement et de délicatesse, que bien souvent il paroisse qu'on en
> soit fort éloigné, et que méme on les ait entierement abandonnez; et
> le genie du Theatre est tel, que d'ordinaire, ce qui ne paroist point, en
> est le plus grand art; un Sentiment qu'on aura presque imperceptible-
> ment jetté dans l'esprit des Auditeurs, une Avanture commencée en
> apparence sans dessein, une Narration imparfaite, ou quelque autre
> conduite ingenieuse, sont capables de soûtenir une partie de tout un
> Poëme, d'en fonder les plus belles passions, et d'en préparer une
> illustre Catastrophe.[47]

The genius of an effective poem, "le genie du Theatre," is said by
d'Aubignac to portray the illusionary inadequacy and deficiency of
its visible parts, rather than the visible potency of either author or
patron. It is noteworthy, moreover, that d'Aubignac aligns this presentation of the genius of incomplete imagery with the art of rhetoric, whereas modern readers like Cassirer associate dramatic unity,
the *discours classique*, and "genius" with the Cartesian paradigm of
logical, rational perception. The eyes are thought by most literary
historians to underlie the experience of seventeenth-century French
theatre. But it is with the figures of rhetoric, so d'Aubignac contends, that the theatre best shows its particular genius.

The Rhetoric of Desire

> En un mot, si la Poësie est l'Empire des Figures, le The-
> atre en est le Thrône; c'est le lieu où par les agitations
> apparentes de celuy qui parle et qui se plaint, elles font

passer dans l'ame de ceux qui le regardent, et qui l'écoutent des sentimens qu'il n'a point.

ABBÉ D'AUBIGNAC,
La Pratique du théâtre [48]

It is the Abbé du Bos who first underscores d'Aubignac's stress on the colors of language: "*Il en est du théâtre comme de l'éloquence,* dit l'Abbé d'Aubignac." [49] As du Bos keenly states, d'Aubignac placed considerable stress on the representational benefits and effects of rhetoric and its particularly theatrical figures. The author of *Discours academique sur l'eloquence*, d'Aubignac asks the playwright to weave the figures of eloquence—what he calls "le genre sublime"—into the fabric of the dramatic poem. Through the economical manipulation of the figures of rhetoric, poets can add more than just visual color to their plays. In considering one particular aspect of rhetoric, deliberation, d'Aubignac outlines how rational dialogue and theatrical exchange are partly the products of subtly crafted rhetorical colors:

> comment donc les Déliberations pourront-elles y prendre part? Elles se font d'un esprit rassis, et tout s'y doit passer avec beaucoup de modération; celuy qui demande conseil, en fait la proposition avec tranquillité, encore que d'ailleurs son ame soit agitée; ceux qui sont appellez pour donner leur avis, doivent estres encore moins troublez d'interests et de passions; ils ne doivent parler qu'avec des raisons épurées; ils doivent estre dans les lumieres, et non pas dans les tempestes, et deslors qu'ils paroistroient émeûs et dans quelque emportement, ils seroient suspects d'entrer par quelque motif secret dans l'un des deux partis, et perdroient la qualité de bons Conseilleurs; enfin dans ces occasions il faut que tout y soit sans agitation, les personnes retenuës, les discours moderez, les expressions douces, et rien qui ressente les mouvemens impetueux de la Scéne: de sorte que sans un grand art, il est impossible que le Theatre ne tombe dans la langueur, comme dans l'immobilité. [50]

The result of such moderation is a scene captivating in the exposition of its figures and pleasurable in its reasonableness, propriety, and admirable turns of phrase and plot. In eliciting the attentive response of its spectator, this sort of rational, centralized dramatic image complements the ideology of the *doctrine classique*. It exemplifies what the abbé termed, in his *Discours academique sur l'eloquence*, the "legitime devoir" to cultivate and promote the study of the science of language in the realm of Louis XIV. [51]

Yet d'Aubignac dissociates himself from his scientific colleagues of the *discours classique* by disputing the effectiveness of the merely grammatical and analytical study of rhetoric. "C'est pourquoy le meilleur avis qu'on puisse donner aux Poëtes, est de se rendre tres-sçavans en la connoissance des Figures par l'étude de ce qu'en ont écrit les Rhétoriciens, qu'il seroit inutile de répeter ici: mais auparavant qu'ils se souviennent, qu'on ne doit pas se contenter de les lire pour en sçavoir le nom et la fabrique."[52] D'Aubignac directs the playwrights' attentions to the more theatrical realm of the throne of figures. Whereas dispassionate analysis is the method of theory, d'Aubignac promotes the *practical* use of figures dependent on the playwrights' engagement in their own medium:

> qu'il . . . faut pénetrer l'énergie [des figures], et y faire de fortes reflexions, et enfin découvrir l'effet qu'elles peuvent produire sur le Theatre. . . . Et pour se rendre subtil et adroit en cét usage des figures, le Poëte en doit rechercher les exemples chez les Anciens, les bien examiner, et ne les pas courir à la légère; et surtout fréquenter les Theatres; car c'est-là où, mieux que dans les Livres, il peut remarquer les bonnes ou mauvaises figures, celles qui languissent, et celles qui font effet.[53]

Although d'Aubignac does not come close to advocating the banishment of book learning, he recommends that rhetorical practice be learned most efficiently from the site of theatre itself. The poet needs to be a theatregoer, to experience the effect of theatrical rhetoric before utilizing it. To write a dramatic poem, in d'Aubignac's view, is less to express one's own genius or control over a body of textual tropes than to write literally from the perspective of the affected spectator. Such a dramatic poem might be said to be the allegorical double of the theatrical experience, just as the author is here understood to take on the guise of the theatregoer. This is the scene of "le genie du Theatre."

If such a stance suggests the partial undermining of a dramatic tradition based on ideals of authorial genius and theatrical portraiture, the rhetorical practice recommended by d'Aubignac hints further at the uneasy paradox of his own textual colors, thus intensifying the ideological implications of his stress on spectatorship. The *Pratique*'s remarks about deliberation make the notable suggestion that control, reasonableness, and self-contained unity compete with other figures of theatre's "mouvements impetueux de la Scéne." When the dramatic poem is colored with the most eloquent figures for representation, it appeals to passion not to reason. For eloquence, as the abbé writes somewhat anxiously in *Discours academique,*

> se gouverne . . . sur l'ame de ceux qui l'ecoutent; car passant insen-
> siblement dans leur coeur, elle s'en rend souveraine, & leur fait perdre
> la connoissance de toute autre chose que de celle qu'elle leur veut
> inspirer: Et cette pensée determine enfin mon incertitude. Oüy sans
> doute la parfaite Eloquence se fait bien sentir agreablement, mais elle
> ne laisse pas le judgement en liberté; ceux qu'elle entreprend de vain-
> cre, ne doivent pas demeurer en estat de discerner les choses sensibles
> qu'ils touchent & qu'ils voyent; de sçavoir ce qu'ils sont & ce qu'ils
> font; ny de la reconnoistre elle-mesme.[54]

As d'Aubignac implies throughout his treatise on eloquence, the rhetorical figures of theatre are likely to work against the spectators' epistemological re-presentations of judgment and controlled reason. For figures aiming at the dispassionate response to images of *bon sens* and *bienséance,* say the figures of written portraiture, are not recommended by d'Aubignac for the theatre. A more representative picture of "la Scéne" envisaged by d'Aubignac is contained in the following passage which argues against the dramatist's use of delib-erative rhetoric:

> Présupposant donc icy pour fondement tout ce qu'on peut apprendre
> ailleurs des Deliberations, je commence par cét avertissement consid-
> erable, Qu'elles sont de leur nature contraires au Theatre; parce que
> le Theatre estant le lieu des Actions, il faut que tout y soit dans l'ag-
> itation, soit par des évenemens qui de moment à autre se contredisent
> et s'embarrassent; soit par des passions violentes qui de tous costez
> naissent du choq, et du milieu des Incidens, comme les éclairs et le
> tonnerre du combat, et du sein des Nuées les plus obscures: en sorte
> que personne ne vient presque sur la Scéne qui n'ait l'esprit inquieté,
> dont les affaires ne soient traversées, et qu'on ne voye dans la neces-
> sité de travailler, ou de souffrir beaucoup; et enfin c'est où règne le
> Démon de l'inquietude, du trouble et du desordre.[55]

The theatrical scene described above shuns the sort of rhetoric that requires a reasoned and disengaged response from the listener. D'Aubignac's theatre means to affect the spectator in a way that dis-misses distance, passive reception, and witnessing. Scattered through the *Pratique* are references, although not always as explicit as above, to an agitated theatricality overseen by the "Démon de l'inquietude, du trouble et du desordre."

An especially interesting case of the demoniacal side of the *Pra-tique* can be found in observing the rhetorical figures recommended by d'Aubignac for theatrical practice. Although the abbé favors "les Figures qu'on peut nommer, *grandes* et *sérieuses*," his choice and description of figures are inconsistent with the Aristotelian emphasis on rhetorical magnitude and eloquence. D'Aubignac demonstrates little interest, for example, in tropes and figures that work metonymically to exemplify, clarify, and heighten heroic qualities and poetic eloquence, such as pleonasm, epithet, adjunction, and alliteration. Theatrical figures, in his opinion, portray grand qualities of a different kind. In selecting his catalogue of especially theatrical tropes, d'Aubignac follows the lead of Scaliger in giving priority to apostrophe:

> le Poëte en pourra bien trouver quelques-unes plus propres au Theatre que les autres: par exemple, l'*Apostrophe*, que j'y ay toûjours remarquée fort éclatante, quand elle est bien placée et bien conduitte; Elle suppose toûjours presente, ou une veritable personne, quoy qu'absente en effet, ou une fausse personne, qui ne l'est que par fiction, comme est la *Patrie*, la *Vertu*, et autres choses semblables; car elle les suppose si bien presentes, que celuy qui discourt, leur adresse sa parole, comme si veritablement il les voyoit: ce qui est tout à fait Theatral; attendu que cela fait deux Personnages où il n'y en a qu'un, l'un visible, et l'autre imaginaire; l'un qui parle, et l'autre à qui il semble qu'on parle: Or quoy que la feinte soit connuë, neantmoins comme c'est un effet de l'emportement de l'esprit de l'Acteur, elle emporte avec elle l'imagination de ceux qui l'écoutent.[56]

D'Aubignac favors a figure that provokes the theatregoer to make present imaginatively a character who is either off-stage or nonexistent. Rather than heighten the colorful depiction of the characters visible on stage, the purpose of apostrophe is said by d'Aubignac to accentuate a theatricality of invisibility and absence supplemented by the imaginative involvement of the theatregoer. This view of apostrophe, by the way, may appear especially familiar to readers of Paul de Man, Jonathan Culler, and Cynthia Chase, who follow d'Aubignac's path in insisting that "to read apostrophe as a sign of a fiction which knows its own fictive nature is to stress its optative character, its impossible imperatives: commands which in their explicit impossibility figure events in and of fiction."[57]

Throughout the *Pratique*, d'Aubignac promotes figures that enhance the representational role of the theatregoer, whose participation in the staging of spectacle is an essential aspect of theatrical fiction. Apostrophe is not an isolated example of the sort of theatrical trope favored by d'Aubignac. The other figures recommended for dramatic practice portray absence, anxiety, trouble, disorder, and other sentiments or notions identified by d'Aubignac as particularly theatrical:

> L'Ironie est encore une figure du Poëme Dramatique, et de sa nature elle est Theatrale; car en disant par moquerie le contraire de ce qu'elle veut faire entendre serieusement, elle porte avec soy un déguisement, et fait un jeu qui n'est pas desagréable.
>
> L'Exclamation est d'autant plus propre au Theatre, qu'elle est la marque sensible d'un esprit touché de quelque violente passion qui le presse.
>
> L'Hyperbole est de ce méme rang, parce que les paroles portant l'imagination plus loin que leur propre sens, elle est convenable au Theatre, où toutes les choses doivent devenir plus grandes, et où il n'y a qu'enchantement et illusion.
>
> L'Interrogation, que Scaliger dit n'estre figure que par usage et non pas de sa nature, est aussi bonne au Theatre; parce qu'elle est la marque d'un esprit agité.
>
> Or entre toutes, l'Imprécation sera jugée certainement Theatrale, à cause qu'elle procede d'un violent transport d'esprit; aussi faut-il que le discours soit fort impetueux, l'impression hardie, et les choses extrémes.[58]

All of the figures listed above magnify "les mouvements impetueux de la Scéne." The fabric of rhetorical theatricality consists of ruses, disguises, and illusions that heighten the agitated and violent imaginative experience of spectacle. The effect of this kind of rhetoric is to dis-place the representation of theatrical imagery from the stage to the *parterre*.[59]

Underlying the ornamental unity and illusionary wholeness of the dramatic image, then, is the *force* of rhetoric.[60] It obliges the theatregoer, who is otherwise comfortable with either the passive observation or absorptive contemplation of a colorful "object" (*le vrai*), to recognize the incompletion or invisibility of the dramatic image (*le semblable*). In one of the passages dismissing narration from the dramatist's repertoire, d'Aubignac further illustrates this forceful nature of representational practice:

> Ces longues Narrations ne sont pas meilleures dans la suitte de l'Action, pour les choses qui surviennent depuis l'ouverture du Theatre; car outre ces raisons communes fondées sur le defaut de varieté, sur l'impatience des Spectateurs, et sur le relâchement de leur esprit; il ne sera jamais vray-semblable que tant de choses soient arrivées en si peu de temps, par exemple dans l'intervalle d'un Acte: ce n'est pas qu'il ne soit fort ordinaire d'y supposer une Bataille, une Conjuration,

une Fourbe signalée, ou quelque autre pareil évenement; mais pour le faire avec vray-semblance, il faut tromper l'Auditeur comme nous avons dit ailleurs, en l'occupant à voir quelque autre chose, et à oüyr quelques discours qui servent de preparation à ce qui doit estre raconté apres, qui lui fassent naistre l'impatience de le sçavoir, et qui séduisent agréablement son imagination.[61]

D'Aubignac's strategy is to engross the theatregoers in the contemplation of an image from which they are, in reality, excluded. If the theatregoers are at all satisfied with the scene, it is because the dramatic moment operates as a substitute for an elusive object of desire. The force of such theatricality confuses the theatregoers' contemplation of the dramatic moment with their narcissistic response to their own desires, projections, and repressions. This play of transference even explains for d'Aubignac the psychological paradox of the pleasure experienced by the spectator continually assaulted and frustrated by the portrayal of figures of always already absent desires. "Laissant toûjours le Spectateur dans l'attente de quelque nouveauté, [les couleurs] échauffent son desir, et l'entretiennent dans une agréable impatience."[62] The sadistic, but delightful, nature of the impatience of desire is even said by the abbé to constitute the primary structure of eloquence, which he describes in the *Discours academique* as "un torrent à quoy rien ne peut resister; mais un torrent de delices, qui porte la joye où sa violence le porte."[63] Obscuring the pleasure and pain of the dramatic object with the spectators' own experiences of unfulfilled desires, such a doubling of desire casts d'Aubignac's theatrical colors in a psychologically energetic light. The spectators of theatrical spectacle re-act to the coloration of their own libidinal mechanisms of representation through condensation, displacement, negation, and substitution.

Current readers of d'Aubignac can appreciate the structural complexity of his poetics in view of recent work by Lyotard, Kofman, Green, Lacoue-Labarthe, and others.[64] It is now almost a commonplace that the scene of theatre doubles as the *mise-en-scène* of the unconscious. But theoreticians and historians of seventeenth-century theatre have yet to emphasize d'Aubignac's fascination with the complexities of representational theory. The exception might be d'Aubignac's nineteenth-century reader, Charles Arnaud, who voices an uncanny appreciation of the more fascinating aspects of d'Aubignac's notions of dramatic representation. It is particularly in view of the *Pratique*'s chapter on "Les Intervalles des Actes" that Arnaud emphasizes the abbé's trust in the libidinal re-presentations of the spectators. In this chapter, d'Aubignac goes to considerable lengths to distance himself from La Mesnardière in recommending that each act be followed by a musical interval. While d'Aubignac was partially concerned about suiting the needs of the audience's limited attention span, he defines the interval in terms of the theatregoers' libidinal supplementations of theatrical spectacle:

> Et quand le Poëme Dramatique est venu à sa derniere perfection, ces Intervalles ont esté considerez comme des parties necessaires à la composition de cet Ouvrage; et pour tout dire en un mot, les Poëtes s'en sont servis pour faire et tout ensemble pour cacher tout ce qui ne pouvoit, ou ne devoit point estres veû des Spectateurs. . . . [Le Poëte] en doit supposer toutes les rencontres incommodes derriere la Tapisserie, et surtout dans ces Intervalles qui luy fourniront un temps convenable pour tout executer.[65]

Whether for the pleasure of the theatregoers or for the sake of the poem's unity and verisimilitude, intervals are structural devices through which the play represents its hidden moments and actions. A most interesting feature of the interval is its aim to chase excess from the stage. Yet excess itself constitutes the spectacle of intervals—through imaginative supplementation of what is not shown on the stage, or, even more interestingly, through the libidinal activity stimulated by the music of intervals. I need but mention in passing Nietzsche's similar notion of how music provides the sounds of "all of nature's *excess* in pleasure, grief, and knowledge."[66]

The excess of theatricality in d'Aubignac's method provides the grounds for Arnaud's fascinating analysis. Believing neoclassical theatre to be primarily an expression of originary presence and an endorsement of the ideology of the visible,[67] Arnaud questions the clarity of d'Aubignac's theory of non-visual representation. "On comprend que la durée des moments représentés se mesure à peu près sur celle de leur représentation; mais on comprend moins que la durée des autres, de ceux qui ne sont pas représentés, doive se mesurer sur la durée de leur *non-représentation*."[68] Arnaud questions the possibility that representation might be constituted as much by its intervals and gaps as by its dominating marks of presence. This debate should be especially notable to contemporary readers in view of "la nécessité de l'intervalle, la dure loi de l'espacement,"[69] which Jacques Derrida has exposed as the constitutional foundation of representation, whether theatrical or prosaic:

"Ce qu'on ne peut pas représenter, c'est le rapport de la représentation à la présence dite originaire. La re-preséntation est aussi une dé-preséntation. Elle est liée à l'oeuvre de l'espacement. L'espacement insinue dans la présence un intervalle qui ne sépare pas seulement les différents temps de la voix et du chant mais aussi le représenté du représentant."[70] Arnaud's complex and even contradictory analysis of the absurdity of *non-représentation* so remarkably foreshadows contemporary debates over the poststructuralist assessment of "dé-présentation" that its further citation should almost be sufficient in itself to clarify the ideological impact of d'Aubignac's notions of representation and its "plaisirs legitimes":

> Ce n'est donc plus sur une représentation sensible, c'est sur une représentation *supposée, imaginée*, que d'Aubignac détermine la durée de l'action; c'est-a-dire que ce ne sont plus les sens seulement qu'il prend pour juges de la poésie représentative, mais, avec eux, l'imagination; c'est-a-dire enfin qu'il abandonne encore et contredit le principe de sa démonstration, à savoir, que le poème dramatique est "un tableau qui tombe sous les sens" et "dont l'oeil seul est le juge." Et c'est à l'abandon de ce principe qu'il faut toujours en venir. Vouloir, en effet, se passer de l'imagination des spectateurs, "poser pour fondement," avec Chapelain, que l'art dramatique ne s'adresse qu'aux sens et doit leur faire illusion, c'est tout simplement rendre l'art dramatique impossible. Il n'y a qu'à considérer les moyens dont il se sert, pour s'apercevoir qu'il n'est matériellement que "feintise," qu'il a besoin de faire suppléer par notre imagination ce qui manque à ses "images," qu'il ne peut et ne veut nous donner le sentiment du vrai qu'en nous laissant la sensation du faux, qu'il n'existe enfin qu'en vertue d'une convention perpetuelle entre le poète et le spectateur ... et le spectateur, accordant tout cela, et plus encore, se faisant le collaborateur, le complice, le compère du poète.[71]

When the poet works to legitimize the pleasure of the spectator, neoclassical theatre is destroyed. The distinction between dramatic object and viewing subject, "dont l'oeil seul est le juge," is eclipsed by the disquieting notion of a theatre endorsing the goal of libidinal (non-)representation. Neither the poet, the patron, the dramatic image, nor even the eye (I) of the spectator functions here as a rational and dependable *représentant* of theatrical practice.[72] Rather, d'Aubignac's theatre strengthens the appreciation of a *représentant* of a different color, once again "le Démon de l'inquietude, du trouble et du desordre."

Re-Placing Theatre

Although Arnaud's complaints exemplify the assumption of critical history that seventeenth-century French dramatic treatises concern themselves with *what* image *should be shown* on the stage, the *Pratique* sidesteps this critical history in favor of positing the problem of representational method: *how* a theatrical image is shown and *how* it is received. When d'Aubignac compares himself to his contemporaries, he laments their insensitivity to the force of theatrical representation, that one need not show on the stage what can be said or suggested.[73] But even though the abbé is bothered by his colleagues' blindness to the fruitfulness of theatrical invisibility, absence, and desire, his text does not totally reject the neoclassical tradition. Rather, d'Aubignac adapts the codes of classical theory to his almost poststructural conception of theatrical practice. I have discussed, for instance, how the principles of *pratique* depend on the seventeenth-century concept of *vraisemblance*. It is essential for what is not performed on the stage to be just as verisimilar and therefore as seductive as what the playwright chooses to show. Another prime example of the *Pratique*'s subtle transformation of the *doctrine classique* is its adaptation of the convention of *bienséance* (propriety and moderation). Whereas the classical theoreticians limit the reference of this concept to the ideological realm of public mores, d'Aubignac extends it to his rhetoric of desire. In discussing the dramatic weakness of long narrations, for example, he cites their lack of moderation. They place too many obstacles between the theatrical moment and the spectator's "dernier plaisir."[74] The sustained seduction of the theatregoer, so the *Pratique* repeats time and again, should not be hindered by an overcharged discourse and rhetoric: "se sentant la memoire accablée de tant de chose et l'imagination confuse, il se fâche contre soy-même, et ensuitte contre le Poëte, et enfin il abandonne tout sans plus écouter."[75] Textual moderation, so important to the *discours classique*, might well be described as a regulating convention of d'Aubignac's theatrical rhetoric. As d'Aubignac sees it, "il ne faut pas laisser le Spectateur sur son appétit, aussi ne faut-il pas le souler; il faut le combler de satisfaction, et non pas l'accabler."[76] The structure of theatrical desire described by d'Aubignac is a delicate system dependent on the balanced introduction of images, action, and rhetorical figures. Too much or too little of a good thing diminishes one's desire to consume it. D'Aubignac's theatre soothes, teases, strokes, and frustrates—all very gently.

The predominance of neoclassical notions in the *Pratique* could well account for the widespread misalignment of d'Aubignac's text as an apparatus faithful only to the ideology of theatrical portraiture. If we merely cite the book for passages that display the conventional vocabulary of theatre history, the *Pratique* is likely to be classical. But even though d'Aubignac preaches moderation, his text is excessive to the core. It not only indirectly challenges the ideology of the visible, but goes so far as to deny the legitimacy of dramatic mimesis. D'Aubignac insists that theatrical practice and method concern much more than imitation, re-production, and visual presentation. The novelty of the *Pratique*—whether in its seventeenth-century context or in view of its Italian, humanist precursors—stems from D'Aubignac's unique elaboration of the many different methods of "non-representation," of "le genie du theatre." It hardly needs to be said that the message of the *Pratique* not only enlarges the scene of theatricality to include the psychology of the theatregoer, as the Jansenists charged, but also complicates the subject matter and idiom of our contemporary critical discussions of seventeenth-century theatre and its theatrical tradition. To historians who look to *Le Prince* instead of *Le Peuple* in studying the genius of early French dramatic literature, it may seem odd that d'Aubignac would undermine the privileged position of the princely literary subject by stressing the performance of the spectators. Yet, d'Aubignac sets his dramatic norm according to "ces Ames vulgaires" with little concern for drawing class boundaries. Smacking of ideological betrayal, the abbé's theatre project might even be argued to go as far as enhancing the bourgeoisie's ability to think representationally, to see colors *as* colors, ideology as ideology, and "plaisirs legitimes" as its own privileged terrain of desire and legitimation. Perhaps the most fitting way to summarize the theoretical effect of the *Pratique* on neoclassical theatre and its modern commentators is to cite d'Aubignac's own anxieties about the paradox of his brand of theatrical legitimation:

> On pourroit peut-estre s'imaginer que le Discours où nous allons entrer, ne seroit pas une instruction avantageuse au Poëte, mais plustost au contraire une pratique capable de détruire tous les agrémens du Theatre.[77]

11

Subliminal Genius:
Energetic Spectating,
Deconstructive Praxis

> Je m'attens bien qu'il y en aura plusieurs qui déclineront la jurisdiction de Longin, qui condamneront ce qu'il approve, et qui loüeront ce qu'il blâme. C'est le traitement qu'il doit attendre de la plûpart des Juges de nostre siecle. Ces Hommes accoûtumez aux débauches et aux excés des Poëtes modernes, et qui n'admirant que ce qu'il n'entendent point, ne pensent pas qu'un Auteur se soit élevé, s'ils ne l'ont entierement perdu de veuë; ces petits Esprits, dis-je, ne seront pas sans doute fort frappez des hardiesses judicieuses des Homeres, des Platons et des Demosthenes. Ils chercheront souvent le Sublime dans le Sublime.
>
> BOILEAU, "Préface" to Longinus[1]

Boileau directs the above comments at seventeenth-century writers, like the Abbé d'Aubignac, who spurn blind identification with "les Regles des Anciens." Endorsing the position that contemporary method and practice should provide at least some of the models for seventeenth-century artistic endeavors, d'Aubignac's texts are outspoken opponents of unquestioning loyalty to classicism. His *Conjectures academiques*, for example, denies the existence of Homer and challenges uncritical acquiescence to classical writings on poetry. "Mais quoi, dira-t-on, Aristote étoit-il capable d'être ébloüi par ces petits esprits, & n'a-t-il pas assez bien examiné les oeuvres d'Homere, puisqu'il en a tiré les regles de son art poëtique? Le nom de cet illustre Philosophe pourroit faire tomber les armes des mains de ceux qui suivroient aveuglément l'autorité; mais d'ailleurs ceux qui ne veulent déferer qu'à la raison, sans que les exemples fameux, ni les grands noms les puissent engager contre elle, ne se rendent pas, qu'ils ne soient entierement convaincus, & j'ay des scrupules qui m'empêchent de suivre le sentiment d'Aristote dans le sujet dont nous parlons."[2] The abbé here expresses skepticism of the authority carelessly attributed to certain classical authors and warns of the critical dangers inherent in the acceptance of unchallenged ancient paradigms. Reasonable "moderns" are asked by d'Aubignac to reread the classics with a cautious mind. They are asked, so Boileau might charge, to seek "le Sublime dans le Sublime."

The quarrel over the ancients and the moderns continues today; only now the moderns of the seventeenth-century constitute the classical academy. Twentieth-century (post)moderns, subscribing to the precepts of deconstructive philosophy and Freudian representational theory, ponder the legitimacy of French neoclassical notions of communication, referentiality, and subjectivity—the notions underlying the allegories of seventeenth-century English and French authorship and patronage, as well as the discourses of authority and power. Contemporary readers from Jean-Luc Nancy and Philippe Lacoue-Labarthe to Louis Marin and Michel Foucault delineate carefully and laboriously the paradigms upon which French neoclassicism is often understood to depend: Cartesian subjectivity and perception, univocal linguistic signification, sociological and metaphysical hierarchy, and, most pertinent to my concluding remarks on theatrical legitimation, the valorization of neoclassical authorship and theoretical uniformity in view of norms of critical, even semiotic, "reason." It is this set of highly charged referents which we suspiciously classify as the neoclassical "ideal" or "*épistemé*."

Reason Sublime

Our cautious attentiveness to this *épistemé* derives in part from its acceptance and institutionalization by our philosophical predecessors. If we turn to Ernst Cassirer's elaborate systematization of French neoclassical aesthetics, to cite one extremely influential writer on the history of philosophy, we will hear resonances of aesthetic principles discussed throughout the preceding analysis of forms of theatrical legitimation. In *The Philosophy of the Enlightenment*, Cassirer prefaces his sensitive discussion of early eighteenth-century aesthetics with a less astute overview of the neoclassical system. He understands neoclassicism to consist of a code of ideal scientific principles which had to be adopted by the seventeenth-century producers and consumers of aesthetic objects (and, he implies, principles which should be imitated by twentieth-century readers). He writes that precise principles of reason, logic, grammar, and perception regulate the creation and the experience of a neoclassical work of art. My preceding discussions of theatrical legitimation also turn repeatedly to reflections on the regulatory role of grammar, logic, and reason in aesthetic practice, but in a way significantly different from Cassirer's inscription of grammatical regulation as a "deep" representational structure of aesthetics. Although my text dwells on the complex sets of aesthetic rules and methods generated by seventeenth-century French and, to a lesser degree, English culture, it does so to emphasize how the English and French antitheatrical activists appropriated logical and grammatical methods to regulate the less predictable rhetorical and subliminal performances underlying the rational (super-)structures of seventeenth-century aesthetics. In a more thorough summary of Cassirer's understanding of early French norms of dramatic aesthetics, I wish to retrace these relations one last time.

Citing Descartes's *Règles pour la direction de l'esprit*, Cassirer stresses "pure" thought and "rational" perception as the essential factors of French neoclassical aesthetics. The goal of such artistic representation is, in Cassirer's words, "to keep the imagination in check and to regulate it deliberately":

> Seen in this light all sense properties and qualities are sifted out and regulated from the realm of truth to that of subjective illusion. What then remains as the real nature of the object is not that which the object presented to direct perception but certain pure relations which can be expressed in terms of exact and universal rules. These rules, which apply to general relations and proportions, are therefore the fundamental framework of all being. They are the norm from which being cannot deviate and which it cannot abandon without sacrificing its real character as being, that is, as objective truth. Classical aesthetics was modeled after this theory of nature and after this mathematical theory point by point.[3]

To appreciate the "being" of the aesthetic object and to represent it faithfully, so this argument maintains, the interlocutors of neoclassical drama must be able to imitate, to trace point by point (*perspectiva legitima*), the epistemological method of its authorial invention. Above all, this method entails control over the imagination through the exercise of the rational codes governing the poet. The spectator or reader must be attentive at all times to the illusions of sense perception beyond which lie the pure forms, the objective truth, of aesthetic artifacts, beauty, and order. The neoclassical critic, asserts Cassirer,

> cannot compete with the creations of nature, he cannot breathe real life into his forms unless he knows the laws of this order, and unless he is completely imbued with these laws. The fundamental conviction of classical criticism is summed up and brought to a focus in a didactic poem by M. J. Chénier: "It is good sense, reason, which achieves all: virtue, genius, spirit, talent, taste. What is virtue? It is reason put into practice. And talent? Reason brilliantly set forth. Spirit? Reason well expressed. Taste is simply refined good sense, and genius is reason sublime."[4]

Such a prescription for neoclassical criticism returns us once again to an allegory of genius. In Cassirer's view, any legitimate criticism of neoclassical theatre is itself sustained by genius, or more specifically, by genius as "reason sublime."

Of particular interest to my discussion is the fact that Cassirer turns to d'Aubignac in citing precedents for the formulation of critical genius: "This parallelism [of the arts and sciences] had been explained on the grounds of the common derivation of the arts and sciences from the absolutely homogeneous and sovereign power of 'reason.' This power knows no compromise and tolerates no qualification. Not to acknowledge the power of reason as an integral and undivided whole and not to entrust oneself to this power without reserve, is to deny and destroy its real nature. 'In all matters which depend on reason and common sense, such as the rules of the theater,' says d'Aubignac in his work *Theatrical Practice* . . . , 'license is a crime which is never permitted.'"[5] By limiting the discussion of theatrical legitimation to the sovereign power of reason over criticism (which my introductory chapter introduces as the will of Habermas), Cassirer rests content with emphasizing the epistemological certainties of d'Aubignac's theory. It would not be difficult to stress d'Aubignac's own references to the poetic powers of "reason sublime." His readers could cite, for example, his attentiveness to poetic mastery and order: "Je sçay bien que le Poëte en est le Maistre, qu'il dispose l'ordre et l'oeconomie de sa piece comme il luy plaist."[6] And they could develop this citation by emphasizing the relation of such economy to d'Aubignac's own veiled reference to an allegory of sublime genius: "Longin nous a dit, comme nous l'avons observé, que [l'Odysée] n'est pas d'un stile si fort, ni d'un genre d'écrire si relevé que l'Iliade. . . . Voila juger d'un auteur, d'une maniere assez nouvelle; car pour le stile, les differens sujets que l'on traite en font presque toûjours la difference; quand il est grand, les pensées, les expressions, les figures, les termes, tiennent du genre sublime; & pour peu qu'un Poëte ait de genie, la matiere l'y porte d'elle-même."[7] D'Aubignac's "novel" manner of evaluating authorship thus gauges genius in relation to the poet's scientific mastery of the sublime.

Consideration of other seventeenth-century, French theoreticians reveals a similar attentiveness to such an economy of sublime reason. Prior to the publication of d'Aubignac's treatise, the Abbé du Pures also hinted at an unspoken prescriptive relation of aesthetics to authorial reason and the sublime: "Je sçay bien que tous ses moments sont precieux et destinez à de sublimes pensées, d'où [quelque Idée d'un divertissement digne de V. M.] ne descende que par raison."[8] This stress on the power of reason is later taken up by Boileau who is remembered today especially for his prescription to the poet: "Aimez donc la Raison. Que toûjours vos écrits / Empruntent d'elle seule et leur lustre et leur prix."[9] Finally, we could follow Cassirer's path to the Enlightenment by stressing du Bos's remarks that "la plupart des Peintres & des Poëtes ne jugent point par voie de sentiment, ni en déférant au goût naturel perfectionné par les comparaisons & par l'expérience, mais par voie d'analyse. Ils ne jugent pas en hommes doués de ce sixiéme sens dont nous avons parlé, mais en Philosophes spéculatifs."[10] From du Pures to du Bos, the codes of aesthetic production and judgment reflect notions of the sublime reason of philosophical speculation. Regardless of the obvious critical differences distinguishing the French theoreticians writing during the century-long development of neoclassical aesthetics, these citations illustrate the theorists' common fascination with the garb of reason.

Still, my previous chapter suggests that d'Aubignac shows colors compromising his membership in this classical club of speculative philosophy, this club which "knows no compromise and tolerates no qualifications." Although he juxtaposes the poet's power or "reason sublime" with the colorful rhetoric of the "genre sublime," the figures and effects of eloquence stimulate representations Other than those provided by speculative reflections on authorship. *La Pratique du théâtre* goes so far as to describe a sort of precarious balancing act between the libidinal pleasure of spectacle and the rational power of authorship. If a play's representation is pleasing, the authorial source remains hidden. The spectators become engrossed in the delights of their imaginations, not in speculation on the rational order of a poet's creation. But the moment that eloquence, the "genre sublime," reveals the slightest fault, thus calling attention to the play's fictionality, the spectators shift their attention to the authorial source of displeasure: "Dés-lors que la Catastrophe est prévenuë par la faute du Poëte, les Spectateurs sont dégoûtez, non pas tant de ce qu'ils sçavent la chose, que de s'appercevoir qu'on ne devroit pas leur dire; leur mécontentement procedant moins en ces occasions de leur connoissance, quoy que certaine, que de l'imprudence du Poëte."[11] Such an imperfect dramatic presentation lacks sufficient color to eclipse its source, "reason sublime." When a representation is thus marred, the spectator substitutes reason for imagination and unpleasantly ponders the character of the flawed poetic master, "l'imprudence du Poëte." Spectatorial desires for pleasure here yield the stage to judgments of method and authorial reason.

The Sublime Turn

This last point is crucial for an understanding of the almost prophetic nature of d'Aubignac's complex concept of theatrical practice. His discourse indirectly calls for the reevaluation of the critical primacy of the allegory of authorial genius, not to mention the portraiture of patronage. D'Aubignac displaces these two important figures of genius—authorship and patronage—both as the definitive categories of critical reflection and as the legitimate subjects of dramatic literature. This is not to say that d'Aubignac lacks respect for authors, whether poetic or princely; he claims to write his treatise "pour faire connoistre au Peuple, l'excellence de leur Art. . . . En quoy, certes, il me semble que je pourray contribuer quelque chose, non seulement à la gloire de nos Poëtes; mais encore au plaisir de tout le Monde."[12] Yet, this citation reminds us that whenever d'Aubignac dwells on the author's natural endowment with "reason sublime," he frames his remarks in the context of another kind of epistemological structure, the spectator's "plaisirs legitimes." In juxtaposition with authorial reason, the subliminal pleasures of spectating here assume the critical position of aesthetic measure.

In view of the tendency of the critical tradition to judge neoclassical aesthetics according to the criteria of its epistemological certainty, we arrive at the allegorical threat of a poetics sustained by the deceits and ruptures of its own interpretational enterprise. For d'Aubignac's paradoxical position, so I want to stress in these closing remarks, was not atypical of the poetics we know as constituting the neoclassical *épistemé*. As Cassirer himself suggests, the representation of "reason sublime" was compromised throughout the late seventeenth century by the growing legitimation of subliminal pleasure as the criteria of aesthetic experience. From Jonson and Richelieu to d'Aubignac, Boileau, Bouhours, du Bos, and other contemporary allegorizers of genius, the scene of theatrical legitimation favors a critical enterprise dependent, however reluctantly, on a two-faced figure of genius: one constitutive of the aesthetics of reason and the other embodied in a critical move toward reproductive pleasure. The early-modern acknowledgment of criticism's figurations of and through desire reflects what Boileau ironically coined as "le sublime dans le sublime." Or, in a more contemporary frame, this double face of the sublime resembles the literary thread rewoven by Neil Hertz in *The End of the Line: Essays on Psychoanalysis and the Sublime*. In Hertz's words, this is "the movement of disintegration and figurative reconstitution I have been calling the sublime turn."[13]

In drawing a rough sketch of the Janus-faced image of genius, we need to remember that the critics figuratively reconstructed throughout this book always balance notions of authorship—a certain weighty idea of rationalized genius—with corresponding, but not necessarily epistemologically synonymous, notions of spectatorship. We might first take a closer look at the picture of authorship which is most familiar to literary history. Among the French writers of the late seventeenth and early eighteenth century, Dominique Bouhours and the Abbé du Bos draw particularly sharp sketches of the rational side of genius. First, Bouhours, in *Les entretiens d'Ariste et d'Eugene*, develops his well-known equation of genius with the enigmatic "je ne sçay quoy":

> le génie est une habileté particuliere, & un talent que la nature donne
> à quelques hommes pour de certaines choses ... il ne suffit pas
> d'avoir de l'esprit & de l'imagination pour exceller dans la poësie; il
> faut estre né Poëte, & avoir ce naturel qui ne dépend ni de l'art, ni de
> l'étude; & qui tient quelque chose de l'inspiration.... C'est un don
> du ciel où la terre n'a point de part; c'est je ne sçay quoy de divin, qui
> rend un bel esprit.[14]

Bouhours's presentation of poetic genius as a primary condition of theatrical legitimation depicts writers (like Jonson) and political figures (like Richelieu) as endowed with a certain phantasmatic "something," a "je ne sçay quoy" distinguishing them from their peers and spectators.

This "something" points, moreover, to two underlying epistemological, as well as ideological, traditions which my analyses have noted on numerous occasions, if only in passing. First, and some literary historians might want to say foremost, the echoes of the metaphysical tradition of the tense religious challenges to theatrical practice resound throughout Bouhours's reminder that the "je ne sçay quoy" is a working trace of religious roots. At a later moment in *Les entretiens d'Ariste et d'Eugene*, Bouhours elaborates on this relation: "pour parler chrestiennement du je ne sçay quoy, n'y en a-t-il un dans nous, qui nous fait sentir, malgré toutes les foiblesses & tous les desordres de la nature corrompuë, que nos ames sont immortelles; que les grandeurs de la terre ne sont pas capables de nous satisfaire; qu'il y a quelque chose au dessus de nous, qui est le terme de nos desirs, & le centre de cette felicité que nous cherchons par tout, & que nous trouvons nulle part."[15] Underlying such a notion of genius is the ideology of religious presence which both the Jansenists and the Puritans fought hard to protect. Threatened by the many aspects of theatrical performance, this legacy channels desire into a theology through which the sublime signifies grace in the guise of genius.[16] Second, I turn to another ideological structure understandable only through the graceful lens of metaphysics. The overbearing representation of grace remained juxtaposed sociologically with the differing public and court productions of theatrical inspiration. Aesthetic performances by Jonson and Richelieu, as well as by the critical enterprises surrounding them, lent themselves less to theological transcendence than to secular ideological phantasms of critical and governmental centralization. While Ben Jonson's folio transferred the allure of "aura" from the Biblical scriptures to the original scripts of a playwright's book, Richelieu's theatrical performances turned the psychology of religious passion, defined by the Jansenist opponents of the stage, to the advantage of his obvious political transformation from cardinal to prince. In these cases, writers and politicians skilled in the subtle performance of allegorical representation successfully adapted the representational structures of theological belief to the secular scene of theatrical legitimation.[17]

By the time of the Abbé du Bos's early eighteenth-century texts, any such representational shifts expressed less a tension between theological and secular positions than the significant epistemological difference between speculative philosophy and libidinal poetics. The Abbé du Bos's *Réflexions critiques sur la poësie et sur la peinture* includes a particularly pointed discussion of the philosophical foundation of reason sublime. Du Bos highlights the epistemological background of late seventeenth-century aesthetics in linking genius with philosophical method: "l'esprit philosophique, qui n'est autre chose que la raison fortifiée par la réflexion & par l'expérience, & dont le nom seul auroit été nouveau pour les Anciens, est excellent pour composer des livres qui enseignent à ne point faire de fautes en écrivant, il est excellent pour mettre en évidence celles qu'aura faites un Auteur."[18] Du Bos asserts that the philosophical enterprise equips criticism with the analytical tools of reason, and gives rise to its own distinctive performativity through the technical evaluation of dramatic poetry, what du Bos calls its *mise-en-évidence.* Unlike any theatrical *mise-en-scène,* philosophy's performance of poetic evidence generates a literary analysis which Derrida has coined as "la production d'une idéalité objective," a production (or performance) in which aesthetics becomes a calculable and objective science.[19] The early-modern, institutional reproduction of the rules of art through standardized codes of aesthetic writing and reading stands forth as a dependable and quantifiable enterprise of "une idéalité objective." Most importantly, such "une idéalité objective," which brings to mind the codified presentations of both Jonson and Richelieu, sustains the neoclassical tradition of reason sublime. As Derrida suggests, the modern notion of quantifiable aesthetic truth stems from the Cartesian trust in language as the certain propositional connection of subject and predicate, as the production of the knowledge of truth. Thus, the differing mental and rhetorical spaces of the theatrical *mise-en-scène* can be understood to be stabilized through propositions of evidence and rules— through reason sublime. This process, moreover, bears a strong resemblance to most of the productions of theatrical legitimation discussed in the preceding pages, productions which tend to diminish the psycho-political variants of theatricality and its institutional manifestations by relegating them to an epistemology of the same.

In admiring philosophy's *mise-en-évidence*, the Abbé du Bos, however, emphasizes a curiously performative distinction between speculative philosophy and aesthetic evaluation. He writes that "[l'esprit philosophique] apprend mal à juger d'un poëme en général. Les beautés qui en font le plus grand mérite, se sentent mieux qu'elles ne se connoissent par la regle & par le compas."[20] More than once du Bos stresses the critical hazards posed by an overdependence on philosophical speculation which is given more to verifiable technical prognosis than to artistic and affective evaluation. Judgment of either a painting or a theatrical performance is a quite different activity for du Bos from the methodical measurement of an artifact's conformity to aesthetic rules and method. In emphasizing that "la réputation d'un poëme s'établit par le plaisir qu'il fait à tous ceux qui le lisent," du Bos stresses the potential danger of sublime reason as a hard and fast code of reading: "les hommes ne sont donc pas autant exposés à être dupés en matiere de poësie qu'en matiere de Philosophie."[21] Offering a particularly notable warning to his modern readers, du Bos makes the subtle observation that "la prévention du genre humain, en faveur d'un systême de Philosophie, ne prouve pas même qu'il doive continuer d'avoir cours durant les trente années suivantes. Les hommes peuvent être désabusés par la vérité."[22] The clarifying truth of aesthetics, moreover, is less a result of philosophical reason than of theatrical pleasure and aesthetic sensibility: "Le mérité réel consiste à plaire & à toucher. Le mérite de comparaison consiste à toucher autant ou plus que certains Autheurs dont le rang est déja connu."[23]

The reader begins to recognize, then, that the legitimation of reason by the aesthetic theory of the period does not occur without a paradoxical counter-nurturing of spectatorship and its psycho-political idiosyncracies. This is nowhere more poignant than in Boileau's *L'art poétique*, which indirectly undercuts the rational foundation of aesthetics by insisting that "le secret est d'abord de plaire et de toucher: / Inventez des ressorts qui puissent m'attacher."[24] As suggested by my close reading of *La Pratique du théâtre*, similar neoclassical displacements of authorial control into the realm of pleasure and desire are just as likely to undermine critical centralization as to sustain it. Take for example Bouhours's analysis of the phenomenological infelicity of authorial genius. It suggests that any aesthetic presentation nurtures mechanisms more libidinal than representational: "le je ne sçay quoy est de la nature de ces choses, qu'on ne connoist que par les effets qu'elles produisent. . . . Il attire les coeurs les plus dures, il excite quelque fois de violentes passions dans l'ame, il y produit quelque fois de tres-nobles sentimens."[25] In relegating the representation of genius to the realm of libidinal passion and affection, Bouhours positions the "je ne sçay quoy" on extremely uncertain terrain. In his words, "il ne se fait jamais connoistre que par là. Son prix et son avantage consiste à estre caché."[26]

Appreciation of this other side of aesthetic method leads the critic into delicate of areas of performance and perception where aesthetic measure and political control might always be eclipsed by the grandeur of pleasure or effect. Such a sublime turn suggests not only Bouhours's understanding of the aesthetic experience but also his methods as a critical writer. No longer bound merely by the dictates of epistemological certainty and speculative reason, this spectator of theatre and art is forced by the nature of the sublime (and I might also say, following Lacan, by the lure of interpretive transference)[27] to alter the geometric codes, the *perspectiva legitima*, of analytical practice. It is in *La Maniere de bien penser dans les ouvrages d'esprit* that Bouhours most vividly reveals the seduction as well as the threat of the critical sublime. In this text, Bouhours maintains that "la sublimité, la grandeur dans une pensée est justement ce qui emporte, & ce qui ravit,"[28] thereby shifting the boundaries of aesthetic genius from the representational certainty of reason to the less predictable side of the sublime, to the "je ne sçay quoy" of aesthetic ravishment. Yet, in acknowledging the force of the sublime, Bouhours seems to attempt to regain a critical foothold by supplementing and thus sublimating his notion of the sublime with the terminology of measure: "la délicatesse ajoûte je ne sçay quoy au sublime & à l'agréable."[29] Here the "je ne sçay quoy" stands apart from the sublime, as its supplement, signifying a sociocritical category, "la délicatesse." Now the unframable sublime is bound, sublimated, by the ordering conventions of the *discours classique.*[30]

But what happens if the reader positions this moment in Bouhours's text in relation to Freud's warning about the relative insufficiency of the psychological countermeasures of sublimation. "Sub-limation," writes Freud in *Introductory Lectures in Psychoanalysis*, "is never able to deal with more than a certain fraction of libido, quite apart from the fact that many people are gifted with only a small amount of capacity to sublimate."[31] Sublimation can work to enhance as well as to block the fertility of the libidinal functions. In this context, further consideration of Bouhours's definition of "la délicatesse" may suggest more about the method of narrative sub-limation than about its ability to give measure to the sublime. For it is precisely when Bouhours turns aside from the sublime that his text activates "the sublime turn" as the critical apparatus from which it cannot escape:

> Mais quand vous me demandez ce que c'est qu'une pensée délicate, je ne sçay où prendre des termes pour m'expliquer. Ce sont de ces choses qu'il est difficile de voir d'un coup d'oeil, & qui à force d'estre subtils nous échapent lors que nous pensons les tenir. Tout ce qu'on peut faire, c'est de les regarder de prés, & à diverses reprises, pour parvenir peu à peu à les connoistre.[32]

Varying perspectives and repeated study present the viewer with alternating visions of "la délicatesse" as both difference and as *différance*, insofar as critical sight of the sublime here inscribes itself in deferral. The sublime turn in this instance is generated by its ulti-mate product, not the nominal stability of "la délicatesse," but the critical infelicity of its foundational terms: "je ne sçay où." Follow-ing this position, we would need to admit that neither the phantas-matic gaze of any perspectival theatre nor the instillation of belief in the rational recovery of authorial perspective guarantees aesthetic representation.

Bouhours himself affirms the ever-present threat of critical "double sens" when cautioning iconographers against the polysemy of allegorical representation. Political emblems, he writes, "pris en un sens allegorique ou hieroglyphique ne sont point legitimes."[33] But even while warning critics to beware of "les pures équivoques," Bouhours counters himself by admitting that "toutes les figures qui renferment un double sens, ont chacune en leur espece des beautez & des graces qui les font valoir."[34] In a curious and fascinating way, Bouhours's own experience as a critical writer leads him to acknowledge the powerful seduction of subliminal praxis. Or, as expressed in the philosophical language of Cassirer, "aesthetic 'rea-son,' as Bouhours points out, is not tied to this limit of the 'clear

and distinct.'. . . That strictly 'linear' thought which classical aesthetics established as its norm is insufficient here, for the straight
line is the shortest distance between two points only in geometry,
not in aesthetics. Bouhours's aesthetics, which is based on the principle of '*délicatesse*,' seeks rather to teach the art of indirection and
to maintain its validity and fruitfulness. An aesthetically valuable
thought almost always makes use of this art in arriving at its goal,
which is to startle the mind, and so to imbue it with a new impulse
and new energy."[35]

Tearful Readers

Similar enraptured efforts to juxtapose aesthetic grace and subliminal energy, the less predictable determinants of genius and its
reception, dominate French treatises on aesthetics penned during
the late seventeeth century's proliferation of theory and criticism.
Critical measurements of subliminal effects are especially pro-
nounced in treatises concerning art. One particularly interesting
presentation on "le sublime dans le sublime" appears in Antoine
Coypel's *L'excellence de le peinture*. To Coypel, aesthetic genius
does more than elicit pleasure-filled responses to reasonably measured artistic creations. As if exaggerating d'Aubignac's and Boileau's more cautious pronouncements, Coypel excitedly proclaims
that,

> Le grand peintre ne doit pas seulement plaire, mais il doit émouvoir
> et ravir, comme les grands poètes et les grands orateurs. Il doit, sem-
> blable à ces musiciens si vantés par l'antiquité, tantôt inspirer la tris-
> tesse jusqu'à tirer des larmes, tantôt exciter les ris, enflammer de col-
> ère, et forcer les spectateurs de témoigner leur admiration et leur
> étonnement, en exprimant non seulement les passions, mais encore
> en les excitant. En effet, c'est là le sublime de la peinture et le plus
> grand mérite du peintre.[36]

Perhaps more than any other passage I have noted so far, this one
situates the sublime in the realm of an active critical enterprise. For
here, the aim of the sublime is no longer merely to excite the passions, to engage the spectator in subliminal performance, but to
force the spectators to read through their tears, to acknowledge
through their display of admiration that the greatest merit of art lies
in their exciting coproduction of subliminal effects.

Especially striking about Coypel's description of the sublime is its exaggerated emphasis on theatricalized tears and laughter as a critical discourse, indeed as the only discourse truly capable of expressing sublime genius. Such an implosion of rational speculation and critical sublimation not only calls to mind the antitheatricalists' deepest fears of the passionate effects of theatre, but also emphasizes the very high stakes of the period's discourse on the sublime. If tears are the products of sublime genius, something Other than the rational norms of centralized authorship or patronage becomes legitimized by Coypel's doubling of sublime art with subliminal re-presentation.

For a particularly intense and fascinating attempt to formulate this "je ne sçay quoy," I could hardly do better than return to du Bos's *Réflexions critiques sur la poësie et sur la peinture*. Du Bos's text provides perhaps the most balanced and direct discussion of the double sublime. Du Bos follows tradition in discussing how some writers and painters may judge aesthetic products according to objective criteria of method and norms, what he calls "son mérite étranger."[37] But he also steps aside from this tradition by dismissing such alien objectivity as the essential factor of critical judgment:

> L'ouvrage plaît-il, ou ne plaît-il pas? L'ouvrage est-il bon ou mauvais en général? C'est la même chose. Le raisonnement ne doit donc intervenir dans le jugement que nous portons sur un poëme ou sur un tableau en général, que pour rendre raison de la décision du sentiment, & pour expliquer quelles fautes l'empêchent de plaire.[38]

Stressing the crucial role of pleasure in critical judgment, du Bos favors the desirous spectator as aesthetics' best judge. He explains that "non-seulement le public juge d'un ouvrage sans intérêt, mais il en juge encore ainsi qu'il en faut décider en général, c'est-à-dire, par la voie du sentiment, & suivant l'impression que le poëme ou le tableau font sur lui."[39]

To present his view of the aesthetic sublime, du Bos turns to consideration of what "Coypel en a tiré": "c'est le caractere propre de ces inventions sublimes [de Poussin] que le génie seul fait trouver, que de paroître tellement liées avec le sujet, qu'il semble qu'elles ayent dû être les premieres idées qui se soient présentées aux Artisans, qui ont traité le sujet."[40] To both Coypel and du Bos, sublime invention is less a technical apparatus of reason than an imaginative performance of genius. Invention here inscribes itself in the economy of desire and pleasure whereby the codes of aesthetics shift in accordance with the sublimal economy of the psyche. Stressing the sublime fluidity of both Poussin's painting of the Crucifixion and La Fontaine's fables, du Bos declares that critical access to these inventions is as open to the spectator as it is to the author: "le premier mouvement du Lecteur est de croire qu'il les eût trouvés aussi bien que [La Fontaine]."[41] This reciprocality of sublime invention puts the spectator on a performative plane as productive as the author's.[42]

To du Bos, the generation of critical energy constitutes the primary aim of the aesthetic enterprise. Considering authorship, he cherishes Aristotle's mention of the poet "qui ne composoit jamais mieux, que lorsque sa fureur poëtique alloit jusques à la frénésie."[43] Shifting his focus to the dramatic production of similar fury, he favors theatrical performance over silent reading: "Dès que la simple récitation ajoute tant d'énergie au poëme, il est facile de concevoir quel avantage les pieces qui se déclament sur un théâtre, tirent de la représentation."[44] In contrast to the antitheatricalists who condoned dramatic reading only as a measured literary enterprise of the college or cabinet, du Bos validates recitation's rhetorical forcefulness on the stage. He acknowledges the (non)representational energies of imagination and passion, however slight or extreme, to be the sole force of poetics, its "mérite réel," deserving of ultimate critical legitimation.

Although these early-modern references to desire and pleasure sound hollow in their lack of the symbolic specificity of post-Kantian critique, du Bos is actually somewhat precise in delineating the sublime features of spectatorship. In fact his treatise is unusual in its development of an allegory of spectatorial genius. On one level, du Bos praises the ability of all spectators to experience aesthetic pleasure. On another, however, he differentiates between mere viewing and spectatorial invention:

tant que les traits propres à ce caractere [théâtral], & qui doivent servir à le dessiner, demeurent noyés & confondus dans une infinité de discours & d'actions que les bienséances, la mode, la coutume, la profession & l'intérêt font faire à tous les hommes à peu près du même air, & d'une maniere si uniforme que leur caractere ne s'y décele qu'imperceptiblement, il n'y a que ceux qui sont nés avec le génie de la Comédie, qui puissent les discerner. Eux seuls peuvent dire quel caractere résulterait de ces traits, si ces traits étoient détachés des actions & des discours indifférens, si ces traits rapprochés les uns des autres, étoient immédiatement réunis entr'eux. Enfin discerner les caracteres de la Nature, c'est invention.[45]

The reader might be tempted to see this passage as an illustration of du Bos's retreat to the essentialist position of Bouhours—that some of us have genius, some of us don't. Yet du Bos's notion of "génie de la Comédie" remains quite different from Bouhours's emphasis on "la délicatesse," on sublimation as the figure of poetic inspiration. Genius here operates in view of, but also aside from, the sublimational blur and confusion of the *discours classique*: "les bienséances, la mode, la coutume."

A particular feature of du Bos's treatise is its stress on genius as a trait of spectatorship, more than of creative authorship. Du Bos even could be said to be austere in his rejection of the idea of any innate superiority of writers over readers. "Les Artisans sans génie jugent moins sainement que le commun des hommes."[46] "Leur attention," he adds, "se porte toute entiere sur l'exécution méchanique, & c'est par-là qu'ils jugent tout l'ouvrage."[47] In repositioning invention as an activity of spectating or reading rather than writing, *Réflexions critiques* lends its support to an aesthetic involvement in which inventive discernment is wrapped in the fabric of pleasure, in contrast to poetry's rule merely by mechanical technique and the repetitive execution of the same aesthetic norms. The "génie de la Comédie" excels at reading because she performs critical invention in the realm of the senses. Discernment, then, sidesteps the ideality of objectivity and enters the subliminal side of the sublime.

Armed with his allegory of the "génie de la Comédie," du Bos challenges sublime reason as the dominant code of viewing or reading. I stress reading here since the theatrical genius performs her inventions beyond the generic boundaries of the playhouse. Throughout *Réflexions critiques*, this allegory of genius appears as a newly remembered figure of the history of aesthetic reception. This is especially notable when du Bos turns his attention to the *Aeneid*:

> Il est facile de prouver historiquement & par les faits, que Virgile & les autres Poëtes excellens de l'antiquité ne doivent point aux Colléges, ni aux préjugés, leur premiers admirateurs.... Les premiers admirateurs de Virgile furent ses compatriotes & ses contemporains. C'étoient des femmes, c'étoient des gens du monde, moins lettrés peut-être que ceux qui bâtissent à leur mode l'histoire de la réputation des grands Poëtes.[48]

Du Bos argues vigorously that aesthetic merits lie outside the borders of institutional codes of poetic mimesis and the history of critical sublimation. Turning aside from the melancholic repetition of rules of times past, as expressed through the deadly reason of the patriarchal colleges and philosophers, his treatise calls for a "lively" (female) aesthetics much like Virgil's, and recalling Samuel Johnson's disquieting "feminine arts." This would energize rather than numb the sensibilities of spectatorial genius:

> La langue dans laquelle l'Enéïde étoit écrite, étoit la langue vivante. Les femmes commes les hommes, les ignorans comme les sçavans, lurent ce poëme, & ils en jugerent par l'impression qu'il faisoit sur eux.... Ainsi ce fut l'impression que l'Enéïde faisoit sur tout le monde; ce furent les larmes que les femmes verserent à sa lecture, qui la firent approuver comme un poëme excellent.[49]

We return again to the tears of women, to the flowing waters of the passionate side of the sublime. These are the tears designating the mysterious psychic activity of representation in the wake of formal recognition of an energetic poetic style and merit. These are the traces par excellence of the pleasure of the text as it doubles with poetic invention.

In many respects, this evocation of an ideal, female reader might sound similar to a previous construct developed by Perrault in *Parallèle des anciens et des modernes*. As read critically by Elizabeth L. Berg, Perrault's treatise aligns early modernism with the potentially feminist voice of authoritative women readers more intuitively gifted than their male counterparts. In Berg's view, however, this favorable regard of female readers works only to foster the sociological authority of "a group of men seeking power—through the intermediary of women."[50] This happens, Berg argues, because the authority of female readers "is based precisely on a lack of education, which allows their instinctive good taste to operate unhampered by erudition or tradition."[51] Women here remain excluded from the dominant social hierarchy, the College of the Ideality of Objectivity, which the female torchbearers refuel at their own expense. To some degree, du Bos's treatise provides a concrete example of such institutional displacement when it distinguishes between the judgment of a play's "mérite réel" and its "mérite de comparaison." Du Bos asserts that "les contemporains jugent très bien du mérite réel d'un ouvrage, mais ils sont sujets à se tromper, quand ils jugent de son mérite de comparaison."[52] Ironically the public's strength at determining the "real" quality of a poem, "qui les touchent & qui lui plaisent," can work to undermine any consensus regarding a poem's proper merit in the scholarly annals of

Comparative Literature. Although du Bos continues to locate comparison in the realm of the senses, "le mérite de comparaison consiste à toucher autant ou plus que certains Autheurs dont le rang est déja connu,"[53] touch becomes a measure of professional, rather than theatrical, evaluation:

> On voit bien qu'il faut laisser juger au tems & à l'expérience quel rang doivent tenir les Poëtes nos contemporains parmi les Ecrivains qui composent ce recueil des livres qui font les hommes des Lettres de toutes les nations, & qu'on pourroit appeller *La Bibliothèque du genre humain.*[54]

Already in the eighteenth century, du Bos delimits the legitimate enterprise of literary comparison to a selective, historical branch of the academy of letters. Further confirming Berg's suspicions, the lasting, instinctual authority of contemporary spectators deserves but a marginal place in the eternally dominant "Bibliothèque du genre humain." While Comparative Literature may have its roots in the pleasure of the text, it derives its authority from the distanced (reasoned) collections assembled by "les hommes des Lettres de toutes les nations."

While I do not want to ignore these sociologically disturbing traces of the discipline of Comparative Literature, further consideration of du Bos's treatise on epistemological grounds might enact a more affirmative, subliminal erasure of the patriarchal specter of comparative literary history. In the context of the epistemological framework of the double sublime, du Bos's figure of the tearful "Genie de la Comédie" gives shape to a reader whose energetic inventions can be understood to deconstruct the figure of comparative authority per se.

I find it helpful to read *Réflexions critiques*'s paradoxical attempt to articulate a "real" poetics of energy—one deferring any "comparative" claims of historical ideality—in relation to *La Pratique du théâtre*'s experimentation with non-representational structures of desire. The parallel is particularly evident when du Bos, in clarifying the aesthetic structure of energy, echoes d'Aubignac's distinction between the logical grammar of argument and the energetic rhetoric of performance. In the first volume of *Réflexions critiques*, the early, eighteenth-century aesthetician compares the non-representationality of musical energy to the nature of the linguistic sign:

> Tous ces sons [de la Musique] . . . ont une force merveilleuse pour nous émouvoir, parce qu'ils sont les signes des passions, institués par

> la nature dont ils ont reçu leur énergie; au lieu que les mots articulés
> ne sont que des signes arbitraires des passions. Les mots articulés ne
> tirent leur signification & leur valeur que de l'institution des hommes,
> qui n'ont pu leur donner cours que dans un certain pays.[55]

In locating the naturalness of passion in the site of music, du Bos
echoes d'Aubignac's theory of the interval which maintains that the
musical presentation of what is not directly shown on stage often
comprises the most forceful and "pure" moments of performance.
Still, the most interesting aspect of this passage is how du Bos dis-
misses spoken words as but the arbitrary signs of the passions, thus
clearly articulating the sublimational function of language later discussed by Freud, Lacan, and most recently, Kristeva, who writes
that "la *sublimation* . . . n'est rien d'autre que la possibilité de nommer le pré-nominal, le pré-objectal, qui ne sont en fait qu'un trans-
nominal, un trans-objectal."[56] Du Bos makes his gesture to such a
trans-nominal referent of sublimation by stressing the (non-), (de-),
or (trans-)representational structure on which theatricality depends:
energy, the empty signifier and force of passion, the flip-side of the
ideological institution of objectivity, the Other of the symbolic institution of arbitrary signification.[57]

Sensus Communis / Sensual Division

In operation here is an aesthetics juxtaposing the institutional benefits of signification with the marvelous, performative power of theatrical energy. Yet, prolonged consideration of the epistemological
structures of du Bos's texts suggests that the trans-nominal referent
may well be fleeting at best. There are many moments in *Réflexions
critiques* that suggest the kind of sublime turn discussed by Hertz: a
literary movement of disintegration and figurative reconstitution.
This drive toward reconstitution, moreover, may well engineer the
ultimate structural domination of the symbolic over its Other. In
addition to the formal dominance of the "comparative" over the
"real," du Bos's text provides evidence of such literary trans-gres-
sion when it attempts the now somewhat familiar alignment of the
energies of passion with the sublimational machinery of *bon sens*:
"Le spectateur y conserve donc son bon sens, malgré l'émotion la
plus vive. C'est sans extravaguer qu'on s'y passione."[58] These turns
in du Bos's aesthetics may call to mind more recent reflections on

the sublime that emulate *Réflexions critiques* in describing the field of linguistic signification as the bar or limit between "l'émotion" and "bon sens." A case in point is a critical relation articulated in Thomas Weiskel's theoretically inspiring book, *The Romantic Sublime*. Weiskel astutely discusses the eighteenth-century discourse of the sublime, itself a potentially "general" or "universal" structure, in terms of a linguistic (legitimation) crisis. "The true function of the sublime," Weiskel suggests, "is to legitimate the necessary discontinuities in the classical scheme of signification and to justify the specific affective experience which these discontinuities entailed."[59] While such an alignment of the sublime with the effects of significational discontinuity amounts to an important shift away from the sublime as an engine of reason, its privileging stress on thoughts of legitimation reinscribes the sublime as a figure of the dominant modernist tradition led by Kant, who turns to the judgment of taste, *sensus communis aestheticus*, to delineate the horizon of law underlying the sublime.[60]

The psycho-political implications of the Kantian sublime are discussed by Lyotard in his recent book, *Le Différend*. In operating apart from the restrictions of logical cognition, the *sensus communis aestheticus* refers, Lyotard writes, "à la communauté qui se fait *a priori*, et qui se juge sans règle de présentation directe; simplement, la communauté est requise dans l'obligation morale par la médiation d'un concept de la raison, l'Idée de liberté, tandis que la communauté des destinateurs et des destinataires de la phrase sur le beau est appelé immédiatement, sans médiation d'aucun concept, par le seul sentiment, en ce qu'il est partageable *a priori*. Elle est déjà là comme goût, mais pas encore là comme consensus raisonnable."[61] While the *sensus communis aestheticus* may not depend directly on rational thought, it remains contingent on symbolic norms, what we recognize today as the Ground or Law of the Father. As Kant explains in the *Critique of Judgment*:

All intuitions which we supply to concepts *a priori* are therefore either *schemata* or *symbols*. . . . Thus the words *ground* (support, basis), *to depend* (to be held up from above), to *flow* from something (instead of, to follow), *substance* (as Locke expresses it, the support of accidents), and countless others are . . . symbolical hypotyposes and expressions for concepts, not by means of a direct intuition, but only by analogy with it, i.e. by the transference of reflection upon an object of intuition to a quite different concept to which it can never directly correspond.[62]

The modernist thrust of the discourse of taste has been to sustain the symbolical and its legal horizons by forgetting the very ground of transference, of hypotyposes, upon which it rests.

This tradition would dwell on the moments in Kant's "Analytic of the Sublime" that outline the refiguration of genius in the guise of taste. On its own grounds, genius is said to operate as an undisciplined enunciational mechanism: "it shows itself, not so much in the accomplishment of a definite concept, as in the enunciation or expression of aesthetical ideas which contain abundant material for that very design; and consequently it represents the imagination as free from all guidance of rules and yet as purposive in reference to the presentment of the given concept. . . . In accordance with these suppositions, genius is the exemplary originality of the natural gifts of a subject in the *free* employment of his cognitive faculties."[63] Still, the "freedom" of the Kantian Subject is encrusted with the many layers of the modernist reception of genius. In Kant's words, the transference of the literary product of genius through the field of enunciation "produces for other good heads a school, i.e. a methodical system of teaching according to rules."[64] Such schooled taste constitutes "the discipline (or training) of genius; it clips its wings, it makes it cultured or polished."[65]

This striking figure of disciplined genius, now fettered with clipped and cultured wings, re-turns my book circuitously to its much earlier, introductory discussion of the phantasm of symbolical consensus, of legitimation as a structure of institutional authority, accord, and domination. Indeed, the citation of Kant's reference to the inevitable offspring of genius, "a methodical system of teaching according to rules," echoes this book's different readings of the allegory of genius as its inscription in the complex epistemology of theatrical legitimation. This echo rings especially true in relation to my opening quotation of a passage from the *Legitimation Crisis* by Habermas. Cited again in this context, this passage now reads as almost a parody of Berg's warning about the symbolical, patriarchal power of early modernism, a power potentially fed by du Bos's two sides of the sublime (passionate energy and its institutional sublimation): "This transformation [of needs and feelings into normative expectations (precepts and values)] produces the distinction, rich in consequences, between the subjectivity of opinion, wanting, pleasure and pain, on the one hand, and the utterances and norms that appear with a *claim to generality* on the other. Generality means objectivity of knowledge and legitimacy of valid norms. Both insure the *community or shared meaning* that is constitutive for the socio-cultural life-world."[66] The ultimate critical product for Habermas is the chain of normative meaning sustaining the ideology of consensus, the cultured or polished products derived from Kant's symbolic judgment of taste.

Lyotard's reading of "The Analytic of the Sublime," however, places less stress on the *a posteriori*, the symbolic manifestations themselves, than on the figure of the *a priori*, the hypotyposes, the site of transference, "le seul sentiment, en ce qu'il est partageable a priori." On this level, the school of symbolical consensus, the college of objective ideality, quakes on its own divided ground, threatened by the disfigurations of transference, as exemplified in Lyotard's view by a specific historico-political example of hypotyposes: "l'enthousiasme populaire devant la Révolution."[67] Here the sublime genius begins to resemble du Bos's "Génie de la Comédie" as the site of transference, the divisible [*le partage*] per se. This is the fragile, energetic terrain sustaining any ideology of consensus, the site of reconstitution itself that always already undermines the figure of consensual authority. This is the cavity of "le sublime dans le sublime."

I would not want to conclude my study without recalling again how *Réflexions critiques* situates—whether strategically or unconsciously—such genius in the figures of the woman and the unlearned, in the figures of cultural and intellectual differentiation which remain juxtaposed with the "institution *des hommes*," the formal discipline of *Comparative* Literature. What is suggestive here is how the figure of the "Génie de la Comédie" evades the symbolic regime of (male) genius, the realm of the Subject exemplified throughout the pages of this book by the allegories of authorship and patronage. Du Bos's most evocative signs of division are those silent (dumb) tears of women, which manifest themselves openly as the wet site or springlike source of reading, the space of the divisible. This fecund feminine aspect of sublime genius might not only catch our eye but might recall contemporary, poststructural accounts of significant analogues of du Bos's "Génie de la Comédie."

I turn first to Kristeva's *Pouvoirs de l'horreur* which points to the sublime as the site of departure of any concept of subjectivity: "Non pas en deçà mais toujours avec et à travers la perception et les mots, le sublime est un *en plus* qui nous enfle, qui nous excède et nous fait être à la fois *ici*, jetés, et *là*, autres et éclatants. Écart, clôture impossible. Tout manqué, joie: fascination."[68] Replaying the primal scene of sublime fascination, the "Génie de la Comédie" might be said by Kristeva to be less a negative representation of the patriarchal symbolism dominating it—Law and Reason—than a performance on the other side of the Lacanian borderline: "un défi à la symbolisation. Que nous lui donnions le nom d'*affect* ou que nous le renvoyions à une sémiotisation infantile—pour laquelle les articulations pré-signifiantes ne sont que des *équations* et non pas des *équivalences* symboliques des objets, nous devons indiquer une nécessité de l'analyse. Cette nécessité, accentuée devant ce type de structure, consiste à ne pas réduire l'écoute analytique du langage à celle de l'idéalisme philosophique et de la linguistique à sa suite; il s'agit, bien au contraire, de poser une *hétérogénéité de la signifiance*. Il va de soi qu'on ne peut rien dire de cet hétérogène (affect ou sémiotique) sans l'homologuer au signifiant linguistique. Mais c'est précisément cette *impuissance* que viennent marquer le signifiant 'vide', la dissociation du discours."[69] This powerlessness, this heterogeneity returns Kristeva's reader to consideration of the maternal, the abject covered over by narcissism and symbolic law.

In a much different but analogous philosophical context, a reading of the relation between "Identité et tremblement" in Hegel, Jean-Luc Nancy reflects on the implications of Hegel's depiction of the mother as the (disfigured) genius of the child. The essence of the representation of such genius, division [*le partage*] as Subjectivity, is its sole presentational aspect:

> Le sujet, ici, naît. Il n'y a pas de présent de sa naissance—et il n'y en a pas non plus de représentation. Mais la naissance est le mode de la présence du coeur, c'est-à-dire du partage. Le Genius n'est pas l'individu, parce qu'il le partage: il le fait trembler, et il le partage d'avec et avec l'autre. Ce n'est pas une communauté immédiate et totale—comme s'il y avait un unique Genius de l'humanité—, car le Genius *est* la différence de l'individu, sans être l'individu lui-même. La naissance a lieu dans une communauté du partage—celle du sein de la mère, celle de l'amour, celle de l'être-ensemble-et-à-plusieurs. Le partage lui-même signifie la naissance (*partum*). Naître, ne pas avoir la naissance derrière soi, mais naître incessamment, dans le tremblement, c'est être partagé.[70]

It is in similar terms that du Bos distinguishes the singular act of thinking and writing from the incessant feminine energy of reading. The continual operation of reading generates responsive differentiation and hybrid reaction in contrast to institutional legitimation of standardized norms of reason or taste. The "Génie de la Comédie" is less a thinking Subject or institutionalized norm than a production of trembling, continually re-presenting the "sublime dans le sublime." Or, to turn once more to Nancy, "le tremblement n'est pas une image, il est le rythme de l'âme affectée, et le partage de l'inconscient, c'est-a-dire l'"inconscient' comme notre partage. Cela veut dire notre communauté, notre destin, notre Genius. Cela veut dire partagé par le génie de la 'nature féminine.' Mais ce Genius n'est pas *un*."[71]

Seen through the multiple mists of passion and female tears (the vapors feared by the eighteenth-century English school of Jonson & Johnson), the theoretical performance of genius in *Réflexions critiques* stands out as an historically specific example of allegorical praxis. Especially in regard to what might appear as philosophical imprecision in its allegorical turn to figures of "energy" and "female readers," *Réflexions critiques*'s articulation of the sublime stands aside from those later positions of Kant and Hegel, which incorporate, however differently, the sublime into the epistemology of the Subject. Du Bos's treatise sketches out a terrain and praxis of representational theory which is perhaps more akin to poststructural reading than to its own scene of early-modern, postCartesian epistemology. Its emphasis on libidinal energy is curiously evocative of Kristeva's psychoanalytical account of the sublime and Nancy's philosophical figure of Unconscious-Genius-Feminine Nature, both of which are foreshadowed by Lyotard's prolonged project of a deconstructive psycho-political criticism. In tracing the figures of desire in discourse, Lyotard's *Discours, figure*, for example, stresses an aspect of discourse Other than the sublimes of taste and reason which remain privileged by the complex tradition of speculative philosophy:

> une énergie autre s'y fait voir. Mais elle ne s'y fait pas *reconnaître*, évidemment; la reconnaissance appartient à l'ordre du préconscient, ordre du discours et ordre de la réalité. Cette énergie se manifeste de façon negative, menaçante, angoissante: désordre. Mais aussi elle dénonce l'ordre, elle annonce un autre "ordre," d'une autre nature; elle démasque la bonne forme, le bon objet, le discours clair. Ainsi la représentation onirique vue en état de veille ne pourrait être qu'une "mauvaise" représentation: une représentation dans laquelle notre désir ne pourrait pas s'accomplir, qui nous le renverrait réflechi. Et ainsi la même image illusioniste du rêve serait, transcrite dans la réalité (dans l'oeuvre), une image désillusionniste. Critique.[72]

As Lyotard, Kristeva, du Bos, and Nancy all argue in their radically differentiating ways, the allegory of impassioned genius clouds up the window of speculative philosophy with a tearful, implosive performance of itself. Energetic spectating always already critiques or, more specifically, deconstructs the mechanisms of reason and taste sublime.

At the same time, deconstructive praxis embraces the (il)logic of its own representational struggles. Du Bos would add that it operates much like the agonistic performance of the sort of love feared by Samuel Johnson, "on se querelle sans sujet, on se raccommode sans raison. Les idées des amans n'ont point de liaison suivie. Le cours de leurs sentimens n'est pas mieux réglé que les cours de ces vagues qu'un vent capricieux souleve à son gré durant la tempête. Vouloir assujettir ces sentimens à des principes, vouloir les ranger dans un ordre certain, c'est vouloir qu'un frénétique ait des visions suivies dans ses délires."[73] As discussed throughout the preceding readings, the incomplete attempt of the allegory of genius and its ideology of consensus to situate and fix its energies in speculative structures of grammar, taste, and space is what, in fact, enacts this allegory's own highly frenetic and theatrical (self-)critique.

It may seem paradoxical that such a deconstructive praxis, which I suggest is indigenous to seventeenth-century theatricality, has had such an inconsequential effect on the historical articulation of the norms of neoclassical and baroque dramatic literature. The institutional powers of reason and grammar seem to have veiled the subliminal forces of rhetorical tropes and theatrical figures. But we might lose sight of the differentiating energies of the illusive "Génie de la Comédie" by desiring nostalgically to reappropriate genius's many ruins in order to reshape them into an ideal and legitimate object of historical, literary study. At issue throughout this book has been the consideration of the epistemological structures displacing any notion of either the historical object or the speaking Subject independent of their ideological conditions of representation. In view of this concern, I wish to conclude this final essay of *Theatrical Legitimation* by stressing the threat of entrapment in the masterful discourse of reconstitution that always hangs over deconstructive and allegorical reading. To do so, I will engage in narrative transference for one final time by recalling the words ending Paul de Man's subtle essay on an influential, nineteenth-century discussion of the sublime:

Hegel's *Aesthetics,* an essentially prosaic discourse on art, is a discourse of the slave because it is a discourse of the figure rather than of genre, of trope rather than of representation. As a result it is also politically legitimate and effective as the undoer of usurped authority. The enslaved place and condition of the section on the sublime in the *Aesthetics* . . . are the symptoms of their strength. Poets, philosophers, and their readers lose their political impact only if they become, in turn, usurpers of mastery. One way of doing this is by avoiding, for whatever reason, the critical thrust of aesthetic judgment.[74]

❧ Notes

Chapter 1

1. Louis Althusser, "Idéologie et appareils idéologiques d'état (notes pour une recherche)," *La Pensée*, 151 (June 1970), 24. "Ideology represents the imaginary relationship of individuals to their real conditions of existence." *Lenin and Philosophy and Other Essays*, trans. Ben Brewster (New York: Monthly Review Press, 1971), p. 163.

2. Fredric Jameson, *The Political Unconscious: Narrative as a Socially Symbolic Act* (Ithaca: Cornell University Press, 1981), p. 79.

3. Francis Bacon, *The New Organon and Related Writings* (Indianapolis: Bobbs-Merrill, 1960), p. 49.

4. John Bullokar, *An English Expositor: Teaching the Interpretation of the hardest words used in our Language* (London: John Legatt, 1616), H.

5. Bacon, *The Great Instauration*, in *The New Organon and Related Writings*, p. 14.

6. Ibid., p. 23.

7. Ibid., p. 28.

8. Ibid., p. 27.

9. Bacon, *The New Organon*, p. 107.

10. Jürgen Habermas, *Legitimation Crisis*, trans. Thomas McCarthy (Boston: Beacon Press, 1973), p. 10.

11. For a broad articulation of this position see Gerald Graff, *Literature Against Itself: Literary Ideas in Modern Society* (Chicago: University

of Chicago Press, 1979). I critique Graff's position in "Terror and Judgment: Consenting With Hassan, Graff (and Now Booth!)," *boundary 2*, 12, No. 3/ 13, No. 1 (Spring/Fall 1984), 215–34. Jean-François Lyotard analyzes the ideology of consensus in two recent books, *La Condition postmoderne* (Paris: Éditions de Minuit, 1979) and *Le Différend* (Paris: Éditions de Minuit, 1983).

12. Habermas, *Legitimation Crisis*, p. 11.

13. Bacon, *The New Organon*, p. 107.

14. Walter Benjamin, *The Origin of German Tragic Drama*, trans. John Osborne (London: NLB, 1977), pp. 170–71.

15. Maureen Quilligan, in *The Language of Allegory: Defining the Genre* (Ithaca: Cornell University Press, 1979), pp. 25–33, makes a strong case for maintaining the difference between "allegoresis" and "narrative allegory." This distinction, moreover, is vital to her confinement of allegory to the master Christian narrative: "All allegories incorporate the Bible into their texts," thus leading "the reader back to the values presented by the sacred book," pp. 96, 135. Her argument eventually aims to refute Angus Fletcher's more provocative conclusion of *Allegory: The Theory of a Symbolic Mode* (Ithaca: Cornell University Press, 1964), p. 368: "allegories are the natural mirrors of ideology."

16. Benjamin, *The Origin of German Tragic Drama*, p. 182.

17. Paul de Man, *Allegories of Reading: Figural Language in Rousseau, Nietzsche, Rilke, and Proust* (New Haven: Yale University Press, 1979), p. 116.

18. De Man, "Pascal's Allegory of Persuasion," in *Allegory and Representation. Selected Papers from the English Institute, 1979–80*, ed. Stephen J. Greenblatt (Baltimore: Johns Hopkins University Press, 1981), p. 2.

19. Ibid., p. 1. For a substantial analysis of de Man's theory of allegory, see Rodolphe Gasché, "'Setzung' and 'Übersetzung': Notes on Paul de Man," *Diacritics*, 11, No. 4 (Winter 1981), 36–57.

20. Louis Marin, *Le Portrait du roi* (Paris: Éditions de Minuit, 1981), p. 10. "Power of institution, authorization, and legitimation."

21. Sigmund Freud, "Transference," *Introductory Lectures on Psychoanalysis*, in *The Standard Edition of the Complete Psychological Works of Sigmund Freud*, trans. and ed. James Strachey (London: Hogarth Press, 1953–74), XVI, 444. See also "The Dynamics of Transference," *The Standard Edition*, XII, 108.

22. Jacques Lacan, "L'intervention sur le transfert," in *Écrits* (Paris: Éditions du Seuil, 1966), pp. 215–226.

23. For specific discussions of transference and text, see Cynthia Chase, "Anecdote for Fathers: The Scene of Interpretation in Freud and Wordsworth," in *Textual Analysis: Some Readers Reading*, ed. Mary Ann Caws (New York: Modern Language Association of America, 1986), pp.

182–206; and her Review of Julia Kristeva's work in *Criticism*, 26, No. 2 (1983), 193–200; Michel de Certeau, *Heterologies: Discourse on the Other*, trans. Brian Massumi (Minneapolis: University of Minnesota Press, 1986), pp. 3–34; Peter Brooks, *Reading for the Plot: Design and Intention in Narrative* (New York: Random House, 1984), pp. 216–37; and Dominick LaCapra, *History and Criticism* (Ithaca: Cornell University Press, 1985), pp. 72–94.

24. In *La Vérité en peinture* (Paris: Flammarion, 1978), pp. 23–24, Jacques Derrida emphasizes how deconstructionist praxis involves the analysis of internal philosophical systems as well as their external institutionalization as critical norms. Deconstruction, he writes,"s'attaque non seulement à l'édification interne, à la fois sémantique and formelle, des philosophèmes, mais à ce qu'on lui assignerait à tort comme son logement externe, ses conditions d'exercice extrinsèques: les formes historiques de sa pédagogie, les structures sociales, économiques ou politiques de cette institution pédagogique. C'est parce qu'elle touche à des structures solides, à des institutions 'matériels,' et non seulement à des discours ou à des représentations signifiantes, que la déconstruction se distingue toujours d'une analyse ou d'une 'critique.' Et pour être pertinente, elle travaille, le plus strictement possible, en ce lieu où l'agencement dit 'interne' du philosophique s'articule de façon nécessaire (interne *et* externe) avec les conditions et les formes institutionnelles de l'enseignement. Jusqu'au point où le concept d'institution lui-même serait soumis au même traitement déconstructeur." "Confronts not only the internal edification of *philosophèmes*, both semantic and formal, but also what will wrongly be cited as its external dwelling, its extrinsic conditions of exercise: the historical forms of its pedagogy, the social, economic, and political structures of this pedagogical institution [the French university]. It is because deconstruction tampers with solid structures, with 'material' institutions, and not only with discourses or signifying representations, that it always distinguishes itself from an analysis or a 'criticism.' And to be relevant, it works as strictly as possible in this area where what is called the 'internal' ordering of the philosophical is connected in a necessary (internal *and* external) way with the institutional conditions and forms of teaching. To the point where the concept of the institution itself will be submitted to the same deconstructive treatment." For particularly acute American discussions of this deconstructive project, see Rodolphe Gasché, "Deconstruction as Criticism," *Glyph*, 6 (1979), 177–215; Philip Lewis, "The Post-Structuralist Condition," *Diacritics*, 12, No. 1 (1982), 2–24; Jonathan Culler, *On Deconstruction: Theory and Criticism after Structuralism* (Ithaca: Cornell University Press, 1982).

25. Lyotard, *Instructions païennes* (Paris: Éditions galilée, 1977), p. 35.

26. Lyotard, *La Condition postmoderne*, p. 33.

27. Ibid., p. 97. "Postmodern science—by concerning itself with such things as undecidables, the limits of precise control, conflicts characterized

by incomplete information, '*fracta*,' catastrophes, and pragmatic para-doxes—is theorizing its own evolution as discontinuous, catastrophic, non-rectifiable, and paradoxical. It is changing the meaning of the word *knowledge*, while expressing how such a change can take place. It is producing not the known, but the unknown. And it suggests a model of legitimation that has nothing to do with maximized performance, but has as its basis difference understood as paralogy." *The Postmodern Condition: A Report on Knowledge*, trans. Geoff Bennington and Brian Massumi (Minneapolis: University of Minnesota Press, 1984), p. 60.

Chapter 2

1. Philip Sidney, *An Apologie for Poetrie* (Oxford: Clarendon Press, 1907), p. 10

2. Ibid., p. 23.

3. Cited in E. K. Chambers, *The Elizabethan Stage* (Oxford: The Clarendon Press, 1923), IV, 198–99.

4. Stephen Gosson, *The School of Abuse*, in Arthur F. Kinney, *Markets of Bawdrie: The Dramatic Criticism of Stephen Gosson* (Salzburg: Institut für Englische Sprache und Literatur, 1974), p. 195.

5. For perceptive discussions of antitheatricality, see Jonas Barish, *The Antitheatrical Prejudice* (Berkeley: University of California Press, 1981); as well as David Leverenz, "Why Did Puritans Hate Stage Plays?" in *The Language of Puritan Feeling: An Exploration in Literature, Psychology, and Social History* (New Brunswick: Rutgers University Press, 1980). The following essays discuss English Renaissance drama's reference to the social threat of its own theatricality: Timothy Murray, "*Othello's* Foul Generic Thoughts and Methods," in *Persons in Groups: Social Behavior as Identity Formation in Medieval and Renaissance Europe*, ed. Richard C. Trexler (Binghamton: Medieval & Renaissance Texts & Studies, 1985), pp. 67–77; Jonathan V. Crewe, "The Theatre of the Idols: Marlowe, Rankins, and Theatrical Images," *Theatre Journal*, 36, No. 3 (October 1984), 321–33; and John Gordon Sweeney III, *Jonson and the Psychology of the Public Theater: To Coin the Spirit, Spend the Soul* (Princeton: Princeton University Press, 1985.)

6. William Prynne, *Histriomastix, The Players Scourge or, Actors Tragedie* (London: A.E. and W.I. for Michael Sparke, 1633), p. 124. In *Drama of a Nation: Public Theater in Renaissance England and Spain* (Ithaca: Cornell University Press, 1985), p. 185, Walter Cohen presents a Marxist interpretation of theatre's threat: "only because of the contradiction between base and superstructure in the theater . . . did the actors' mastery of more powerful methods of impersonation and representation present a danger to moralists of the time."

7. On authorship, see Roland Barthes, "Authors and Writers," *Critical Essays*, trans. Richard Howard (Evanston: Northwestern University Press, 1972), pp. 143–50; and Michel Foucault, "What is an Author?," in *Textual Strategies: Perspectives in Post-Structuralist Criticism*, ed. Josué V. Harari (Ithaca: Cornell University Press, 1980), pp. 141–60.

8. Gosson, *Playes Confuted in Five Actions*, in Kinney, *Markets of Bawdrie*, p. 146.

9. Samuel Johnson, "PROPOSALS for Printing, by SUBSCRIPTION, The DRAMATICK WORKS of William Shakespeare," *Johnson on Shakespeare*, Vols. VII and VIII of *The Yale Edition of the Works of Samuel Johnson*, ed. Arthur Sherbo (New Haven: Yale University Press, 1968), VII, 51.

10. Ibid., 55.

11. Ibid., 52.

12. Gerald Eades Bentley, *The Profession of Dramatist in Shakespeare's Time, 1590–1642* (Princeton: Princeton University Press, 1970).

13. John Dryden, *An Essay of Dramatick Poesie*, in Vol. XVII of *The Works of John Dryden*, ed. Samuel Holt Monk (Berkeley: University of California Press, 1971), p. 57.

14. Ben Jonson, *Timber: or, Discoveries*, in Vol. VIII of *Ben Jonson*, eds. C. H. Herford, Percy and Evelyn Simpson (Oxford: Oxford University Press, 1925–52), p. 639. All citations of Jonson will be from this edition and will be cited hereafter as "H & S."

15. George Puttenham, *The Arte of English Poesie* (London: Alex. Murray & Son, 1869), p. 21. For an interesting discussion of the difference between Sidney's and Puttenham's notions of imitation and counterfeit, with additional remarks on Ben Jonson, see Lawrence Manley, *Convention 1500–1750* (Cambridge, Mass.: Harvard University Press, 1980), pp. 137–202.

16. Mr. Mason, *Reflections on Originality in Authors . . . with a word or two on The Character of Ben Jonson and Pope* (London, 1766), p. 64. Richard S. Peterson, in *Imitation and Praise in the Poems of Ben Jonson* (New Haven: Yale University Press, 1981), p. 20, is more generous than Mason in explaining Jonson's position concerning plagiarism: "The offense of plagiarism is especially reprehensible because, as the root meaning suggests, it is like the theft of a living thing, indeed of a child from its father. . . . The good writer, far from stealing another's child, creates a work recognizably his own even while, as imitator, he (and his writing) becomes the child or inheritor of those he consults." In *Originality and Imagination* (Baltimore: The Johns Hopkins University Press, 1985), Thomas McFarland dwells on the fine lines shading the eighteenth-century confusions of originality, plagiarism, and genius. The offense of plagiarism also provided material for Marston's and Dekker's attacks on Jonson; Joseph Loewenstein, in *Responsive Readings: Versions of Echo in Pastoral, Epic, and the Jonsonian*

Masque, Yale Studies in English, 192 (New Haven: Yale University Press, 1984), pp. 78–92, develops an intriguing reading of *Cynthia's Revels* in view of Jonson's "defensiveness about the attractions and dangers of renovation and innovation."

17. Johnson, *Johnson on Shakespeare,* VII, 52–53. E. K. Chambers discusses Shakespeare's plot imitations in *William Shakespeare: A Study of Facts and Problems* (Oxford: The Clarendon Press, 1930), I, 218.

18. How intertextuality itself might have been thought to be the source of the obscurity of plays is suggested by Ben Jonson in *Volpone* and *The Alchemist.* Scoto Mantuano, in *Volpone,* attributes his rare and unverifiable knowledge to his youthful endeavors "to get the rarest secrets, and booke them" (H & S, V, 54). Like Prospero in *The Tempest,* only Scoto has the key to the interpretation of his book of allusions. Similarly, *The Alchemist*'s Mammon defends the wisdom of alchemy by spewing forth the many sources of its textual tradition, "all abstract riddles of our *stone*" (H & S, 317).

19. Gosson, *Playes Confuted in Five Actions,* p. 169.

20. In *La Dissémination* (Paris: Éditions du Seuil, 1972), p. 12, Derrida makes explicit the distinction between *différance* and the dialectics of univocal, homogenous models of thought and practice which prefigures any allegorical narrative of legitimation: "Le mouvement par lequel Hegel détermine la différence en contradiction . . . est précisément destiné à rendre possible la relève ultime (onto-théo-téléo-logique) de la différence. La *différance*—qui n'est donc pas la contradiction dialectique en ce sens hegelien—marque la limite critique des pouvoirs idéalisants de la relève partout où ils peuvent, directement ou indirectement, opérer. Elle *inscrit* la contradiction ou plutôt, la différance restant irréductiblement différenciante et disséminante, *les* contradictions. Marquant le mouvement "producteur" (au sens de l'économie générale et compte tenu de la perte de présence) et différenciant, le "concept" *économique* de la différance ne réduit donc pas les contradictions à l'homogénéité d'un seul modèle." "The movement by which Hegel determines difference as contradiction . . . is designed precisely to make possible the ultimate (onto-theo-teleo-logical) sublation of difference. *Differance*—which is thus by no means dialectical contradiction in this Hegelian sense—marks the critical limit of the idealizing powers of relief wherever they are able, directly or indirectly, to operate. Differance *inscribes* contradiction, or rather, since it remains irreducibly differentiating and disseminating, contradictions. In marking the 'productive' (in the sense of general economy and in accordance with the loss of presence) and differentiating movement, the *economic* 'concept' of differance does not reduce all contradictions to the homogeneity of a single model." *Dissemination,* trans. Barbara Johnson (Chicago: University of Chicago Press, 1981), pp. 6–7.

21. Perhaps more than any of his communal peers, Wayne Booth is

most upfront in locating pluralistic antagonism toward deconstruction in the figure of anxiety: "Renewing the Medium of Renewal: Some Notes on the Anxieties of Innovation," in *Innovation/Renovation: New Perspectives on the Humanities*, ed. Ihab Hassan and Sally Hassan (Madison: University of Wisconsin Press, 1983), pp. 131–59. I respond to his essay in "Terror and Judgment: Consenting with Hassan, Graff (and Now Booth!)," *boundary 2*, 12, No. 3/ 13 No. 1 (Spring/Fall 1984), 215–34.

22. Prynne, *Histriomastix*, pp. 130, 935.

23. Stephen Greenblatt, in *Renaissance Self-Fashioning: From More to Shakespeare* (Chicago: University of Chicago Press, 1980), p. 253, emphasizes the stage's relation to the monarchical order sustaining it: "The theater is widely perceived in the period as the concrete manifestation of the histrionic quality of life, and, more specifically, of power—the power of the prince who stands as an actor upon a stage before the eyes of the nation, the power of God who enacts His will in the Theater of the World. The stage justifies itself against recurrent charges of immorality by invoking this normative function: it is the expression of those rules that govern a properly ordered society and displays the punishment, in laughter and violence, that is meted out upon those who violate the rules." Stephen Orgel develops the scope of Elizabethan royal dissimulation in "The Spectacles of State," *Persons in Groups*, ed. Trexler, pp. 101–22; also see Robert Weimann's discussion of the crown's protection of the stage, in *Shakespeare and the Popular Tradition in the Theater: Studies in the Social Dimension of Dramatic Form and Function* (Baltimore: The Johns Hopkins University Press, 1978), pp. 172–73. On the actual threat of polysemy itself, see Steven Mullaney, "Lying Like Truth: Riddle, Representation and Treason in Renaissance England," *ELH*, 47, No. 1 (Spring 1980), 32–47.

24. Jonathan Goldberg, *James I and the Politics of Literature: Jonson, Shakespeare, Donne, and Their Contemporaries* (Baltimore: The Johns Hopkins Press, 1983), pp. 68–69. Goldberg's wide-ranging analysis of the secretive representations typifying the age of James I is but one example of his book's subtle demystifications of Tudor authority and power. Puttenham's emphasis on the figure *Allegoria* as "false semblant" is also prominent in Frank Whigham's essay, "Interpretation at Court: Courtesy and the Performer-Audience Dialectic," *New Literary History*, 14, No. 3 (Spring 1983), 623–39.

25. Robert Dallington, *Aphorismes Civill and Militarie* (London: Edward Blount, 1613), p. 176.

26. Bacon, *The New Organon*, p. 84.

27. Bacon, *The Advancement of Learning*, ed. Arthur Johnston (Oxford: The Clarendon Press, 1974), p. 26.

28. Bacon, *The New Organon*, p. 49.

29. H. S. Bennett, *English Books and Readers 1603–1640* (Cambridge: Cambridge University Press, 1970), p. 61; and Marjorie Plant, *The English*

Book Trade: An Economic Sale of Books (London: Unkins Brothers, 1939), pp. 73–74.

30. The English theatre was unique in terms of the diminutive status that it granted to authors. In both Italy and France, a dramatic text was likely to be published by its authors before its release into the hands of the shifty players. And regardless of whether the play was printed before or after its performance, the author usually authorized publication, if he did not directly prepare the text for the printer. In these countries, authority over texts was assumed to belong to the playwrights. The following texts include forewords of French and Italian printed plays that clarify this privileged status of authorship: Louise George Clubb, *Italian Plays (1500–1700) in The Folger Library* (Florence: Leo S. Olschki, 1968); Antoine de Ferreul, *Catalogue des livres: une collection presque universelle de pièces de Théâtre* (Paris: Le Clerc, 1774); Isidor Justin Déverin Taylor, *Catalogue de la bibliothèque dramatique* (Paris: Librarie Techener, 1893); Frédéric Lachèvre, *Bibliographie des recueils collectifs de poésies publiées de 1597 à 1700* (Paris: Librarie Ancienne Honoré Champion, 1922).

31. Johnson, *Johnson on Shakespeare*, VII, 51–52.

32. Bentley, *The Profession of Dramatist in Shakespeare's Time*, p. 87.

33. Alexander Pope, "Preface to 'The Works of Shakespear,'" in *Eighteenth Century Essays on Shakespeare*, ed. D. Nichol Smith (Oxford: The Clarendon Press, 1963), p. 54.

34. Bentley, *The Profession of Dramatist in Shakespeare's Time*, p. 236.

35. W. W. Greg, *The Shakespeare First Folio* (Oxford: The Clarendon Press, 1955), pp. 106–7. For an analysis of the influence of censorship on early modern authorship, see Annabel Patterson, *Censorship and Interpretation: The Condition of Writing and Reading in Early Modern England* (Madison: University of Wisconsin Press, 1984).

36. Steven Urkowitz, *Shakespeare's Revision of "King Lear"* (Princeton: Princeton University Press, 1980); and Gary Taylor and Michael Warren, eds., *The Division of the Kingdoms: Shakespeare's Two Versions of "King Lear"* (Oxford: The Clarendon Press, 1983).

37. Weimann, *Shakespeare and the Popular Tradition in the Theater*, p. 214, asserts that "the principal of joint authorship and joint responsibility accorded fully with the implications and spirit of the Elizabethan theatrical experience."

38. H & S, IV, 215–16.

39. Prynne, *Histriomastix*, pp. 834–35, 928–29. A curious modern corollary of this trust in recitation surfaces in Roger Shattuck's anti-deconstructionist essay, "How To Rescue Literature," *The New York Review of Books*, April 17, 1980, pp. 33, 35. Sounding much like Prynne, Shattuck maintains that "the practical attention to the physical words enforced by reading aloud protects a work from being usurped by the ambitious cate-

gories of much contemporary criticism." Aligning oral reading with the ideology of consensus, he adds that "if literature is to be valued as a shared
enterprise we must find a common ground of meaning and a limit on the
splash and performance of divergent interpretations. Even information theory sets a ceiling to the number of "bits" the human mind can process;
every channel has a capacity. Oral interpretation can serve as a kind of test
or verification that will suggest just how much of a work can be transmitted
by speech to a community of listeners."

40. Prynne, *Histriomastix*, p. 930.

41. Ibid., p. 5.

42. H. S. Bennett, *English Books and Readers 1558–1603* (Cambridge:
Cambridge University Press, 1965), p. 255.

43. In *The Shakespeare First Folio*, p. 71, Greg stresses that approxi-
mately one-third of the printed books from the period 1607–1637 were not
entered in the Stationer's Register. This includes *Mucedorus, Volpone*
(1607), and *Catiline* (1611).

44. Joseph Loewenstein, "The Script in the Marketplace," *Representations*, 12 (Fall 1985), 105, writes that, to combat piracy, "Henslowe and
others occasionally took to paying registration fees to the Stationer's Court
of Assistants simply in order to secure exclusive rights to print texts (rights
that they had no intention of exercising)."

45. Richard Jhones, "To the Gentlemen Readers: and others that take
pleasure in reading Histories," *Tamburlaine the Great* (London, 1590), A$_2$.

46. George Chapman, *The Memorable Maske of the two Honorable
Houses or Inns of Court; the Middle Temple, and Lyncolns Inne* (London,
1613), A$_1$v.

47. It was not until July 1637 that printers were banned from signing
books with counterfeit names without the consent of the author. See Bennett, *English Books and Readers 1603–1640*, p. 46. "Counterfeiting" also
was accomplished by printing the author's name without consent. Ben Jonson refused to recognize *The Case is Altered* which was so published under
his name without permission (H & S, I, 21).

48. Barish, *The Antitheatrical Prejudice*, pp. 132–33.

49. Greg, *A Bibliography of the English Printed Drama to the Restoration* (London: Oxford University Press, 1939), Cat. 151, I, 248.

50. Bentley, *The Profession of Dramatist in Shakespeare's Time*, p.
245.

51. Bacon, *The Great Instauration*, in *The New Organon and Related
Writings*, p. 12.

Chapter 3

1. H & S, I, 13–17; George Parfitt, *Ben Jonson: Public Poet and Private Man* (New York: Harper & Row, 1976), pp. 11–13.

2. Marchette Chute, *Ben Jonson of Westminster* (New York: E.P. Dutton, 1953), pp. 75–76.

3. Barish, "Jonson and the Loathèd Stage," in *The Antitheatrical Prejudice*, pp. 132–33.

4. H & S, V, 19–20.

5. Barish, *The Antitheatrical Prejudice*, p. 137. In "Jonson and the (Re-)Invention of the Book," Richard C. Newton discusses Jonson's turn to printing to protect his authorship. Newton's essay diverges from my reading of Jonson's printing activities, however, in making Jonson more of a classicist than an allegorist. This difference will become especially clear in the next chapter's consideration of Jonson's printed epistles and masques.

6. H & S, VIII, 44–45.

7. Ibid., 628.

8. Ibid., 629.

9. Ibid.

10. Ibid., 625.

11. L. J. Potts, "Ben Jonson and the Seventeenth Century," *English Studies 1949* (London: John Murray, 1949), pp. 7–24. D. J. Gordon, "Poet and Architect: The Intellectual Setting of the Quarrel between Ben Jonson and Inigo Jones," *The Renaissance Imagination: Essays and Lectures by D. J. Gordon*, ed. Stephen Orgel (Berkeley: University of California Press, 1975), pp. 77–101. Richard C. Newton, "'Ben./ Jonson': The Poet in the Poems," in *Two Renaissance Mythmakers: Christopher Marlowe and Ben Jonson*, ed. Alvin Kernan, *Selected Papers from The English Institute 1975–76*, NS 1 (1979), 165–69. Don E. Wayne, *Penshurst: The Semiotics of Place and the Poetics of History* (Madison: University of Wisconsin Press, 1984). Manley, *Convention 1500–1750*, pp. 188–96.

12. Bacon, *The New Organon*, p. 102.

13. Murray Cohen, *Sensible Words: Linguistic Practice in England 1640–1785* (Baltimore: Johns Hopkins University Press, 1977), p. 8.

14. Manley and Helgerson argue especially hard for Jonson's tug toward custom and convention.

15. Although Jonson includes a large number of extracts from grammars written in Latin, primarily those of Ramus and Scaliger, he paraphrases all quotations in an English lacking sophistication.

16. This is part of the subtitle of William Bullokar's *Booke at Large* (London: Henrie Denham, 1580).

17. This is part of the subtitle of John Hewes's *A Perfect Survey of the English Tongue* (1624; rpt. Menston, England: The Scholar Press, 1972).

18. This is the subtitle of *The English Grammar*, H & S, VIII, 463.

19. For a thorough discussion of early English grammars, see Ian Michael, *English Grammatical Categories and the Tradition to 1800* (Cambridge: Cambridge University Press, 1970), pp. 151–54.

20. Ibid., pp. 187, 409.

21. H & S, VIII, 465.

22. See Wilbur Samuel Howell, *Logic and Rhetoric in England, 1500–1700* (New York: Russell & Russell, 1961), pp. 157–58, for a discussion of the tradition begun by Thomas Wilson's *Rule of Reason, conteinyng the Arte of Logique* (London: R. Grafton, 1551), John Seton's *Dialectica* (1545; rpt. London, 1611), and Ralph Lever's *The Arte of Reason, rightly termed, Witcraft* (London: H. Bynneman, 1573).

23. H & S, VIII, 502.

24. Ibid., 480.

25. Ibid., 622.

26. Ibid., 517.

27. Barish's book, *Ben Jonson and the Language of Prose Comedy* (Cambridge, Mass.: Harvard University Press, 1960), continues to provide the most informative discussion of the artistic results of Jonson's proportioning of natural language. Equally impressive is Martin Elsky's discussion of Jonson's grammar book in "Words, Things, and Names: Jonson's Poetry and Philosophical Grammar," in Summers and Pebworth, ed., *Classic and Cavalier: Essays on Jonson and the Sons of Ben* (Pittsburgh: University of Pittsburgh Press, 1982), pp. 91–104.

28. See Michel Foucault, *Les mots et les choses* (Paris: Gallimard, 1966), pp. 92–136.

29. H & S, VIII, 517.

30. Ibid.

31. Ibid., 625.

32. Bacon, *The New Organon*, p. 130.

33. For analyses of the commonplace tradition, see D. C. Allen's introduction to Francis Meres, *Palladis Tamia, Wits Treasury* (1598; rpt. Delmar, N.Y., 1938); and Joan Marie Lechner, *Renaissance Concepts of the Commonplaces* (Westport, Conn.: Greenwood Press, 1974).

34. Walter J. Ong, *Ramus, Method, and the Decay of Dialogue* (Cambridge, Mass.: Harvard University Press, 1958), p. 119.

35. Allen, introduction, *Palladis Tamia*, p. vi.

36. Wolfgangus Musculus, "The Preface," *Common places of Christian Religion* (London, 1613).

37. Newton, "'Ben./Jonson,'" p. 182.

38. H & S, VIII, 561. Because *Discoveries* was first published in the 1640 folio, there is no evidence that these words were written by Jonson.

39. Allen, introduction, *Palladis Tamia*, p. iv.

40. Greg, *A Bibliography*, Cat. 163, I, 264.

41. H & S, V, 283. John J. Enck, in *Jonson and the Comic Truth* (Madison: University of Wisconsin Press, 1957), p. 45, suggests that Jonson's use of a Latin motto is in itself antitheatrical: "The second bait, that of offering more than acted on the stage, may have stimulated literary curiosity. The Latin motto seems a quaint flourish, but Jonson's example helped launch

the practice later popular in printed drama. The kinds of books most highly respected at the time served as models. For a dramatist to publish his script was infra dig; serious works, of course, deserved Latin mottoes, but not a popular playbook, which, among the literate, enjoyed a reputation not much higher than collections of comic strips command at present."

42. Greg, *A Bibliography*, Cat. 172, I, 278–79.

43. H & S, VI, 16.

44. Stephen Orgel, "The Poetics of Spectacle," *New Literary History*, 2, No. 3 (Spring 1971), 382–83.

45. H & S, IV, 350–51.

46. Ibid., VIII, 391.

47. Richard Helgerson, *Self-Crowned Laureates: Spenser, Jonson, Milton, and the Literary System* (Berkeley: University of California Press, 1983), pp. 139–40.

48. H & S, IV, 294.

49. Ibid., V, 20–21.

50. Bentley, *The Profession of Dramatist in Shakespeare's Time*, p. 261.

51. Bennett, *English Books and Readers, 1603–1640*, p. 195.

52. Prynne, "To the Christian Reader," *Histriomastix*.

53. On the complex relations of the ideology of textual form to commodification and interpretative authority, see Pierre Macherey, *Pour une théorie de la production littéraire* (Paris: François Maspero, 1980); Peter Uwe Hohendahl, *The Institution of Criticism* (Ithaca: Cornell University Press, 1982); and Walter Cohen, *Drama of a Nation*.

54. H & S, IX, 46.

55. Ibid., 47.

56. In *The Masque of Blacknesse*, for example, Jonson explains his classical interests in the couples' fans, "in one of which were inscribed their mixt *Names*, in the other a mute *Hieroglyphick* . . . Which manner of *Symbole* I rather chose, then *Imprese*, as well for strangenesse, as relishing of antiquitie, and more applying to that originall doctrine of sculpture, which the *AEgyptians* are said, first, to have brought from the *AEthiopians*," H & S, VII, 177. For comprehensive discussions of the classical nature of Jonsonian verse, see Orgel, *The Jonsonian Masque* (Cambridge, Mass.: Harvard University Press, 1965); Wesley Trimpi, *A Study of the Plain Style* (Stanford: Stanford University Press, 1962); Richard S. Peterson, *Imitation and Praise in the Poems of Ben Jonson* (New Haven: Yale University Press, 1980); and Katharine Eisaman Mauss, *Ben Jonson and the Roman Frame of Mind* (Princeton: Princeton University Press, 1984).

57. Johan Gerritsen, rev. of *Ben Jonson* (H & S), *English Studies*, 38 (1957), 122.

58. Ben Jonson, *Epicoene or The Silent Woman*, ed. L. A. Beaurline (Lincoln, Nebr.: University of Nebraska Press, 1966), p. xxi.

59. Gerritsen, p. 122; H & S, IV, 333. I might note that Greg expresses doubts about Jonson's editing in some of his reviews of H & S—see especially *Review of English Studies*, 14 (1938), 216–18. But his reservations concern, for the most part, particular claims about editorial decisions of H & S. I need not stress the importance of the crucial matters of Jonson's authorial presence to current theoretical discussion. In "The Computerized *Ulysses*: Establishing the Text Joyce Intended," *Harpers*, April 1980, pp. 89–95, Hugh Kenner makes a similar point about authorship and print in discussing how the editorial decisions made by Joyce in reading proofs altered the "original" manuscript as submitted to the publisher. Kenner argues that editing became for Joyce another way of writing the original text, a way in which repetition means iteration, in which reading means rereading.

60. The discussions of Barish, Wayne, Newton, and Helgerson rigorously explore Jonson's interest in printing. In *Renaissance Self-Fashioning*, pp. 74–114, Greenblatt discusses the relevance of Benjamin's work to the printed texts of More and Tyndale.

61. Walter Benjamin, "The Work of Art in the Age of Mechanical Reproduction," in *Illuminations*, ed. Hannah Arendt, trans. Harry Zohn (New York: Schocken Books, 1969), p. 220.

62. Ibid.

63. Ibid., pp. 220–21.

64. See especially, Walter J. Ong, "From Allegory to Diagram in the Renaissance Mind: A Study in the Significance of the Allegorical Tableau," *The Journal of Aesthetics and Art Criticism*, 17, No. 4 (June 1959), 423–40, and *Ramus, Method, and the Decay of Dialogue*.

65. Elizabeth L. Eisenstein, *The Printing Press as an Agent of Change: Communications and Cultural Transformations in Early Modern Europe*, 2 vols. (Cambridge: Cambridge University Press, 1979).

66. Ong, *Ramus, Method, and the Decay of Dialogue*, pp. 89–90.

67. H & S, IV, 293.

68. Ibid.

69. Frances Yates, *The Art of Memory* (Chicago: University of Chicago Press, 1966), p. 234.

70. Rosemond Tuve, *Elizabethan & Metaphysical Imagery* (Chicago: University of Chicago Press, 1947), p. 386. I thank Victoria Kahn for calling my attention to Tuve's differences with Yates. In *Rhetoric, Prudence, and Skepticism in the Renaissance* (Ithaca: Cornell University Press, 1985), p. 236, Kahn briefly discusses Ramism's appropriation of rhetoric and how "Ramus's goal, like that of the rhetoricians who followed him, was to methodize instruction in both rhetoric and logic, thereby making these skills accessible not to courtiers, but to 'the common people.'" I will return to the theme of rhetoric and "the common people" in Chapter 10.

71. Richard Dutton, *Ben Jonson: To the First Folio* (Cambridge: Cambridge University Press, 1983), p. 14.

72. Yates, *The Art of Memory*, p. 234.

73. Derrida, *Limited Inc a b c...* (Baltimore: The Johns Hopkins University Press, 1977), pp. 25–26. "There is no doubt that the 'permanence' or the 'survival' of the document (*scripta manent*), when and to the degree (always relative) that they take place, imply iterability or remaining in general. But the inverse is not true. Permanence is not a necessary effect of remaining. I will go even further: the structure of the remainder, implying alteration, renders all absolute permanence impossible." "Limited Inc a b c...," trans. Samuel Weber, *Glyph* 2 (1977), p. 191.

74. Ibid., p. 28. "Intention or attention, directed towards something iterable which in turn determines it as being iterable, will strive or tend in vain to actualize or fulfill itself, for it cannot, by virtue of its very structure, ever achieve this goal. In no case will it be fulfilled, actualized, totally present to its object and to itself. It is divided and deported in advance, by its iterability, towards others, removed [*écartée*] in advanced from itself. This re-move makes its movement possible. Which is another way of saying that if this remove is its condition of possibility, it is not an eventuality, something that befalls it here and there, by accident. Intention is a priori (at once) *différante*: differing and deferring, in its inception." "Limited Inc a b c...," p. 194. For Derrida's analyses of *différance* in the scene of theatre, see "La parole soufflée" and "Le théâtre de la cruauté et la clôture de la représentation" in *L'écriture et la différence* (Paris: Éditions du Seuil, 1967), pp. 253–92, 341–368.

Chapter 4

1. See D. J. Gordon, "Poet and Architect," pp. 77–101.

2. Stephen Orgel, "The Poetics of Spectacle," 371. In *Responsive Readings*, pp. 94–95, Joseph Loewenstein argues that "it would be more fruitful to inquire initially into how Jones's particular scenic art managed to hold Jonsonian ambivalence in check.... Jonson was so beguiled by the architect's devices for their first production that he went further than he ever had or ever would toward an endorsement of gaze."

3. H & S, VII, 313.

4. On the play of figure and the figural, from image to code, see Jean-François Lyotard, *Discours, figure* (Paris: Éditions Klincksieck, 1971).

5. Margery Corbett and Ronald Lightbown, *The Comely Frontispiece: The Emblematic Title-Page in England 1550–1660* (London: Routledge & Kegan Paul, 1979), p. 148.

6. Louis Adrian Montrose, "Of Gentlemen and Shepherds: The Politics of Elizabethan Pastoral Form," *ELH*, 50, No. 3 (Fall 1983), 415–59.

7. Corbett and Lightbown, *The Comely Frontispiece*, p. 150.

8. In his article, "The Stigma of Print: A Note on the Social Bases of Tudor Poetry," *Essays in Criticism*, 1, No. 2 (April 1951), 139–64, J. W. Saunders addresses the issue of print and social status. Although it was undesirable for amateur poets of the court to print their poems, it was often the professional poet's only avenue toward "personal profit, social promotion and a national reputation." Also see Saunders, *The Profession of English Letters* (London: Routledge & Kegan Paul, 1964); and Phoebe Sheavyn, *The Literary Profession in the Elizabethan Age*, ed. J. W. Saunders (Manchester and New York: Manchester University Press and Barnes & Noble, 1967). Jonson's shaping of a princely self-image through poetry has been discussed more recently by W. David Kay, "The Shaping of Ben Jonson's Career: A Reexamination of Facts and Problems," *Modern Philology*, 67, No. 3 (February 1970), 224–37; Richard C. Newton, "Jonson and the (Re-)Invention of the Book," in *Classic and Cavalier: Essays on Jonson and the Sons of Ben*, ed. Summers and Pebworth, pp. 31–55; Richard Helgerson, *Self-Crowned Laureates*; and E. Pearlman, "Ben Jonson: An Anatomy," *ELR*, 9, No. 3 (Autumn 1979), 364–93.

9. L. C. Knights, "Public Attitudes and Social Poetry," in *A Celebration of Ben Jonson*, ed. William Blissett, Julian Patrick, and R. W. Van Fossen (Toronto: University of Toronto Press, 1975), p. 169.

10. Helgerson, *Self-Crowned Laureates*, p. 166.

11. John Mennes, *Wits recreations. Selected from the finest fancies of moderne muses* (London: Printed by R. H. for Humphrey Blunden, 1640), Sonnet 269.

12. Bacon, *The New Organon*, p. 70.

13. Ibid, p. 71.

14. Mennes, *Wits Recreations*, Sonnet 270.

15. H & S, VIII, 311.

16. Walter Benjamin, *The Origin of German Tragic Drama*, p. 179.

17. In contrast, the generic ordering of plays in the Shakespeare folio places much more emphasis on the theatrical classification of the plays.

18. H & S, IV, 55.

19. Bentley, *The Profession of Dramatist in Shakespeare's Time*, p. 290, adds to this list: "Four of the early ones written for Henslowe, mostly collaborations, *Hot Anger Soon Cold*, *Robert II*, *King of Scotts*, *The Page of Plymouth*, and *Richard Crookback*, he chose to suppress and never mentioned in his numerous discussions of his work."

20. H & S, IV, 351.

21. In England, collections of plays did not become popular until well after the collection of Jonson's folio. Even then, save a few exceptions, like Thomas Heywood's quarto edition of the *Pleasant Dialogues & Drammas, selected out of Lucian, Erasmus, Textor, Ovid, etc.* (London: R. O. Printed

for Hearne & Slater, 1637), the collections published in the 1630s tended to be limited to the plays of single authors. See John Lyly, *Sixe Court Comedies . . . By the onely Rare Poet of that Time, the Wittie, Comicall, Facetiously-Quicke, and unparalleled John Lilly* (London: William Stansby, 1632) and *The WORKES of JOHN MARSTON* (London: William Sheares, 1633). This bookish promotion of individual authors stands in sharp contrast to the collective activities of the acting companies. The actors nurtured an intellectual spirit akin to the intertextual thought stimulated by printed collections on the Continent (see Eisenstein, "Some Conjectures about the Impact of Printing on Western Society and Thought"). Jonson's folio, by its symbolic rejection of plays written in collaboration with others, endorses a conservative mode of collective dramatic literature. It purposely calls attention to the exclusive model of only one English man of letters.

22. For provocative theoretical analyses developing the relation of Jonson's method to his writing of the *Epigrammes*, see Don Wayne, "Poetry and Power in Ben Jonson's *Epigrammes*: The Naming of 'Facts' or the Figuring of Social Relations?," *Renaissance and Modern Studies*, 23 (1979), 79–103; Judith Kegan Gardiner, *Craftsmanship in Context* (The Hague: Mouton, 1975), pp. 12–53; and Jennifer Brady, "'Beware the Poet': Authority and Judgment in Jonson's *Epigrammes*," *Studies in English Literature*, 23, No. 1 (Winter, 1983), 95–112.

23. Prynne, *Histriomastix*, p. 120.

24. Newton, "Jonson and the (Re-)Invention of the Book," p. 37. In *Ben Jonson: To the First Folio*, p. 34, Richard Dutton similarly suggests that "the development of Jonson's career as it is reflected in his first folio can be seen as a series of attempts to resolve the problems posed by *Every Man In His Humour* . . . which must in some way mean involving the audience in the judgement, making it a communal process rather than a matter of individual taste and assertion."

25. Gosson, *Playes Confuted in Five Actions*, p. 164.

26. In *The English Grammar*, H & S, VIII, 551, Jonson writes that "a *Comma* is a distinction of an *imperfect* Sentence." In "The Catalogue," titles of plays made incomplete by commas are perfected by the dedicatory clause followed by a period. On the significance of Jonson's attentiveness to commas, also see Ian Donaldson's introduction to Jonson's *Poems* (Oxford: Oxford University Press, 1975), p. xix; and G. K. Hunter, *The Marking of "Sententiae" in Elizabethan Printed Plays, Poems, and Romances* (London: The Bibliographical Society, 1951).

27. H & S, V, 432.

28. Ibid.

29. Claude Lévi-Strauss, *La Pensée sauvage* (Paris: Plon, 1962), p. 240. "At one extreme, the name is an identifying mark which, by the application of a rule, establishes that the individual who *is named* is a member of a

preordained class (a social group in a system of groups, a status by birth in a system of statuses)." *The Savage Mind* [no trans.] (Chicago: University of Chicago Press, 1966), p. 181.

30. Ibid. "At the other extreme, however, the name is a free creation on the part of the individual who *gives the name* and expresses a transitory and subjective state of his own by means of the person he names. But can one be said to be naming in either case? The choice seems only to be between identifying someone else by assigning him [or a play] to a class, or under cover of giving him a name, identifying oneself through him."

31. As Don E. Wayne writes in *Penshurst*, pp. 18–19, "the only freedom from a rigidly hierarchical system attainable for [Jonson] depended on the willing subjection of his power as a writer to the legitimation of the existing hierarchy. Yet in serving that function in exchange for the recognition and conservation of his genius, the writer became an embodiment of a new ideology, one that asserted the possibility of individual transcendence."

32. Henry Peacham, *The Compleat Gentleman* (London: Francis Constable, 1627), p. 54.

33. Angel Day, *The English Secretary* (London: O.S. for C. Burbic, 1599), p. 1. For theoretical discussions of forewords, prefaces, and epistles as authorial devices for the recuperation of written texts already free of the limiting hand of the writer, see Jacques Derrida, "Hors livre: préfaces," in *La dissémination*, pp. 7–67; Louis Marin, "Avant-Propos," *Études sémiologiques: écritures, peintures* (Paris: Éditions Klincksieck, 1971), pp. 7–14; Timothy C. Murray, "Kenneth Burke's Logology: A Mock Logomachy," *Glyph* 2 (1977), 144–61.

34. H & S, IV, 33.

35. Ibid., VIII, 26.

36. Barish, *The Antitheatrical Prejudice*, p. 139.

37. Newton, "Jonson and the (Re-)Invention of the Book," p. 40. This distinction corresponds to Sweeney's perceptive point, in *Jonson and the Psychology of Public Theater*, p. 130, that "we admit to our idea of theater as a social experience valued for its ability to affirm human community, the suggestion that theater might actually exclude its audience from the communal experience it seems to promise." Stanley Fish, in "Authors-Readers: Jonson's Community of the Same," in *Lyric Poetry: Beyond New Criticism*, ed. Chaviva Hosek and Patricia Parker (Ithaca: Cornell University Press, 1985), pp. 132–47, argues that Jonson's poetry, in stripping its readers of judgment, actually establishes a "community of the same." If this is the case, I would argue that Jonson stands aside as the figure of authorial difference.

38. H & S, VIII, 25.

39. H & S, VIII, 26.

40. In "'Beware the Poet': Authority and Judgement in Jonson's *Epi-*

grammes," 106, Jennifer Brady writes that "the grammatical structures of the [Pembroke] dedication, in its inward quality, make it clear that we have been prejudged. Jonson places the burden of deciphering his assertions on us." My reading of the passage suggests, moreover, that the reader's burden here, like that of Sisyphus, is everlasting.

41. H & S, V, 431.

42. Newton, "Jonson and the (Re-)Invention of the Book," p. 40.

43. See Orgel, "The Royal Theatre and the Role of the King," in *Patronage in the Renaissance,* ed. Guy Fitch Lytle and Stephen Orgel (Princeton: Princeton University Press, 1981), pp. 261–73.

44. H & S, IV, 301.

45. Ibid., V, 19.

46. Ibid., 17.

47. Émile Benveniste, *Le Vocabulaire des institutions indo-européennes* (Paris: Éditions de Minuit, 1969), II, 121. "[An arbiter] does not make decisions according to formulas and laws, but by his/her own sentiment and in the name of fairness. The *arbiter* is in reality a *iudex* who acts as *arbiter*; she judges by coming between the parties unexpectedly, by coming from outside as someone who assisted in the business without being seen, who can thus judge freely and without appeal of the case, beyond all precedent and in terms of the circumstances. This liaison with the first sense of 'witness who was not a third party' permits comprehension of the specialized sense of *arbiter* in juridical language."

48. H & S, VII, 313.

49. Ibid., VIII, 386.

50. Ibid., 400.

51. For a discussion of Ramistic "Dialectic as Art or Doctrine," and its "Invention: Questions, Arguments, Places," see Ong, *Ramus, Method, and the Decay of Dialogue,* pp. 171–213.

52. Jonathan Goldberg, *James I and the Politics of Literature,* p. 57.

53. Jacques Derrida, *De la Grammatologie* (Paris: Éditions de Minuit, 1967), p. 404. "The movement of idealization: an algebrizing, de-poeticizing formalization whose operation is to repress—in order to master it better—the charged signifier or the linked hieroglyph," *Of Grammatalogy,* trans. Gayatri Chakravorty Spivak (Baltimore: The Johns Hopkins University Press, 1976), p. 284.

54. H & S, VII, 229.

55. Orgel, *The Jonsonian Masque,* pp. 81–83.

56. Ibid., p. 87.

57. Goldberg, *James I and the Politics of Literature,* p. 59.

58. H & S, VII, 250.

59. Ibid., 90–91. On narrative theory of description, see the special issue of *Yale French Studies,* "Towards a Theory of Description," 61 (1981); Marc Eli Blanchard, *Description: Sign, Self, Desire: Critical Theory*

in the Wake of Semiotics (The Hague: Mouton, 1980); Georg Lukács, "Narrate or Describe?" in *Writer & Critic and Other Essays*, trans. Arthur D. Kahn (New York: Grosset & Dunlap, 1971), pp. 110–48.

60. H & S, VII, 306.

61. Ibid., 308–09.

62. Orgel, *The Jonsonian Masque*, p. 69.

63. H & S, VII, 213.

64. For theoretically acute discussions of this ideological shift, see Wayne, *Penshurst*, p. 148; and Loewenstein, *Responsive Readings*, p. 117.

65. Benjamin, "The Author As Producer," *Reflections*, ed. Peter Demetz (New York: Harcourt Brace Jovanovich, 1978), pp. 234–35.

66. H & S, VII, 109.

67. Ibid., 221.

68. Ibid., 286.

69. Loewenstein, *Responsive Readings*, p. 115, suggests that Jonson's poetic strategy in *The Masque of Queenes* "points both to his own figurative energies and shows the king the many ways in which what he watches is distinct from himself."

70. H & S, VII, 343.

71. N. G. L. Hammond and H. H. Scullard, eds., *Oxford Classical Dictionary* (Oxford: The Clarendon Press, 1970), p. 989.

72. H & S, VIII, 561. In *James I and the Politics of Literature*, p. 124, Goldberg undertakes a fascinating analysis of the role of Silenus in *Oberon*. In arguing for Silenus's contribution to the ideology of royalist centralization, Goldberg makes a point which also suggests the workings of a more authorial allegory of reading: "The masque is not structured like earlier, dualistic masques, as a series of exclusions rising to a final truth. Rather, it is constructed by layerings and deepenings, a study in mediation and dissolution."

73. Derrida, *La vérité en peinture*, p. 81. "Do violence to the interior of the system and distort its own articulations."

74. Loewenstein's similar observations about the actual performance-dialectic of perspective and diffused visions further suggest the impressive breadth of his analysis in *Responsive Readings*, pp. 61–132. I propose a specifically anamorphic theory of reading in "A Marvelous Guide to Anamorphosis: *Cendrillon ou La Petite Pantoufle de Verre*," *MLN*, 91, No. 6 (December 1976), 1276–95.

75. H&S, VII, 282.

76. In *Trials of Desire: Renaissance Defenses of Poetry* (New Haven: Yale University Press, 1983), p. 161, Margaret W. Ferguson discusses Sidney's similar allegorical positioning and the attendant inconstancy of allegorical transference: "Neither the courtier nor the author of a written text, however, can make an audience 'note' his words, and Sidney's ambivalent recognition of this fact makes his discourse oscillate between two modes of

allegory—an 'old' one associated with classical oratory (with its emphasis on 'clarity'), and a new one closer to what Puttenham recommended to those who would safely address the Queen: 'Allegoria,' the 'courtly figure,' to 'speake one thing and thinke another.' Indeed the passage about Menenius and Nathan is an 'allegory of allegory' in which both modes dialogically confront one another: it is a complex mirror that refracts not only Sidney's desires for a golden world but his awareness of a brazen one. 'My only service is speech, and that is stopped,' he wrote in 1580. In the *Defence*, his efforts to serve both himself and the Queen take many shapes of 'false semblant.'" Christopher Pye, in "The Sovereign, the Theater, and the Kingdome of Darknesse: Hobbes and the Spectacle of Power," *Representations*, 8 (Fall 1984), 85–106, looks beyond Jonson in analyzing a similar allegory of genius for Hobbes.

77. H & S, VII, 412.
78. Ibid., VIII, 616.

Chapter 5

1. Bentley, *The Profession of Dramatist in Shakespeare's Time*, p. 52.
2. Ibid., pp. 55–56.
3. John Dryden, *Of Dramatick Poesie, An Essay*, in Vol. XVII of *The Works of John Dryden*, ed. Samuel Holt and A. E. Wallace Maurer (Berkeley: University of California Press, 1971).
4. Loewenstein, in *Responsive Readings*, pp. 11–12, 119–25, discusses printing's alienation from the exclusivity of the court.
5. John Locke, "Of Property," *Two Treatises of Government* (London: Dent, 1977), pp. 129–41. See also C. B. MacPherson's substantial, Marxist explication of Locke's essay, *The Political Theory of Possessive Individualism: Hobbes to Locke* (Oxford: The Clarendon Press, 1962).
6. In *Penshurst*, p. 160, Wayne summarizes the "painful contradiction that is generally characteristic of Jonson's work: that is, while merit based on intellectual accomplishment is the means through which the poet-commoner asserts his freedom, and while the accomplishment is held to be an external sign of the interior quality of the man, the recognition of such merit depends finally on the same system of rationalized commodity exchange that Jonson satarizes in its more acquisitive forms." On Jonson and these acquisitive forms, see Wayne's Ph.D. dissertation, *Ben Jonson, The 'Anti-Acquisitive Attitude' and the Accumulated Discourse: Contribution to a Historico Semiotics*, Diss. University of California, San Diego, 1975; and Walter Cohen, *Drama of a Nation*, pp. 292–301.
7. Samuel Johnson, "Preface to Shakespeare," *Jonson on Shakespeare*, VII, 90.
8. Ibid., 84.

9. Ibid., 88.

10. Ibid., 62–63.

11. In *Samuel Johnson and Neoclassical Dramatic Theory: The Intellectual Context of the Preface to Shakespeare* (Lincoln: University of Nebraska Press, 1973), R. D. Stock discusses how Lockian epistemology influences Johnson's reading of Shakespeare.

12. On the confusing relation of originality and plagiarism, see Stephen Orgel, "The Renaissance Artist as Plagiarist," *ELH* 48, No. 3 (Fall 1981), 484; and Thomas McFarland, "The Originality Paradox," *New Literary History* 5, No. 3 (Spring, 1974), 460.

13. Johnson, *Johnson on Shakespeare*, VII, 55.

14. Ibid., 91.

15. Alexander Pope, "Preface to 'The Works of Shakespear,'" *Eighteenth Century Essays on Shakespeare*, ed. D. Nichol Smith (Oxford: The Clarendon Press, 1963), p. 48.

16. John Dennis, "On the Genius and Writings of Shakespear," *Eighteenth Century Essays on Shakespeare*, p. 23.

17. Pope, "Preface," p. 44.

18. James Boswell, *Boswell's Life of Johnson*, ed. George Birkbeck Hill, revised by L. F. Powell (Oxford: The Clarendon Press, 1934–1950), I, 196.

19. Ibid., 167. In *The Antitheatrical Prejudice*, p. 280, Barish makes an interesting argument for the Platonic overtones of Johnson's prejudice against actors.

20. For an illuminating discussion of the ideological transformation of this period's dramatic form, see Laura Brown, *English Dramatic Form, 1660–1760: An Essay in Generic History* (New Haven: Yale University Press, 1981).

21. Johnson, *Johnson on Shakespeare*, VII, 65.

22. Leopold Damrosch, Jr., *Samuel Johnson and the Tragic Sense* (Princeton: Princeton University Press), p. 201.

23. Johnson, *Johnson on Shakespeare*, VII, 63–64.

24. William Prynne, *Histriomastix,* p. 208. Also see David Leverenz, "Why Did Puritans Hate Stage Plays?"

25. Dryden, "Preface to *Troilus and Cressida*," in *Four Centuries of Shakespearian Criticism*, ed. Frank Kermode (New York: Avon, 1965), p. 48.

26. Johnson, *Johnson on Shakespeare*, VII, 64.

27. Johnson, "Notes on *Antony and Cleopatra*," in *Johnson on Shakespeare*, VIII, 873.

28. Laura Brown, in *English Dramatic Form, 1660–1760*, pp. 81–86, analyzes Cleopatra's questionable character in Dryden's *All For Love* as "a seductrice, a courtesan, a liar, a conniver, and a traitor."

29. James Barclay, *An examination of Mr. Kenrick's review* (1766), rpt. in *On Johnson's Shakespeare, 1765–1766. Johnsoniana II* (New York: Garland Publishing, 1975), pp. 22–23.

30. Johnson, *Johnson on Shakespeare*, VII, 159.

31. *Boswell's Life of Johnson*, I, 201, suggests that the "feminine arts" posed as much a literal as a figural problem for Johnson: "He for a considerable time used to frequent the *Green Room*, and seemed to take delight in dissipating his gloom, by mixing in the sprightly chit-chat of the motley circle then to be found there. Mr. David Hume related to me from Mr. Garrick, that Johnson at last denied himself this amusement, from considerations of rigid virtue; saying, 'I'll come no more behind your scenes, David; for the silk stockings and white bosoms of your actresses excite my amorous propensities.'" Boswell also recounts, II, 464–65, how Johnson's anxieties over love stemmed from an early experience with the theatre: "When we were by ourselves he told me, 'Forty years ago, Sir, I was in love with an actress here, Mrs. Emmet, who acted Flora, in 'Hob in the Well'.' What merit this lady had as an actress, or what was her figure, or her manner, I have not been informed: but, if we may believe Mr. Garrick, his old master's taste in theatrical merit was by no means refined; he was not an *elegans formarum spectator*." I thank Neil Hertz for calling these passages to my attention.

32. Boswell, *Boswell's Life of Johnson*, II, 89.

33. Ibid., II, 88.

34. Jacques Derrida, *L'Écriture et la différence*, pp. 284–85. "Europe lives upon this ideal of the separation between force and meaning as text, at the very moment when . . . in purportedly elevating the mind above the letter, it states a preference for metaphorical writing. This derivation of force within the sign divides the theatrical act, exiles the actor far from any responsibility for meaning, makes of him an interpreter who lets his life be breathed into him, and lets his words be whispered to him, receiving his delivery as if he were taking orders, submitting like a beast to the pleasure of docility. Like the seated public, he is but a consumer, an aesthete, a 'pleasure-taker.' The stage is no longer cruel, is no longer the stage, but a decoration, the luxurious illustration of a book. In the best of cases, another literary genre." *Writing and Difference*, trans. Alan Bass (Chicago: University of Chicago Press, 1978), p. 189.

Chapter 6

1. "A portrait is a rather inconsequential picture for those who do not know the person it represents; but this portrait is a precious picture for those who love the person portrayed."

2. Jacques de Bie, "Au Roy" [dedication], *Les vrais PORTRAITS des ROIS DE FRANCE. Tirez de ce qui nous reste de leurs Monumens, sceaux, medailles, ou autres Effigies, conservées dans les plus rares & plus curieux Cabinets du Royaum* (Paris: J. Camusat, 1636). "I am confident that those, who will see your Name on the frontispiece of this admirable structure, will not be able to refrain from entering it in order to regard its marvels with delight. If they are capable of appreciating them properly, they will acknowledge that your Image, which I have placed at the farthest end of this Sanctuary, as in the most honorable place, is truly the perfect ornament and the Guardian Genius of this entire work. I know, Sire, that Time, however powerful it is, has no mastery over your Royal Virtues which of themselves are more durable than the Medals of the Alexanders and the Cesars. Accordingly I have placed your image in this Book, only to propose it as a model of what has ever been the most Majestic in the World, and as an examplar after which the greatest Kings of the Earth are obliged to fashion themselves."

3. For a discussion of forms of portraiture in seventeenth-century France, see Erica Harth, *Ideology and Culture in Seventeenth-Century France* (Ithaca: Cornell University Press, 1983), pp. 68–128. I should point out, however, that the following analyses are closer in allegorical tone and critical purpose to Louis Marin's intricate study, *Le Portrait du roi*. In critiquing Marin's book because "there is no historical dimension to this analysis," p. 77, Harth strips from her study attentiveness to the most complex historical manifestations of portraiture: the rhetorical and allegorical shapes of sovereignty and patronage. Indeed, in looking past the representational structures of rhetoric, Harth's sensitive socio-political analysis undervalues the allegorical depth of seventeenth-century portraiture, and the import of historical transference, the regeneration of fact through theoretical narration and representation.

4. John Gordon Sweeney III, in *Jonson and the Psychology of Public Theater*, offers a wide-ranging discussion of Jonson's unsuccessful attempts to manipulate poetics for the sake of altering his relationship to his audience.

5. See Marin, *Le Portrait du roi*, pp. 171–205, a version of which appears in English: "The Inscription of the King's Memory: On the Metallic History of Louis XIV," *Yale French Studies*, 59 (1980), 17–36; Jean-Marie Apostolidès, *Le roi-machine: spectacle et politique au temps de Louis XIV* (Paris: Éditions de Minuit, 1981), pp. 25–35.

6. Charles-H. Boudhors, "Notice," the preface to Nicolas Boileau-Despréaux, *Art Poétique* (Paris: Société Les Belles Lettres, 1967), p. 258. "It should not be forgotten that the Académie Française, as early as its founding, promised a *Grammar* and a *Poetics*. An effort was constantly pursued to regulate language, to classify the 'works of the mind,' to define the 'genres.' What we see now as only deceptive and illusory ambition was consid-

ered at that time as the legitimate and necessary measure of progress and order."

7. For varying discussions of the Académie's attentiveness to the neo-classical dramatic text, see Henry C. Lancaster, *A History of French Dramatic Literature in the Seventeenth Century*, 12 vols. (Baltimore: Johns Hopkins University Press, 1929–42); René Bray, *La formation de la doctrine classique in France* (1927; rpt. Paris: Nizet, 1951); Jean Jacquot, *La vie théâtrale du temps de la Renaissance* (Paris: Institut Pédagogique Nationale, 1963); and *Le lieu théâtral à la Renaissance* (Paris: Éditions du Centre de la Recherche Scientifique, 1964).

Chapter 7

1. Paul Robert, *Dictionnaire alphabétique et analogique de la langue française* (Paris: Société du Nouveau Littré, 1959), IV, 228. "Acknowledgment of powers (of a sovereign, of an envoy)."

2. Ibid. "Action of legitimizing, of justifying."

3. My emphasis on acknowledgment is indebted strongly to two essays by Stanley Cavell, "Knowing and Acknowledging" and "The Avoidance of Love: A Reading of *King Lear*," both in *Must We Mean What We Say?* (Cambridge: Cambridge University Press, 1976), pp. 238–353. See also Cavell's *The Claim of Reason: Wittgenstein, Skepticism, Morality, and Tragedy* (New York: Oxford University Press, 1979), pp. 329–496.

4. For a discussion of the contemporary relation of legitimation and aesthetics, see Lyotard's previously cited texts along with David Craven, "Hans Haacke and the Aesthetics of Legitimation," *Parachute* 23 (Summer 1981), 4–11.

5. *Le dictionnaire de l'Académie Française*, 2 (Paris: Jean Baptiste Coignard, 1964). "To declare legitimate by sovereign authority, to make publicly known as legitimate."

6. François Parfaict, *Histoire du théâtre françois* (Paris: Lemercier and Saillant, 1746), VI, 132–33. "We decree that their practice, which can innocently distract our people from numerous injurious pursuits, can neither bring blame on them nor harm their reputation in public affairs."

7. The notion of performative discourse, or speech act, is developed in J. L. Austin, *How To Do Things With Words*, 2d ed. (Oxford: Oxford University Press, 1962), and in John R. Searle, *Speech Acts: An Essay in the Philosophy of Language* (London: Cambridge University Press, 1969). My later emphasis on the figural importance of performatives as simulacra rather than as dependable realities accords with recent deconstructive readings of speech act theory. See Jacques Derrida, "Signature événement contexte," *Marges de le philosophie* (Paris: Éditions de Minuit, 1972), pp. 365–93, and "Limited Inc abc . . ."; Samuel Weber, "It," *Glyph*, 4 (1978), 1–31;

Gayatri Chakravorty Spivak, "Revolutions That As Yet Have No Model: Derrida's *Limited Inc*," *Diacritics*, 8 (Winter 1980), 29–49; Barbara Johnson, "Poetry and Performative Language: Mallarmé and Austin," *The Critical Difference* (Baltimore: The Johns Hopkins University Press, 1980), pp. 52–66; and Stanley E. Fish, "With the Compliments of the Author: Reflections on Austin and Derrida," *Critical Inquiry*, 8 (Summer 1982), 693–721.

8. For analyses of the relation of speech acts and self-representation, see Jean-François Lyotard, *Rudiments païens: genre dissertatif* (Paris: 10/18, 1977); Louis Marin, *Le récit est un piège* (Paris: Éditions de Minuit, 1978), and *Le Portrait du roi*; Paul de Man, *Allegories of Reading*, pp. 119–31; Shoshana Felman, *Le Scandale du corps parlant: Don Juan avec Austin, ou La séduction en deux langues* (Paris: Éditions du Seuil, 1980); Monique Schneider, "The Promise of Truth—the Promise of Love," *Diacritics*, 11 (Fall 1981), 27–38; Stanley E. Fish, "How To Do Things with Austin and Searle: Speech Act Theory and Literary Criticism, *MLN*, 91 (October 1976), 983–1025; Donald K. Hedrick, "Merry and Weary Conversation: Textual Uncertainty in *As You Like It*, II. iv.," *ELH*, 46 (Spring 1979), 21–34.

9. Parfaict, VI, 128. "[theatregoers who] talk, whistle, and shout constantly, and . . . go to the theatre only because they have nothing better to do."

10. T. E. Lawrenson, *The French Stage in the XVIIth Century* (Manchester: Manchester University Press, 1957), pp. 81–85.

11. I should point out that Antoine Adam argues against the radical generic difference between the plays performed at the Marais and at the Bourgogne, in *Histoire de la littérature française au XVIIᵉ siècle* (Paris: Éditions Domat-Montchrestien, 1948), I, 460–61. Although the Marais was not entirely different from the Bourgogne, it did emphasize tragedy, while the Bourgogne specialized in tragicomedy and farce. For further discussions emphasizing the difference between these two theatres, see Lawrenson, *The French Stage in the XVIIth Century*; Sophie Wilma Deierkauf-Holsboer, *L'histoire de la mise en scène dans le théâtre français à Paris, de 1600 à 1673* (Paris: Librarie A. Nizet, 1960); and W. L. Wiley, *The Early Public Theater in France* (Cambridge, Mass.: Harvard University Press, 1960).

12. Charles Arnaud, *Étude sur la vie et les oeuvres de l'Abbé d'Aubignac et sur les théories dramatiques au XVIIᵉ siècle* (Paris: Alphonse Picard, 1887), p. 184. This might be an opportune moment to mention Timothy J. Reiss's interesting comparison of Richelieu's notion of government and later seventeenth-century Racinian tragedy. In *Tragedy and Truth: Studies in the Development of a Renaissance and Neoclassical Discourse* (New Haven: Yale University Press, 1980), p. 220, Reiss discusses *Bajazet* in terms of how "the political theory of the period (my examples will be drawn from Richelieu and Hobbes) argues that power must be accompanied by will and by knowledge, that real power consists in action, that these ele-

ments may be situated in a general field wherein reason is pitted against passion: 'passion' will cause the search for power and its practice to be utterly ineffectual (Richelieu)." While Reiss's discussion of neoclassical tragedy in view of Hobbes provides us with a refreshing outlook, I will soon make clear how I understand Richelieu's exercise of power to rely as much on desire as on reason.

13. Adam, *Histoire de la littérature française au XVII° siècle*, I, 464.

14. Lancaster, *A History of French Dramatic Literature in the Seventeenth Century*, Part 2, I, 128–44.

15. *L'ami du Cid à Claveret* in *Recueil des bonnes pièces qui ont esté faites pour & contre le Cid, Par les bons esprits de ce temps* (Paris: Nicolas Traboulliet, 1637), p. 4. "It is completely ridiculous that . . . you would wish to write and to compare yourself to one of the greatest men of our century for the theatre and that you would doubt, moreover, the approbation *Le Cid* received at both the Louvre and the Hôtel de Richelieu."

16. Pierre Corneille, *Lettre apologétique du S' Corneille, contenant sa response aux observations faites par le S' Scudéry sur le Cid*, in *Recueil des bonnes pièces*, p. 4. Also reprinted in Corneille, *Théâtre complet* (Paris: Éditions Garniers Frères, 1971), 1, 717–18. "Did you not remember that *Le Cid* was played three times at the Louvre and two times at the Hôtel de Richelieu? When you called poor Chimène lewd, whorish, parricidal, and monstrous, did you not remember that she was received and embraced as an honorable girl by the Queen, the Princesses, and the most virtuous Women of the Paris Court?"

17. Corneille, *Lettre apologétique*, p. 5; *Théâtre complet*, I, 178. "I even took the original Spanish text to his Grace, the Cardinal, your Master and mine."

18. Adam, *Histoire de la littérature française au XVII° siècle*, I, 467. "Under the control of a domineering genius."

19. Before the Salle de la Comédie was constructed, there were probably a number of small private theatres in and around Paris. Richelieu himself had two. A small theatre on his estate at Rueil was used for rehearsals and impromptu performances. The cardinal also maintained a larger theatre, seating 600, at the Palais Cardinal. However, the grandeur of this theatre's spectacle was limited by its size. Neither theatre, moreover, was equipped like the Salle to signify the political stature of its patron.

20. Lawrenson, *The French Stage in the XVIIth Century*, pp. 172–73.

21. Henry Sauval, *Histoire et recherches des antiquités de la Ville de Paris* (Paris: Moette Chardon, 1724), II, 163. "Oak beams of such an extraordinary and prodigious length."

22. Michel de Marolles, *Memoires* (Amsterdam: n.p., 1755), I, 236. "One entered the room only by tickets, and these tickets were given only to those who were recorded in his Eminence's memorandum, each according

to his condition; thus there were tickets for the Ladies, for the Lords, for the Ambassadors, for the Foreigners, for the Prelates, for the Officers of Justice, and for the Men of War."

23. *Gazette*, 19 January 1641, cited by Léopold Lacour, *Richelieu dramaturge et ses collaborateurs* (Paris: Librarie Ollendorff, 1925), p. 115. "Generals Jean de Werth, Enkenfort and Dom Pedro de Léon, prisoners of war, were included, having been taken [to the theatre] from the Vincennes Woods."

24. Sauval, *Histoire et recherches des antiquités de la Ville de Paris*, II, 162.

25. Lawrenson, *The French Stage in the XVIIth Century*, p. 171.

26. Orgel, "The Poetics of Spectacle," 378.

27. Although Louis XIII came to various performances at the Palais Cardinal and joined Richelieu on the dais, Richelieu's performance tended to upstage the king. See my "Richelieu's Theater: The Mirror of a Prince," *Renaissance Drama*, NS 8 (1977), 296–97.

28. De Marolles, *Memoires*, I, 235–36. "The machines that caused the sun and the moon to rise and showed a distant sea filled with vessels." The *Gazette* prints a more elaborate description of the spectacle: "dont la perspective apportât plus de ravissement aux yeux des spectateurs . . . de fort délicieux jardins, ornés de grottes, de statues, de fontaines et de grands parterres en terrasses sur la mer, avec des agitations, qui semblaient naturelles, aux vagues de ce vaste élément, et deux grandes flottes, dont l'une paraissait éloignée de deux lieues, qui passèrent toutes deux à la vue des spectateurs. La nuit sembla arriver ensuite par l'obscurcissement imperceptible tant du jardin que de la mer et du ciel qui se trouva éclairé de la lune." "Whose perspective produced more rapture in the eyes of the spectators . . . incredibly delightful gardens, made more beautiful with grottoes, statues, fountains, and large terraced flower beds, overlooking the sea, a vast element whose movements appeared as natural as tossing waves, and two large fleets, one that seemed two leagues away, passing within the view of the spectators. Then nighttime appeared to arrive with the imperceptible darkening of the garden as well as of the sea and the sky lit by the moon." Cited by Lancaster, *A History of French Dramatic Literature in the Seventeenth Century*, Part 2, II, 376. These scenic devices are illustrated in a series of engravings by della Bella that depicts a scene from each act of *Mirame* (Paris: Le Gras, 1641), reproduced in Alexandre de Vesme and Phyllis Dearborn Massar, *Stefano della Bella* (New York: Collectors Editions, 1971), Prints Nos. 937–41, II, 200–02.

29. Paul Pellison-Fontanier, *Relations concernant l'histoire de l'Académie Francoise* (Paris: Augustin Courbé, 1653), p. 178. "Whose production cost him two or three hundred crowns."

30. Sebastiano Serlio, *The first [-fifth] Booke of Architecture* (London: R. Peake, 1611), Book 2, Chap. 3, fol. 26.

31. Orgel, *The Illusion of Power: Political Theater in the English Renaissance* (Berkeley: University of California Press, 1975), p. 37.

32. The Salle de la Comédie also boasted the first French proscenium arch curtain, which called attention to the hidden wonders of the stage. See Lawrenson, *The French Stage in the XVIIth Century*, p. 138; and Wiley, *The Early Public Theater in France*, p. 198.

33. De Marolles, *Memoires*, I, 236, even complained that the emphasis on perspective diminished the quality of spectacle in the Salle de la Comédie: "je n'en trouvai pas l'action beaucoup meilleure pour toutes ces belles machines, & grandes perspectives. Les yeux se lassent bientôt de cela, & l'esprit de ceux qui s'y connoissent, n'en n'est guere plus satisfait." "I did not find the action of the play to be any better for all of these pretty machines and vast perspectives. The eyes tire of that soon enough, and the minds of those knowledgeable about theatre were not at all satisfied."

34. Jean Duvignaud, *Sociologie du théâtre* (Paris: Presses Universitaires de France, 1965), pp. 262–78. More recently, Orgel, in *The Illusion of Power* and "The Poetics of Spectacle," discusses the significance of such perspectival centering in the English court theatre.

35. Roland Fréart, Sieur de Chambray, *Idée de la perfection de la peinture demonstrée par les principes de l'art* (Le Mans: J. Ysambart, 1662), p. 20. "This indispensable art, which the learned have named 'Optique' and which painters and all designers commonly call 'Perspective,' provides the infallible means to represent with precision on a surface (such as the canvas of a painting, a wall, a piece of paper, or something comparable) all that the eye sees and can encompass in a single glance while remaining fixed in the same place."

36. Ibid., p. 40. "That the point of view represents the eye that sees the painting."

37. Ibid., p. 19. "Geometricians, who are the real masters of this question, use the word *optique* to express the intelligence, meaning by this term the art of seeing things by reason and with the eyes of understanding: for it would be quite impertinent to imagine that the body's eyes were themselves capable of such a sublime operation as being able to be judges of the beauty and the excellence of a painting."

38. Although it is not my intention to become engrossed in a complex discussion of seventeenth-century painting theory, I wish to note that the relation *portrait:perspective* is stressed repeatedly in theoretical texts of the period. Granted, these texts often refer to the process of painting a portrait *in* perspective. But, still, the insistence on the common nomination of portraiture and perspective by such a central critic as Abraham Bosse is suggestive: "l'on remarquera que j'ay dit que le nom de Perspective, Pourtrait, Pourtraiture, ou Representation platte, signifient tous une mesme chose." "One will notice that I said that the names *perspective, pourtrait, pourtraiture, representation platte* all signify the same thing." *Traité des pratiques*

*geometrales & perspectives enseignées dans l'Académie Royale de la Pein-
ture et Sculpture* (Paris: chez l'Auteur, 1665), p. 3. Moreover, in Fréart's text
cited above, the correlation of portrait and perspective includes not only
the process of painting but also the act of viewing the portrait in perspective. Bosse also insists on the double relation of painting and visual
perspective:

> le but de la Regle de la Perspective est, de faire, former & figurer, toucher &
> colorer une Pourtraiture, en façon que veüe de sa distance reglée, elle fasse
> avoir à l'oeil qui la regarde toute la mesme sensation & expression visuelle
> que le sujet qu'elle represente luy feroit avoir, si au lieu de cette Pourtraiture,
> il regardoit le sujet mesme aussi de sa distance reglée; qui est ce en quoy con-
> siste l'essentiel effet de ce qu'on nomme le Pourtrait d'un tel sujet ou objet.

> the purpose of the rule of perspective is to make, form, and figure, to depict
> and color a portraiture so that when viewed from the correct distance it causes
> the beholder's eye to experience the same sensation and visual expression that
> the subject represented by the portrait would provoke if, instead of the por-
> trait, the subject itself were viewed also from the correct distance; this is what
> constitutes the essential effect of what we call the portrait of a given subject or
> object. (p. 44)

If perspective is the application and signification of all that is implied by
the notion of "optique," it should not only create for the viewer a mimetic
picture of the subject portrayed but also provide the idea of the mental perspective ("entendement") portrayed. In brief, one perspective leads to
another. The optical perspective of the viewer imitates the perspective of
the canvas, and the mental perspective of the viewer reflects that shown by
the portrait. A similar reflection of perspective functioned in the Salle de la
Comédie between the vanishing point, Richelieu, and his beholders.

39. Lyotard discusses the representational structure of simulacra in
Économie libidinale (Paris: Éditions de Minuit, 1974), pp. 57–115. In his
fascinating essay treating similar sovereign, perspectival representation in
Hobbes, "The Sovereign, the Theater, and the Kingdome of Darknesse:
Hobbes and the Spectacle of Power," 103, Christopher Pye suggests that
"we discern the king's represented eye as a separate eye, an eye we see but
which doesn't see us. By separating the distinct powers of our gaze, by figuring our sight at once as the sight of the narcissist and the onlooker, the
spectacular figure enables us to complete a fantasy of absolute visibility, of
sight seeing itself seeing."

40. What I am describing is analogous to Edgar Wind's concept of
composite portraiture, presented in "Studies in Allegorical Portraiture I,"
Journal of the Warburg and Courtauld Institutes, 1 (1937–38), 139. Erica
Harth discusses literal examples of the artistic portraiture of Richelieu in
Ideology and Culture in Seventeenth-Century France, pp. 70–71, 81–82.

41. "The Comic Poet thus recounts to us adventures of our equals, and
he presents us with portraits whose originals we see every day. Pardon me
the expression: he brings the groundlings themselves up on the stage."

42. Corneille, *Théâtre complet*, I, 238. "Comedy is but a portrait of our actions and our words."

43. François Hédelin, Abbé d'Aubignac, *Dissertation sur la condamnation des théatres* (Paris: N. Pepingué, 1666), p. 139. "As a magnificent and tangible portrait of the fortune of the great."

44. Adam, I, 560. "A certain number of bizarre characters, probably easily recognizable by an informed audience. Thus, it involved neither a drama of intrigue, nor a comedy of manners, nor a study of character. What Richelieu expected was hardly even a play, but a series of portraits."

45. D'Aubignac, *Le Martyre de Ste Catherine* (Caën: Eleazar Mangeant, 1650), p. 85.

> Ha! Madam, here is what will put you to the test,
> Valere does not come unintentionally to find you.
> The Sentence of your doom is painted on his countenance.

46. Ibid., p. 103.

> I dare not suspect your spirit of other charms,
> It has never resorted to such cowardly armes;
> All of the spell it practices is written in your eyes.

47. Ibid., p. 112. "You who see the pleasure I receive from it in my soul, Incomparable object of an eternal flame!"

48. D'Aubignac, *Le Roman des lettres* (Paris: Baptiste Loyson, 1667), pp. 378–79. "All the eyes arrested on your person, seek there less the traits of your visage than the secrets of your soul."

49. Antoine Coypel, *L'excellence de la peinture*, in Nicolas Jouin, ed., *Discours prononcés dans les conferences de l'Académie Royale de Peinture et de Sculpture* (Paris: J. Collombat, 1721), p. 258. "Molière was able to paint the character of men so well that many people whom he had never considered took the portraits painted after nature in general to be their own; these were the ones who fled his performances in order to spare themselves the secret displeasure aroused in them by the vivid painting of the faults that they knew they had and that they had had the misfortune to cherish too dearly."

50. Cited by Léopold Lacour, *Richelieu dramaturge et ses collaborateurs*, p. 116. "The Cardinal . . . was so engrossed in the plot of his play that he could only admire himself in his own work."

51. Agne Beijer, in "Une maquette de décor récemment retrouvée pour le 'Ballet de la prosperité des armes de France,'" in *Le lieu théâtral à la Renaissance*, ed. Jean Jacquot, p. 378, suggests that this engraving, which she attributes to van Lochon, is modelled after the sketch "Intérieur du Théâtre du Palais Cardinal" (Musée des Arts Décoratifs, Paris).

52. Corneille, *Théâtre complet*, I, 825–26. "Certainly, my Grace, what is the visible change noticed in my works since I have had the honor of being in the service of your Eminence, if not an effect of the lofty thoughts

you inspire in me when you deign to allow me to present you with what is your due? And to what can be attributed the flaws mixed here except to the unrefined hues I revert to when I remain left to my own weakness? Everyone, My Grace, who dedicates his labors to the theatre must join me in proclaiming loudly that we owe two very obvious debts to you: one, to have ennobled the purpose of art; the other, to have made our understanding it easier . . . since to do so we no longer need any study other than fixing our eyes on your Eminence when you honor the reading of our poems with your presence and your attention. It is, then, by reading on your visage what pleases and displeases that we teach ourselves with assurance what is good and what is bad and draw infallible rules concerning what should be observed and what should be avoided: it is then that I often have learned in two hours what my books could not have taught me in ten years."

53. Georges de Scudéry, *Observations sur le Cid*, in *Recueil des bonnes pieces*, pp. 1–2. "I am not very surprised that the people, who pass judgment with their eyes, let themselves be fooled by that which is the easiest of all of the senses to deceive: But this gross vapour, which takes shape among the Groundlings, could have risen to the Galleries, and that a phantom had deluded knowledge as it does ignorance, and the Court as well as the Bourgeois, I admit that this marvel astonishes me."

54. Stephen Greenblatt, in *Renaissance Self-Fashioning* and "Invisible Bullets: Renaissance Authority and Its Subversion," *Glyph*, 8 (1981), 40–61, maintains that theatricality, in showing and disguising paradox and ambiguity, is one of royal power's essential modes.

55. Armand de Bourbon, Prince de Conti, *Traité de la comedie et des spectacles selon la tradition de l'eglise* (Paris: Louys Billaine, 1666), pp. 23–4. "Thus only in treatises on poetics does instruction still remain the end of dramatic poetry. This is no longer true, either in the intentions of the poet or in those of the spectator. The desire to please guides the former, and the latter is guided by the pleasure of seeing passions depicted on the stage which resemble one's own: for our self-love is so infirm that *we love to see the portraits of our passions as well as those of our persons*. Our self-love is even so incomprehensible that, through a strange reversal, it often *makes these portraits into our models* and that, in painting the passions of others, the theatre stirs our soul in such a way that it gives rise to our own passions and nourishes them once they have come alive."

56. Barish discusses various aspects of the psychology of the actor in *The Antitheatrical Prejudice*. Henry Philips presents an overview of the French antitheatrical position in *The Theatre and its Critics in Seventeenth-Century France* (Oxford: Oxford University Press, 1980). For illuminating discussions of the French psychology of self-love, see Marin, *La critique du discours* (Paris: Éditions du Minuit, 1975), pp. 215–38; Philip E. Lewis, *La Rochefoucauld: The Art of Abstraction* (Ithaca: Cornell Univ. Press, 1977), pp. 55–61. And on the relation of self-love to literary expression and pro-

duction, see Domna C. Stanton, *The Aristocrat As Art: A Study of the Hon-nête Homme and the Dandy in Seventeenth- and Nineteenth-Century French Literature* (New York: Columbia University Press, 1980).

57. Pierre Nicole, "De la connoissance de soy-même," *Essais de morale* (Paris: Guill. Desprez, 1675), III, 7–8. "Man likes to see himself because he is vain. He avoids seeing himself because, being vain, he cannot bear the sight of his faults and miseries. Therefore, to reconcile these desires, he turns to an artifice worthy of his vanity that provides him the means to satisfy both desires at once. This is the artifice of covering all his faults with a veil, obscuring them in some way with the image he has of himself, and including only those qualities that can enhance him in his own eyes. If he actually lacks the qualities, he acquires them through his imagination; and if he cannot find them in his own self, he will seek them in the opinions of others or in exterior objects that he associates with his idea as if they were part of it; and by means of this illusion, he is always absent from himself and present to himself: he constantly looks at himself, and he never truly sees himself, because in place of his self he sees only the vain phantom that he has made for himself."

58. Marin, *La critique du discours*, p. 219.

59. Nicole, "De la comédie," in *Les visionnaires* (Liège: Adolphe Beyers, 1667), p. 484. "That is enough to force all who have any care for their health to flee the Dramas, the Ball, and the Novels, there being nothing at all that drives the soul more outside of itself, that makes it more incapable of attending to God, and that replenishes it more with vain phantoms. Strange prayers are those which one utters in exiting these spectacles, having the head full of all of the forms of folly which one saw there."

60. Ibid., pp. 462–63. "Were it true that the theatre has no ill effect on some minds, they nevertheless could not take it to be an innocent pastime or believe that they are not guilty in attending it. Theatre is not performed for a single person: it is a spectacle that is presented before all sorts of minds, most of which are weak and corrupt and for whom theatre is consequently extremely dangerous. One may say that they are to blame for attending in this condition. This is true; but you legitimize them by your example . . . the more you are disciplined in your actions, the more they are impudent in imitating you in this one . . . and if theatre itself does not harm you, you harm yourself through the harm that others receive from your example."

61. A similar position concerning the moral influence of viewers was voiced by Jacques-Bénigne Bossuet in *Maximes & réflexions sur la comédie* (Paris: J. Anisson, 1694), p. 46: "quant à ceux qui frequentent les comedies, comme il y en a de plus innocens les uns que les autres, & peut-estre quelques-uns qu'il faut plûtost instruire que blasmer, ils ne sont pas reprehensibles en mesme degré, & il ne faut pas fulminer également contre tous. Mais de là s'il ne s'ensuit pas, qu'il faille autoriser les perils publics." "As

for those who frequent the theatres, since there are some who are more innocent than others, and perhaps some whom we should educate instead of criticize, they are not reprehensible to the same degree and we must not fulminate equally against all of them. But it cannot be concluded from this that one must sanction public dangers."

62. Nicole, "De la connoissance de soy-même," p. 17. "How many people make up the portrait of a prince! For him, all his kingdom, all the foreign countries are an academy of painters, for whom he is the model."

63. Ibid., p. 16. "To understand better how man could be compelled to see himself on his own through the objects outside himself and what he does to ensure this, we must consider that he sees himself no less according to a certain being that he has in the imagination of others than according to what he actually is; and he bases his portrait not only on what he knows of himself on his own but also on the perception of the portraits that he discovers in the minds of others. For we are all with regard to one another like the man who serves as a model for the pupils at the academies of painters. Everyone around us creates his own portrait of us; and the different ways in which our actions are viewed provide the occasion to create an almost infinite diversity of portraits."

64. Cited in *Le Dictionnaire universel d'Antoine Furetiere*, 1690 edition (Paris: Le Robert, 1978), II, s.v. "Miroir." "I did see myself in another as one sees oneself in a mirror, and much better than I saw myself introspectively."

Chapter 8

1. Pierre Nicole, "De la comédie," p. 494. "If temporal things are nothing but figures and shadows without solidity, one can say that Dramas are shadows of shadows, and figures of figures, since they are nothing but vain images of temporal things, and often of false things."

2. Ibid., p. 465. "Dramas and Novels excite not only the passions, but they also teach the language of the passions, that is to say, the art of expressing them and of making them appear in an agreeable and ingenious fashion, which is no small evil."

3. Nicole, "De la connoissance de soy-même," p. 17. "A common man . . . who lives with his family is painted only by the small number of those who know him, and the portraits made of him barely leave the confines of his Town."

4. Nicole, "De la comédie," p. 484.

5. Nicole, *Les Visionnaires*, p. 51. "You misuse the word *Comedies* and confuse him who writes them for the Theatre with him who translates them only for the Schools; but there is such a difference between the two

that one can draw no inferences about one from the other. The Translator has in his mind only the rules of Grammar which are not bad in themselves, and which a good purpose can render very favorable; but the Poet has very different ideas in his imagination, he feels all of the passions he conceives and even endeavors to experience them in order to better conceive them." Even a casual reference to the complex scenes of seventeenth-century Jesuit, school theatre would go far beyond the margins of this study. For comprehensive analyses, however, see François de Dainville, *L'Éducation des jésuites (XVIᵉ–XVIIIᵉ siècles)* (Paris: Éditions de Minuit, 1978), and William H. McCabe, S.J., *An Introduction to the Jesuit Theatre* (St. Louis: Institute of Jesuit Sources, 1983).

6. Nicole's example echoes my previous suggestion that Ben Jonson's interests in grammar were essentially antitheatrical. This chapter will discuss, even if sometimes only in passing, many similar examples of how grammarians place theatrical rhetoricity in opposition to the more favorable codes of reason and orderly grammatical praxis.

7. Nicole, *Les Visionnaires*, p. 51.

8. Du Marsais, *Traité des tropes* (Paris: Le Nouveau Commerce, 1977), p. 7. "It is generally said that *figures are manners of speaking removed from those that are natural and ordinary; that there are certain expressions and manners of speaking, which distance themselves in some fashion from the common and simple manner of speaking*: this means only that figures are manners of speaking removed from what is not figured, and that, in a word, figures are figures, and are not what is not a figure."

9. Cited by Louis Dimier in *Le Portrait en France au XVIIᵉ siècle* (Paris & Brussels: C. Van Oest et Cie, 1924), I, 177. "To say, paint my portrait, the prince exclaims: Write me."

10. Mademoiselle de Montpensier, *Recueil des portraits et eloges en vers et en prose* (Paris: Charles de Sercy et Claude Barbin, 1659), I, 11. "Marks and designates so well those whose lives it undertook that it seems we see them, that we speak with them, and that we enter into a very close intimacy with them." I will refer to this collection throughout as "Montpensier." Erica Harth, in her chapter "Of Portraits," *Ideology and Culture in Seventeenth-Century France*, pp. 68–128, discusses the sociological implications of the importance of written portraiture to women of the bourgeoisie. I might mention again, however, that Harth's disinterest in rhetoric as a structure of historical representations sometimes aligns her analyses in strategy and tone with the rational codes favored by the Port Royalists and other antitheatricalists. For discussions more sensitive to the rhetoric of female portraiture, see Gabrielle Verdier, "Mademoiselle de Montpensier et le plaisir du texte," *Papers on French Seventeenth Century Literature*, 18 (1983), 11–34; Verdier, "Les 'Lucrèces' sortent du 'grenier': portraits de femmes dans les *Lettres* de Madame de Sévigné, *Papers on French Seven-*

teenth Century Literature, 15, No. 2 (1981), 71–88; Domna Stanton, "On Female Portraiture in Sévigné's Letters," *Papers on French Seventeenth Century Literature*, 15, No. 2 (1981), 89–94.

11. "I prefer to say that [Voiture] agreeably makes sport with his subject, and that love Letters do not require a truthfulness as austere as that of dedicatory Epistles, which are grave and serious in themselves."

12. Edouard La Calprenède, "À Monseigneur L'Eminentissime Cardinal Duc de Richelieu," *La Mort des enfans d'Herodes ou suite de Mariane* (Paris: Augustin Courbé, 1639). "Certainly, Sir, when I consider the marvels of your life, I no longer believe that men have the power to describe things so infinitely above them; men can speak of them only as the Persians spoke of the Sun, and the most prudent, in imitation of the Painter, will no doubt cover with a veil what they cannot convey adequately; thus what satisfaction can one derive from one's nightly labors by bringing to light that which posterity will take only to be fables, since the marvels giving them shape seem so distant from the truth that they make things seem only apparent . . . and all of Europe is a table on which the history of your life is engraved in eternal characters. It is on this vast Theatre that you appeared with such pomp, and have obliged all of the world to suspend its own concerns to observe with what prudence and what command you discern our own."

13. This is a conventional method of introducing written portraits. In addition to heightening the praise and glory of the subject, such a declaration of the subject's indescribability frees the author from any criticism of his or her misrepresentation of the subject: "La Divine Reyne dont vous voulez que je vous fasse le Portrait, n'est pas une chose qui puisse estre peinte: & quand la Fortune vous osta l'occasion de la voir, vous ne deûtes pas vous promettre que tout ce qui est en elle vous pût jamais estre representé, puis qu'il faudroit des yeux propres à regarder fixement le Soleil, pour les oser lever sur elle, sans en estre ébloüis. Ne jugez donc pas de la Reyne du Nord, par ce que Je vous en vais dire, mais seulement de mon amitié pour vous, qui me fait entreprendre au delà du possible, vous donnant un Portrait qui feroit dans son entreprise trembler le plus hardy pinceau." "The Divine Queen, whose portrait you wish me to create, is not a thing which is able to be painted; and when Fortune deprived you of the opportunity of seeing her, you must not have anticipated that everything in her could ever be represented for you, since one must have eyes suitable for looking directly at the Sun in order to dare to look up on her without being dazzled. Therefore, do not judge the Queen of the North by what I will tell you of her, but judge only by my friendship for you that makes me undertake the impossible by giving you a Portrait whose attempt would make the most hardy brush tremble." Anonymous, *Portrait de la Reyne de Suede*, Montpensier, I, 59.

14. Leon Battista Alberti, *On Painting*, trans. John R. Spencer (New Haven: Yale University Press, 1966), pp. 68–69.

15. Ibid., p. 69.

16. Friedrich Nietzsche, *The Birth of Tragedy*, trans. Walter Kaufmann (New York: Vintage, 1967), p. 45.

17. Distinguishing between the immediate present of *énonciation* and the abstract time of universal maxims (*énoncé*), Philip E. Lewis uses the term "durative present," in *La Rochefoucauld: The Art of Abstraction*, p. 171.

18. See Gérard Genette, *Figures III* (Paris: Seuil, 1972); and Christian Metz, *Essais sur la signification au cinéma* (Paris: Klincksieck, 1968).

19. Aristotle, *The "Art" of Rhetoric*, trans. John Henry Freese (Cambridge, Mass.: Harvard University Press, 1939), pp. 34–35.

20. For a general discussion of rhetorical theory in seventeenth-century France, see A. Kibedi-Varga, *Rhétorique et littérature: études de structures classiques* (Paris: Didier, 1970), Parts 1 and 2. In Part 3, Varga presents a formalist analysis of the use of Aristotle's rhetorical genres in classical drama. Varga's discussion of seventeenth-century linguistic theory is challenged and rightly complicated by Genette in *Figures III*, p. 22.

21. Anonymous, "Lettre à la Mesme, en luy envoyant l'original de ce sonnet," *Portrait de Mademoiselle de Beauvais*, Montpensier, I, 294. "Most Authors applied themselves less to resemblance than to amplification."

22. In "Les 'Lucrèces' sortent du 'grenier,'" 77–78, Verdier suggests that "ce sont les métamorphoses du sujet plutôt que son essence qui attirent l'attention de l'épistolière." "The metamorphoses rather than the essence of the subject attract the attention of the epistle writer." In *A Rhetoric of Motives* (Berkeley: University of California Press, 1969), p. 71, Kenneth Burke suggests a formal way in which epideictic transformations call attention to themselves: "Often this third kind [epideictic], as a rhetoric of 'display,' was aimed at praise, not as an attempt to win an audience's praise for the subject discussed, but as an attempt to win praise for the oratory itself. The appropriate time for such oratory could then be called the present in the sense that the appeal was directed to the very presence of the words and speaker themselves." The delight of reading such ornate fictions might be said to enhance the pleasure of the reader's narcissistic identification with the subject of praise. As the portrait is more enticing, its fictional qualities, its transformations, are more desirable than its essence.

23. Monsieur Perrin, *Portrait de Madame la Comtesse D.....*, Montpensier, II, 87. "I would speak your Praise, and not your Portrait, if I were to say more; and that is neither your intention, nor mine."

24. Madame Desjardins, *Portrait de Mademoiselle Gaboury*, Montpensier, I, 316. "And if I recounted all the thoughts to which they give rise,

I would not be able to speak about the rest of her person without composing a Book instead of a Portrait."

25. The fictional neutrality of portraiture also appears to have been enhanced by conventions limiting the time of the text's composition. Madame la Marquise de Mauny, distinguishing between a personal confession and a more "neutral" self-portrait (a genre deserving a study of its own), refers to the appropriate writing-time of a portrait: "si je disois à quoy je l'establis, ce seroit plutost faire une Confession qu'un Portrait; & voila tout ce que je veux mettre en main, afin de ne luy donner que le quart d'heure que je viens d'employer à le faire." "If I were to speak on what I based it, I would make more of a Confession than a Portrait; and thus this is all that I wish to undertake, in order to give it only the quarter of an hour that I have just taken to make it." Montpensier, I, 123.

26. I should point out that, in keeping with epideictic discourse's option of praise or blame, written portraits were also used for vehement attacks on the character of the subject. Retz and La Rochefoucauld, for example, turned to portraiture to embellish their attacks against each other. See Cardinal du Retz, *Mémoires* (Paris: Éditions Gallimard, 1965); and La Rochefoucauld, *Portrait du Cardinal du Retz*, in *Maximes, suivies . . . du Portrait de La Rochefoucauld par lui-même* (Paris: Éditions Garnier Frères, 1967).

27. "In the sense of Aristotle, Leibniz, Locke, the 'virgin' state of mind, before all representation." "Mass of data in which each article can be identified by means of one or many arguments (abscissa, ordinance; figures, symbols)." "Collection of information, of data . . . grouped systematically for easy consultation." For Foucault's discussion of *tableau*, see *Les Mots et les choses*, pp. 86–91.

28. Dominique Bouhours reports, in *La Maniere de bien penser dans les ouvrages d'esprit* (Amsterdam: Abraham Wolfgang, 1688), p. 37, that this sort of economical portrait appeared again as an epitaph of Richelieu: "Arreste, Passant; tout ce que tu verras, tout ce que tu entendra en quelque lieu du monde que ce soit, est icy renfermé." "Stop, Passerby; all that you will see, all that you hear, wherever in the world it might be, is enclosed here."

29. The fragment is reconstructed by Roy Strong in *Tudor & Jacobean Portraits* (London: Her Majesty's Stationery Office, 1969), I, 106:

> The prince of light. The Sonne by whom thin[ngs]
> Of heaven the glorye, and of earthe the [grace?]
> Hath no such glorye as [ ] grace to go [
> Where Correspondencie May have no plac[e]
> Thunder the Ymage of that power dev[ine?]
> Which all to nothinge with a worde c[
> Is to the earthe when it doth ayre r[
> Of power the Scepter, not of wr

This yle of such both grace [ ] power
The boundles ocean [ ] em[
P[ ]p[rince?] [ ] the [ ]ll[
Rivers of thanckes retourne for Springes [
Rivers of thanckes still to that oc[ean]

30. The Ditchley portrait is described and explicated in detail by Strong, pp. 104–07, and by Frances A. Yates, *Astraea: The Imperial Theme in the Sixteenth Century* (London: Routledge & Kegan Paul, 1975), pp. 218–19.

31. Discussing miniature portraits in *The Savage Mind* (Chicago: University of Chicago Press, 1966), p. 24, Claude Lévi-Strauss makes a similar point regarding the role of economy as an interlocutory device. Louis Marin, *Le Portrait du roi*, p. 76, attributes the miniaturized figure's rhetorical engagement of the reader to the rhetorical trope *litotes:* "le passage par le simulacre du lecteur universel permet et réalise la transformation des acteurs principaux . . . en manières de portraits ou de caractère, en formes-de-réception, représentations ou idées dans le procès de lecture. Là encore, la règle essentielle de cette transformation repose sur l'équivalence de deux mouvements discursifs, symétriques et inversés, dont le second est la représentation du premier, son effet dynamique: une *litote*, abréviation, diminution de l'objet du discours émis dont l'effet dans le discours reçu est expansion, *augmentation*. La litote opère la transformation du référentiel, la matière du discours en manière ou forme de son écoute." "Recourse to the simulacrum of the universal reader permits and realizes the transformation of the principal actors . . . in the form of portraits or of character, in forms-of-reception, representations or ideas in the reading process. There also, the essential rule of this transformation is based on the equivalence of two discursive movements, symmetrical and inverted, in which the second is the representation of the first, its dynamic effect: a *litotes*, abbreviation, dimunition of the object of the discourse uttered, whose effect in the received discourse is expansion, augmentation. Litotes performs the transformation of the discourse into the manner or form of its reception."

32. Montpensier, "Dedicace: à son Altesse Royale, Mademoiselle," I, 4–5. "If the most difficult and the most bizarre [Ladies of the Kingdom] preserve the respect and veneration for the Paintings of Heros and Heroines, who ordinarily make the rich ornaments of their Palaces? How esteemed our Portraits should be, since they depict not only, like the others, the beauties and traits of the face, but also the wisdom of the mind, and the noble qualities of the soul. The first are masterpieces of Painters excelling in their Art, which only give fame to the Artist. The second glorify the represented Heroes, and bring to light their objects' merit, inclinations, and virtues. These are great models of beauty, sweetness, piety, prudence, love, generosity and modesty, which are given to the public. As there are many more victorious men than men of wisdom, and as it is much easier to van-

quish than to live honorably, we can say that it is much more difficult to
represent well the generous inclinations and the grand qualities of a divine
soul, such as that of your R. H., than to describe combats and triumphs that
indeed make Heroes more glorious, but not always more prudent and more
virtuous. Thus, one can say that, in this summary of all the marvels of our
Court, our Princesses, and our Ladies, we bid for our Poets and Orators
above all others."

33. Roger de Piles, *Remarques sur l'Art de Peindre de Charles Alfonse
du Fresnoy* (Paris: Nicolas Langlois, 1673), p. 220. "The point is to express
the veritable temperament of the persons one represents and to show their
Physiognomy."

34. De Piles, *Cours de peinture par principes* (Paris: C-A. Jombart,
1766), pp. 218–20. "It is above all necessary that the figures which are not
occupied appear to wish to satisy the desire of those curious to see them,
and thus that they are shown in the action most suitable to their temperament and their state, as if they wished to instruct the spectator about what
they are in reality; and since most people pride themselves on their sincer-
ity, honesty and magnanimity, one must avoid all sorts of affectations in
the attitudes, make everything be free and natural and usher in some measure of pride, nobility, and majesty: . . . I am this valorous captain who
spreads terror everywhere, or rather, who has displayed many glorious suc-
cesses by my good conduct. . . . Thus, attitudes constitute the language of
portraits."

35. Op. cit. "That it seems we see them, that we speak with them."

36. Nicolas Poussin, *Lettres et propos sur l'art* (Paris: Hermann, 1964),
p. 36. "The first seven figures on the left will tell you everything that is
written here and everything else is of the same cloth: read the story and
painting in order to know whether each thing is appropriate to the subject."

37. For a summary of the issues of *ut pictura poesis* in seventeenth-
century French painting and poetic theory, see Rensselaer W. Lee, *Ut Pictura Poesis: The Humanistic Theory of Painting* (New York: W. W. Norton,
1967).

38. For my understanding of Montpensier's claims for portraiture, I
am indebted to Émile Benveniste's discussion of a corollary linguistic structure, in his essay "La Phrase nominale," *Problèmes de linguistique générale*
(Paris: Éditions Gallimard, 1966), I, 151–67.

39. Puget de La Serre, "À Madame, Madame La Duchesse d'Esguillon," *Thomas Morus ou le triomphe de la foy et de la constance* (Paris:
Augustin Courbé, 1642). "I am very satisfied that [this Work] gives me the
opportunity to show the Public that I know how to submit with all due
respect to the Law of its Oracles, when they publish throughout the World
that you are one of its richest ornaments."

40. See Lewis, *La Rochefoucauld*, pp. 141–87.

41. Bouhours, *Les Entretiens d'Ariste et d'Eugène* (Paris: Mabre-Cra-
moisy, 1671), p. 290. "There is also another kind of noble mind, which one

can call the mind of negotiation and ministry. These are enlightened, judicious, agile geniuses, and appropriate for the business: with a glance they penetrate to the essence, and uncover there all of the circumstances and consequences; they find in an instant all of the expedients and all of the ways to arrange the most difficult matters and make them succeed. But they see only what they need to see, and no more, to reach a good decision and to make a reasonable choice."

42. In *Le roi-machine*, p. 81, Apostolidès chooses to delimit the impact of such representational, even libidinal, transference to the stage of French neoclassical rationality: "la poétique du XVIIe préconcise l'emploi monosémique des termes; cela engendre une plus grande rationalité du discours, au détriment du pouvoir incantatoire du verbe." "Seventeenth-century poetics sanctioned the monosemic use of terms; that engenders a greater rationality of discourse to the detriment of the incantatory power of the verb." My argument suggests that auto-signification is striking for provoking the opposite effect, for stimulating the "pouvoir incantatoire du verbe."

43. Aristotle, *The Art of Rhetoric*, pp. 33–35.

44. De La Serre, "À Madame, Madame La Duchesse d'Esguillon." "The most ambitious for honor aspire only to be able to imitate you."

45. Kenneth Burke, in *A Rhetoric of Motives*, p. 39, refers to this imitation as a *moralizing* process of *socialization*: "The individual person, striving to form himself in accordance with the communicative norms that match the cooperative ways of his society, is by the same token concerned with the rhetoric of identification. To act upon himself persuasively, he must variously resort to images and ideas that are formative. Education ("indoctrination") exerts such pressure upon him from without; he completes the process from within. If he does not somehow act to tell himself (as his own audience) what the various brands of rhetorician have told him, his persuasion is not complete. Only those voices from without are effective which can speak in the language of a voice within."

46. Genette provides an economical discussion of this difference in "La rhétorique des figures," his introduction to Pierre Fontanier, *Les Figures du discours* (Paris: Flammarion, 1977), pp. 5–17. See also Paul De Man, "Semiology and Rhetoric," *Allegories of Reading*, pp. 3–19.

47. Du Marsais, *Traité des tropes*, pp. 180–81. "It is certainly much more useful to observe [the errors] that sin against good conduct, against precision in reasoning, against honesty, uprightness, and good morals. It would be desirable were examples of these latter sorts of errors less rare, or rather that they were unknown."

48. Fontanier, *Les Figures du discours*, p. 111. "*Personification* consists in making *a sort of real and physical being, endowed with sensation and life from an inanimate, insensible being, or an abstract and purely ideal being, in sum what is called a* person; *and doing that by a simple manner of speaking or by a fiction completely* verbal."

49. Lewis, *La Rochefoucauld*, p. 155, cites Arthur-Herman Fink's con-

tention in *Maxime und Fragment* (Munich, 1934) that nominal style is inherently related to personification.

50. The figural essence of the model is emphasized by Fontanier's classification of personification as the *primary* rhetorical trope of "figures d'expression par fiction," *Les Figures du discours*, p. 111.

51. In *A Rhetoric of Motives*, pp. 268–69, Burke discusses the usefulness of epideictic rhetoric as an ideological tool. Because its nominal praise promotes "pure" fictional models, the rhetoric is also attractive as pure in itself, seeming to seek no advantage over the listener.

52. Of course the exception of Ben Jonson comes immediately to mind; Jonson worked hard to neutralize epistolary praise to *his* advantage.

53. Anonymous, *Portrait de Madame de la Calprenede*, Montpensier, I, 252. "All Men are Catos or at least Cesars; and Women are Lucretias or Octavias."

54. Boisrobert, Abbé de Chastillon, "À Monsieur Le Marquis de Richelieu," *Le Jalousie d'elle-mesme* (Paris: Augustin Courbé, 1650). "That I published it only out of the sole jealousy I have of the honor of your friendship."

55. Jules de La Mesnardière, *La Poétique* (Paris: Antoine Sommoville, 1639), p. 10. "We intentionally banish Rhythms and Music from our Definition, which Aristotle places in his; since our Tragedy does not make use of these splendors as necessary items, but employs Actions, real Representation accompanied by Discourse only in imitation."

56. Abbé d'Aubignac, *Dissertation sur la condamnation des théatres*, p. 95. "One views poems only as masterpieces of a wit, and as a perfect imitation of the virtue of Heroes."

57. Op. cit. "Masterpieces of Painters excelling in their Art, which only give fame to the Artist."

58. Corneille, "Au lecteur," *Mélite*, in *Théâtre complet*, I, 83. "I know well that printing a play weakens its reputation; publishing it degrades it."

59. André Mareschal, "Au lecteur," *Le Railleur ou le satyr du temps* (Paris: Toussainct Quinet, 1638). ". . . the reason that put an end to its representation. I am much more at a loss to know how you are bound to receive it, since it is true that for purely Comic plays like this one the paper deprives them of much of their grace, and that action is their soul. These truncated lines and all of these interrupted phrases peculiar to Comic play and which, due to their familiarity, enter so easily into the imagination when they are energetically spoken, languish when they are written."

60. So writes either Nicolas or Jean de la Coste to the reader of the quarto edition of de Pradès, *La Victime d'estat, ou la mort de Plautius Silvanus Pretuer Roman, par le Sieur D. P.* (Paris: Nicolas & Jean de la Coste, 1649): "J'assemble trois pieces rares & merveilleuses, Annibal, la Victime d'Estat, & le Recueil des Vers qui les suit: La moindre estant capable de vous rendre mon obligé, je vous laisse à penser quelle reconnaissance vous me devez pour toutes trois. Elles partent de la mesme main, comme il est

aisé de voir à l'excellence de l'Ouvrage qui s'y montre par tout égale. L'Autheur toute fois, n'a pas voulu qu'elles ayent porté son nom. . . . Quoy qu'il en soit, c'est toute la faute que je luy voy commettre en ses Oeuvres: il devoit soufrir qu'elles donnassent a son Nom l'esclat que son Esprit leur a donné." "I assemble three rare and marvelous pieces, Hannibal, the Victim of State, and the collection of verse following them; the least being capable of obligating you to me, I leave you to determine the gratitude you owe me for all three. They come from the same hand, as is easy to see from the Work's excellence which is unvarying throughout. The author nevertheless did not wish for them to bear his name. . . . Be that as it may, it is the only fault I see him commit in his Works: he ought to have allowed them to give his Name the renown that his Mind gave them."

61. In his "Advis des libraires au lecteur," following the anonymous title page of d'Aubignac's *Zenobie, où la verité de l'Histoire est conservée dans l'observation des plus rigoreuses reigles du Poëme Dramatique* (Paris: Augustin Courbé, 1647), Augustin Courbé writes: "si tu n'y trouves point d'Epistre, de Preface, ny d'Argument, qui d'ordinaire accompagnent les pieces de cette sorte, & dont souvent elles reçoivent autant de lumiere & de grace que leur propre merite, c'est un effet de son extreme douleur. . . . Si nous le pouvons tirer des mains de l'Autheur avec la *Pratique du Theatre* achevée depuis long-temps, nous ne refuserons pas nos soins pour en enricher le public." "If you do not find here any Epistle, Preface, or Summary, which ordinarily accompanies plays of this sort, and from which plays often receive as much insight and grace as from their own merit, it is an effect of his extreme sadness. . . . If we are able to take it from the hands of the Author along with the *Pratique du Théâtre* finished a long time ago, we will not withhold our attentions so that the public may profit from these works."

62. Mareschal. "À tres-illustre Seigneur Messire Robert Sidney, Comte de Leycestre," *La Cour bergere, ou L'ARCADIE de Messire Philippes Sidney* (Paris: Toussainct Quinet, 1640). "Sir, this play is so legitimately worthy of YOUR EXCELLENCE, since it bears this illustrious and glorious Name of SIDNEY, and since it even belongs to your House . . . to show that the protection of this Book is in your decorum. . . . You will be its Judge and its Patron; you, Sir, who possess the doctrine and the insight to judge it, and enough goodness as well to excuse the few faults which you might find in it."

63. Corneille, "À la Reine Régente," *Polyeucte, Théâtre complet*, II, 4. "This is only a theatre play which I present to you, but which will speak to you of God: the dignity of its content is so elevated, that the incompetence of the artisan cannot debase it; and your royal soul takes too much pleasure in this sort of discourse to take offense at the faults of a work in which your spirit will encounter the delights of its heart. It is by this means, MADAME, that I hope Your Majesty will pardon me for having waited so long to pay you homage of this type. Every time I placed moral and political virtues on

our stage, I always believed their representation to be too unworthy of appearing before Your Majesty, when I considered that however carefully I chose them from history, and with whatever ornaments artifice was able to enrich them, Your Majesty saw greater examples of them in Herself."

64. Verdier, "Mademoiselle de Montpensier et le plaisir du texte," 20, similarly terms Montpensier's function of writing as "le produit d'un débordement, l'expression d'un épanouissement inscrit dans le texte même." "It is the product of an excess, the expression of an expansion in the text itself."

65. Bouhours, *La Maniere de bien penser*, p. 64. "What do you think about these personages which a writer introduces in dedicatory Epistles? Listen to me, if you will. The Author of a work that treats the conquests of Caesar, or the adventures of Hippolitus, does not hesitate to say to a Prince, when dedicating the book to him: *Here is the conqueror of the Gauls who comes to pay his homage to you. Hippolitus emerges from the heart of the forest to court you.*"

66. Boisrobert, "À Monsieur le Marquis de Richelieu." "Sir, since I owe my entire good fortune to the illustrious Name that you bear, I believe that I owe all of my projects to it as well, all of my inclination, and my thoughts, and that from now on I must behold only this grand Name in the world, through which I have seen established my honor, my leisure, and my tranquillity, along with the well-being of France. Do not find it strange, then, that if I dare dedicate to you this small Comic Work, it seems to be so little worthy of this illustrious Name."

67. Louis Althusser, "Idéologie et appareils idéologiques d'état," p. 24. "Ideology represents the imaginary relationship of individuals to their real conditions of existence," *Lenin and Philosophy and other essays*, p. 163.

68. Bouhours, *La Maniere de bien penser*, p. 163. "An Epistle addressed to Cardinal Richelieu, in which a Writer of the previous reign flatters him in these terms which remain in my memory. 'As our wonders increase so our strength fails; and as was once said of a valiant man, that he could no longer be wounded except on the wounds he had received, your praises can only be repetition; since truth, which has its limits, has said about you everything that falsehood, which has none, has invented for the others.'"

69. Ibid., p. 259. "In truth, when the cardinal had died, the Author omitted all these praises in a second edition, and even dedicated his book to Jesus Christ, as if to disavow publicly the flattering thoughts which had something excessive and even a little religious about them."

Chapter 9

1. "I know that you have occasionally written Verse and Prose, and that you sometimes have had a share of the Theatre's applause, and I will

admit, if you wish, that Parnassus is covered with your Creatures. . . . One is not at all responsible for the sermons one makes in Dedicatory Epistles; it is permissible to lie with impunity in them, and this is but a drug that is given without guarantee, and is of no better quality than the tales of La Fontaine."

2. Charles Arnaud, *Étude sur la vie et les oeuvres de l'Abbé d'Aubignac*, pp. 15–16.

3. D'Aubignac, *Troisième et quatrième dissertation, en forme de remarques sur la tragédie de M. Corneille, intitulée OEdipe, et de réponses à ses calomnies* (Paris: Jacques Du Brueil, 1663), pp. 167–68. D'Aubignac's *JUGEMENT De la Tragédie intitulée PENTHÉE écrit sur le champ, et envoyé à Monseigneur le Cardinal de Richelieu par son ordre exprez* is included in the Pierre Martino edition of *La Pratique du théâtre* (Alger: Jules Carbonel, 1927), pp. 379–85. I refer throughout to this edition of *La Pratique du théâtre* unless otherwise noted.

4. D'Aubignac, *Troisième et quatrième dissertation*, p. 182.

5. D'Aubignac, *La Pratique du théâtre*, pp. 15–16.

6. Ibid., p. 11. "Spectacles of course must be very important to the government of States."

7. Ibid., p. 10.

8. Ibid., p. 8. "The beautiful representations of Theatre which one can truly call the School of the People." The link between theatre and public surveillance is worth further consideration. Although I have seen no evidence suggesting that early French theatre was used by the authorities specifically for the purpose of surveillance, a study of seventeenth-century French police records might reveal interesting data in this domain. On a theoretical level, theatre was described by Jules de La Mesnardière, in "Discours," *La Poétique* (Paris: Antoine Sommoville, 1639), as responsible for the transmission of the revered classical institutions of religion, economics, morality, and, interestingly enough, the police: "les loix de la plus sainte Republique que les Payens ayent établie, lui ont été communiquées par le ministre des Vers. Mais ce n'est pas le seul service qu'ils ont rendu au public. La Religion & la Police n'ont pas été les seuls thresors que la Poësie à découvers. Tout ce qu'il y a d'admirable dans les hautes speculations, & de commode dans les Arts, a eu besoin de ce langage pour se faire connoître aux hommes . . . celle qui a mis dans le monde la Religion & la Police, la Morale & l'Economie, ne doit pas estre effacée du nombre des connaissances que l'on appelle profitable." "The laws of the most sacred Republic which the Pagans had established were handed down by the minister of Verses. But this is not the only service that Verses offered to the public. Religion and Regulation were not the only treasures revealed by Poetry. Everything admirable in lofty speculations and agreeable in the Arts required this language to make itself known to men."

9. D'Aubignac, *La Pratique du théâtre*, p. 6. "This shows conspicuously that the State has inexhaustible riches and Men as well."

10. Lancaster, *A History of French Dramatic Literature in the Seventeenth Century*, Part 2, II, 762.

11. D'Aubignac, *La Pratique du théâtre*, p. 10 "Sovereigns can do nothing more advantageous to their glory and for the good of their Subjects than to establish and maintain Spectacles and Public Games with noble order and the splendors worthy of their Crown."

12. Ibid., pp. 15–17. "The Stage has taken on a new look, and the wrinkles which its age engraved on its brow have lost much of their deformity. Its good fortune was not to have displeased the most marvelous Mind in the world, I mean the Great Cardinal Richelieu, and also to have had enough charm to merit his graces. Through his generosity the Stage acquired new strengths and began to regain its former rights, original beauty, nobility, and splendor. And due to his attentions, everything learned, ingenious, and magnificent known to Antiquity gradually reappeared in our Theatre. . . . But since the same hand that so warmly welcomed Theatre did not complete its restoration, it hardly seems that our Theatre will ever arrive at its perfection, or even that it can be sustained for long. And its setback will be even more dangerous, since every Age does not possess Geniuses with self-sufficiency, liberality, purity of morals, and the other qualities necessary for this project. This Great Man's life shaped an Age of great and new things. Anything that was not perfected or strengthened under him will have difficulty finding the opportunity to become so. Indeed, it rested with no one to offer France these legitimate pleasures, except with the one who multiplied day by day France's Palms and Laurels. It was certainly just that he who made himself the equal of the Caesars and Pompeys in his victories should also have imitated them in the restoration of Theatre and its illustrious diversions. In short, the glory and grandeur of Spectacles could have no better source than he who made himself the most glorious and greatest Spectacle in the World."

13. D'Aubignac's stress on the political nature of theatre should be understood as novel, of course, only in the context of early French theatre treatises. Discussion of the ideological utility of theatre is a commonplace in sixteenth-century Italian tracts on theatre and goes as far back as Vitruvius.

14. Gabriel Gueret, *La Guerre des auteurs anciens et modernes* (Paris: Theodore Girard, 1671), p. 137. "It is permissible to lie with impunity in them, and this is but a drug that is given without guarantee."

15. D'Aubignac, *Aristandre ou histoire interrompuë* (Paris: Iacques du Brueil, 1664), p. 5. "You indeed know my dear Reader that I am beholden to no one in what I present to the public, and that you have no right to examine a gift as if it were a means that I employ for clearing some debts."

16. Letter of Chapelain, 29 July 1641, cited by Arnaud, *Étude sur la vie et les oeuvres de l'Abbé d'Aubignac*, p. 43. "He would have been received first, had he not written a satire about Desmarets's *Roxane*, in which he

reproached the taste of His Eminence and of Madame d'Aiguillon who found it of value."

17. D'Aubignac, *Troisième et quatrième dissertation*, p. 124. "I share with ten thousand people of birth, condition, and virtue, who merit more than you, but who are not known to his Majesty, no more than I, who for seventeen years have not even seen the gates of the Louvre."

18. D'Aubignac, *Le Roman des lettres*, pp. 542–43. "If I dare speak as Balzac on this occasion, I would say that you give us something more excellent than a King [I received the two last volumes which you released]. But I leave all of these noble thoughts to your colleagues of the Academy: I lack the strength to make them legitimate and to support myself."

19. For a brief summary of Guez de Balzac's absolutism, see Nannerl O. Keohane, *Philosophy and the State in France* (Princeton: Princeton University Press, 1980), pp. 197–202.

20. D'Aubignac, *Discours au Roy sur l'establissement d'une seconde Academie dans la Ville de Paris* (Paris: Jacques de Brueil, 1664), pp. 30–31. "Those who find themselves pledged to this necessity to instruct the public, these learned Masters of so many different Faculties, have become remiss in two matters that harm the progress of the Sciences and which have almost completely disfigured them. First, they cling doggedly to the maxims which the ancients left in their writings, and persuading themselves that they possess the certitude of all truths, they will search for nothing further. They condemn everything that does not agree with their principles; they pronounce anathema against anyone contradicting them; and no matter how strongly innovations are supported by demonstrations, and with whatever experiments old errors are swept aside, a proposition need only be new for them to reject it."

21. In "Classical Criticism and Ideology," *Papers on French Seventeenth Century Literature*, 18 (1983), 149–71, Timothy J. Reiss presents the interesting argument that, regardless of the vast seventeenth-century struggles for intellectual power exemplified by such debates between academies, or by the more extensive debate between the ancients and moderns, the dominance of a particular centralized discourse remained untarnished. While my following discussion of spectatorship will recall Reiss's emphasis on a neoclassical bedrock of authority, it will maintain that the socio-political position of the enunciator of authority can shift the locale and import of authority's seat. In striving for critical authority, D'Aubignac's second academy, if implemented, could have worked to disfigure the streamlined monolith of Louis XIV's centralized academies.

22. D'Aubignac, *Discours au Roy*, p. 7. "It is the Learned who know and say that the Sovereigns are the perceptible images of the living God, or to speak in the terms of the Sacred Scripture, that they are the earth's visible Gods; that one can never violate the respect due to them without injuring the orders of Divine Providence; and that we no more have the right to

examine their wishes, than to contradict their foundation, which has no other principle than the all-powerful hand of the Eternal." In reading d'Aubignac's *Discours au Roy* as a text that endorses monarchical centralization, Apostolidès, in *Le roi-machine*, pp. 24–25, 121, ignores its status as a marginal and subversive document penned by an intellectual who had been spurned by the court. D'Aubignac is the sort of figure described by Apostolidès as "the individuals dispossessed of their learning and traditional privileges," p. 34.

23. D'Aubignac, *Troisième et quatrième dissertation*, p. 176.

24. D'Aubignac, *Troisième et quatrième dissertation*, pp. 162–63. "When I undertook this work, I resolved to copy nothing from those who have given us poetics since Aristotle, and to teach only new things, or to correct by learned innovations those that were known; and you know that you never saw elsewhere what you found in this book, which the disinterested experts truly call a book, and a new book at that."

25. D'Aubignac, *La Pratique du théâtre*, p. 33. "As for me, without repeating in this discourse what one can learn in Aristotle, in his Interpreters and in the ancients and the moderns, I will endeavor to treat only new Matters, or at least to provide some new instructions on those things which the others have treated."

26. *Le Journal littéraire*, first issue, 4 (1715), 31–32. "Although this is only a reprint of a Work older perhaps and better known than any of us, we will not fail to give an extended Extract from it. We said in our Preface that 'we could sometimes give Extracts of certain books which by their merit or rarity are worth our providing an exact idea of them.' *La Pratique du Théâtre*, by *François Hedelin*, Abbé *d'Aubignac*, has both of these qualities. This Book has always been held in high esteem, and it had become very rare. Moreover, we believe that no one will be displeased to find gathered here in a single Extract the principal rules of the Dramatic Poem. Everyone speaks about these rules, but few people know of what they consist; here we will provide a general idea of them. Those who wish to instruct themselves in more depth can consult the book itself."

27. D'Aubignac, *La Pratique du théâtre*, p. 270. "One must not acquire exact knowledge of ancient Plays on the notes and specious distinctions which are in our publications, but on an exact reading of these excellent works."

Chapter 10

1. In *La Critique du discours*, Marin coins the term "intermediary" to discuss the representationality of ideology.

2. D'Aubignac, *La Pratique du théâtre*, pp. 72–73. "One must not forget (and this is, perhaps, one of the more significant observations I have

made on Theatre Plays) that the Subject will never succeed if it does not conform to the morals and sensibilities of the Spectators, regardless of the care employed by the Poet and whatever ornaments he uses to support it; this is because Dramatic Poems must be different according to the People before whom they are to be represented; and this is why the plays' success may sometimes differ, even though they are still alike. . . . Among us, the respect and love we have for our Princes does not allow these Spectacles full of horror to be offered to the Public; we do not wish to believe that Kings could be wicked, nor suffer that their Subjects, although abused in appearance, touch their sacred Persons or rebel against their Power, not even in painting."

3. See especially Hans-Jörg Neuschäfer, "D'Aubignacs *Pratique du théâtre* und der Zusammenhang von *imitatio, vraisemblance* und *bienséance*," in his edition, *La pratique du théâtre und andere Schriften zur Doctrine classique* (Munich: Wilhelm Fink Verlag, 1971), pp. vii-xxvii.

4. D'Aubignac, *La Pratique du théâtre*, p. 76. "In a word, it must be put thus, Verisimilitude is the essence of the Dramatic Poem, without which nothing reasonable can be done or said on the Stage."

5. Ibid., pp. 76-77. "(1) It is a general maxim that *Truth* is not the subject of Theatre, because there are many true things that must not be viewed on the stage, and many that cannot be represented there: this is why Synesius was correct when he said that Poetry and the other Arts founded only on imitation do not follow truth, but the opinion and common sensibility of men." "Nor will the *Possible* be its subject, because there are many things that can happen, whether through the confluence of natural causes or through the adventures of Morality, which however would be ridiculous and barely believable if represented."

6. Ibid., p. 68. "It is quite ridiculous to think of going to the Theatre to learn History. The Stage does not at all present things as they were, but as they should be, and the Poetry must restore in the subject whatever cannot be accommodated to the rules of his Art." Derrida, *De la grammatologie*, p. 416, discusses the structural role of such a "should" as the agent of "une réappropriation totale de la présence. *Devrait:* c'est le mode et le temps d'une anticipation téléologique et eschatalogique." "A total reappropriation of presence. *Should:* it is the mode and tense of a teleological and eschatological anticipation." *Of Grammatology*, p. 295.

7. In "Classicisme et vraisemblance," *Papers on French Seventeenth Century Literature*, 8 (1977-78), 65-78, Selma A. Zebouni argues that *vraisemblance*, not truth, is the fundamental element of the neoclassical *épistémè*.

8. Neuschäfer, "D'Aubignacs *Pratique du théâtre*," pp. xx-xxi. D'Aubignac himself had plenty of reasons to forget the Fronde. His exclusion from the court of Louis XIV, reported in the *Quatrième dissertation*, was probably a result of his known association with the Cardinal de Retz. As

the nineteenth-century literary historian Charles-Louis Livet writes, in *Précieux et précieuses* (Paris: Didier, 1870), pp. 166–67, "rien dans les écrits de l'abbé d'Aubignac ne laisse percer son opinion sur les dissensions funestes de la Fronde. . . . Mais il est remarquable cependant que les discours qu'il fait à cette époque sont destinés surtout à flatter le parti opposé à la cour. Ainsi le maréchal de Rantzau avait payé par un emprisonnement de onze mois son attachement à la Fronde . . . c'est lui que nous trouvons portant la parole au cardinal de Retz, à l'occasion de sa promotion au cardinalat, au nom de la congrégation pour la Propagation de la foi. Ses relations avec le cardinal de Retz mirent fréquemment l'abbé d'Aubignac en présence de Gilles Ménage." "Nothing in the writings of the Abbé d'Aubignac makes manifest his opinion of the disastrous dissensions of the Fronde. . . . But it is notable nevertheless that his discourses during this period were chiefly designed to humor the side opposed to the court. Thus, for his attachment to the Fronde, the Maréchal de Rantzau paid with eleven months of imprisonment . . . it is he whom we find speaking to Cardinal de Retz in the name of the congregation of the Propagation of faith on the occasion of his promotion to the cardinalate. Because of his relations with Cardinal de Retz the Abbé d'Aubignac was frequently in the presence of Gilles Ménage."

9. D'Aubignac, *La Pratique du théâtre*, p. 313. "The Subject who rebels against his sovereign is a criminal."

10. Ibid., p. 339. "Living in a monarchical State, we hold the person of Kings sacred, even if they were unjust."

11. Ernst Cassirer, *The Philosophy of the Enlightenment*, trans. Fritz C. A. Koelln and James P. Pettegrove (Princeton: Princeton University Press, 1951), p. 282.

12. Arnaud, *Étude sur la vie et les oeuvres de l'Abbé d'Aubignac*, pp. 232–33. "Works inspired by fashion are condemned to be quickly outmoded and antiquated . . . the flatterer and the accessory of prejudices, passions or the ignorances of the crowd."

13. Abbé (Michel) du Pures, *Idée des spectacles anciens et nouveaux* (Paris: Michel Brunet, 1668), p. 162. "We make no distinction here between the diverse genres of Plays, because the common and universal Idea ordinarily confuses them, and because these notions, too subtle for the People and for the members of Court, perplexes them much more than instructs them."

14. Abbé du Bos, *Réflexions critiques sur la poësie et sur la peinture*, 7th edition, (Paris: Pissot, 1770), II, 347. "Are Professors who have taught Logic all their lives those who know best when a man speaks sensibly and when he reasons with precision?"

15. Ibid., p. 349. "Without knowing the rules, the groundlings judge a theatre play as well as do professionals. *The same holds for theatre as for eloquence*, said the Abbé d'Aubignac, *their perfections are no less perceptible to the ignorant than to the* learned, even though they may not equally know the reason why."

16. D'Aubignac, *La Pratique du théâtre*, p. 8. "The minds of those who are of the meanest rank and the lowest conditions of a State have so little commerce with elegant notions that the most general maxims of Morality are absolutely useless to them. In vain might one wish to bring them to virtue with a discourse upheld by reasons and authorities; for they can neither understand the first, nor wish to defer to the latter." "The sublime speculations of the Learned and the ingenious distinctions of the Philosophers certainly remain far beyond the capacity of these common souls. . . . All of these truths of Wisdom are lights too strong for their weak eyes. They remain paradoxes for them, which renders Philosophy suspect and even ridiculous to them. They require a much plainer instruction. Reason cannot conquer them except through means which appeal to the senses. Such are the beautiful representations of Theatre which one can truly call the School of the People."

17. Ibid., p. 320. "I would not approve using many verses to say to a Sovereign,

That a King possesses power which no one should resist.

But I would find it more agreeable for him to say,

You do not know the rights of your Crown, your power has no limits, and whoever might wish to resist you will become a criminal.

Because these discourses are different in appearance from general instructions and so closely embrace the Action of Theatre, they cannot be boring."

18. Ibid., p. 313. "Here is a new topic in Poetic Art and one that I have not found in the thick Volumes of Authors who have written on it: I am the first to have observed it, and I have offered reflections that are not found elsewhere and that contain opinions which the Poet should not scorn."

19. Citing Castelvetro, d'Aubignac reveals his debt to the Italian theoretician's attentiveness to the common spectator and the pleasures of artistic reception. Bernard Weinberg outlines Castelvetro's poetics in *A History of Literary Criticism in the Italian Renaissance* (Chicago: University of Chicago Press, 1961), I, 502–11. For a more detailed discussion, consult H. B. Charlton, *Castelvetro's Theory of Poetry* (Manchester: University of Manchester Publications, 1913). Regardless of d'Aubignac's personal investment in arguing for the novelty of his theory, readers recognize his debts to the Italian humanists throughout the *Pratique*. I am less concerned, however, with the obvious sources of d'Aubignac's influence than with the ideological/epistemological implications of this claim of novelty within his seventeenth-century French context.

20. D'Aubignac, *La Pratique du théâtre*, pp. 314–15. "One must admit as certain that all these instructive Discourses are ordinarily defective in the Theatre because they are cold and lifeless by nature; and that general Maxims which, to instruct, address only the mind without at all touching the heart, illuminate but do not arouse; and even though they are often beau-

tiful enough and well expressed, they only touch the ear without moving the soul: so that the Action of Theatre, where we seek something that stirs our affections and makes some impression on our heart, becomes hardly sensible to us, and consequently barely capable of entertaining us."

21. Ibid., p. 38. "In the same manner, the Poet, in considering the Spectacle or the Representation in his Tragedy, does all that his Art and Mind can provide him with to make it win the Spectators' admiration: for he works only to please them."

22. D'Aubignac does not admit the closeness of his position to that voiced a century earlier by the critic Francesco Robortello. In his commentary, *In librum Aristotelis de arte poetica explicationes* (1548), Robortello suggests that spectacle is the most important part of dramatic poetry. See Weinberg, *A History of Literary Criticism in the Italian Renaissance*, I, 389–403; and "Robortello on the *Poetics*," *Critics and Criticism: Ancient and Modern*, ed. R. S. Crane (Chicago: University of Chicago Press, 1952), pp. 319–48.

23. D'Aubignac, *La Pratique du théâtre*, p. 34. "He must keep them in mind when he works for the Theatre."

24. Arnaud, *Étude sur la vie et les oeuvres de l'Abbé d'Aubignac*, p. 235. "Everything for the specators! d'Aubignac said. It is in the name of the spectators, of the power of their imagination, of the impossibility of dispensing with their cooperation, that one must reject demonstration."

25. D'Aubignac, *La Pratique du théâtre*, p. 36. "To understand how the Poet should govern himself with regard to the Spectators, and how they are important to him or not, we need only reflect on what we have said about a Painting. For in considering the picture as a painting, or a work of Art, the Painter does everything possible to render it excellent; because it will be seen, and because he does everything with the intention of being admired."

26. Ibid., p. 282. I should point out, in agreement with Bobra Goldsmith's phenomenological study, *L'Abbé d'Aubignac's "Pratique du Théatre": An Analysis in the Light of Twentieth-Century Aesthetics*, Diss., University of Colorado, 1972, that d'Aubignac maintains that a well-written dramatic poem should give rise to a pleasurable reading. But his treatise, pp. 222–23, 233, 282, 310, 330–31, emphasizes the quality of the representational experience of spectacle as it is played out in the theatre hall.

27. Arnaud, *Étude sur la vie et les oeuvres de l'Abbé d'Aubignac*, p. 224. "Concerning the representation, the *sentiments* of the spectators on the contrary are determined, in the theatre itself, by organic impressions, by *sensations* they receive there. While the epic poem addresses itself directly to the imagination, the dramatic poem is a picture 'which is evident to the senses,' and of which 'the eye is the judge,' as Chapelain said. Verisimilitude requires, then, that the *sensations* and *sentiments* of the spectators never contradict each another, and consequently that everything evident to the senses be made identical in the action and representation."

28. D'Aubignac, *La Pratique du théâtre*, p. 37. "He will use the most vivid colors for this; so that the eye finds more satisfaction in viewing it. . . . He will not represent her at the bottom of a steep crag, since she could not be seen, but at the entrance to a Grotto; and in this he will govern himself thus because he considers his work as a painting which must please and be evident to the senses."

29. Ibid., p. 34. "I take up here the comparison with a Picture, of which I have resolved to make use frequently in this Treatise, and I say that one can consider it in two ways. The first as a painting, that is to say, inasmuch as it is produced by the Painter's hand, and where there are only colors and not things, shadows and not bodies, artificial lights, false elevations, and Perspective distances, illusory foreshortenings, and simple appearances of what does not exist. The second inasmuch as it contains a thing painted, whether real or supposed to be so, whose places are certain, whose qualities are natural, whose actions are unquestionable, and all the circumstances are in accordance with order and reason."

30. Rensselaer W. Lee, *Ut Pictura Poesis: The Humanistic Theory of Painting* (New York: Norton, 1967), p. 8.

31. Svetlana Alpers, "Describe or Narrate? A Problem in Realistic Representation," *New Literary History*, 8, No. 1 (Autumn 1976), 28.

32. D'Aubignac, *La Pratique du théâtre*, p. 39. "I know well that the Poet does not work on the Action as if true, but only insofar as it can be represented; from this one might conclude that there may be some mixture of these two considerations, but here is how he must distinguish between them. He examines everything he wants and must make known to the Spectators by the ears and eyes, and resolves to have it recited or shown to them, because he must take heed of them in considering the Action as represented. . . . He must search in the Action considered as if true a motive or an apparent reason, called color, to makes these Narrations and Spectacles happen verisimilarly in this way."

33. Ibid., p. 39. "And I dare say that the greatest Art of the Theatre consists in finding all of these colors."

34. This debate is discussed in detail by Bernard Teyssèdre in *Roger de Piles et les débats sur le coloris au siècle de Louis XIV* (Paris: Bibliothèque des arts, 1957).

35. Alpers, "Describe or Narrate?," 27-8.

36. Ibid., 28.

37. D'Aubignac, *La Pratique du théâtre*, pp. 39-41. "It is the duty and even the principal intention of the Poet to work on the Action as represented. But he must disguise it under some color which depends on the Action as if true. . . . For in the Theatre of the Ancients there is no action, no speech, no narration, no passion, no intrigue without its color, taking the Story as if true, even though it is invented by the Poet only in order to be represented."

38. On the relation of truth to the irrational real, see Julia Kristeva,

"La productivité dite texte," *Communications*, 11 (1968), 59–83, and "Le vréel," in *Folle vérité: vérité et vraisemblance du texte psychotique*, ed. Jean-Michel Ribettes (Éditions du Seuil, 1979), pp. 11–35.

39. D'Aubignac, *La Pratique du théâtre*, p. 85. "And by representing a single part make everything pass artfully again before the eyes of the Spectators without multiplying the principal action."

40. Ibid., p. 89. "Although dependent to some degree on a principal one, all of these actions were so great and powerful that each could have been the subject of a Poem."

41. Ibid., p. 83. "Theatre is nothing but an Image."

42. Ibid., p. 100. "Theatre is nothing other than a representation, one must not imagine that there is anything to what we see there, but rather the things themselves whose images we find."

43. Ibid., p. 43. "I call Representation, the collection of everything which might serve to represent a Dramatic Poem, and which must be found there, considering them in themselves and according to their own nature, such as the Players, the Painters, the Scenes, the Violinists, the Spectators and such like."

44. Ibid., p. 282. "Considering tragedy strictly and in its own nature, in view of the genre of Poetry according to which it is constituted, one might say that it is so attached to the actions that speeches do not appear to belong to it. This poem is called *Drama*, this is to say, *Action* and not *Narration*; Those who perform it are called *Actors*, and not *Orators*; Those who are found present there are called *Spectators* or *Beholders*, and not *Listeners*; Finally, the Place used for its Representations is called a *Theatre*, and not an *Auditorium*, that is, *a Place where one watches what happens*, and not where *one Listens to what is said there*. Thus, it is true that the Speeches made there ought to be like the Actions of those appearing on the Stage; because *To Speak* there is *To Act*."

45. Ibid., p. 259.

46. Ibid., pp. 282–83. "In a word, Speeches in the Theatre are nothing but the accessories of the Action, even though the entire Tragedy in its Representation might consist only of Speech; herein lies the entire work of the Poet and to what he principally directs the energies of his mind; and if he stages some actions in his Theatre, it is to take the opportunity to perform some agreeable speech; everything he invents is for the sake of having it spoken."

47. Ibid., p. 304. "The Dramatic Poem is like a quintessence of all the precepts one reads in the Authors who have taught us the art of speaking well in prose and verse; this is because one must employ them with such judgment and refinement that it often appears that one has wandered far away from these precepts, and even abandoned them completely; and the genius of Theatre is such that, ordinarily, what does not appear is its greatest art; a Sentiment which will have been cast almost imperceptibly in the

minds of the Auditors, an Adventure begun apparently without design, an imperfect Narration, or some other ingenious scheme are all capable of sustaining a part of an entire Poem, of laying the foundation for its strongest passions, and of preparing for its illustrious Catastrophe."

48. Ibid., pp. 347–48. "In a word, if Poetry is the Realm of Figures, Theatre is its Throne; it is the place where, through the outward agitations of him who speaks and complains of his fate, figures convey into the souls of those watching the action and listening to it sentiments that he does not at all possess."

49. Abbé du Bos, *Réflexions critiques*, II, 349. "Theatre resembles eloquence, said the Abbé d'Aubignac."

50. D'Aubignac, *La Pratique du théâtre*, p. 305. "How then might Deliberations be able to be part of the Theatre? They are produced by a sedate spirit, and everything must happen in great moderation; one who requests counsel makes this proposition with tranquillity, even though his soul might be otherwise agitated; those who are called upon to give their advice must be even less troubled by interests or passions; they must speak only with clear reason; they must be lit by wisdom and not be storm-tossed; and once they appear moved and impassioned, they will be suspected of sharing some secret motive favoring one of the two parties, and will lose the quality of dependable Counselors; finally on these occasions, everything must be without agitation, persons must be reserved, discourse moderate, expressions gentle, and nothing must resemble the impetuous movements of the Stage: thus without great art, it is impossible for the Theatre not to fall into languor, as well as immobility."

51. D'Aubignac, *Discours academique sur l'eloquence* (Paris: Pierre Colin, 1669), p. 3.

52. D'Aubignac, *La Pratique du théâtre*, p. 346. "This is why the best advice one can give to Poets is to become very learned in the knowledge of Figures by studying what the Rhetoricians wrote on the subject, which should be unnecessary to repeat here: but first they must remember not to be content simply to read the Rhetoricians to learn how to name and make figures." In *Terence iustifié*, pp. 59–60, D'Aubignac describes bad criticism as: "la chicane de la Republique des Lettres, elle n'estend guere plus loing que la Grammaire, & n'ose passer au delà, parce qu'elle n'a pas assez de force pour se soustenir dans les sciences plus solides. Son employ n'est qu'à feüilleter diverses leçons, qu'un examen de nottes & de commentaires, un rapport de plusieurs passages que bien souvent elle n'entend pas, une recherche de diverses impressions, & pour chef-d'oeuvre l'observation d'un manuscrit. . . . Telle est la suffisance des Grammairiens, & presque de tous les Scholiastes & Glossateurs, qui fait dire à Scaliger qu'il n'y a rien de si miserable qu'un Grammarien." "The chicanery of the Republic of Letters hardly extends beyond Grammar, and dares go no further because it lacks the strength to succeed in more solid sciences. Its task is only to leaf through

various lessons, only an examination of notes and commentaries, an analysis of several passages which it usually does not understand, a study of various impressions, and as the masterpiece, the commentary upon a manuscript. . . . Such is the sufficiency of Grammarians, and almost all the Scoliasts and Glossarists, who provoked Scaliger to say that there is nothing more miserable than a Grammarian."

53. Ibid., pp. 346–47. "That it is necessary to understand the energy of figures, reflect deeply upon them, and finally, discover the effect they can produce on the Stage. . . . And to become subtle and skilled at this use of figures, the Poet must seek and carefully study examples of their use by the Ancients, and not skim these sources casually; and most of all, he must frequent the Theatres; because it is there, better than in Books, that he can observe good or bad figures, those that languish and those that make an impression."

54. D'Aubignac, *Discours academique sur l'eloquence*, p. 12. "[Eloquence] directs itself according to the soul of its listeners; since eloquence passes imperceptibly into the heart, it comes to rule the heart and causes the auditors to lose consciousness of everything except what eloquence wishes to inspire in them; And this notion causes my uncertainty. Yes, doubtless, perfect Eloquence makes an agreeable impression, but it does not leave the powers of judgment free; those whom eloquence undertakes to conquer must not remain capable of discerning the sensual things they touch or see, or of knowing what they are or what they do, nor even of recognizing eloquence itself."

55. D'Aubignac, *La Pratique du théâtre*, p. 304–5. "Presupposing here as a basis everything that one can learn elsewhere about Deliberations, I begin with this important warning: that by their nature they are harmful to the Theatre. Since the Theatre is the place of Actions, everything must be in a state of agitation there, whether from events that from one moment to the next contradict or obstruct one another, or from violent passions springing up on all sides from collision and from the midst of Plot devices like the lightning and thunder of battle, and from the heart of the darkest Clouds; so that scarcely anyone comes on Stage without a troubled mind, thwarted plans, and seen as having to struggle and suffer greatly. Finally, the Demon of anxiety, confusion, and disorder reigns at the Theatre."

56. Ibid., p. 349. "The Poet may well find some Figures more fitting for the Theatre than others: well placed and conveyed *Apostrophe*, for example, which I have always noticed to be very striking on the stage; it always alleges as present either a real person, even though absent in fact, or a feigned person only there through fiction, as is the *Fatherland*, *Virtue* and other similar things; this is because Apostrophe so effectively alleges them present that the speaker addresses his speech to them as if he truly saw them: this is completely Theatrical; whereas this creates two characters when there is only one, one visible and the other imaginary; one speaking

and the other to whom he appears to speak: even though the ruse is obvious, it nevertheless carries off the imagination of those who hear it since it is an effect of the actor's impassioned mind."

57. Jonathan Culler, "Apostrophe," *The Pursuit of Signs: Semiotics, Literature, Deconstruction* (Ithaca: Cornell University Press, 1981), p. 146. See also Paul de Man, *Allegories of Reading*; and Cynthia Chase, *Decomposing Figures: Rhetorical Readings in the Romantic Tradition* (Baltimore: The Johns Hopkins University Press, 1986), pp. 65–112.

58. D'Aubignac, *La Pratique du théâtre*, p. 353. "Irony is also a figure of the Dramatic Poem, and is Theatrical by nature; this is because, in saying in jest the contrary of what it wishes to have understood, it carries with itself a disguise and creates a not unpleasant play.

Exclamation is all the more suitable to the Theatre, since it is the tangible mark of a mind touched by some violent passion oppressing it.

Hyperbole is of the same order. Because the words carry the imagination farther than does their own meaning, Hyperbole is appropriate for the Theatre where everything must appear larger than life and where there is but enchantment and illusion.

Interrogation, which Scaliger claims to be a figure only by custom and not by its nature, is also good for the Theatre since it is the mark of an agitated mind.

But above all, Imprecation will certainly be judged as Theatrical, since it proceeds from a violent delirium of the mind; thus it requires a very impetuous discourse, a strong impression, and extreme things."

59. Although Robert Morrissey, in "*La Pratique du théâtre* et le langage de l'illusion," *XVIIᵉ Siecle*, 146 (January/March, 1985), 17–27, argues that "the interior space of the spectators becomes the space of the play for the duration of the spectacle," he disregards the potential epistemological subversiveness of such spectatorial space by aligning it only with "a certain reigning rationalism."

60. D'Aubignac, *La Pratique du théâtre*, p. 319.

61. Ibid., p. 292. "These long Narrations are not more suitable in the course of the Action [to depict] what happens from the opening Act. For besides the well-known reasons based on the lack of variety, the Spectators' impatience, and the loosening of their attention, it will never be credible that so many things could happen in so little time, during the interval of an Act for example. Not that it would be terribly uncommon to assume that a Battle, a Conspiracy, a remarkable deceit or some similar event could happen in such a short time; but to perform it verisimilarly, as we have said elsewhere, one must fool the Auditor, in busying him with the sight of some other thing and the sounds of accounts that prepare for what must be recounted later and arouse the auditor's impatience to know the events and which agreeably seduce his imagination."

62. Ibid., p. 297. "Always leaving the Spectator in anticipation of some

novelty, colors heighten his desire and keep him in a state of agreeable impatience." D'Aubignac's mixture of pleasure with pain here calls to mind André Green's subtle analysis of the pleasurable pains we desire in tragedy, *Un Oeil en trop: le complexe d'Oedipe dans la tragédie* (Paris: Éditions de Minuit, 1969).

63. D'Aubignac, *Discours academique sur l'eloquence*, pp. 18–19. "A torrent which nothing can resist; but a torrent of delights, which brings joy where its violence leads the auditor."

64. See Lyotard, *Discours, figure*; *Économie libidinale*; *Des dispositifs pulsionnels* (Paris: 10/18, 1973); "The Unconscious as Mise-en-scène," in *Performance in Postmodern Culture*, ed. Michel Benamou and Charles Caramello, trans. Joseph Maier (Madison: Coda Press, 1977), pp. 87–98; Sara Kofman, *L'enfance de l'art: une interprétation de l'esthétique freudienne* (Paris: Éditions Payot, 1970); Green, *Narcissisme de vie, narcissisme de mort* (Paris: Éditions de Minuit, 1983); *Hamlet et Hamlet: une interprétation psychoanalytique de la représentation* (Paris: Balland, 1982); and *Un Oeil en trop*.

65. D'Aubignac, *La Pratique du théâtre*, pp. 235, 238. "And when the Dramatic Poem arrived at its last perfection, these Intervals were considered as parts necessary for the composition of this Work. To say all in a word, the Poets made use of them to portray and hide simultaneously everything that could not or should not be seen by the Spectators. . . . The Poet must suppose that all inconvenient encounters take place behind the Curtain and, especially, during these Intervals that will furnish an appropriate time for their execution."

66. Nietzsche, *The Birth of Tragedy*, p. 46.

67. The ideology of the visible is the subject of Jean-Louis Baudry's *L'effet du cinema* (Paris: Éditions Albatros, 1978). I discuss the relation of the ideology of the visible to the ideology of consensus in "Screening the Camera's Eye: Black and White Confrontations of Technological Representation," *Modern Drama*, 28, No. 1 (March, 1985), 110–24.

68. Arnaud, *Étude sur la vie et les oeuvres de l'Abbé d'Aubignac*, p. 234. "It is understandable that the duration of the moments represented should be more or less equivalent to that of their representation; but it is less understandable how the duration of the others, those which are not represented, is supposed to be equivalent to the duration of their *non-representation*."

69. Derrida, *De la grammatologie*, pp. 286. "The necessity of interval, the harsh law of spacing." *Of Grammatology*, p. 200.

70. Ibid., p. 289. "What one cannot represent is the relationship of representation to so-called originary presence. The re-presentation is also a de-presentation. It is tied to the work of spacing. Spacing insinuates into presence an interval which not only separates the different times of speech and of song but also the represented from the representer." *Of Grammatology*, pp. 203.

71. Arnaud, *Étude sur la vie et les oeuvres de l'Abbé d'Aubignac*, pp. 234–35. "Thus, it is no longer according to a perceptible representation, but according to a *supposed, imagined* representation that d'Aubignac determines the duration of the action; this is to say that he no longer allows only the senses to be the judges of representational poetry, but, with them, the imagination; this is to say, finally, that he again abandons and contradicts the principle of his demonstration, namely, that the dramatic poem is 'a picture which is evident to the senses' and 'of which the eye is the only judge.' And one must always return to his abandonment of this principle. To wish, in fact, to do without the imagination of the spectators, 'to establish as the foundation,' with Chapelain, that dramatic art is addressed only to the senses and must present illusions to them is simply to make dramatic art impossible. One need only consider the means dramatic art uses to understand that it is materially only a 'ruse,' that it needs to have our imagination supplement what its 'images' lack, that it can and wants to give the sensation of the real only by leaving us with the sensation of the false, that it exists, finally, only by virtue of a perpetual pact between the poet and the spectator . . . and granting all of this, and more still, the spectator makes himself the collaborator, the accomplice, the confederate of the poet."

72. *Représentant* is used by d'Aubignac to mean the illusionary presence of the dramatic image (*La Pratique du théâtre*, p. 44). In "Non-Representation in *La Pratique du théâtre*," *Papers on French Seventeenth Century Literature*, 16 (1982), 57–74, I develop the implications of making a distinction between a libidinal poetics and the kind of rational, phenomenological model proposed for Diderot by Michael Fried's *Absorption and Theatricality: Painting and Beholder in the Age of Diderot* (Berkeley: University of California Press, 1980).

73. D'Aubignac, *La Pratique du théâtre*, p. 289.

74. Ibid., p. 293.

75. Ibid., p. 291. "Feeling his memory overtaxed and his imagination confused by so much detail, he becomes angry with himself, then with the Poet, and finally abandons everything without listening to another word."

76. Ibid., p. 341. "One must not leave the Spectator hungry, nor should he be given too much to drink; he must be entirely satisfied, but not overwhelmed."

77. Ibid., p. 128. "One might imagine, perhaps, that the Discourse we are about to undertake will not give advantageous instructions to the Poet, but on the contrary will be a practice capable of destroying all the charms of Theatre."

Chapter 11

1. "I anticipate that there will be many readers who will refuse to recognize the jurisdiction of Longinus, who will condemn what he approves

and who will laud what he criticizes. This is the treatment he must expect from most Judges of our century. These men, accustomed to the debauches and excesses of the modern Poets, and who admire only what they fail to comprehend, do not believe that an Author is elevated unless they have entirely lost sight of him; these small Minds, I say, will no doubt fail to be strongly struck by the bold judiciousness of the Homers, Platos, and Demosthenes. They will often seek the Sublime in the Sublime."

2. Abbé d'Aubignac, *Conjectures academiques ou Dissertation sur L'Iliade* (Paris: François Fournier, 1715), pp. 25–26. "But after all, they will say, Aristotle could have been bewildered by these small minds, and didn't examine the works of Homer well enough since he took from them the rules of his poetic art? The name of this illustrious Philosopher could totally disarm those who would blindly follow authority; however, those who wish to defer only to reason, without famous examples or great names capable of pitting them against reason, will not surrender until they are entirely convinced. And I have scruples that prevent me from following Aristotle's opinion on the subject in question."

3. Ernst Cassirer, *The Philosophy of the Enlightenment*, trans. Fritz C. A. Koelln and James P. Pettegrove (Princeton: Princeton University Press, 1951), p. 284.

4. Ibid., pp. 282–83.

5. Ibid., pp. 280–81.

6. D'Aubignac, *La Pratique du théâtre*, p. 35. "I know that the Poet is the Master of theatre, that he establishes the order and economy of his play as he sees fit."

7. D'Aubignac, *Conjectures academiques*, p. 345. "As we have noted, Longinus told us that the *Odyssey*'s style is not as strong nor its type of writing so lofty as is the *Iliad*'s. . . . This is how to judge an author in a rather new way; in terms of the style, the different subjects one treats almost always make the difference; when the style is great, the thoughts, expressions, figures, and terms belong to the sublime genre. And if a Poet possesses any genius, the subject-matter alone will carry him there."

8. Abbé du Pures, *Idée des spectacles anciens et nouveaux* (Paris: Michel Brunet, 1668), "Au Roy." "I know well that all of his moments are precious and destined to sublime thoughts, from which [some Idea of an entertainment worthy of Your Majesty] will issue only through reason."

9. Nicolas Boileau-Despréaux, *L'art poétique* (Paris: Société Les Belles Lettres, 1967), p. 82. "Therefore love Reason. May your writings always / borrow both their luster and their value only from it."

10. Abbé Du Bos, *Réflexions critiques*, II, 399. "Most Painters and Poets do not judge according to sentiment or by deferring to natural taste perfected by comparisons and experience, but by the path of analysis. They do not judge as men gifted with the sixth sense discussed above, but as speculative Philosophers."

11. D'Aubignac, *La Pratique du théâtre*, p. 139. "The spectators are disgusted as soon as they foresee the Catastrophe through the fault of the Poet, not so much because they know what will follow, but because they realize they should not have been told; their dissatisfaction proceeding less on these occasions from their knowledge, however certain, than from the imprudence of the Poet."

12. Ibid., p. 18. "To make known to the People the excellence of their Art. . . . In which, of course, it seems to me that I could contribute something, not only to the glory of our Poets but also to everyone's pleasure."

13. Neil Hertz, "A Reading of Longinus," *The End of the Line: Essays on Psychoanalysis and the Sublime* (New York: Columbia University Press, 1985), p. 14.

14. Bouhours, *Les Entretiens d'Ariste et d'Eugene*, pp. 298–300. "Genius is a special aptitude and a talent which nature gives to a few men for certain things . . . it does not suffice to be endowed with wit and imagination to excel in poetry; one must be born a Poet and possess a natural quality that depends neither on art nor study; and which draws something from inspiration. . . . It is a gift from heaven in which the earth plays no part; it is something divine that creates a mind of genius."

15. Ibid., pp. 342–43. "To speak in Christian terms about this something, is it not that in us which makes us feel that our souls are immortal, regardless of all the weaknesses and disorders of corrupt nature; that earthly marvels cannot satisfy us; that there is something beyond us, which is the term of our desires and the center of the happiness which we seek everywhere and find nowhere?"

16. Sebastian de Senlis, in *Le Flambeau du iuste. Pour la conduite des esprits sublimes* (Paris: n.p., 1640), discusses the sublime as an expression of faith. In terms of Jansenist concerns, Louis Marin develops the complex theoretical relation of theology and desire in *La Critique du discours*, pp. 314–16.

17. In *Rhetoric, Prudence, and Skepticism in the Renaissance*, p. 190, Victoria Kahn discusses the philosophical analysis of this adaptation as developed by Hobbes, "who, like the humanists sees the analogies between prudence, poetry, and religious faith, but who unlike the humanists want precisely for this reason to subordinate these unpredictable and potentially disruptive aspects of human experience to the arbitrary authority of the sovereign."

18. Du Bos, *Réflexions critiques*, II, 528. "The philosophical mind, which is nothing more than reason strengthened by reflection and experience, and whose name alone would have been unknown to the Ancients, is excellent for composing books that instruct how not to make mistakes in writing; it is excellent for showing those that an Author has made."

19. Derrida, "Psyche: Inventions de l'autre," unpublished manuscript, p. 24. "The production of an objective ideality."

20. Du Bos, *Réflexions critiques*, II, 528. "But the philosophical mind teaches poorly how we should judge a poem in general. The beauties constituting a poem's greatest merit can be better felt than known with a ruler and compass."

21. Ibid., p. 516. "The reputation of a work is founded on the pleasure it gives to all who read it." "Men are thus less likely to be duped in matters of poetry than in matters of Philosophy."

22. Ibid., p. 515. "The prejudice of humanity in favor of a system of Philosophy does not even prove that it must continue to be valid over the next thirty years. Men are able to be disabused by truth."

23. Ibid., p. 444. "Real merit consists of pleasing and touching. Comparative merit consists of touching as much as or more than particular Authors whose position is already established."

24. Boileau, *L'art poétique*, p. 96. "The secret is first to please and affect: / Invent the dynamics that might engage me." In *Detours of Desire: Readings in the French Baroque* (Columbus: Ohio State University Press, 1984), Mitchell Greenberg emphasizes the structures of desire endemic to the Baroque.

25. Bouhours, *Les Entretiens d'Ariste et d'Eugene*, pp. 329–30. "The *je ne sçay quoy* is like one of those things which one knows only through the effects they produce. . . . It attracts the hardest of hearts, it sometimes excites violent passions in the soul, and it sometimes produces very noble sentiments."

26. Ibid., p. 330. "It never makes itself known any other way. Its value and its advantage consist in remaining hidden."

27. In "L'intervention sur le transfert," pp. 215–26, Lacan stresses the dialectical process of psychoanalytical transference which includes, as the negative operation, the operation of the interpreting analyst. Counter-transference, moreover, is defined by Lacan as "the sum total of the prejudices, passions, and difficulties of the analyst, or even of his insufficient information, at any given moment of the dialectical process."

28. Bouhours, *La Maniere de bien penser*, p. 79. "The sublimity, the grandeur of a thought, is precisely what sweeps us away and ravishes us."

29. Ibid., p. 159. "Refinement adds *je ne sçay quoy* to the sublime and to the pleasing."

30. Daniel Brewer's extremely provocative essay, "Stages of the Enlightened Sublime: Narrating Sublimation," *Theatre Journal*, 38, No. 1 (March 1986), 5–18, provoked me to revise this chapter in view of its analysis of the important function of sublimation in the narrative of the sublime.

31. Freud, *The Standard Edition*, XVI, 346.

32. Ibid., p. 158. "But when you ask me what is a delicate thought, I do not know where to find the terms to explain myself. It is one of those things which are difficult to see at a glance and which, by virtue of their

subtlety, escape us when we think we grasp them. All that one can do is to observe them closely and repeatedly in order gradually to know them."

33. Bouhours, *Les Entretiens d'Ariste et d'Eugene*, p. 358. "Taken in an allegorical or hieroglyphical sense are not legitimate."

34. Bouhours, *La Maniere de bien penser*, p. 21. "All figures containing a double meaning each in their own way have beauties and graces that enhance them."

35. Cassirer, *The Philosophy of the Enlightenment*, p. 301. Hertz develops the relation of the sublime to the activity of startled reading in "The Notion of Blockage in the Literature of the Sublime," *The End of the Line*, pp. 40–60. For a discussion of blockage in the seventeenth-century narrative of painting, see Marin, "La description du tableau et le sublime en peinture," *Communications*, 34 (1981), 61–84.

36. Coypel, *L'excellence de la peinture*, p. 365. "The great painter must not only please but also move and enrapture, as do great poets and great orators. Like those musicians so praised by antiquity, he must sometimes inspire sadness to the point of drawing tears, sometimes provoke laughter, sometimes inflame anger and force the spectators to display their admiration and surprise. In fact, this is what is sublime in painting and the painter's greatest merit."

37. Du Bos, *Réflexions critiques*, II, 379. "His foreign merit."

38. Ibid., 340. "Does the work please or not? Is the work good or bad in general? It amounts to the same thing. Reasoning must not then intervene in our judgments of a poem or a painting in general, unless to explain the decision made by sentiment and to explain what faults prevent it from pleasing."

39. Ibid., 339. "The public not only judges a Work without self-interest, but it also judges the way such decisions must be made in general, this is, by the path of sentiment and by following the impression which the poem or painting has on it."

40. Ibid., I, 235–36. "Coypel concluded": "the particular character of [Poussin's] sublime inventions to which genius alone can lead is that of appearing so connected to the subject that they seem to have been the first ideas that occurred to the Artisans who treated the subject."

41. Ibid., 236. "The Reader's first reaction is to believe that he might have discovered [the sublime inventions] as well as [La Fontaine]."

42. See Suzanne Guerlac, "Longinus and the Subject of the Sublime," *New Literary History*, 16, No. 2 (Winter 1985), 275–89.

43. Du Bos, *Réflexions critiques*, II, 14. "Who never composed better than when his poetic fury led as far as madness."

44. Ibid., I, 433. "When a simple recitation adds so much energy to the poem, it is easy to understand the advantage gained from theatrical representation by plays delivered on the stage."

45. Ibid., I, 246. "As long as the particular traits of this [theatrical]

character and what must serve to delineate it remain blurred and mixed together with an infinity of discourses and actions which the *bienséances*, fashion, custom, profession, and interest make all men perform in much the same way and in a manner so uniform that their character only reveals itself imperceptibly, only those born with the genius of Theatre can discern them. They alone can say what character will follow from traits, whether these traits were separate from unimportant actions and discourses, and whether they were immediately united when drawn together. Finally, invention is to discern the characters of Nature."

46. Ibid., II, 384. "Artisans without genius judge less soundly than the common person."

47. Ibid. "Their attention is focused entirely on mechanical execution, and they judge the entire work on this basis."

48. Ibid., II, 522. "It is easy to prove historically and by facts that Virgil and the other esteemed Poets of antiquity are in no way indebted to the Colleges or to prejudices, as their first admirers. Virgil's first admirers were his compatriots and contemporaries. They were women, wordly people, less educated perhaps than those who build as they wish the history of the reputation of the great Poets."

49. Ibid. "The language in which the *Aeneid* was written was his living language. Women as well as men, the uneducated as well as the learned, read this poem and judged it according to the impression it made on them. . . . Thus, this was the impression made by the *Aeneid* on everyone; the tears of women shed at its reading were what won its acceptance as an excellent poem."

50. Elizabeth L. Berg, "Recognizing Differences: Perrault's Modernist Esthetic in *Parallèle des anciens et des modernes*," *Papers on French Seventeenth Century Literature*, 18 (1983), 145.

51. Ibid., 144.

52. Du Bos, Réflexions critiques, II, 444–45. "Contemporaries judge perfectly well the real merit of a work, but they are subject to mistake when they judge its comparative merit."

53. Ibid. "Comparative method consists of touching as much as or more than a particular Author whose position is already established."

54. Ibid. "One clearly must leave to time and experience judgment of what position our contemporary Poets should occupy among the Writers who fashion this collection of books made by men of letters of all nations, which might be called *The Library of Mankind*."

55. Ibid., I, 467. "All of these sounds [of Music] . . . possess a marvelous power to move us because they are signs of the passions, established by nature from which they received their energy. Spoken words, on the other hand, are only arbitrary signs of the passions. Spoken words derive their signification and value only from their institution by men, who were able to give them value only in a particular country."

56. Kristeva, *Pouvoirs de l'horreur: Essai sur l'abjection* (Paris: Éditions du Seuil, 1980), p. 19. "*Sublimation* . . . is nothing else than the possibility of naming the pre-nominal, the pre-objectal, which are in fact only a trans-nominal, a trans-objectal." *Powers of Horror: An Essay On Abjection*, trans. Leon S. Roudiez (New York: Columbia University Press, 1982), p. 11.

57. The paradox of such an aesthetics struggling against "l'institution des hommes" is that it is formulated by the writer who later penned *Histoire critique de l'établissement de la monarchie française dans les Gaules* (1742). In my opinion, du Bos's aesthetics, much like d'Aubignac's, undermines the epistemological structures necessarily fueling the author's sincere belief in centralized monarchy. For a brief and informative analysis of du Bos's "Romanist" position, see Nannerl O. Keohane, *Philosophy and the State in France: The Renaissance to the Englightenment* (Princeton: Princeton University Press, 1980), pp. 347–48.

58. Du Bos, *Réflexions critiques*, I, 452–53. "The spectator thus retains his common sense at the theatre regardless of the strongest emotion. One becomes impassioned there, yet within bounds."

59. Thomas Weiskel, *The Romantic Sublime: Studies in the Structure and Psychology of Transcendence* (Baltimore: The Johns Hopkins University Press, 1976), p. 17.

60. Immanuel Kant, *Critique of Judgment*, trans. J. H. Bernard (New York: Hafner Press, 1951), pp. 135–38.

61. Lyotard, *Le Différend* (Paris: Éditions de Minuit, 1983), p. 243. "To the community which establishes itself *a priori*, and which judges itself without the rule of direct presentation; it's simply that community is morally called for through the mediation of a concept of reason, the Idea of liberty; whereas the community of speakers and addressees of a sentence on beauty is named immediately, without the mediation of any concept, by sentiment alone, in that it can be shared *a priori*. Community is already present as taste, but not already present as rational consensus." Lyotard here echoes—thereby setting in motion the politico-critical *différend*—an earlier reading of Kant by Derrida, in *La Vérité en peinture*, pp. 129–30. Derrida reads the *a priori* status of taste in view of archi-taste: "Bien que la troisième *Critique* (lieu de l'esthétique) dissocie le plaisir et la connaissance, bien qu'elle fasse de cette dissociation une frontière juridique rigoureuse entre le goût et la connaissance, l'esthétique et le logique, il faut bien que le principe du plaisir ait quelque part, dans un temps immémorial (concept dont le statut reste fort incertain dans une *Critique*), commandé la connaissance, qu'il l'ait conditionnée et accompagnée partout où elle était possible, déterminée comme expérience (au sens kantien), précédant ainsi l'écart entre le jouir et le connaître. Comment situer ici le temps de cet archi-plaisir soudant l'imagination (esthétique) à l'entendement (logique)?" "Although the third *Critique* (place of the aesthetic) disassociates pleasure and knowl-

edge, although it creates from this disassociation a rigorous juridical border between taste and knowledge, aesthetics and logic, the pleasure principle must certainly have governed knowledge, in an immemorial time (a concept whose status remains extremely uncertain in a *Critique*), it must have conditioned and accompanied it everywhere knowledge was possible, determined as experience (in the Kantian sense), preceding thus the gap between enjoying it and knowing it. How does one situate here the time of the archipleasure joining imagination (aesthetic) and understanding (logic)?

62. Kant, *Critique of Judgment*, p. 198.

63. Ibid., p. 161.

64. Ibid., p. 162.

65. Ibid., p. 163.

66. Habermas, *Legitimation Crisis*, p. 10.

67. Lyotard, *Le différend*, p. 246.

68. Kristeva, *Pouvoirs de l'horreur*, p. 19. "Not at all short of but always with and through perception and words, the sublime is *something added* that expands us, overstrains us, and causes us to be both *here*, as dejects, as *there*, as others and sparkling. A divergence, an impossible bounding. Everything missed, joy—fascination." *Powers of Horror*, p. 12.

69. Ibid., p. 62. "A challenge to symbolization. Whether we call it an *affect* or link it with infantile semiotization—for which the pre-signifying articulations are merely *equations* rather than symbolic *equivalences* for objects, we must point to a necessity within analysis. This necessity . . . consists in not reducing analytic attention to language to that of philosophical idealism and, in its wake, to linguistics; the point is, quite to the contrary, to posit a *heterogeneity of significance*. It stands to reason that one can say nothing of such (effective or semiotic) heterogeneity without making it homologous with the linguistic signifier. But it is precisely that *powerlessness* that the 'empty' signifier, the dissociation of discourse . . . come to indicate." *Powers of Horror*, p. 51. For further discussion of Kristeva's text, see Hertz, *The End of the Line*, pp. 217–39; and Cynthia Chase's 1983 review in *Criticism*.

70. Jean-Luc Nancy, "Identité et tremblement," *Hypnoses* (Paris: Editions galilée, 1984), p. 44. "The subject, here, is born. There is no presence of its birth—nor is there representation of it. But birth is the heart's mode of presence, that is, of division. Genius is not the individual, because it divides the individual; it makes him tremble, and it divides him from and with the other. It is not an immediate and total community—as if there were a single Genius of humanity—because Genius *is* the difference of the individual, without being the individual itself. Birth takes place in a community of division—that of the mother's breast, of love, of being-together-and-many. Division itself signifies birth [*partum*]. Being born, not having birth behind one, but being born unceasingly, in trembling, is to be divided."

71. Ibid., p. 45. "Trembling is not an image, it is the rhythm of the affected soul and the division of the unconscious, that is, the 'unconscious' as our division. This means our community, our destiny, our Genius. This means divided by the genius of 'feminine nature.' But this Genius is not *one*."

72. Lyotard, *Discours, figure*, p. 323. "Inversion in the function of deconstruction corresponds to this inversion in the place of the subject. Condensations, displacements, distortions in general now come to shape a material which one expects to be governed by the preconscious rules of discourse and action: how could they not make themselves felt? They are reflected on the preconscious material as are figures in a mirror or waves against a breakwater. An other energy shows itself here. But it does not make itself *recognized*, obviously; recognition belongs to the preconscious order, the order of discourse and the order of reality. The way this energy manifests itself is negative, menacing, anguishing: disorder. But it also denounces order, it announces another 'order,' of another nature; it unmasks good form, the proper object, clear discourse. Thus oeniric representation seen in a waking state could only be a 'bad' representation; a representation in which our desire could not fulfill itself, which should *send it back* to us as a reflected image. And so, transcribed into reality (into the work), the same illusionist dream-image would be a demystifying image. A critical one."

73. Du Bos, *Réflexions critiques*, I, 141. "In love, one quarrels without cause and reconciles for no reason. The ideas of lovers possess no coherent interconnection. The flow of their sentiments is no better controlled than the flow of waves whipped up by a capricious stormy wind. To wish to subjugate these sentiments to principles, to wish to organize them in a specific way is to wish that a madman might have coherent visions in his ravings."

74. De Man, "Hegel on the Sublime," in *Displacement: Derrida and After*, ed. Mark Krupnick (Bloomington: Indiana University Press, 1983), p. 153.

✑ Index

A

Absence, 58, 121, 185–91
Academies: French, 109–10, 129;
   Académie Française, 110, 112–15,
   125, 161–62; Académie des Belles
   Lettres, 162–63
Acknowledgment, 111–16, 120, 122,
   126, 157. *See also* Legitimation
Actors: English companies and textual
   conventions, 32–36, 69–70, 116,
   150, 233 *n*; French companies,
   112–15, 150; psychology of, 129–
   30, 248 *n*. *See also*
   Antitheatricality; Psychology
Adam, Antoine, 122, 242 *n*
Alberti, 120, 136
Allegory: as narrative and
   representational practice, 12–20,
   28, 48, 63, 130, 152, 157–58, 200,
   219 *n*; of genius, 30, 65, 97, 153,
   196, 203–6, 212–16; of reading, 65,
   81, 83–84, 121–22, 126, 164, 207–
   8, 216; of spectatorship, 183; and
   ideology, 14, 30, 109, 130, 158, 219
   n; and transference, 95, 145;
   "Académie des Allegoriques,"
   163. *See also* Narration;
   Representation; Genius; Reading;
   Spectatorship; Ideology;
   Transference
Allen, D. C., 48
Alpers, Svetlana, 176–77
Althusser, Louis, 7, 153, 167
Antitheatricality: English, 16, 23–24;
   28–29; 98–104; French: 17, 126–30,
   146, 295; and philosophy, 8–9, 18;

linguistic fear, 28–29, 131–33; and
   Ben Jonson, 40, 47, 68, 74–78, 228
   n; and oral reading, 78, 206;
   endorsement of grammar, 131–33,
   145–46, 194; and misogyny, 100–
   102; inscription in English drama,
   221 *n*; and psychology of acting,
   129–30, 248 *n*. *See also* Actors;
   Grammar; Jonson; Reading;
   Women
Apelles, 135
Apostolidès, Jean, 240 *n*; 257 *n*,
   264–65 *n*
Apostrophe, 185. *See also* Figure;
   Rhetoric
Aristophanes, 53
Aristotle, 23, 122, 130, 137, 145, 163–
   64, 185, 192–93, 206, 252 *n*
Arnaud, Charles, 159, 170, 173–74,
   187–90
Art theory. *See* Painting; Portraiture
Artaud, Antonin, 103
Aubignac, Abbé de (François Hédelin),
   17–19, 14, 122–23, 134, 158–93; *La
   Pratique du théâtre*, 159–61, 163–
   91, 196–97, 202, 209; Académie
   des Belles Lettres, 162–63; color
   174–81; eloquence, 182–84, 187;
   authorship, 148–49, 195–98, 204;
   spectatorship, 169–93; "le genie du
   Theatre," 181–93; the rhetoric of
   desire, 181–91; intervals, 187–89,
   210, 259 *n*; grammar, 271–72 *n*.
   See also Authorship; Genius;
   Grammar; Spectatorship;
   Sublime
Aubigny, Lord, 76